NO EASY ANSWERS

Should schools be integrated? Or are Black
children better off staying apart from Whites?

*Can Blacks work effectively with White
liberals?* Or is this the path to corruption?

*Is Black capitalism the solution to economic
oppression?* Or is a Marxist revolution the
only cure?

*Can the Black find worthwhile values in
America?* Or must he turn to Africa?

*These are among the questions to
which the Black leaders, thinkers, and
writers in this volume address themselves. Upon their answers hang the
future and very survival of the Black
in the United States.*

VIEWPOINTS

SIGNET and MENTOR Black Anthologies

☐ **HARLEM edited by John Henrik Clarke.** America's foremost Black writers recreate the people, the landscape, the joy, and the horror of their ghetto heartland. A unique and superb collection of tales which recapture the essence of Harlem and its people. (#Q4336—95¢)

☐ **THE BLACK WOMAN: An Anthology edited by Toni Cade.** This volume presents the eloquent writings of Abbey Lincoln, Joanne Grant, Kay Lindsay and others—all discussing such topics as politics, the Black man, sex, child-raising in the ghetto and much more. (#Q4317—95¢)

☐ **RIGHT ON! An Anthology of Black Literature edited by Bradford Chambers and Rebecca Moon.** The authors describe this book as "the works of more than forty authors . . . presented in these pages, from the plaintive cries of the first Black poet to be stolen from Africa to the angry, fiery voices of today's Black Militants." This book will be welcomed both in schools and libraries. (#MQ1005—95¢)

☐ **BLACK VOICES: An Anthology of Afro-American Literature edited by Abraham Chapman.** Fiction, autobiography, poetry, and literary criticism by American Blacks selected from the work of well-known authors as well as younger writers whose work is being published here for the first time. Contributors include **Ralph Ellison, Richard Wright, James Weldon Johnson, James Baldwin, Gwendolyn Brooks, Langston Hughes and Margaret Walker.** (#MW866—$1.50)

Black
Viewpoints

Edited by
ARTHUR C. LITTLETON
and
MARY W. BURGER

A MENTOR BOOK from
NEW AMERICAN LIBRARY
TIMES MIRROR
New York and Scarborough, Ontario
The New English Library Limited, London

SECOND PRINTING

 MENTOR TRADEMARK REG. U.S. PAT. OFF. AND FOREIGN COUNTRIES
REGISTERED TRADEMARK—MARCA REGISTRADA
HECHO EN CHICAGO, U.S.A.

SIGNET, SIGNET CLASSICS, SIGNETTE, MENTOR, AND PLUME BOOKS are published *in the United States* by
The New American Library, Inc.,
1301 Avenue of the Americas, New York, New York 10019,
in Canada by The New American Library of Canada Limited,
81 Mack Avenue, Scarborough, 704, Ontario,
in the United Kingdom by The New English Library Limited,
Barnard's Inn, Holborn, London, E.C. 1, England.

FIRST PRINTING, MAY, 1971

PRINTED IN THE UNITED STATES OF AMERICA

Acknowledgments

JULIAN BOND, "Uniting the Races." Originally appeared in
Playboy Magazine. Copyright © 1969 by HMH Publishing Co. Inc.

JULIAN BOND, BOBBY SEALE, excerpts from "Other Voices,
Other Strategies." Copyright © 1970 by Time, Inc. Reprinted by
permission.

EDWARD W. BROOKE, "After a Long Hot Summer." By permission of the editors. From the September 5, 1967, issue of *Look*
Magazine. Copyright © 1967 by Cowles Communications, Inc.
Copyright © 1966 by Edward W. Brooke. From *The Challenge
of Change* by Edward W. Brooke, by permission of Little, Brown
and Co., Boston.

H. RAP BROWN, reprinted from *Die Nigger Die* by H. Rap
Brown. Copyright © 1969 by Lynne Brown and used by permission
of the publisher, The Dial Press, New York.

STOKELY CARMICHAEL, "Toward Black Liberation." Reprinted
from *The Massachusetts Review,* © 1966 The Massachusetts
Review, Inc. Excerpted from *Black Power,* by Stokely Carmichael
and Charles Hamilton. Copyright © 1967 by Stokely Carmichael
and Charles Hamilton. Reprinted by permission of Random House,
Inc., New York.

SHIRLEY CHISHOLM, "Black Is an Attitude." Copyright ©
1969, reprinted by permission of Congresswoman Shirley Chisholm.

KENNETH B. CLARK, "Fifteen Years of Deliberate Speed."
Copyright © 1969 by Saturday Review, Inc. "The Present Dilemma
of the Negro." Copyright © by the Association for the Study of
Negro Life and History, Inc. Published in the January 1968 *Journal
of Negro History*.

ELDRIDGE CLEAVER, "Revolution in the White Mother Country." Copyright © 1968 by Eldridge Cleaver. "The White Race
and Its Heroes," from *Soul On Ice* by Eldridge Cleaver. Copyright
© 1968 by Eldridge Cleaver. Used with permission of McGraw-
Hill Book Company, New York.

(*The following pages constitute an extension of this copyright page.*)

W. E. B. Du BOIS, "The Immediate Program of the American Negro," *The Crisis*, April, 1915. "Segregation," *The Crisis*, January, 1934. Reprinted with permission of the Crisis Publishing Company, Inc.

CHARLES EVERS, "Black Americans and the Press: Comment." Reprinted by permission of the author and the Ward Ritchie Press, Los Angeles, from *The Black American and the Press*.

CHARLES EVERS, "Notes and Comments." Reprinted by permission of the author and *The New Yorker*. Copyright © 1969, The New Yorker Magazine, Inc.

JAMES L. FARMER, "Are White Liberals Obsolete in the Black Struggle?" Reprinted by permission of the author and *The Progressive*, January, 1968. "Education Is the Answer." Reprinted by permission of the author and N.E.A. from *Today's Education*, April, 1969.

MARCUS M. GARVEY, excerpts from the *Philosophy and Opinions of Marcus Garvey*. Reprinted by permission of Mrs. Amy Jacques Garvey and the publisher, Frank Cass & Co., Ltd., London, 1967.

DICK GREGORY, "One Less Door." From the book *Nigger: An Autobiography*, by Dick Gregory with Robert Lipsyte. Copyright © 1964 by Dick Gregory Enterprises, Inc. Reprinted with permission of E. P. Dutton & Co., Inc., publishers. "Divine Libel," from *Black Manifesto: Religion, Racism, and Reparations*, edited by Robert S. Lecky and H. Elliott Wright. Copyright © Sheed and Ward, Inc., 1969.

NATHAN HARE, JR., "The Case for Black Separatism: Black Perspective." Copyright Newsweek, Inc., 1969.

ROY INNIS, "Separatist Economics: A New Social Contract," from William F. Haddad and G. Douglas Pugh, editors, *Black Economic Development* © 1969 by The American Assembly, Columbia University, New York, New York. Reprinted by permission of Prentice-Hall, Inc., Englewood Cliffs, N.J.

JESSE L. JACKSON, "Black Power and White Churches." Reprinted by permission of the author.

LEROI JONES, excerpts from "Tokenism: 300 Years for Five Cents" in *Home: Social Essays by LeRoi Jones*. Reprinted by permission of William Morrow and Company, Inc., New York. Copyright © 1962, 1966 by LeRoi Jones. From "The Legacy of Malcolm X, and the Coming of the Black Nation" in *Home: Social Essays by LeRoi Jones*. Reprinted by permission of William Morrow and Company, Inc., New York. Copyright © 1965, 1966 by LeRoi Jones.

Dedication

To the parents of the editors, George W. and Elizabeth M. Littleton and William H. and Ethel M. Williams, who have long worked to instill in their children intellectual curiosity as well as a genuine commitment to the Black struggle.

Contents

Introduction

We are currently witnessing a nationwide expansion of interest and concern about the rightful place of Blacks in American society. This increased concern is not at all limited to the newly created black studies programs in our high schools and colleges; it is also very evident, in a different form, on the community level. People from all walks of life with varied interests and equally varied attitudes toward the Black Movement are looking for answers and solutions. For this reason we must not falsely assume that the current demand for black texts and materials is merely a fad. If books are written from this vantage point, the probability of their being shallow, simplistic, and dated is greatly increased.

Because we feel this interest is genuine and pervasive, we reject a second assumption which has limited the number of truly useful books on the market. There is a tendency in this country to seek a monolithic movement or a single leader of black people. This is certainly misleading, for one person or one small group of persons cannot speak for millions of individuals. There is now, in fact, a dynamic multifaceted debate among black leaders over the means for achieving complete freedom and justice in twentieth-century America and over the role of the Black man in this changing nation. As a result, a number of articulate, young black activists have risen to national prominence, while many black establishment leaders also remain as recognized spokesmen for their people. It is this latter group, however, that has most readily been provided a forum. For this reason, presentation of the viewpoints of several Blacks who represent all major facets of the Black Movement would seem to be a realistic and timely approach. Perhaps out of such a diversity of thoughts, some commonality of goals, objectives, and philosophy can be discerned which would be beneficial for those readers seeking not only to increase their understanding of Blacks, but also to sharpen their ability to think critically and reach independent decisions on controversial subjects and individuals.

Without a comprehensive source, the task of comparing and contrasting the viewpoints of black leaders is certainly not an easy one. This state of affairs is largely due to the inaccessibility of these viewpoints in a single volume. For the most part, one interested in analyzing and evaluating the Black Movement is confronted with the herculean task of searching for single and fragmentary excerpts of various leaders' thinking. This book is therefore designed to meet the existing need for a well-organized book of readings which captures the essence of the thoughts and ideas of several contemporary black spokesmen. The book is divided into seven parts which point toward the major programs and strategies offered by thirty-one prominent black spokesmen. The more than fifty selections included deal almost exclusively with the Black man in the twentieth century, his aspirations and his frustrations, his victories and his defeats, and his image of himself and modern America. The viewpoints are divergent. They vary not only in terms of the general programs and strategies but also within these categories in terms of focus and philosophical orientation. There are also differences in emphasis, vocabulary, and prose technique. Some offer a neat step-by-step analysis of the subject, while the style and rhetoric of others is impatient and emotional as they examine the ideas in question.

Because we recognize the difficulty as well as the inherent danger of isolating specific spokesmen for a book which has the above purpose and design, it was necessary to impose certain restrictions on our choices. Those finally chosen are persons whose viewpoints are representative of a large number of persons. They are writers, orators, and activists with national or regional prominence among members of their race. In short, they are men with an audience and with a mechanism for disseminating their thoughts and activating their programs. More importantly, they are men who have spoken out, who have addressed themselves to the economic, social, and political needs of their people at a crucial time.

Too often books seeking to represent viewpoints from various sources rely on personalities and stereotypical labels such as militant, moderate, and conservative as a means of categorization. Such approaches cloud basic issues and make it difficult for the reader to objectively appraise ideas and their significance. We have sought a more meaningful and pragmatic means of grouping men and ideas. We have utilized a system of categorization which deals with the basic strategies and approaches which are repeatedly expressed. These categories are: Self-Awareness and Self-Determination; Education; Black-White Coalition; Government, Politics and Courts; Social and Institutional Reform; Revolutionary Action. Preceding these sections is one which presents the ideas of early and pretwentieth-century spokesmen. The inclusion of these forerunners, we feel, allows the reader to place the contemporary representatives in a proper perspective and to identify, in many cases, origins of ideology and tactics. Additionally, such an order enables the reader to see a continuity of thought in the Black Movement through the years.

Even with precautions to avoid the traditional pitfalls of organization, we encountered difficulties. For example, there is some overlapping in the categories in that some essays might have been included in more than one section. We also recognize that the categories themselves are not mutually exclusive. One spokesman might very well fit into two or more, as some of the discussion questions indicate. By way of illustration, although one may see education as a primary means of solving our problems he might also emphasize black awareness or institutional reform.

We feel that this book is unique in its total commitment to the reader. It provides a structure within which readers of various educational backgrounds and interests can see the interrelationship of the ideas and thoughts presented. For each section a brief introductory statement is included. This statement defines the rationale for the particular heading by showing the commonalities of the positions and programs therein, thus enabling diverse readers to establish a common ground for understanding and interpretation.

There are biographical sketches which should be beneficial to both the novice and the experienced reader as a means of revealing the activities and the growth which led to the spokesman's prominence and the prominence of his ideas.

One of the special features of the book is the use of a short quotation from each spokesman following his biography. These quotations, taken from one of the essays included in this text, will allow the reader to focus instantly on the spokesman's general approach and orientation to the Black Movement. Another useful feature is the discussion questions which conclude each section. These questions can lead the reader to a more penetrating analysis of the essays and, therefore, to a more critical understanding of the relationships among them and those in other parts of the book.

As a whole, this book should be enjoyable and useful to a general audience as well as to an academically oriented audience and in all cases where intellectul discourse is an essential part of the learning process. The essays are thought-provoking, challenging, perhaps even inciting, and always interesting and informative. They are not guidelines for the reader; rather they are presentments of answers to the many questions he undoubtedly has on one of the most-discussed but misunderstood problems of our time—racism and the Black Movement. These readings are offered as motivating forces to the reader's formulation of useful and workable ideas and as a means of gaining greater insight into himself and the world for which he is being prepared. In this book, the reader will find himself confronted by the Black man, speaking for himself, about himself, and for the good of his people.

The passing of time will undoubtedly and rightfully result in the emergence of new spokesmen and new statements. Consequently, some of those persons identified here will be eliminated in one way or another while others will merely fade into obscurity. Yet, the ideas and philosophies will remain, if not with active significance, certainly with historicity. Since this is true, our book emphasizes thoughts and ideas as well as spokesmen, for ideas are more resistant to mortality than are men.

Forerunners

Forerunners

The ideas expressed by the forerunners serve as a springboard to all other parts of the book. The spokesmen included represent some of the real pioneers of the present Black Movement. Their essays reflect a wide array of conceptual approaches such as black pride, self-help, the development of an intelligentsia, Pan-Africanism, industrial education, and communal activities. The strategies range from a genuine conciliatory approach to the most militant demands. In general, these writings reveal the origins of several presently used concepts—integration, separatism, nationalism, black consciousness, black studies, black manifestos.

Douglass' letter to Harriet Beecher Stowe, for example, proposes that the elevation of free blacks come through learning agricultural and mechanical skills. Although Washington expresses the same concern for black industrial education, the occurrence of the Civil War and the freedom of blacks make his ideas seem less practical and more conciliatory. Du Bois' essay on education is a direct answer to Washington's program. He looks toward the college-educated and the exceptional members of his race to lead the masses. His feeling is that an entire race trained to be artisans would only lead to further degradation.

On the issue of social justice, Douglass' second essay, written at the time of the Civil War, calls for complete civil and political equality for the emancipated black man. The question of social assimilation seems unimportant in this essay but, according to Douglass, it too must be a future goal. Washington's address calls for social separatism and economic cooperation, with the black man supplying the industrial and agricultural labor. Du Bois gives a specific program for the black man's fight for human equality and stresses the value of organizing. In another essay, he makes a very good distinction between segregation and discrimination by pointing out that segregation is not in itself undesirable. In a related manner,

Marcus Garvey's appeal for black consciousness and self-reliance can be seen as precursory ideas for black independence and self-determination.

While we have included only four spokesmen from the early and pretwentieth century, numerous others have made valuable and lasting contributions to the black struggle for complete freedom. By way of illustration, one may recall the revolutionary activities of Harriet Tubman and her underground railroad, Denmark Vesey and Nat Turner's slave rebellions, Mary McLeod Bethune's educational innovations, George Washington Carver's scientific and agricultural discoveries, and James Weldon Johnson's creative writings reflecting the cultural and social life of the Negro in America.

FREDERICK DOUGLASS,
Slave, Freedom Orator, Author

America has never known a more militant nor a more realistic spokesman for black people than Frederick Douglass. He was born into slavery as Frederick Augustus Baily in 1817, but escaped bondage in 1838 and changed his name as he fled to New Bedford, Massachusetts. Because of existing laws and customs, Douglass had to learn to read and write in secrecy while still enslaved. This self-education served him well, however, for he developed into an intelligent and most articulate orator. Following his escape, Douglass worked with the Massachusetts Anti-Slavery Society as a lecturer traveling all over New England and the North as well as abroad in England. His formal freedom was purchased with money he raised during this time.

Organizing reform groups and speaking and writing about the evils of slavery and the merits of active resistance, Douglass won many whites to abolitionism and inspired blacks to continue their fight for educational and economic equality after the Civil War. His newspapers, the North Star and the Douglass' Monthly, were the media through which he spoke to America, denouncing the evils of institutional slavery and the lack of effective programs after the war. He has also written several inspiring books which include the story of his life in three autobiographical accounts: Narrative of the Life of Frederick Douglass, A Fugitive Slave, My Bondage and My Freedom, *and* Life and Times of Frederick Douglass. *In the later years of his life, he was very influential in politics, holding such offices as Secretary of the Santo Domingo Commission and U.S. Consul General to Haiti.*

As the outstanding black orator of the nineteenth century and as an eloquent and forceful leader in the antislavery movement before the war and in black suffrage afterwards, Douglass is, today, a living symbol of black pride and uncompromising resistance to oppression.

"POVERTY, IGNORANCE, AND DEGRADATION ARE THE COMBINED EVILS . . . THESE CONSTITUTE THE SOCIAL DISEASE OF THE FREE COLORED PEOPLE OF THE UNITED STATES."

Letter to Harriet Beecher Stowe*

Rochester, March 8, 1853.

My Dear Mrs. Stowe:

You kindly informed me, when at your house a fortnight ago, that you designed to do something which should permanently contribute to the improvement and elevation of the free colored people in the United States. You especially expressed an interest in such of this class as had become free by their own exertions, and desired most of all to be of service to them. In what manner and by what means you can assist this class most successfully, is the subject upon which you have done me the honor to ask my opinion. . . . I assert, then, that *poverty, ignorance,* and *degradation* are the combined evils; or in other words, these constitute the social disease of the free colored people of the United States.

To deliver them from this triple malady is to improve and elevate them, by which I mean simply to put them on an equal footing with their white fellow-countrymen in the sacred right to *"Life, Liberty,* and the pursuit of happiness." I am for no fancied or artificial elevation, but only ask fair play. How shall this be obtained? I answer, first, not by establishing for our use high schools and colleges. Such institutions are, in my judgment, beyond our immediate occasions and are not adapted to our present most pressing wants. High schools and colleges are excellent institutions, and will in due season be greatly subservient to our progress; but they are the result, as well as they are the demand, of a point of progress which we as a people have not yet attained. Accustomed as we have been to the rougher and harder modes of living, and of gaining a livelihood, we cannot and we ought not to hope that in a single leap from our low condition, we can reach that of *Ministers, Lawyers, Doctors, Editors, Merchants,* etc. These

* Reprinted from *Life and Times of Frederick Douglass,* DeWolfe and Fiske Company, 1892.

will doubtless be attained by us; but this will only be when we have patiently and laboriously, and I may add successfully, mastered and passed through the intermediate gradations of agriculture and the mechanic arts. Besides, there are (and perhaps this is a better reason for my view of the case) numerous institutions of learning in this country, already thrown open to colored youth. To my thinking, there are quite as many facilities now afforded to the colored people as they can spare the time, from the sterner duties of life, to judiciously appropriate. In their present condition of poverty, they cannot spare their sons and daughters two or three years at boarding schools or colleges, to say nothing of finding the means to sustain them while at such institutions. I take it, therefore, that we are well provided for in this respect; and that it may be fairly inferred from the fact, that the facilities for our education, so far as schools and colleges in the Free States are concerned, will increase quite in proportion with our future wants. Colleges have been open to colored youth in this country during the last dozen years. Yet few, comparatively, have acquired a classical education; and even this few have found themselves educated far above a living condition, there being no methods by which they could turn their learning to account. Several of this latter class have entered the ministry; but you need not be told that an educated people is needed to sustain an educated ministry. There must be a certain amount of cultivation among the people, to sustain such a ministry. At present we have not that cultivation amongst us; and, therefore, we value in the preacher strong lungs rather than high learning. I do not say that educated ministers are not needed amongst us, far from it! I wish there were more of them! but to increase their number is *not* the largest benefit you can bestow upon us.

We have two or three colored lawyers in this country; and I rejoice in the fact; for it affords very gratifying evidence of our progress. Yet it must be confessed that, in point of success, our lawyers are as great failures as our ministers. White people will not employ them to the obvious embarrassment of their causes, and the blacks, taking their *cue* from the whites, have not sufficient confidence in their abilities to employ them. Hence educated colored men, among the colored people, are at a very great discount. It would seem that education and emigration go together with us, for as soon as a man rises amongst us, capable, by his genius and learning, to do us great service, just so soon he finds that he can serve himself better by going elsewhere. In proof of this, I might instance the Russwurms, the Garnetts, the Wards, the Crummells, and others, all men of superior ability and attainments, and capable of removing mountains of prejudice against their race, by their simple presence in the country; but these gentlemen, finding themselves embarrassed here by the peculiar disadvantages to which I have referred, disadvantages in part growing out of their education, being repelled by ignorance on the one hand, and prejudice on the other, and having no taste to continue a contest against such odds, have sought more congenial climes, where they can live more peaceable and quiet lives. I regret their election, but I cannot blame them; for with an equal amount of education, and the hard lot which was theirs, I might follow their example. . . .

There is little reason to hope that any considerable number of the free colored people will ever be induced to leave this country, even if such a thing were desirable. The black man (*un*like the Indian) loves civilization. He does not make very great progress in civilization himself, but he likes to be in the midst of it, and prefers to share its most galling evils, to encountering barbarism. Then the love of country, the dread of isolation, the lack of adventurous spirit, and the thought of seeming to desert their "brethren in bonds," are a powerful check upon all schemes of colonization, which look to the removal of the colored people, without the slaves. The truth is, dear madam, we are *here*, and here we are likely to remain. Individuals emigrate—nations never. We have grown up with this republic, and I see nothing in her character, or even in the character of the American people, as yet, which compels the belief that we must leave the United States. If, then, we are to remain here, the question for the wise and good is precisely that which you have submitted to me—namely: What can be done to improve the condition of the free people of color in the United States? The plan which I humbly submit in answer to this inquiry (and in the hope that it may find favor with you, and with the many friends of humanity who honor, love and cooperate with you) is the establishment in Rochester, N.Y., or in some other part of the United States equally favorable to such an enterprise, of an INDUSTRIAL COLLEGE in which shall be taught several important branches of the mechanic arts. This college shall be open to colored youth. I will pass over the details of such an institution as I propose. . . . Never having had a day's schooling in all my life, I may not be expected to map out the details of a plan so comprehensive as that involved in the idea of a college. I repeat, then, that I leave the organization and administration of the institution to the superior wisdom of yourself and the friends who second your noble efforts. The argument in favor of an Industrial College (a college to be conducted by the best men, and the best workmen which the mechanic arts can afford; a college where colored youth an be instructed to use their hands, as well as their heads; where they can be put in possession of the means of getting a living whether their lot in after life may be cast among civilized or uncivilized men; whether they choose to stay here, or prefer to return to the land of their fathers) is briefly this: Prejudice against the free colored people in the United States has shown itself nowhere so invincible as among mechanics. The farmer and the professional man cherish no feeling so bitter as that cherished by these. The latter would starve us out of the country entirely. At this moment I can more easily get my son into a lawyer's office to study law than I can into a blacksmith's shop to blow the bellows and to wield the sledge-hammer. Denied the means of learning useful trades, we are pressed into the narrowest limits to obtain a livelihood. In times past we have been the hewers of wood and drawers of water for American society, and we once enjoyed a monopoly in menial employments, but this is so no longer. Even these employments are rapidly passing away out of our hands. The fact is (every day begins with the lesson, and ends with the lesson) that colored men must learn trades; must find new employments; new modes of usefulness to society, or that they must decay under the pressing wants to which their condition is rapidly bringing them.

We must become mechanics; we must build as well as live in houses; we must make as well as use furniture; we must construct bridges as well as pass over them, before we can properly live or be respected by our fellow men. We need mechanics as well as ministers. We need workers in iron, clay, and leather. We have orators, authors, and other professional men, but these reach only a certain class, and get respect for our race in certain select circles. To live here as we ought we must fasten ourselves to our countrymen through their everyday, cardinal wants. We must not only be able to *black* boots, but to *make* them. At present we are, in the Northern States, unknown as mechanics. We give no proof of genius or skill at the county, State, or national fairs. We are unknown at any of the great exhibitions of the industry of our fellow-citizens, and being unknown, we are unconsidered.

The fact that we make no show of our ability is held conclusive of our inability to make any, hence all the indifference and contempt with which incapacity is regarded fall upon us, and that too when we have had no means of disproving the infamous opinion of our natural inferiority. I have, during

the last dozen years, denied before the Americans that we are
an inferior race; but this has been done by arguments based
upon admitted principles rather than by the presentation of
facts. Now, firmly believing, as I do, that there are skill,
invention, power, industry, and real mechanical genius among
the colored people, which will bear favorable testimony for
them, and which only need the means to develop them, I am
decidedly in favor of the establishment of such a college as I
have mentioned. The benefits of such an institution would not
be confined to the Northern States, nor to the free colored
people. They would extend over the whole Union. The slave
not less than the freeman would be benefited by such an
institution. It must be confessed that the most powerful argument now used by the southern slaveholder, and the one most
soothing to his conscience, is that derived from the low condition of the free colored people of the North. I have long
felt that too little attention has been given by our truest friends
in this country to removing this stumbling-block out of the
way of the slave's liberation.

The most telling, the most killing refutation of slavery is
the presentation of an industrious, enterprising, thrifty, and
intelligent free black population. Such a population I believe
would rise in the Northern States under the fostering care of
such a college as that supposed.

To show that we are capable of becoming mechanics I
might adduce any amount of testimony; but, dear madam, I
need not ring the changes on such a proposition. There is no
question in the mind of any unprejudiced person that the
Negro is capable of making a good mechanic. Indeed, even
those who cherish the bitterest feelings toward us have admitted that the apprehension that Negroes might be employed
in their stead dictated the policy of excluding them from
trades altogether. But I will not dwell upon this point, as I
fear I have already trespassed too long upon your precious
time, and written more than I ought to expect you to read.
Allow me to say in conclusion that I believe every intelligent
colored man in America will approve and rejoice at the establishment of some such institution as that now suggested. There
are many respectable colored men, fathers of large families,
having boys nearly grown up, whose minds are tossed by
day and by night with the anxious inquiry, What shall I do
with my boys? Such an institution would meet the wants of
such persons. Then, too, the establishment of such an institution would be in character with the eminently practical
philanthropy of your transatlantic friends. America could
scarcely object to it as an attempt to agitate the public mind

on the subject of slavery, or to *dissolve the Union*. It could not be tortured into a cause for hard words by the American people, but the noble and good of all classes would see in the effort an excellent motive, a benevolent object, temperately, wisely, and practically manifested.

Wishing you, dear madam, renewed health, a pleasant passage and safe return to your native land,

I am, most truly, your grateful friend,

FREDERICK DOUGLASS.

BOOKER T. WASHINGTON,
Educator, Orator

Booker T. Washington, by his account, was not sure of the precise place or date of his birth. However, historians have indicated that he was born a slave April 5, 1856, in Franklin County, Virginia. After the Civil War his family moved to Malden, West Virginia, where he attended school on an ir- regular basis and worked in salt furnaces and coal mines. Sheer determination and hard work enabled him to complete his education at Hampton Normal and Agricultural Institute. In 1881 he was selected to head the Tuskegee Normal and Industrial Institute, a school modeled after Hampton Institute. From a very meager beginning he developed Tuskegee into one of the leading centers of Negro education in the world. Philosophically he felt the interest of the Negro could best be realized through education, thrift, and practical skill in industry and agriculture rather than by emphasizing equality and agitating for civil rights. Washington, a champion of co- operation between the races, died at Tuskegee on November 14, 1915.

"PROGRESS IN THE ENJOYMENT OF ALL THE PRIVI- LEGES THAT WILL COME TO US MUST BE THE RESULT OF SEVERE AND CONSTANT STRUGGLE RATHER THAN OF ARTIFICIAL FORCING."

vidual makes all efforts to surround himself throughout life
with the evidence of it. As of the individual so should it be
of the race and nation. His glittering career of Rockefeller

Industrial Education for the Negro*

One of the most fundamental and far-reaching deeds that
has been accomplished during the last quarter of a century
has been that by which the Negro has been helped to find himself
and to learn the secrets of civilization—to learn that there are
a few simple, cardinal principles upon which a race must start
its upward course, unless it would fail, and its last estate be
worse than its first.

It has been necessary for the Negro to learn the difference
between being worked and working—to learn that being
worked meant degradation, while working means civilization;
that all forms of labor are honorable, and all forms of idle-
ness disgraceful. It has been necessary for him to learn that all
races that have got upon their feet have done so largely by
laying an economic foundation, and, in general, by beginning
in a proper cultivation and ownership of the soil.

In what I say here I would not by any means have it understood that I would limit or circumscribe the mental development of the Negro student. No race can be lifted until its mind
is awakened and strengthened. By the side of industrial training should always go mental and moral training, but the pushing of mere abstract knowledge into the head means little. We
want more than the mere performance of mental gymnastics.
Our knowledge must be harnessed to the things of real life. I
would encourage the Negro to secure all the mental strength,
all the mental culture—whether gleaned from science, mathematics, history, language or literature that his circumstances
will allow, but I believe most earnestly that for years to come
the education of the people of my race should be so directed
that the greatest proportion of the mental strength of the
masses will be brought to bear upon the every-day practical
things of life, upon something that is needed to be done, and
something which they will be permitted to do in the com-

* Reprinted from *The Negro Problem*, James Potts and Company,
1903.

munity in which they reside. And just the same with the professional class which the race needs and must have, I would say give the men and women of that class, too, the training which will best fit them to perform in the most successful manner the service which the race demands.

I would not confine the race to industrial life, not even to agriculture, for example, although I believe that by far the greater part of the Negro race is best off in the country districts and must and should continue to live there, but I would teach the race that in industry the foundation must be laid— that the very best service which any one can render to what is called the higher education is to teach the present generation to provide a material or industrial foundation. On such a foundation as this will grow habits of thrift, a love of work, economy, ownership of property, bank accounts. Out of it will grow moral and religious strength. Out of it will grow wealth from which alone can come leisure and the opportunity for the enjoyment of literature and the fine arts.

I would set no limits to the attainments of the Negro in arts, in letters or statesmanship, but I believe the surest way to reach those ends is by laying the foundation in the little things of life that lie immediately about one's door. I plead for industrial education and development for the Negro not because I want to cramp him, but because I want to free him. I want to see him enter the all-powerful business and commercial world.

Early in the history of the Tuskegee Institute we began to combine industrial training with mental and moral culture. Our first efforts were in the direction of agriculture, and we began teaching this with no appliances except one hoe and a blind mule. From this small beginning we have grown until now the Institute owns two thousand acres of land, eight hundred of which are cultivated each year by the young men of the school.

Many seem to think that industrial education is meant to make the Negro work as he worked in the days of slavery. This is far from my conception of industrial education. If this training is worth anything to the Negro, it consists in teaching him how not to work, but how to make the forces of nature—air, steam, water, horse-power and electricity— work for him. If it has any value it is in lifting labor up out of toil and drudgery into the plane of the dignified and the beautiful. The Negro in the South works and works hard; but too often his ignorance and lack of skill causes him to do his work in the most costly and shiftless manner, and this keeps him near the bottom of the ladder in the economic world.

I close, then, as I began, by saying that as a slave the Negro was worked, and that as a freeman he must learn to work. There is still doubt in many quarters as to the ability of the Negro unguided, unsupported, to hew his own path and put into visible, tangible, indisputable form, products and signs of civilization. This doubt cannot be much affected by abstract arguments, no matter how delicately and convincingly woven together. Patiently, quietly, doggedly, persistently, through summer and winter, sunshine and shadow, by self-sacrifice, by foresight, by honesty and industry, we must re-enforce argument with results. One farm bought, one house built, one home sweetly and intelligently kept, one man who is the largest taxpayer or has the largest bank account, one school or church maintained, one factory running successfully, one truck garden profitably cultivated, one patient cured by a Negro doctor, one sermon well preached, one office well filled, one life cleanly lived—these will tell more in our favor than all the abstract eloquence that can be summoned to plead our cause. Our pathway must be up through the soil, up through swamps, up through forests, up through the streams, the rocks, up through commerce, education and religion!

WILLIAM E. B. DUBOIS,
Historian, Intellectual, Social Justice Advocate

W. E. B. Du Bois became involved in the Black Movement, at least partially, in reaction to the conciliatory tactics of Booker T. Washington. Born in Great Barrington, Massachusetts, in 1868, he received his Ph.D. from Harvard in 1895, and taught history and economics at Atlanta University for several years, between 1896 and 1910.

Du Bois has at times been considered the father of modern black militancy. As one of the founders of the Niagara Movement and the National Association for the Advancement of Colored People, he recognized early the need for organized protest. Du Bois was the editor of the magazine Crisis *for several years and has to his scholarly credit many outstanding books and articles. For instance, he wrote* The Souls of Black Folk, Suppression of the Black African Trade, Black Reconstruction, The Philadelphia Story: A Social Study *and his autobiography,* Dusk of Dawn.

One of his primary interests was to inspire a vanguard of college-educated blacks to become leaders for their people. Later in life, however, he became disillusioned with the prospects of complete freedom for black people in this country through the existing democratic process and looked toward Communism as a solution to the political and economic problems of blacks. He spent the last years of his life in Ghana editing a newspaper and working on the Encyclopedia Africana. *In 1963, he died at the age of 95.*

"THE NEGRO MUST HAVE POWER; THE POWER OF MEN, THE RIGHT TO DO, TO KNOW, TO FEEL AND TO EXPRESS THAT KNOWLEDGE. . . ."

35

The Talented Tenth*

The Negro race, like all races, is going to be saved by its exceptional men. The problem of education, then, among Negroes must first of all deal with the Talented Tenth; it is the problem of developing the Best of this race that they may guide the Mass away from the contamination and death of the Worst, in their own and other races. Now the training of men is a difficult and intricate task. Its technique is a matter for educational experts, but its object is for the vision of seers. If we make money the object of man-training, we shall develop money-makers but not necessarily men; if we make technical skill the object of education, we may possess artisans but not, in nature, men. Men we shall have only as we make manhood the object of the work of the schools—intelligence, broad sympathy, knowledge of the world that was and is, and of the relation of men to it—this is the curriculum of that Higher Education which must underlie true life. On this foundation we may build bread winning, skill of hand and quickness of brain, with never a fear lest the child and man mistake the means of living for the object of life.

It is the fashion of to-day to sneer at them and to say that with freedom Negro leadership should have begun at the plow and not in the Senate—a foolish and mischievous lie; two hundred and fifty years that black serf toiled at the plow and yet that toiling was in vain till the Senate passed the war amendments; and two hundred and fifty years more the half-free serf of to-day may toil at his plow, but unless he have political rights and righteously guarded civic status, he will still remain the poverty-stricken and ignorant plaything of rascals, that he now is. This all sane men know even if they dare not say it.

And so we come to the present—a day of cowardice and

* Reprinted from *The Negro Problem*, James Potts and Company, 1903.

vacillation, of strident wide-voiced wrong and faint hearted compromise; of double-faced dallying with Truth and Right. Who are to-day guiding the work of the Negro people? The "exceptions" of course. And yet so sure as this Talented Tenth is pointed out, the blind worshippers of the Average cry out in alarm: "These are exceptions, look here at death, disease and crime—these are the happy rule." Of course they are the rule, because a silly nation made them the rule: Because for three long centuries this people lynched Negroes who dared to be brave, raped black women who dared to be virtuous, crushed dark-hued youth who dared to be ambitious, and encouraged and made to flourish servility and lewdness and apathy. But not even this was able to crush all manhood and chastity and aspiration from black folk. A saving remnant continually survives and persists, continually aspires, continually shows itself in thrift and ability and character.

Can the masses of the Negro people be in any possible way more quickly raised than by the effort and example of this aristocracy of talent and character? Was there ever a nation on God's fair earth civilized from the bottom upward? Never; it is, ever was and ever will be from the top downward that culture filters. The Talented Tenth rises and pulls all that are worth the saving up to their vantage ground. This is the history of human progress; and the two historic mistakes which have hindered that progress were the thinking first that no more could ever rise save the few already risen; or second, that it would better the unrisen to pull the risen down.

How then shall the leaders of a struggling people be trained and the hands of the risen few strengthened? There can be but one answer: The best and most capable of their youth must be schooled in the colleges and universities of the land. We will not quarrel as to just what the university of the Negro should teach or how it should teach it—I willingly admit that each soul and each race-soul needs its own peculiar curriculum. But this is true: A university is a human invention for the transmission of knowledge and culture from generation to generation, through the training of quick minds and pure hearts, and for this work no other human invention will suffice, not even trade and industrial schools.

All men cannot go to college but some men must; every isolated group or nation must have its yeast, must have for the talented few centers of training where men are not so mystified and befuddled by the hard and necessary toil of earning a living, as to have no aims higher than their bellies, and no God greater than Gold.

I would not deny, or for a moment seem to deny, the paramount necessity of teaching the Negro to work, and to work steadily and skillfully; or seem to depreciate in the slightest degree the important part idustrial schools must play in the accomplishment of these ends, but I *do* say, and insist upon it, that it is industrialism drunk with its vision of success, to imagine that its own work can be accomplished without providing for the training of broadly cultured men and women to teach its own teachers, and to teach the teachers of the public schools.

But I have already said that human education is not simply a matter of schools; it is much more a matter of family and group life—the training of one's home, of one's daily companions, of one's social class. Now the black boy of the South moves in a black world—a world with its own leaders, its own thoughts, its own ideals. In this world he gets by far the larger part of his life training, and through the eyes of this dark world he peers into the veiled world beyond. Who guides and determines the education which he receives in his world? His teachers here are the group-leaders of the Negro people—the physicians and clergymen, the trained fathers and mothers, the influential and forceful men about him of all kinds; here it is, if at all, that the culture of the surrounding world trickles through and is handed on by the graduates of the higher schools. Can such culture training of group leaders be neglected? Can we afford to ignore it? Do you think that if the leaders of thought among Negroes are not trained and educated thinkers, that they will have no leaders? On the contrary a hundred half-trained demagogues will still hold the places they so largely occupy now, and hundreds of vociferous busybodies will multiply. You have no choice; either you must help furnish this race from within its own ranks with thoughtful men of trained leadership, or you must suffer the evil consequences of a headless misguided rabble.

I am an earnest advocate of manual training and trade teaching for black boys, and for white boys, too. I believe that next to the founding of Negro colleges the most valuable addition to Negro education since the war, has been industrial training for black boys. Nevertheless, I insist that the object of all true education is not to make men carpenters, it is to make carpenters men; there are two means of making the carpenter a man, each equally important: the first is to give the group and community in which he works, liberally trained teachers and leaders to teach him and his family what life means; the second is to give him sufficient intelligence and technical skill to make him an efficient workman; the first object demands the Negro college and college-bred men—not a quantity of such colleges, but a few of excellent quality; not too many college-bred men, but enough to leaven the lump, to inspire the masses, to raise the Talented Tenth to leadership; the second object demands a good system of common schools, well-taught, conveniently located and properly equipped.

Men of America, the problem is plain before you. Here is a race transplanted through the criminal foolishness of your fathers. Whether you like it or not the millions are here, and here they will remain. If you do not lift them up, they will pull you down. Education and work are the levers to uplift a people. Work alone will not do it unless inspired by the right ideals and guided by intelligence. Education must not simply teach work—it must teach Life. The Talented Tenth of the Negro race must be made leaders of thought and missionaries of culture among their people. No others can do this work and Negro colleges must train men for it. The Negro race, like all other races, is going to be saved by its exceptional men.

The Present and Future of the Colored Race in America*

By FREDERICK DOUGLASS

I think that most of you will agree with me in respect to the surpassing importance of the subject we are here to consider this evening though you may differ from me in other respects. It seems to me that the relation subsisting between the white and colored people of this country, is of all other questions, the great, paramount, imperative, and all commanding question for this age and nation to solve.

All the circumstances of the hour plead with an eloquence, equaled by no human tongue, for the immediate solution of this vital problem. 200,000 graves.—A distracted and bleeding country plead for this solution. It cannot be denied, nobody now even attempts to deny, that the question, what shall be done with the negro, is the one grand cause of the tremendous war now upon us, and likely to continue upon us, until the country is united upon some wise policy concerning it. When the country was at peace and all appeared prosperous, there was something like a plausible argument in favor of leaving things to their own course. No such policy avails now. The question now stands before us as one of life and death. We are encompassed by it as by a wall of fire. The flames singe and burn us on all sides, becoming hotter every hour.

Men sneer at it as the "nigger question," endeavoring to degrade it by misspelling it. But they degrade nothing but themselves. They would much rather talk about the Constitution as it is, and the Union as it was, or about the Crittenden, or some other impossible compromise, but the negro peeps out at every flash of their rhetorical pyrotechnics and utterly

* Reprinted from the *Douglass' Monthly*, V (1863), pp. 833-36.

refuses to be hid by either fire, dust or smoke. The term, negro, is at this hour the most pregnant word in the English language. The destiny of the nation has the negro for its pivot, and turns upon the question as to what shall be done with him. Peace and war, union and disunion, salvation and ruin, glory and shame all crowd upon our thoughts the moment this vital word is pronounced.

You and I have witnessed many attempts to put this negro question out of the pale of popular thought and discussion, and have seen the utter vanity of all such attempts.—It has baffled all the subtle contrivances of an ease loving and selfish priesthood, and has constantly refused to be smothered under the soft cushions of a canting and heartless religion. It has mocked and defied the compromising cunning of so called statesmen, who would have gladly postponed our present troubles beyond our allotted space of life and bequeath them as a legacy of sorrow to our children. But this wisdom of the crafty is confounded and their counsels brought to naught. A divine energy, omniscient and omnipotent, acting through the silent, solemn and all-pervading laws of the universe, irresistible, unalterable and eternal, has ever more forced this mighty question of the negro upon the attention of the country and the world.

What shall be done with the negro? meets us not only in the street, in the Church, in the Senate, and in our State Legislatures; but in our diplomatic correspondence with foreign nations, and even on the field of battle, where our brave sons and brothers are striking for Liberty and country, or for honored graves.

This question met us before the war; it meets us during the war, and will certainly meet us after the war, unless we shall have the wisdom, the courage, and the nobleness of soul to settle the status of the negro, on the solid and immovable basis of Eternal justice.

I stand here tonight therefore, to advocate what I conceive to be such a solid basis, one that shall fix our peace upon a rock. Putting a side all the hay, wood and stubble of expediency, I shall advocate for the negro, his most full and complete adoption into the great national family of America. I shall demand for him the most perfect civil and political equality, and that he shall enjoy all the rights, privileges and immunities enjoyed by any other members of the body politic. I weigh my words and I mean all I say, when I contend as I do contend, that this is the *only solid, and final solution* of the problem before us. It is demanded not less by the terrible exigencies of the nation, than by the negro himself for the negro and the nation, are to rise or fall, be killed or cured, saved or lost together. Save the negro and you save the nation, destroy the negro and you destroy the nation, and to save both you must have but one great law of Liberty, Equality and Fraternity for all Americans without respect to color.

There are at least four answers, other than mine, floating about in the public mind, to the question what shall be done with the negro.

1st. It is said that the white race can, if they will, reduce the whole colored population to slavery, and at once make all the laws and institutions of the country harmonize with that state of facts and thus abolish at a blow, all distinctions and antagonisms. But this mode of settling the question, simple as it is, would not work well. It would create a class of tyrants in whose presence no man's Liberty, not even the white man's Liberty, would be safe. The slaveholder would then be the only really free man of the country.—All the rest would be either slaves, or be poor white trash, to be kept from between the wind and our slaveholding nobility. The non-slaveholder would be the patrol, the miserable watch dog of the slave plantation.

2nd. The next and best defined solution of our difficulties about the negro is colonization, which proposes to send the negro back to Africa where his ancestors came from.—This is a singularly pleasing dream. But as was found in the case of sending missionaries to the moon, it was much easier to show that they might be useful there, than to show how they could be got there. It would take a larger sum of money than we shall have to spare at the close of this war, to send five millions of American born people, five thousand miles a cross the sea.

It may be safely affirmed that we shall hardly be in a condition at the close of this war to afford the money for such costly transportation, even if we could consent to the folly of sending away the only efficient producers in the largest half of the American union.

3d. It may be said as another mode of escaping the claims of absolute justice, the white people may Emancipate the slaves in form yet retain them as slaves in fact just as General Banks is now said to be doing in Louisiana, or then may free them from individual masters, only to make them slaves to the community. They can make of them a degraded caste. But this would be about the worst thing that could be done. It would make pestilence and pauperism, ignorance and crime, a part of American Institutions. It would be dooming the colored race to a condition indescribably wretched and the dreadful contagion of their vices and crimes would fly like cholera and small pox through all classes. Woe, woe! to this land, when it strips five millions of its people of all motives for cultivating an upright character. Such would be the effect of abolishing slavery, without conferring equal rights. It would be to lacerate and depress the spirit of the negro, and make him a scourge and a curse to the country. Do anything else with us, but plunge us not into this hopeless pit.

4th. The white people of the country may trump up some cause of war against the colored people, and wage that terrible war of races which some men even now venture to predict, if not to desire, and exterminate the black race entirely. They would spare neither age nor sex.

Now, I hold that there is but one way of wisely disposing of the colored race, and that is to do them right and justice. It is not only to break the chains of their bondage and accord to them personal liberty, but it is to admit them to the full and complete enjoyment of civil and political Equality.

The mere abolition of slavery is not the end of the law for the black man, or for the white man. To emancipate the bondman from the laws that make him a chattel, and yet subject him to laws and deprivations which will inevitably break down his spirit, destroy his patriotism and convert him into a social pest, will be little gain to him and less gain to the country. One of the most plausible arguments ever made for slavery is that which assumes that those who argue for the freedom of the negro, do not themselves propose to treat him as an equal fellow citizen. The true course is to look this matter squarely in the face and determine to grant the entire claims of justice and liberty keeping back no part of the price.

But the question comes not only from those who hate the colored race, but from some who are distinguished for their philanthropy: can this thing be done? can the white and colored people of America ever be blended into a common nationality under a system of equal Laws?

Mark, I state the question broadly and fairly. It respects civil and political equality, in its fullest and best sense: can such equality ever be practically enjoyed?

The question is not can there be social equality? That does not exist anywhere.—There have been arguments to show that no one man should own more property than another. But no satisfactory conclusion has been reached. So there are those who talk about social Equality, but nothing better on that subject than *"pursuit,"* the right of pursuit has been attained.

The question is not whether the colored man is mentally equal to his white brother, for in this respect there is no equality among white men themselves.

The question is not whether colored men will be likely to reach the Presidential chair. I have no trouble here: for a man may live quite a tolerable life without ever breathing the air of Washington.

But the question is: Can the white and colored people of this country be blended into a common nationality, and enjoy together, in the same country, under the same flag, the inestimable blessings of life, liberty and the pursuit of happiness, as neighborly citizens of a common country?

I answer most unhesitatingly, I believe they can.

Let me give a few of the reasons for the hope that is within me.

The first is, despite all theories and all disparagements, the negro is a man. By every fact, by every argument, by every rule of measurement, mental, moral or spiritual, by everything in the heavens above and in the earth beneath which vindicates the humanity of any class of beings, the negro's humanity is equally vindicated. The lines which separate him from the brute creation are as broad, distinct and palpable, as those which define and establish the very best specimens of the Indo-Caucasian race. I will not stop here to prove the manhood of the negro. His virtues and his vices, his courage and his cowardice, his beauties and his deformities, his wisdom and his folly, everything connected with him, attests his manhood.

If the negro were a horse or an ox, the question as to whether he can become a party to the American government, and member of the nation, could never have been raised. The very questions raised against him confirm the truth of what they are raised to disprove. We have laws forbidding the negro to learn to read, others forbidding his owning a dog, others punishing him for using fire arms, and our Congress came near passing a law that a negro should in no case be superior to a white man, thus admitting the very possibility of what they were attempting to deny.

That the interests of all the people would be promoted by the full participation of colored men in the affairs of government seems very plain to me. The American government rests for support, more than any other government in the world, upon the loyalty and patriotism of all its people. The friendship and affection of her black sons and daughters, as they increase in virtue and knowledge, will be an element of strength to the Republic too obvious to be neglected and epelled. I predict, therefore, that under an enlightened public entiment, the American people will cultivate the friendship, ncrease the usefulness and otherwise advance the interests f the colored race. They will be as eager to extend the rights nd dignity of citizenship as they have hitherto been eager to eny those rights.

But a word as to objections. The Constitution is interposed. t always is.

Let me tell you something. Do you know that you have een deceived and cheated? You have been told that this overnment was intended from the beginning for white men, nd for white men exclusively; that the men who formed the Jnion and framed the Constitution designed the permanent xclusion of the colored people from the benefits of those nstitutions. Davis, Taney and Yancey, traitors at the south, ave propagated this statement, while their copperhead echoes t the north have repeated the same. There never was a bolder r more wicked perversion of the truth of history. So far rom this purpose was the mind and heart of your fathers, hat they desired and expected the abolition of slavery. They ramed the Constitution plainly with a view to the speedy lownfall of slavery. They carefully excluded from the Constitution any and every word which could lead to the belief hat they meant it for persons of only one complexion.

The Constitution, in its language and in its spirit, welcomes he black man to all the rights which it was intended to guarantee to any class of the American people. Its preamble ells us for whom and for what it was made.

But I am told that the ruling class in America being white, t is impossible for men of color ever to become a part of he "body politic." With some men this seems a final statenent, a final argument, which it is utterly impossible to answer. t conveys the idea that the body politic is a rather fastidious oody, from which everything offensive is necessarily excluded. ., myself, once had some high notions about this body politic nd its high requirements, and of the kind of men fit to enter t and share its privileges. But a day's experience at the polls convinced me that the "body politic" is not more immaculate han many other bodies. That in fact it is a very mixed affair. saw ignorance enter, unable to read the vote it cast. I saw he convicted swindler enter and deposit his vote. I saw the gambler, the horse jockey, the pugilist, the miserable drunkard ust lifted from the gutter, covered with filth, enter and leposit his vote. I saw Pat, fresh from the Emerald Isle, requiring two sober men to keep him on his legs, enter and leposit his vote for the Democratic candidate amid the loud hurrahs of his fellow-citizens. The sight of these things went far to moderate my ideas about the exalted character of what is called the body politic, and convinced me that it could not suffer in its composition even should it admit a few sober, industrious and intelligent colored voters.

It is a fact, moreover, that colored men did at the beginning of our national history, form a part of the body politic, not only in what are now the free states, but also in the slave states. Mr. Wm. Goodell, to whom the cause of liberty in America is as much indebted as to any other one American citizen, has demonstrated that colored men formerly voted in eleven out of the thirteen original states.

The war upon the colored voters, and the war upon the Union, originated with the same parties, at the same time, and for the same guilty purpose of rendering slavery perpetual, universal and all controlling in the affairs of the nation.

Let this object be defeated and abandoned, let the country be brought back to the benign objects set forth in the preamble of the Constitution, and the colored man will easily find his way into the body politic, and be welcome in the jury box as well as at the ballot box. I know that prejudice largely prevails, and will prevail to some extent long after slavery shall be abolished in this country, but the power of prejudice will be broken when slavery is once abolished. There is not a black law on the statute book of a single free state that has not been placed there in deference to slavery existing in the slave states.

But it is said that the negro belongs to an inferior race. Inferior race! This is the apology for all the hell-black crimes ever committed by the white race against the blacks and the warrant for the repetition of those crimes through all times. Inferior race! It is an old argument. All nations have been compelled to meet it in some form or other since mankind have been divided into strong and weak, oppressors and oppressed. Whenever and wherever men have been oppressed and enslaved, their oppressors and enslavers have in every instance found a warrant for such oppression and enslavement in the alleged character of their victims. The very vices and crimes which slavery generates are usually charged as the peculiar characteristic of the race enslaved. When the Normans conquered the Saxons, the Saxons were a coarse, unrefined, inferior race. When the United States wants to possess herself of Mexican territory, the Mexicans are an inferior race. When Russia wants a share of the Ottoman Empire, the Turks are an inferior race, the sick man of Europe. So, too, when England wishes to impose some new burden on Ireland, or excuse herself for refusing to remove some old one, the Irish are denounced as an inferior race. But this is a monstrous argument. Now, suppose it were true that the negro is inferior instead of being an apology for oppression and proscription, it is an appeal to all that is noble and magnanimous in the human soul against both. When used in the service of oppression, it is as if one should say, "that man is weak; I am strong, therefore I will knock him down, and as far as I can I will keep him down. Yonder is an ignorant man. I am instructed, therefore I will do what I can to prevent his being instructed and to with-hold from him the means of education. There is another who is low in his associations, rude in his manners, coarse and brutal in his appetites, therefore I will see to it that his degradation shall be permanent, and that society shall hold out to him no motives or incitements to a more elevated character." I will not stop here to denounce this monstrous excuse for oppression. That men can resort to it shows that when the human mind is once completely under the dominion of pride and selfishness, the reasoning faculties are inverted if not subverted.

I should like to know what constitutes inferiority and the standard of superiority. Must a man be as wise as Socrates, as learned as Humboldt, as profound as Bacon, or as eloquent as Charles Sumner, before he can be reckoned among superior men? Alas! if this were so, few even of the most cultivated of the white race could stand the test. Webster was white and had a large head, but all men have not large heads. The negro is black and has a small head, but all negroes have not small heads. What rule shall we apply to all these heads? Why this: Give all an equal chance to grow.

There are signs of this good time coming all around us. Slavery has overleapt itself.—Having taken the sword it is destined to perish by the sword, and the long despised negro is to bear an honorable part in the salvation of himself and the country by the same blow. It has taken two years to convince the Washington Government, of the wisdom of calling the black man to participate in the gigantic effort now making to save the country. Even now they have not fully learned it— but learn it they will, and learn it they must before this tremendous war shall be ended.—Massachusetts, glorious old Massachusetts, has called the black man to the honor of bearing arms, and a thousand are already enrolled.

Hitherto we have been viewed and have viewed ourselves, as an impotent and spiritless race, having only a mission of folly and degradation before us. To-night we stand at the portals of a new world, a new life and a new destiny.

We have passed through the furnace and have not been consumed. During more than two centuries and a half, we have survived contact with the white race. We have risen from the small number of twenty, to the large number of five millions, living and increasing, where other tribes are decreasing and dying. We have illustrated the fact, that the two most opposite races of men known to ethnological science, can live in the same latitudes, longitudes, and altitudes, and that so far as natural causes are concerned there is reason to believe that we may permanently live under the same skies, brave the same climates, and enjoy Liberty, Equality and Fraternity in a common country.

The Atlanta Exposition Address*

By BOOKER T. WASHINGTON

The Atlanta Exposition, at which I had been asked to make an address as a representative of the Negro race . . . , was opened with a short address from Governor Bullock. After other interesting exercises, including an invocation from Bishop Nelson, of Georgia, a dedicatory ode by Albert Howell, Jr., and addresses by the President of the Exposition and Mrs. Joseph Thompson, the President of the Woman's Board, Governor Bullock introduced me with the words, "We have with us to-day a representative of Negro enterprise and Negro civilization."

When I arose to speak, there was considerable cheering, especially from the coloured people. As I remember it now, the thing that was uppermost in my mind was the desire to say something that would cement the friendship of the races and bring about hearty cooperation between them. So far as my outward surroundings were concerned, the only thing that I recall distinctly now is that when I got up, I saw thousands of eyes looking intently into my face. The following is the address which I delivered:—

MR. PRESIDENT AND GENTLEMEN OF THE BOARD OF DIRECTORS AND CITIZENS

One-third of the population of the South is of the Negro race. No enterprise seeking the material, civil, or moral welfare of this section can disregard this element of our population and reach the highest success. I but convey to you, Mr. President and Directors, the sentiment of the masses of my race when I say that in no way have the value and manhood of the American Negro been more fittingly and generously recognized than by the managers of this magnificent

* Reprinted from *Up From Slavery*, Doubleday and Company, Inc., 1901.

Exposition at every stage of its progress. It is a recognition that will do more to cement the friendship of the two races than any occurrence since the dawn of our freedom.

Not only this, but the opportunity here afforded will awaken among us a new era of industrial progress. Ignorant and inexperienced, it is not strange that in the first years of our new life we began at the top instead of at the bottom, that a seat in Congress or the state legislature was more sought than real estate or industrial skill; that the political convention of stump speaking had more attractions than starting a dairy farm or truck garden.

A ship lost at sea for many days suddenly sighted a friendly vessel. From the mast of the unfortunate vessel was seen a signal, "Water, water; we die of thirst!" The answer from the friendly vessel at once came back, "Cast down your bucket where you are." A second time the signal, "Water, water; send us water!" ran up from the distressed vessel, and was answered, "Cast down your bucket where you are." And a third and fourth signal for water was answered, "Cast down your bucket where you are." The captain of the distressed vessel, at last heeding the injunction, cast down his bucket, and it came up full of fresh, sparkling water from the mouth of the Amazon River. To those of my race who depend on bettering their condition in a foreign land or who underestimate the importance of cultivating friendly relations with the Southern white man, who is their next-door neighbour, I would say: "Cast down your bucket where you are"—cast it down in making friends in every manly way of the people of all races by whom we are surrounded.

Cast it down in agriculture, in mechanics, in commerce, in domestic service, and in the professions. And in this connection it is well to bear in mind that whatever other sins the South may be called to bear, when it comes to business, pure and simple, it is in the South that the Negro is given a man's chance in the commercial world, and in nothing is this Exposition more eloquent than in emphasizing this chance. Our greatest danger is that in the great leap from slavery to freedom we may overlook the fact that the masses of us are to live by the productions of our hands, and fail to keep in mind that we shall prosper in proportion as we learn to dignify and glorify common labour and put brains and skill into the common occupations of life; shall prosper in proportion as we learn to draw the line between the superficial and the substantial, the ornamental gewgaws of life and the useful. No race can prosper till it learns that there is as much dignity in tilling a field as in writing a poem. It is at the bottom of life we must begin, and not at the top. Nor should we permit our grievances to overshadow our opportunities.

To those of the white race who look to the incoming of those of foreign birth and strange tongue and habits for the prosperity of the South, were I permitted I would repeat what I say to my own race, "Cast down your bucket where you are." Cast it down among the eight millions of Negroes whose habits you know, whose fidelity and love you have tested in days when to have proved treacherous meant the ruin of your firesides. Cast down your bucket among these people who have, without strikes and labour wars, tilled your fields, cleared your forests, builded your railroads and cities, and brought forth treasures from the bowels of the earth, and help make possible this magnificent representation of the progress of the South. Casting down your bucket among my people, helping and encouraging them as you are doing on these grounds, and to education of head, hand, and heart, you will find that they will buy your surplus land, make blossom the waste places in your fields, and run your factories. While doing this, you can be sure in the future, as in the past, that you and your families will be surrounded by the most patient, faithful, law-abiding, and unresentful people that the world has seen. As we have proved our loyalty to you in the past, in nursing your children, watching by the sick-bed of your mothers and fathers, and often following them with tear-dimmed eyes to their graves, so in the future, in our humble way, we shall stand by you with a devotion that no foreigner can approach, ready to lay down our lives, if need be, in defence of yours, interlacing our industrial, commercial, civil, and religious life with yours in a way that shall make the interests of both races one. In all things that are purely social we can be as separate as the fingers, yet one as the hand in all things essential to mutual progress.

There is no defence or security for any of us except in the highest intelligence and development of all. If anywhere there are efforts tending to curtail the fullest growth of the Negro, let these efforts be turned into stimulating, encouraging, and making him the most useful and intelligent citizen. Effort or means so invested will pay a thousand per cent interest. These efforts will be twice blessed—"blessing him that gives and him that takes."

There is no escape through law of man or God from the inevitable:—

The laws of changeless justice bind
Oppressor with oppressed;

And close as sin and suffering joined
We march to fate abreast.

Nearly sixteen millions of hands will aid you in pulling
the load upward, or they will pull against you the load downward. We shall constitute one-third and more of the ignorance
and crime of the South, or one-third its intelligence and
progress; we shall contribute one-third to the business and
industrial prosperity of the South, or we shall prove a veri-
table body of death, stagnating, depressing, retarding every
effort to advance the body politic.

Gentlemen of the Exposition, as we present to you our
humble effort at an exhibition of our progress, you must not
expect overmuch. Starting thirty years ago with ownership
here and there in a few quilts and pumpkins and chickens
(gathered from miscellaneous sources), remember the path
that has led from these to the inventions and production of
agricultural implements, buggies, steam engines, newspapers,
books, statuary, carving, paintings, the management of drug
stores and banks, has not been trodden without contact with
thorns and thistles. While we take pride in what we exhibit
as a result of our independent efforts, we do not for a moment
forget that our part in this exhibition would fall far short
of your expectations but for the constant help that has come
to our educational life, not only from the Southern states,
but especially from Northern philanthropists, who have made
their gifts a constant stream of blessing and encouragement.

The wisest among my race understand that the agitation
of questions of social equality is the extremest folly, and
that progress in the enjoyment of all the privileges that will
come to us must be the result of severe and constant struggle
rather than of artificial forcing. No race that has anything
to contribute to the markets of the world is long in any
degree ostracized. It is important and right that all privileges
of the law be ours, but it is vastly more important that we be
prepared for the exercises of these privileges. The opportunity to earn a dollar in a factory just now is worth infinitely
more than the opportunity to spend a dollar in an opera-
house.

In conclusion, may I repeat that nothing in thirty years
has given us more hope and encouragement, and drawn us
so near to you of the white race, as this opportunity offered
by the Exposition; and here bending, as it were, over the
altar that represents the results of the struggles of your race
and mine, both starting practically empty-handed three decades ago. I pledged that in your effort to work out the great

and intricate problem which God has laid at the doors of the South, you shall have at all times the patient, sympathetic help of my race; only let this be constantly in mind, that, while from representations in these buildings of the product of field, of forest, of mine, of factory, letters, and art, much good will come, yet far above and beyond material benefits will be that higher good, that, let us pray God, will come, in a blotting out of sectional differences and racial animosities and suspicions, in a determination to administer absolute justice, in a willing obedience among all classes to the mandates of law. This, then, coupled with our material prosperity, will bring into our beloved South a new heaven and a new earth.

The first thing that I remember, after I had finished speaking, was that Governor Bullock rushed across the platform and took me by the hand, and that others did the same. I received so many and such hearty congratulations that I found it difficult to get out of the building. I did not appreciate to any degree, however, the impression which my address seemed to have made, until the next morning, when I went into the business part of the city. As soon as I was recognized, I was surprised to find myself pointed out and surrounded by a crowd of men who wished to shake hands with me. This was kept up on every street on to which I went, to an extent which embarrassed me so much that I went back to my boarding place. The next morning I returned to Tuskegee. At the station in Atlanta, and at almost all of the stations at which the train stopped between that city and Tuskegee, I found a crowd of people anxious to shake hands with me.

The papers in all parts of the United States published the address in full, and for months afterward there were complimentary editorial references to it. Mr. Clark Howell, the editor of the *Atlanta Constitution*, telegraphed to a New York paper, among other words, the following, "I do not exaggerate when I say that Professor Booker T. Washington's address yesterday was one of the most notable speeches, both as to character and as to the warmth of its reception, ever delivered to a Southern audience. The address was a revelation. The whole speech is a platform upon which blacks and whites can stand with full justice to each other."

The *Boston Transcript* said editorially: "The speech of Booker T. Washington at the Atlanta Exposition, this week, seems to have dwarfed all the other proceedings and the Exposition itself. The sensation that it has caused in the press has never been equalled."

The Immediate Program
of the American Negro*

By WILLIAM E. B. DU BOIS

The immediate program of the American Negro means nothing unless it is mediate to his great ideal and the ultimate ends of his development. We need not waste time by seeking to deceive our enemies into thinking that we are going to be content with a half loaf, or by being willing to lull our friends into a false sense of our indifference and present satisfaction.

The American Negro demands equality—political equality, industrial equality and social equality; and he is never going to rest satisfied with anything less. He demands this in no spirit of braggadocio and with no obsequious envy of others, but as an absolute measure of self-defense and the only one that will assure to the darker races their ultimate survival on earth.

Only in a demand and a persistent demand for essential equality in the modern realm of human culture can any people show a real pride of race and a decent self-respect. For any group, nation or race to admit for a moment the present monstrous demand of the white race to be the inheritors of the earth, the arbiters of mankind and the sole owners of a heritage of culture which they did not create, nor even improve to any greater extent than the other great division of men—to admit such pretense for a moment is for the race to write itself down immediately as indisputably inferior in judgment, knowledge and common sense.

The equality in political, industrial and social life which

* Reprinted from *The Crisis*, IX (April, 1915) pp. 310-12. By permission of the Crisis Publishing Company, Inc.

modern men have in order to live, is not to be confounded with sameness. On the contrary, in our case, it is rather insistence upon the right of diversity;—upon the right of a human being to be a man even if he does not wear the same cut of vest, the same curl of hair or the same color of skin. Human equality does not even entail, as is sometimes said, absolute equality of opportunity; for certainly the natural inequalities of inherent genius and varying gift make this a dubious phrase. But there is a more and more clearly recognized minimum of opportunity and maximum of freedom to be, to move and to think, which the modern world denies to no being which it recognizes as a real man.

These involve both negative and positive sides. They call for freedom on the one hand and power on the other. The Negro must have political freedom; taxation without representation is tyranny. American Negroes of to-day are ruled by tyrants who take what they please in taxes and give what they please in law and administration, in justice and in injustice; and the great mass of black people must stand helpless and voiceless before a condition which has time and time again caused other peoples to fight and die.

The Negro must have industrial freedom. Between the peonage of the rural South, the oppression of shrewd capitalists and the jealousy of certain trade unions, the Negro laborer is the most exploited class in the country, giving more hard toil for less money than any other American, and have less voice in the conditions of his labor.

In social intercourse every effort is being made to-day from the President of the United States and the so-called Church of Christ down to saloons and boot-blacks to segregate, strangle and spiritually starve Negroes so as to give them the least possible chance to know and share civilization.

These shackles must go. But that is but the beginning. The Negro must have power; the power of men, the right to do, to know, to feel and to express that knowledge, action and spiritual gift. He must not simply be free from the political tyranny of white folk, he must have the right to vote and to rule over the citizens, white and black, to the extent of his proven foresight and ability. He must have a voice in the new industrial democracy which is building and the power to see to it that his children are not in the next generation trained to be the mudsills of society. He must have the right to social intercourse with his fellows. There was a time in the atomic individualistic group when "social intercourse" meant merely calls and tea-parties; to-day social intercourse means theaters, lectures, organizations, churches, clubs, excursions, travel, hotels,—it means in short Life; to bar a group from such methods of thinking, living and doing is to bar them from the world and bid them create a new world;—a task to which no single group is to-day equal; it is to crucify them and taunt them with not being able to live.

What now are the practical steps which must be taken to accomplish these ends?

First of all before taking steps the wise man knows the object and end of his journey. There are those who would advise the black man to pay little or no attention to where he is going so long as he keeps moving. They assume that God or his vice-regent the White Man will attend to the steering. This is arrant nonsense. The feet of those that aimlessly wander land as often in hell as in heaven. Conscious self-realization and self-direction is the watch-word of modern man, and the first article in the program of any group that will survive must be the great aim, equality and power among men.

The practical steps to this are clear. *First* we must fight obstructions; by continual and increasing effort we must first make American courts either build up a body of decisions which will protect the plain legal rights of American citizens or else make them tear down the civil and political rights of all citizens in order to oppress a few. Either result will bring justice in the end. It is lots of fun and most ingenious just now for courts to twist law so as to say I shall not live here or vote there, or marry the woman who wishes to marry me. But when to-morrow these decisions throttle all freedom and overthrow the foundation of democracy and decency, there is going to be some judicial house cleaning.

We must *secondly* seek in legislature and congress remedial legislation; national aid to public school education, the removal of all legal discriminations based simply on race and color, and those marriage laws passed to make the seduction of black girls easy and without legal penalty.

Third the human contact of human beings must be increased; the policy which brings into sympathetic touch and understanding, men and women, rich and poor, capitalist and laborer, Asiatic and European, must bring into closer contact and mutual knowledge the white and black people of this land. It is the most frightful indictment of a country which dares to call itself civilized that it has allowed itself to drift into a state of ignorance where ten million people are coming to believe that all white people are liars and thieves, and the whites in turn to believe that the chief industry of Negroes is raping white women.

Fourth only the publication of the truth repeatedly and incisively and uncompromisingly can secure that change in public opinion which will correct these awful lies. *The Crisis,* our record of the darker races, must have a circulation not of 35,000 chiefly among colored folk but of at least 250,000 among all men who believe in men. It must not be a namby-pamby box of salve, but a voice that thunders fact and is more anxious to be true than pleasing. There should be a campaign of tract distribution—short well-written facts and arguments—rained over this land by millions of copies, particularly in the South, where the white people know less about the Negro than in any other part of the civilized world. The press should be utilized—the 400 Negro weeklies, the great dailies and eventually the magazines, when we get magazine editors who will lead public opinion instead of following afar with resonant brays. Lectures, lantern-slides and moving pictures, co-operating with a bureau of information and eventually becoming a Negro encyclopedia, all these are efforts along the line of making human beings realize that Negroes are humans.

Such is the program of work against obstructions. Let us now turn to constructive effort. This may be summed up under (1) economic co-operation (2) a revival of art and literature (3) political action (4) education and (5) organization.

Under economic co-operation we must strive to spread the idea among colored people that the accumulation of wealth is for social rather than individual ends. We must avoid, in the advancement of the Negro race, the mistakes of ruthless exploitation which have marked modern economic history. To this end we must seek not simply home ownership, small landholding and saving accounts, but also all forms of co-operation, both in production and distribution, profit sharing, building and loan associations, systematic charity for definite, practical ends, systematic migration from mob rule and robbery, to freedom and enfranchisement, the emancipation of women and the abolition of child labor.

In art and literature we should try to loose the tremendous emotional wealth of the Negro and the dramatic strength of his problems through writing, the stage, pageantry and other forms of art. We should resurrect forgotten ancient Negro art and history, and we should set the black man before the world as both a creative artist and a strong subject for artistic treatment.

In political action we should organize the votes of Negroes in such congressional districts as have any number of Negro voters. We should systematically interrogate candidates on matters vital to Negro freedom and uplift. We should train colored voters to reject the bribe of office and to accept only decent legal enactments both for their own uplift and for the uplift of laboring classes of all races and both sexes.

In education we must seek to give colored children free public school training. We must watch with grave suspicion the attempt of those who, under the guise of vocational training, would fasten ignorance and menial service on the Negro for another generation. Our children must not, in large numbers, be forced into the servant class; for menial service is still, in the main, little more than an antiquated survival of impossible conditions. It has always been as statistics show, a main cause of bastardy and prostitution and despite its many marvelous exceptions it will never come to the light of decency and honor until the house servant becomes the Servant in the House. It is our duty then, not drastically but persistently, to seek out colored children of ability and genius, to open up to them broader, industrial opportunity and above all, to find that Talented Tenth and encourage it by the best and most exhaustive training in order to supply the Negro race and the world with leaders, thinkers and artists.

For the accomplishment of all these ends we must organize. Organization among us already has gone far but it must go much farther and higher. Organization is sacrifice. It is sacrifice of opinions, of time, of work and of money, but it is, after all, the cheapest way of buying the most priceless of gifts—freedom and efficiency. I thank God that most of the money that supports the National Association for the Advancement of Colored People comes from black hands; a still larger proportion must so come, and we must not only support but control this and similar organizations and hold them unwaveringly to our objects, our aims and our ideals.

Segregation*

By WILLIAM E. B. DU BOIS

The thinking colored people of the United States must stop being stampeded by the word segregation. The opposition to racial segregation is not or should not be any distaste or unwillingness of colored people to work with each other, to cooperate with each other, to live with each other. The opposition to segregation is an opposition to discrimination. The experience in the United States has been that usually when there is racial segregation, there is also racial discrimination.

But the two things do not necessarily go together, and there should never be an opposition to segregation pure and simple unless that segregation does involve discrimination. Not only is there no objection to colored people living beside colored people if the surroundings and treatment involve no discrimination, if streets are well lighted, if there is water, sewerage and police protection, and if anybody of any color who wishes can live in that neighborhood. The same way in schools, there is no objection to schools attended by colored pupils and taught by colored teachers. On the contrary, colored pupils can by our contention be as fine human beings as any other sort of children, and we certainly know that there are no teachers better than trained colored teachers. But if the existence of such a school is made reason and cause for giving it worse housing, poorer facilities, poorer equipment and poorer teachers, then we do object, and the objection is not against the color of the pupils' or teachers' skins, but against the discrimination.

In the recent endeavor of the United States government to redistribute capital so that some of the disadvantaged groups

* Reprinted from *The Crisis*, XLI (January, 1934), p. 20. By permission of the Crisis Publishing Company, Inc.

may get a chance for development, the American Negro should voluntarily and insistently demand his share. Groups of communities and farms inhabited by colored folk should be voluntarily formed. In no case should there be any discrimination against white and blacks. But, at the same time, colored people should come forward, should organize and conduct enterprises, and their only insistence should be that the same provisions be made for the success of their enterprise that is being made for the success of any other enterprise. It must be remembered that in the last quarter of a century, the advance of the colored people has been mainly in the lines where they themselves, working by and for themselves, have accomplished the greatest advance.

There is no doubt that numbers of white people, perhaps the majority of Americans, stand ready to take the most distinct advantage of voluntary segregation and cooperation among colored people. Just as soon as they get a group of black folk segregated, they use it as a point of attack and discrimination. Our counter attack should be, therefore, against this discrimination; against the refusal of the South to spend the same amount of money on the black child as on the white child for its education; against the inability of black groups to use public capital; against the monopoly of credit by white groups. But never in the world should our fight be against association with ourselves because by that very token we give up the whole argument that we are worth associating with.

Doubtless, and in the long run, the greatest human development is going to take place under experiences of widest individual contact. Nevertheless, today such individual contact is made difficult and almost impossible by petty prejudice, deliberate and almost criminal propaganda and various survivals from prehistoric heathenism. It is impossible, therefore, to wait for the millennium of free and normal intercourse before we unite, to cooperate among themselves in groups of like-minded people and in groups of people suffering from the same disadvantages and the same hatreds.

It is the class-conscious working man uniting together who will eventually emancipate labor throughout the world. It is the race-conscious black man cooperating together in his own institutions and movements who will eventually emancipate the colored race, and the great step ahead today is for the American Negro to accomplish his economic emancipation through voluntary determined cooperative effort.

MARCUS M. GARVEY,

Visionary, Black Nationalist

Marcus Garvey preached black separatism at the turn of the last century, a time when many blacks were diligently working for acceptance into the white world which was progressing so rapidly around them. Although he was born in St. Ann's Bay, Jamaica, he moved to New York as a young man and launched his "Back to Africa" movement—a program designed to resettle black Americans in their ancestral homeland. At the height of this movement, Garvey claimed more than two million followers and at various times published The New World *and other newspapers, including* The Watchman *and* Our Own.

Many of the programs being inaugurated by black separatists today are suggestive of those which Garvey initiated. For example, he created the Universal Negro Improvement Association, the African Communities League, and founded "The Black Star Line," a steamship company. In addition, he spearheaded efforts to develop black businesses. Throughout his life he was vitally concerned about the "unity and liberation" of black people throughout the world. To him the racist exploitation of Africa was as intolerable as that in America. Because of his inability to manage his affairs, however, he was imprisoned for mail fraud in 1925 and deported to Jamaica upon his release. Thereafter his movement and his leadership declined. He died in England in 1940, a somewhat obscure figure. Garvey was a visionary, an idealist, and a black nationalist.

"THE EVIL OF INTERNAL DIVISION IS WRECKING OUR EXISTENCE AS A PEOPLE."

An Appeal to the Conscience of the Black Race to See Itself*

It is said to be a hard and difficult task to organize and keep together large numbers of the Negro race for the common good. Many have tried to congregate us, but have failed, the reason being that our characteristics are such as to keep us more apart than together.

The evil of internal division is wrecking our existence as a people, and if we do not seriously and quickly move in the direction of a readjustment it simply means that our doom becomes imminently conclusive.

For years the Universal Negro Improvement Association has been working for the unification of our race, not on domestic-national lines only, but universally. The success which we have met in the course of our effort is rather encouraging, considering the time consumed and the environment surrounding the object of our concern.

It seems that the whole world of sentiment is against the Negro, and the difficulty of our generation is to extricate ourselves from the prejudice that hides itself beneath, as well as above, the action of an international environment.

Prejudice is conditional on many reasons, and it is apparent that the Negro supplies, consciously or unconsciously, all the reasons by which the world seems to ignore and avoid him. No one cares for a leper, for lepers are infectious persons, and all are afraid of the disease, so, because the Negro keeps himself poor, helpless and undemonstrative, it is natural also that no one wants to be of him or with him.

* Reprinted from *The Philosophy and Opinions of Marcus Garvey*, 1967. By permission of Frank Cass and Company, Ltd., London, and Mrs. Amy Jacques Garvey.

Progress and Humanity

Progress is the attraction that moves humanity, and to whatever people or race this "modern virtue" attaches itself, there will you find the splendor of pride and self-esteem that never fail to win the respect and admiration of all.

It is the progress of the Anglo-Saxons that singles them out for the respect of all the world. When their race had no progress or achievement to its credit, then, like all other inferior peoples, they paid the price in slavery, bondage, as well as through prejudice. We cannot forget the time when even the ancient Briton was regarded as being too dull to make a good Roman slave, yet today the influence of that race rules the world.

It is the industrial and commercial progress of America that causes Europe and the rest of the world to think appreciatively of the Anglo-American race. It is not because one hundred and ten million people live in the United States that the world is attracted to the republic with so much reverence and respect—a reverence and respect not shown to India with its three hundred millions, or to China with its four hundred millions. Progress of and among any people will advance them in the respect and appreciation of the rest of their fellows. It is such a progress that the Negro must attach to himself if he is to rise above the prejudice of the world.

The reliance of our race upon the progress and achievements of others for a consideration in sympathy, justice and rights is like a dependence upon a broken stick, resting upon which will eventually consign you to the ground.

Self-Reliance and Respect

The Universal Negro Improvement Association teaches our race self-help and self-reliance, not only in one essential, but in all those things that contribute to human happiness and well-being. The disposition of the many to depend upon the other races for a kindly and sympathetic consideration of their needs, without making the effort to do for themselves, has been the race's standing disgrace by which we have been judged and through which we have created the strongest prejudice against ourselves.

There is no force like success, and that is why the individual makes all efforts to surround himself throughout life with the evidence of it. As of the individual, so should it be of the race and nation. The glittering success of Rockefeller makes him a power in the American nation; the success of Henry Ford suggests him as an object of universal respect, but no one knows and cares about the bum or hobo who is Rockefeller's or Ford's neighbor. So, also, is the world attracted by the glittering success of races and nations, and pays absolutely no attention to the bum or hobo race that lingers by the wayside.

The Negro must be up and doing if he will break down the prejudice of the rest of the world. Prayer alone is not going to improve our condition, nor the policy of watchful waiting. We must strike out for ourselves in the course of material achievement, and by our own effort and energy present to the world those forces by which the progress of man is judged.

A Nation and Country

The Negro needs a nation and a country of his own, where he can best show evidence of his own ability in the art of human progress. Scattered as an unmixed and unrecognized part of alien nations and civilizations is but to demonstrate his imbecility, and point him out as an unworthy derelict, fit neither for the society of Greek, Jew, nor Gentile.

It is unfortunate that we should so drift apart, as a race, as not to see that we are but perpetuating our own sorrow and disgrace in failing to appreciate the first great requisite of all peoples—organization.

Organization is a great power in directing the affairs of a race or nation toward a given goal. To properly develop the desires that are uppermost, we must first concentrate through some system or method, and there is none better than organization. Hence, the Universal Negro Improvement Association appeals to each and every Negro to throw in his lot with those of us who, through organization, are working for the universal emancipation of our race and the redemption of our common country, Africa.

No Negro, let him be American, European, West Indian or African, shall be truly respected until the race as a whole has emancipated itself, through self-achievement and progress, from universal prejudice. The Negro will have to build his own government, industry, art, science, literature and culture, before the world will stop to consider him. Until then, we are but wards of a superior race and civilization, and the outcasts of a standard social system.

The race needs workers at this time, not plagiarists, copyists and mere imitators; but men and women who are able to create, to originate and improve, and thus make an independent racial contribution to the world and civilization.

Monkey Apings of "Leaders"

The unfortunate thing about us is that we take the monkey apings of our "so-called leading men" for progress. There is no progress in aping white people and telling us that they represent the best in the race, for in that respect any dressed monkey would represent the best of its species, irrespective of the creative matter of the monkey instinct. The best in a race is not reflected through or by the action of its apes, but by its ability to create of and by itself. It is such a creation that the Universal Negro Improvement Association seeks.

Let us not try to be the best or worst of others, but let us make the effort to be the best of ourselves. Our own racial critics criticise us as dreamers and "fanatics," and call us "benighted" and "ignorant," because they lack racial backbone. They are unable to see themselves creators of their own needs. The slave instinct has not yet departed from them. They still believe that they can only live or exist through the good graces of their "masters." The good slaves have not yet thrown off their shackles; thus, to them, the Universal Negro Improvement Association is an "impossibility."

It is the slave spirit of dependence that causes our "so-called leading men" (apes) to seek the shelter, leadership, protection and patronage of the "master" in their organization and so-called advancement work. It is the spirit of feeling secured as good servants of the master, rather than as independents, why our modern Uncle Toms take pride in laboring under alien leadership and becoming surprised at the audacity of the Universal Negro Improvement Association in proclaiming for racial liberty and independence.

But the world of white and other men, deep down in their hearts, have much more respect for those of us who work for our racial salvation under the banner of the Universal Negro Improvement Association, than they could ever have in all eternity for a group of helpless apes and beggars who make a monopoly of undermining their own race and belittling themselves in the eyes of self-respecting people, by being "good boys" rather than able men.

Surely there can be no good will between apes, seasoned beggars and independent minded Negroes who will at least make an effort to do for themselves. Surely, the "dependents" and "wards" (and may I not say racial imbeciles?) will rave against and plan the destruction of movements like the Universal Negro Improvement Association that expose them to the liberal white minds of the world as not being representative of the best in the Negro, but, to the contrary, the worst. The best of a race does not live on the patronage and philanthropy of others, but makes an effort to do for itself. The best of the great white race doesn't fawn before and beg black, brown or yellow men; they go out, create for self and thus demonstrate the fitness of the race to survive; and so the white race of America and the world will be informed that the best in the Negro race is not the class of beggars who send out to other races piteous appeals annually for donations to maintain their coterie, but the groups within us that are honestly striving to do for themselves with the voluntary help and appreciation of that class of other races that is reasonable, just and liberal enough to give to each and every one a fair chance in the promotion of those ideals that tend to greater human progress and human love.

The work of the Universal Negro Improvement Association is clear and clean-cut. It is that of inspiring an unfortunate race with pride in self and with the determination of going ahead in the creation of those ideals that will lift them to the unprejudiced company of races and nations. There is no desire for hate or malice, but every wish to see all mankind linked into a common fraternity of progress and achievement that will wipe away the odor of prejudice, and elevate the human race to the height of real godly love and satisfaction.

Excerpts from

Philosophy and Opinions*

Propaganda

We are living in a civilization that is highly developed. We are living in a world that is scientifically arranged in which everything done by those who control is done through system; proper arrangement, proper organization, and among some of the organized methods used to control the world is the thing known as and called "PROPAGANDA."

Propaganda has done more to defeat the good intentions of races and nations than even open warfare.

Propaganda is a method or medium used by organized peoples to convert others against their will.

We of the Negro race are suffering more than any other race in the world from propaganda—Propaganda to destroy our hopes, our ambitions and our confidence in self.

Slavery

Slavery is a condition imposed upon individuals or races not sufficiently able to protect or defend themselves, and so long as a race or people expose themselves to the danger of being weak, no one can tell when they will be reduced to slavery.

When a man is a slave he has no liberty of action; no freedom of will, he is bound and controlled by the will and act of others; as of the individual, so of the race.

Slavery is not a condition confined to any one age or race

* Reprinted from *The Philosophy and Opinions of Marcus Garvey*, 1967. By permission of Frank Cass and Company, Ltd., and Mrs. Amy Jacques Garvey.

67

of people. Slavery has been since man in the different distribution of himself, scattered here, there and everywhere, has grown and developed, wherein one race will become strong and the other race remains weak. The strong race has always reduced the weak to slavery. It has been so in ages past, it is so now in certain parts of the world, and will be so until the end of time.

The great British nation was once a race of slaves. In their own country they were not respected because the Romans went there, brutalized and captured them, took them over to Rome and kept them in slavery. They were not respected in Rome because they were regarded as a slave race. But the Briton did not always remain a slave. As a freed man he went back to his country (Britain) and built up a civilization of his own, and by his self-reliance and initiative he forced the respect of mankind and maintains it until today.

Force

The powers opposed to Negro progress will not be influenced in the slightest by mere verbal protests on our part. They realize only too well that protests of this kind contain nothing but the breath expended in making them.

They also realize that their success in enslaving and dominating the darker portion of humanity was due solely to the element of FORCE employed (in the majority of cases this was accomplished by force of arms).

Pressure of course may assert itself in other forms, but in the last analysis whatever influence is brought to bear against the powers opposed to Negro progress must contain the element of FORCE in order to accomplish its purpose, since it is apparent that this is the only element they recognize.

Education

To be learned in all that is worth while knowing. Not to be crammed with the subject matter of the book or the philosophy of the class room, but to store away in your head such facts as you need for the daily application of life, so that you may the better in all things understand your fellowmen, and interpret your relationship to your Creator.

You can be educated in soul, vision and feeling, as well as in mind. To see your enemy and know him is a part of the complete education of man; to spiritually regulate one's self in another form of the higher education that fits man for a nobler place in life, and still, to approach your brother by the feeling of your own humanity, is an education that softens the ills of the world and makes us kind indeed.

Many a man was educated outside the school room. It is something you let out, not completely take in. You are part of it, for it is natural; it is dormant simply because you will not develop it, but God creates every man with it knowingly or unknowingly to him who possesses it—that's the difference. Develop yours and you become as great and full of knowledge as the other fellow without even entering the class room.

Miscegenation

Some of the men of the Negro race aggravate the race question because they force the white man to conclude that to educate a black man, to give him opportunities, is but to fit him to be a competitor for the hand of his woman; hence the eternal race question.

But not all black men are willing to commit race suicide and to abhor their race for the companionship of another. There are hundreds of millions of us black men who are proud of our skins and to us the African Empire will not be a Utopia, neither will it be dangerous nor fail to serve our best interests, because we realize that like the leopard we cannot change our skins.

The men of the highest morals, highest character and noblest pride are to be found among the masses of the Negro race who love their women with as much devotion as white men love theirs.

Prejudice

Prejudice of the white race against the black race is not so much because of color as of condition; we have built no nation, no government; because we are dependent for our economic and political existence.

You can never curb the prejudice of the one race or nation

against the other by law. It must be regulated by one's own feeling, one's own will, and if one's feeling and will rebel against you no law in the world can curb it.

Prejudice can be actuated by different reasons. Sometimes the reason is economic, and sometimes political. You can only obstruct it by progress and force.

Radicalism

"Radical" is a label that is always applied to people who are endeavoring to get freedom.

Jesus Christ was the greatest radical the world ever saw. He came and saw a world of sin and his program was to inspire it with spiritual feeling. He was therefore a radical.

George Washington was dubbed a radical when he took up his sword to fight his way to liberty in America one hundred and forty years ago.

All men who call themselves reformers are perforce radicals. They cannot be anything else, because they are revolting against the conditions that exist.

Conditions as they exist reveal a conservative state, and if you desire to change these conditions you must be a radical.

I am, therefore, satisfied to be the same kind of radical, if through radicalism I can free Africa.

Government

Government is not infallible. Government is only an executive control, a centralized authority for the purpose of expressing the will of the people.

Before you have a government you must have the people. Without the people there can be no government. The government must be, therefore, an expression of the will of the people.

Poverty

A hellish state to be in. It is no virtue. It is a crime.

To be poor, is to be hungry without possible hope of food; to be sick without hope of medicine; to be tired and sleepy without a place to lay one's head; to be naked without hope of clothing; to be despised and comfortless. To be poor is to be a fit subject for crime and hell.

The hungry man steals bread and thereby breaks the eighth commandment; by this state he breaks all the laws of God and man and becomes an outcast. In thought and deed he covets his neighbor's goods; comfortless as he is he seeks his neighbor's wife; to him there is no other course but sin and death. That is the way of poverty. No one wants to be poor.

Power

Power is the only argument that satisfies man.

Except the individual, the race or the nation has POWER that is exclusive, it means that that individual, race or nation will be bound by the will of the other who possesses this great qualification.

It is the physical and pugilistic power of Harry Wills that makes white men afraid to fight him.

It was the industrial and scientific power of the Teutonic race that kept it for years as dictator of the economic and scientific policies of Europe.

It is the naval and political power of Great Britain that keeps her mistress of the seas.

It is the commercial and financial power of the United States of America that makes her the greatest banker in the world. Hence it is advisable for the Negro to get power of every kind. POWER in education, science, industry, politics and higher government. That kind of power that will stand out signally, so that other races and nations can see, and if they will not see, then FEEL.

Man is not satisfied or moved by prayers or petitions, but every man is moved by that power of authority which forces him to do even against his will.

Race Assimilation

Some Negro leaders have advanced the belief that in another few years the white people will make up their minds to assimilate their black populations; thereby sinking all racial prejudice in the welcoming of the black race into the social companionship of the white. Such leaders further believe that

by the amalgamation of black and white, a new type will spring
up, and that type will become the American and West Indian
of the future.

This belief is preposterous. I believe that white men should
be white, yellow men should be yellow, and black men should
be black in the great panorama of races, until each and every
race by its own initiative lifts itself up to the common standard
of humanity, as to compel the respect and appreciation of all,
and so make it possible for each one to stretch out the hand
of welcome without being able to be prejudiced against the
other because of any inferior and unfortunate condition.

The white man of America will not, to any organized extent,
assimilate the Negro, because in so doing, he feels that he will
be committing racial suicide. This he is not prepared to do.
It is true he illegitimately carries on a system of assimilation;
but such assimilation, as practised, is one that he is not prepared to support because he becomes prejudiced against his
own offspring, if that offspring is the product of black and
white; hence, to the white man the question of racial differences is eternal. So long as Negroes occupy an inferior position
among the races and nations of the world, just so long will
others be prejudiced against them, because it will be profitable
for them to keep up their system of superiority. But when the
Negro by his own initiative lifts himself from his low state
to the highest human standard he will be in a position to stop
begging and praying, and demand a place that no individual,
race or nation will be able to deny him.

Discussion and Study Questions

1. Discuss the difference in educational goals advocated by Washington and Du Bois.

   A. What is their major point of divergence?
   B. Illustrate ways in which these positions could have been synthesized in relationship to the total Black Movement.

2. What is Washington's advice for the blacks and whites of the 1890s? Having a perspective of seventy-five years to observe the progress of the Black man, what disparities, if any, can you see between the results and expectations of Washington's theory?

3. Washington completely rejects the question of social equality. How, on the other hand, can the value and manhood of the American Negro be "fittingly and generously recognized"? How does his reason for rejecting social interaction between the races differ from those of black leaders today who advocate separatism? See essays by Hare, Elijah Muhammad, and Innis.

4. What aspects of Washington's description of blacks in postslavery days have today become symbols of "Tomism"? Can you account for the largely negative connotations of this image today?

5. What is Du Bois' subtle distinction between segregation and discrimination?

   A. Why shouldn't Blacks fight against segregation, according to Du Bois?
   B. In what ways may his notions be considered forerunners to the modern concept of separatism?

6. How does Du Bois define human equality?

   A. What specific freedoms must the Negro have?

B. What steps must be taken to secure these?

7. In your view, which of the current spokesmen or organizations have adopted ideologies most in keeping with that espoused by Garvey?

8. Discuss the factors which might possibly account for the difference in tone and rhetoric in the two essays by Douglass.

9. How would you characterize the spokesmen in this section according to the current labels—conservative, moderate, militant? Explain.

Self-Awareness
and Self-Determination

Self-Awareness
and Self-Determination

Although there are two main concepts presented in this part they are by no means unrelated. In fact, self-awareness is considered to be a prerequisite to self-determination. For too long the Black man has been confused about his self-image. This state of affairs began with his enslavement and has continued to a lesser extent until the present. The whites who have effectively controlled the media have largely defined and interpreted the essence of being black. When one hears a lie and a distortion often enough he begins to accept it as being valid. Thus, the situation of white racism is perpetuated by the Black man's confusion about his identity. After years of conditioning as to his inferiority and lack of worth the Black man has begun, in many cases, to subconsciously hate himself, his blackness, and all that it implies.

Some of the essays presented here are an effort to reject and counteract the adverse effects of such massive negative reinforcement; they point to the need for Blacks to develop singly and collectively a more positive self image. Out of such awareness arises the desire and demand for self-determination. Some of the essays suggest that it is the Black man who must define his problems, develop his programs and select tactics designed to deal with his basic concerns. This means determining priorities which affect all aspects of life such as health, education, politics, housing, and employment. The concept of self-determination does not automatically suggest separatism. It does, however, recognize the inherent difficulty of attaining independence and sovereignty while entangled with a more dominant force. For this reason, many Blacks advocate at least a temporary break with the white world in order to gain a measure of cohesiveness and autonomy.

LeRoi Jones urges Blacks to become aware of how white

liberals and certain black bourgeois have thwarted movement toward complete freedom through their acceptance of tokenism. Farmer urges Blacks to strengthen the ghetto—their economic and political power base—and learn to love blackness. He urges Blacks also to rely less upon white liberals as allies. Clark, while recognizing the deep doubts of Blacks concerning their worth and self-image, contends that Blacks may increase their chances for survival through disciplined intelligence and humanity. In an interview Hare defines black power and discusses this concept in relation to integration. Gregory's essay calls for southern Blacks to stop being afraid of the system and start taking positive steps toward gaining equal constitutional rights. Malcolm explains to the masses how to recognize the enemy and unite against him behind closed doors without his interference and knowledge. Those who offer specific programs for self-determination are McKissick, Elijah Muhammad, and Innis. McKissick calls for the development of rural areas by blacks primarily to meet the needs of Blacks but not exclusively. Elijah Muhammad stresses the importance of unity and land as necessities for black independence and self-determination. While Innis does not emphasize land, he does call for a new social contract between blacks and whites in which whites recognize the validity of black self-determination in community programs and projects. Carmichael feels that Blacks need to redefine themselves, their culture, and their goals in order to refute all the distortions of the white man. He also speaks of the need for a sense of community and group solidarity.

LEROI JONES, Playwright, Poet

LeRoi Jones began his career as an avant-garde writer, rejecting the aesthetics of white America to emerge as a "missionary of blackness." His aesthetic views have become a foundation for his concept of culture, for he is now an active black nationalist who believes that black people should come together as a separate "nation."

Jones was awarded the Whitney Fellowship in 1961–62 and a Guggenheim Award in 1964–65. He was a founder of the Black Arts Repertory Theater in Harlem, and has produced and directed plays in a theater in Newark; he has assisted neighborhood teen-agers in publishing a community newspaper. Among his best-known literary works are Dutchman, *a play;* The System of Dante's Hell, *a novel;* The Dead Lecturer *and* Preface to a Twenty Volume Suicide Note, *books of poems; and* The Blues People *and* Home, *collections of essays.*

Jones was born in Newark, New Jersey, in 1934. He studied at Howard and Columbia universities and the New School of Social Research in New York.

"THE BLACK ARTIST'S ROLE IN AMERICA IS TO AID IN THE DESTRUCTION OF AMERICA AS HE KNOWS IT."

Tokenism: 300 Years for Five Cents*

A rich man told me recently that a liberal is a man who tells other people what to do with their money. I told him that that was right from the side of the telescope he looked through, but that as far as I was concerned a liberal was a man who told other people what to do with their poverty.

I mention this peculiarly American phenomenon, *i.e.,* American Liberalism, because it is just this group of amateur social theorists, American Liberals, who have done most throughout American history to insure the success of tokenism. Whoever has proposed whatever particular social evasion or dilution— to whatever ignominious end—it is usually the liberal who gives that lie the greatest lip service. They, liberals, are people with extremely heavy consciences and almost nonexistent courage. Too little is always enough. And it is always the *symbol* that appeals to them most. The single futile housing project in the jungle of slums and disease eases the liberals' conscience, so they are loudest in praising it—even though it might not solve any problems at all. The single black student in the Southern university, the promoted porter in Marietta, Georgia—all ease the liberals' conscience like a benevolent but highly addictive drug. And, for them, "moderation" is a kind of religious catch phrase that they are wont to mumble on street corners even alone late at night.

Is it an excess for a man to ask to be free? To declare, even vehemently, that no man has the right to dictate the life of another man? Is it so radical and untoward for nations to claim the right of self-determination? Freedom *now!* has become the cry of a great many American Negroes and colonial nations. Not freedom "when you get ready to give it," as some spurious privilege or shabby act of charity; but *now*. The liberal says, "You are a radical." So be it.

Liberals, as good post-Renaissance men, believe whole-

* Reprinted from *Home: Social Essays*, 1966. By permission of William Morrow and Company, Inc., and the author.

heartedly in *progress*. There are even those people who speak knowingly about "progress in the arts." But progress is not, and never has been the question as far as the enslaving of men is concerned. Africans never asked to be escorted to the New World. They never had any idea that learning "good English" and wearing shoes had anything to do with the validity of their lives on earth. Slavery was not anything but an unnecessarily cruel and repressive method of making money for the Western white man. Colonialism was a more subtle, but equally repressive method of accomplishing the same end. The liberal is in a strange position because his conscience, unlike the conscience of his richer or less intelligent brothers, has always bothered him about these acts, but never sufficiently to move him to any concrete action except the setting up of palliatives and symbols to remind him of his own good faith. In fact, even though the slave trade, for instance, was entered into for purely commercial reasons, after a few years the more liberal-minded Americans began to try to justify it as a method of converting heathens to Christianity. (And again, you can see how perfect Christianity was for the slave then; a great number of slave uprisings were dictated by the African's gods or the new slaves' desire to return to the land of their gods. As I put it in a recent essay on the sociological development of blues: "You can see how necessary, how perfect, it was that Christianity came first, that the African was given something 'to take his mind off Africa,' that he was forced, if he still wished to escape the filthy paternalism and cruelty of slavery, to wait at least until he died, when he could be transported peacefully and majestically to 'the promised land.' " I'm certain the first Negro spirituals must have soothed a lot of consciences as well as enabling a little more relaxation among the overseers. It almost tempts me toward another essay tentatively titled *Christianity as a Deterrent to Slave Uprisings*. More tokens.

A Negro who is told that the "desegregation" of a bus terminal in Georgia somehow represents "progress" is definitely being lied to. Progress to where? The bare minimum of intelligent life is what any man wants. This was true in 1600 when the first slaves were hauled off the boats, and it has not changed. Perhaps the trappings and the external manifestations that time and the lessons of history have proposed make some things seem different or changed in the world, but the basic necessities of useful life are the same. If a tractor has replaced a mule, the need to have the field produce has not changed. And if a black man can speak English now, or read a newspaper, whereas (ask any liberal) he could not in 18 so-and-so, he is no better off now than he was then if he still cannot receive the basic privileges of manhood. In fact, he is perhaps worse off than in 18 so-and-so since he is now being constantly persuaded that he *is* receiving these basic privileges (or, at least, he is told that he soon will, *e.g.,* R. Kennedy's high comic avowal that perhaps in forty years a Negro might be president).

But, for me, the idea of "progress" is a huge fallacy. An absurd Western egoism that has been foisted on the rest of the world as an excuse for slavery and colonialism. An excuse for making money. Because this progress the Western slavemaster is always talking about means simply the mass acquisition of all the dubious fruits of the industrial revolution. And the acquisition of material wealth has, in my mind, only very slightly to do with self-determination or freedom. Somehow, and most especially in the United States, the fact that more Negroes can buy new Fords this year than they could in 1931 is supposed to represent some great stride *forward.* To where? How many new Fords will Negroes have to own before police in Mississippi stop using police dogs on them. How many television sets and refrigerators will these same Negroes have to own before they are allowed to vote without being made to live in tents, or their children allowed decent educations? And even if a bus station in Anniston, Alabama, is "integrated," how much does this help reduce the 25 per cent unemployment figure that besets Negroes in Harlem.

If, right this minute, I were, in some strange fit of irrationality, to declare that "I am a free man and have the right of complete self-determination," chances are that I would be dead or in jail by nightfall. But being an American Negro, I am supposed to be conditioned to certain "unfortunate" aspects of American democracy. And all my reactions are supposedly based on this conditioning, which is, in effect, that even as a native born American, etc., etc., there are certain things I cannot do because I have a black skin. Tokenism is that philosophy (of psychological exploitation) which is supposed to assuage my natural inclinations toward complete freedom. For the middle-class Negro this assuagement can take the form it takes in the mainstream of American life, *e.g.,* material acquisition, or the elevating of one "select" coon to some position that seems heaped in "prestige," *e.g.,* Special Delegate to the United Nations, Director of Public Housing, Assistant Press Secretary to the President of the United States, Vice President In Charge of Personnel for Chock Full O' Nuts, Borough President of Manhattan, etc. The "Speaking Of People" column in *Ebony* magazine is the banal chronicler of such "advances," *e.g.,* the first Negro sheriff of Banwood,

Utah, or the first Negro Asst. Film Editor for BRRR films. But the lower class Negro cannot use this kind of tokenism, so he is pretty much left in the lurch. But so effective is this kind of crumb-dropping among the *soi-disant* black middle class that these people become the actual tokens themselves, or worse. Thus when an issue like the treacherous relief cuts in Newburgh, New York, presents itself, the black middle class is actually likely to side with reactionaries, even though, as in the Newburgh case, such a situation harms a great many poorer Negroes. This kind of process reaches perhaps its most absurd, albeit horrible, manifestation when a man like George Schuyler, in the Negro paper *The Pittsburgh Courier,* can write editorials *defending the Portuguese* in Angola, even after the United States Government itself had been pressured into censuring this NATO ally. It is also a man like Schuyler who is willing to support one of the great aphorisms of tokenism (this one begun by the worst elements of racist neo-colonialism) that somehow a man, usually a black man, must "make progress to freedom." That somehow, a man must show he is *"ready* for independence or self-determination." A man is either free or he is not. There cannot be any apprenticeship for freedom. My God, what makes a black man, in America or Africa, or any of the other oppressed colonial peoples of the world, less ready for freedom than the average *Daily News* reading American white man?

But again, while it is true that there is a gulf of tokens seemingly separating the middle-class Negro from the great masses of Negroes (just as there is seemingly a great gulf of tokens separating the "select cadre" of a great many colonial countries from their oppressed people), I insist that it is only an artificial separation, and that the black bourgeosie (and their foreign cousins) are no better off than the poorest Negro in this country. But how to tell the *first* Negro Asst. Film Editor of BRRR films that he is just as bad off as the poorest and most oppressed of his black brothers? Tokenism is no abstract philosophy; it was put into action by hardheaded realists.

But realists or no, there is in the world now among most of its oppressed peoples, a growing disaffection with meaningless platitudes, and a reluctance to be had by the same shallow phrases that have characterized the hypocritical attitude of the West toward the plight of the American black man and all colonial peoples. There will be fewer and fewer tragedies like the murder of Patrice Lumumba. The new nations will no longer allow themselves to be sucked in by these same hackneyed sirens of tokenism or malevolent liberalism. The world, my friends, is definitely changing.

JAMES L. FARMER, Civil Rights Leader, Government Official

Founder of Congress of Racial Equality, James Farmer saw as long ago as 1942 that civil rights action must devise different approaches for relieving the pressures of discrimination.

Born in Marshall, Texas, on January 12, 1920, the son of a minister and college professor, he took degrees at Wiley College in 1938 and Howard University in 1941. Prior to becoming national director of CORE, he had been active in NAACP, worked as an organizer for unions and participated in the first wave of sit-ins during the 1940s.

Farmer left his post with CORE in 1965, but returned to the front in 1968 to run unsuccessfully against Shirley Chisholm for United States Representative in Congress for New York's twelfth district. His subsequent acceptance of the position of Assistant Secretary of the Department of Health, Education, and Welfare seemed to him to be a useful way to continue his leading role in the Negro's struggle to participate fully and meaningfully in every aspect of American life.

Through two and a half decades, Farmer has remained one of black America's most intelligent and articulate spokesmen.

"THE BLACK MAN MUST FIND HIMSELF AS A BLACK MAN BEFORE HE CAN FIND HIMSELF AS AN AMERICAN."

Are White Liberals Obsolete in the Black Struggle?*

Several months ago I received a telephone call from a stranger. The caller identified himself as a Negro and said that he was confused. He felt he was damned if he did and damned if he didn't.

"Just a few years ago," he said, "civil rights leaders were saying that the creative and radical thing to do was to break down Jim Crow by integrating white neighborhoods." So he and his bride met the challenge and battled their way into a lily white suburb. They overcame the vandalism and survived the physical threats and the isolation. They made it. "Now," he went on, "Negroes call us Uncle Toms and ex-colored folk for living out here with all these white people."

Soon the Los Angeles City School Board, after years of prodding by militant civil rights leaders, is expected to come up with plans for total desegregation of the city's schools. If these plans take shape, they will not now be hailed as a victory by the black community. The scattered applause which may greet the change will be smothered by the relentless opposition of those who demand local community control of ghetto schools instead of dispersal of their children.

The agenda of the black ghetto is changing rapidly. Last week's clichés have a hollow ring. Yesterday's answers have lost their relevance. If white America is bewildered by the swirl of shifting demands, it is not alone. There is lack of comprehension among many black folk, too.

Behind the rhetoric and posturing of today, a fundamental debate is rending the black community. The shallow newspaper headlines have done nothing to clarify the controversy, and the news accounts have oversimplified and distorted it.

* Reprinted from *The Progressive*, XXII (January, 1968), pp. 13-16. By permission of *The Progressive* and the author.

The issue is not militancy versus moderation. There are militants indeed and there are moderates, too, in both camps. Nor is "integration versus separation" the definitive division. Which is it—integration or separation—when a black student joins a campus Afro-American association after choosing freely to enter an integrated university? Then, is it youth against age? The young, it is true, carry the burden of the argument on one side, while many of their elders form the bulwark on the other. But chronology must not be confused with ideology.

Is the question, then, "black power"? How does one debate a slogan without a precise statement of its meaning?

There is an issue, however, and it is frighteningly real. The question stripped bare is this: What is the way for black Americans to find a meaning for their existence and to achieve dignity in the American context? Is it through assimilation? Or is it through racial cohesiveness?

This is not an unfamiliar debate on American soil. All immigrant groups have wrestled with it, and it has torn many asunder. In each case there have been voices speaking for group cohesion, for maintaining cultural identity, for a kind of sub-nationalism within this nation. There have also been voices urging dispersal, and assimilation, and pressing the smaller group to enter the larger group of their new national home. Invariably, in the first generation, internal insecurity of the group and external hostility toward it gave ascendancy to the voices favoring group cohesion. The greater the external pressure, the greater the cohesion. Immigrants and their decendants remained Irish-Americans, Italian-Americans, Polish-Americans, Jewish-Americans, with the accent on their original identity. As the external pressure was reduced, the voices of assimilation became more compelling. The ethnic hyphens faded, but they have never completely disappeared.

Among black people, the ideological division has been of longer duration, because of their high visibility and the background of slavery. After emancipation the debate began, but in a low key. Many Negroes wanted then to return to Africa, and some did. But most sought somehow to make their way here—some as a separate people, and some as an assimilated group. What was the American Negro—or the Negro American? A black man who happened, through historical accident, to live in America, or an American who, by genetic accident, happened to be black? In 1903, W. E. B. Du Bois put the dilemma thus:

"One feels his two-ness—an American Negro, two souls,

two thoughts, two unreconciled strivings, two warring ideals, in one dark body. . . .

"The history of the American Negro is the history of this strife—this longing to attain self-conscious manhood, to merge his double self into a better and truer self. . . . He would not Africanize America, for America has too much to teach the world and Africa. He would not bleach the Negro soul in a flood of white Americanism, for he knows that Negro blood has a message for the world. He simply wishes to make it possible for a man to be both a Negro and an American without being cursed and spit upon. . . ."

The ferocious quality of the debate in black America is of recent vintage, and was triggered by three failures—the failure of newly won legal and constitutional civil rights prerogatives to effect any meaningful change in the life situation of black people; the failure of the assault on segregation to halt the trend toward increasing segregation in housing and schools; and the failure of all efforts to have any discernible impact on racism in the nation's society. "Everything has changed, but everything remains the same," one hears constantly in the South. *De facto* segregation throughout the nation continues to rise. The income gap is still widening. Racism, like a miasma, is still breathed with the air.

Throughout this century the ascendancy among the contending Negroes has been held by those who sought dispersal and assimilation. With the Supreme Court school desegregation decision of 1954 this ascendancy rode on a wave of euphoria. Two years ago, however, optimism receded to leave the bitter taste of hollow victories in the mouths of the black masses.

What has been said to the black man throughout this century, by his leaders and by white liberals, is that he must think of himself as an individual and not as a member of a group, and that if, as an individual, he gained education and money he would first be acculturated and then assimilated into a racially integrated society. He would become, in reality, a white man with an invisible black skin in a color-blind community. Men of good will, black and white, bowed to the myth that proximity would, in itself, produce color-blindness. If assimilation were achieved, the black man would have no ethnic or racial identity; he would be an American distributed through every phase of the nation's life. The black ghetto would disappear; the Harlems would become nightmares of the past.

For many years no responsible leader would have suggested

that improvement of educational or housing conditions in the ghetto could possibly serve any useful purpose. The ghettos were seen as an anachronism; to improve them would be to perpetuate the evil of segregation. Privately supported Negro colleges almost went bankrupt. A. Philip Randolph was castigated in the late 1950s for urging formation of a "Negro American Labor Council." White students in integrated colleges complained that black students were not yet truly emancipated, for when two Negroes entered the dining hall they frequently sat together and talked with each other, rather than distributing themselves in the best integrated fashion. The cry was "segregation in reverse."

Efforts to implement this dispersion concept of integration obviously have failed, though some still argue for it—naïvely, I think. It no longer enjoys the widespread acceptance in the black community which it once had. Indeed, it is today under fierce attack. What the dispersion concept required of the black man was a kind of abnegation, a losing of himself as a black man to find himself as an American.

Its opponents argue for an ethnic cohesiveness, a finding of himself as a black man, as the urgent goal. They advocate group self-assertion. They foster pride in pigmentation, rather than white mimicry. Rather than disperse the ghetto and reject self, they would preserve, cherish, and develop the ghetto, and love the black self.

Some of the ethnic unity advocates are separationists and view the ghetto which they seek to upgrade, as a separate community preferably to remain alienated from the body politic. Others see it as an ethnic community among many ethnic communities in our cities, and as a power fulcrum to propel the black man into the political and economic mainstream, thereby changing the mainstream significantly. So, there are debates within debates. The debates are creative and good. The truth, I am sure, will emerge somewhere between the extremes.

The black man must find himself as a black man before he can find himself as an American. He must now become a hyphenated American, discovering the hyphen so that he can eventually lose it. This involves accepting the stark reality that the black ghettos of our cities are not going to disappear in the foreseeable future. Nor is racism.

The Afro-American cannot skip the hyphenated phase in his development, and the losing of his hyphen will be more difficult for him, as I have suggested, because of a racial mystique deeply rooted in both white and Negro, which holds the Negro inferior. Paradoxically, the black man must, I think, strengthen his ghetto on the one hand and continue to provide an exit on the other. He must build the economic and political power of the ghetto as he simultaneously fights for open-occupancy housing, which eventually will destroy the ghetto, but will provide the Negro with a new potency as a full American.

This is bound to be a long and agonizing process, encompassing a series of progressive and regressive steps—some dramatic, some prosaic, some violent, some passive. A thin line separates group self-pride and self-hate. To expect that all will walk that line without crossing it is naïve. To ask that it not be walked because some will step over it is to ask the impossible. If the rhetoric of proponents of black consciousness is sometimes excessive, it is because they are trying to "de-program" themselves. They, too, are creatures of a national culture which has held them worthless. "Black is beautiful and it is so great to be black." If they shout too loudly, it is because they are shouting down the echoes of 400 years of contrary conditioning.

Those least capable of understanding what is happening in the ghetto today are, I hear, the white liberals. Their reaction is more than a matter of unrequited love. The new formulations of black unity fly in the face of their liberal dogmas and challenge every cliché they hold dear. Such a cliché is "breaking up the ghetto." Another is the "color-blindness" mystique. Still another is the shibboleth of inter-racialism, which requires, for instance, that every house party have at least one black guest.

But the white liberal is even more shattered by the redefinition of his role, or, more accurately, the rejection of his former role. Liberals have not hated us; they have loved us. It is the bigots who have hated us, and hate is its own bizarre kind of flattery; it pays its victims the high compliment of worthiness. But paternalistic love depreciates them. Hate says to a man that he is equal; paternalism tells him he is a child. But what happens to paternalism when the child grows up?

The horror of racist programming in America, from womb to tomb, is that it has pictured the black man as an incompetent, a child—the "boy," "girl," and first-name syndrome— or at best it has viewed him as a little brother who must have his big brother as his keeper. Despite all protestations to the contrary, the historic Negro-liberal alliance, from the Abolitionists to today, has been on that basis. We blacks have been junior partners, not equals.

As a liberal friend wrote to me recently in response to my reply to his initial inquiry as to whether we had been wrong all these years he and I had fought together for integration, ". . . some of our long cherished clichés about the civil rights struggle do need updating. [But] . . . some things I continue to believe are absolute truths; among these is the fundamental truth that each man in fact be his brother's keeper, regardless of race . . ." Another cliché. And that is precisely the problem: liberals have been our custodians, guardians, handlers, *keepers*, but not our *brothers*, our eyeball-to-eyeball equals.

A middle-aged white lady, a mover in liberal causes for many years, asked me a few weeks ago why it is that now when the hand of friendship is offered to black people in the ghettos, often as not they bite it. I tried to explain that black people, especially of the lower economic strata, were hitherto silent, pliant, and largely invisible. But now they have found their voice. They are bursting with existence and are willing no longer to have their whole lives ordered by others. They insist upon making for themselves the decisions which determine their lives. They will make mistakes, but they must be their mistakes, their blunders. Free a man and he is not yet free. He must still free himself. This I viewed as a positive development toward participatory democracy. Help and cooperation, I argued, must be given on those terms, their terms, or not at all.

The worst result of the nation's racist programming is that even black people until now have absorbed the concept of themselves as inferior. It has stunted their growth. A child does not mature so long as he plays the role of a child. When he reaches adulthood, it is good that he leaves the household and rejects the parent if the parent does not begin to view him as an adult. Black people have now grown up in their self-image, and they have walked out of the house.

White liberalism has lost its relevance to the black struggle because it is emotionally and ideologically out of date. Some liberals have conquered their paternalism, and a few— a precious few—escaped the virus all along. But liberalism, on the whole, is weak in this respect.

To regain their relevance to the Negro struggle, white liberals must re-orient their feelings and their thinking. They must get over seeing themselves as great white fathers and mothers, brokers of power and patronage for black people. They must learn that if they stoop down to offer, in the missionary way, the hand of friendship, the offer will be rejected, the hand bitten. If they offer it laterally, it will be circled warily, eyed suspiciously, then perhaps taken gingerly and tentatively.

The coming of age of the Negro has been psychological.

But it is also political. The recent elections in Cleveland, Gary, Virginia, and several counties in Mississippi demonstrated that the black vote has matured in the grandest American tradition. The Negro electorate no longer is content to deprecate itself by having whites as its exclusive political custodians. It no longer is willing to be partner to the myth that political decision-making is white men's work. This shakes to its roots the urban coalition which has kept the Democratic kite aloft. The "tail" of the alliance has moved up front to join labor, liberals, ethnic blocs, and professional political machines as part of the kite itself. The Democratic Party must now accommodate to this new development or face disaster in 1968.

The new black maturation, apparent for some time in the psychological sense and now visible in the political arena, has encompassed the economic and educational areas only in demand, not yet in performance. Economically the ghettos are still colonies; the income-producing properties are owned by absentees, and the inhabitants are consumers paying inflated prices. A balance of payments position like theirs would cause England's Prime Minister Harold Wilson to do more than devalue the pound.

Ghetto folk are now demanding that the outward flow of dollars be reversed and that economic control of their communities be turned over to those who share their woes and dreams. None but the lunatic fringe among them clings to the bootstrap illusion that Negroes can do it all alone. Most are keenly aware that they lack the boots—the capital, the technical know-how, the managerial skills. But help from whites must be consultative and advisory; the decisions must be made by the Negroes in the ghettos. They want industries to invest in their communities, and a few are beginning to do so—to build plants, to grant franchises, to train managers. It is mandatory, though, that such properties, when built, be turned over to the local community people—when trained—to run. In Watts, Aerojet Corporation has built a subsidiary, the Watts Manufacturing Company, which makes tents and allied products. Watts people have been trained to run the plant from top to bottom. Plans are being made to allow the five hundred employees to purchase stock in the company. The Watts Manufacturing Company, alone, will not save Watts, but it is a start toward providing ghetto dwellers with some measure of control over their economic destiny.

The demand for control over their own future is nowhere so compelling as in the education realm. After more than a decade of using every device available in a vain attempt to get their children into white schools, in the hope that white power would insure quality education because white children were their classmates, black parents have reversed their field. The demand, as yet unachieved, is now for local community control of ghetto schools. School boards have failed to integrate and failed to educate black children, so now black parents around the country are mounting insistent campaigns for decentralization of authority, giving them control over administrators and curricula in ghetto schools. They could hardly do worse than the school boards—witness the widening gap in learning, from grades one through twelve, between ghetto youngsters and others. They might do much better, for they have one thing which the school boards have lacked: a passionate concern for their children's education and future.

The debate will rage on between cohesiveness and dispersion. Ascendancy of one camp or the other will be determined ultimately not by rhetoric, and not even by leadership, as much as by events. Events today seem to be racing to the side of the spirited new force—cohesion—and I think that is right and good for the black man at this historical juncture.

KENNETH B. CLARK,

Educator, Psychologist

Kenneth Clark has an outstanding academic background which he uses quite effectively toward the betterment of black Americans. Born in the Panama Canal Zone on July 24, 1914, he received the A.B. and the M.A. degrees from Howard University and, in 1940, the Ph.D. from Columbia University. He has since worked as a professor of psychology at City College of New York, and as president of its Metropolitan Applied Research Center, Inc. In 1961 he won the NAACP Spingarn Medal for his research in psychology. Later he organized Harlem Youth Opportunities Unlimited (HARYOU), an antipoverty program for Harlem youngsters. Although he resigned his position with this group in 1964, he has continued to promote programs to combat injustices in ghettos and deprived areas. He served as director of the Social Dynamics Research Institute at the City College of New York and was recently elected president of the American Psychological Association.

As a professor and researcher, Clark has made many contributions to alleviating the problems of Blacks. Especially useful have been his studies of the effects of racial prejudice on children, as seen in his book, Dark Ghettos. His recent psychological analysis of the forces behind the various black movements and their leaders is also noteworthy.

"THE ENEMY WAS NEVER TO BE UNDERSTOOD IN TERMS OF COLOR . . . BUT IN THE MORE DIFFICULT AND ABSTRACT TERMS OF HUMAN IRRATIONALITY, IGNORANCE, SUPERSTITION, RIGIDITY, AND ARBITRARY CRUELTY."

The Present Dilemma of the Negro*

A basic dilemma of America is whether the Negro should be accepted and taken seriously as a human being and permitted the rights and privileges accorded other human beings in our political system. America has endured slave rebellions, developed an underground railroad, fought one of the most bloody wars in human history and is now undergoing a series of urban ghetto implosions in the attempt to resolve this persistent bedeviling question.

The Negro's form of this basic dilemma is whether to persist in his insistence upon his unqualified rights as a human being without regard to the risks or consequences—or whether to accommodate to the resistances by subtle or flagrant forms of withdrawal from the fray. The general acceptance of slavery, the many psychological adjustments and deflection of aggressive reactions to subjugation, the varieties of back-to-Africa movements, the cults, fads, and the recent series of riots in our ghettos are among the many ways in which American Negroes have sought to deal with this basic American dilemma.

The gnawing doubts of white Americans as to their status and worth as human beings—the deep feelings of inferiority coming out of the actual inferior status in the land of their origin in Europe—impelled American whites to develop and enforce social and institutional arrangements designed to inflict upon Negroes an inferior status in American life. This was necessary to bolster the demanding status needs of whites. These needs were powerful enough to counteract the logic, the morality and the powerful political ethics of the egalitarian and democratic rhetoric which is also an important American reality. I differ with early [Gunnar] Myrdal† only in my belief

* Reprinted from *The Journal of Negro History*, LIII (January, 1968), pp 2-11. By permission of ASNIA and the author.

† Myrdal is the author of a comprehensive study of the Negro in America, *An American Dilemma: The Negro Problem and Modern Democracy*, Harper and Brothers Publishers, 1944.

that the American democratic creed and ideals are not psychologically contradictory to American racism. In terms of dynamics and motivation of the insecure, they are compatible.

This critical American dilemma is reflected in Negroes not only in terms of acceptance of the creeds and its promises literally, but also in terms of deep doubts concerning the worth of self. The former aspect of the dilemma stems from the fact of general indoctrination which transcends even the barriers of racially segregated schools and is reinforced by the development of the mass media in the twentieth century. The latter component of the Negro's dilemma arises out of the reality of the inferior status to which he has been subjugated. The walls of segregation are not only humiliating—but given this type of chronic humiliation there develops self doubt, subtle and flagrant forms of self hatred, personal and group frustrations, internationalized hostility, aggressions, self-denial or bombast. Under these conditions the walls of segregation become pathetically protective. Within them the subjugated individuals need not meet the tests of free and open competition—need not expose vulnerable egos to single standards of competence.

The anguish and resistance of anxious, self-doubting white segregationists and the cautious timidity of striving middle class whites with the psyche of affluent peasants are matched only by the anxieties, doubts, and vacillation of vast numbers of Negroes—working and middle class—as they stand at the threshold of nonsegregated society and are confronted by the tremendous psychological challenges for which American history not only did not prepare them but erected seemingly insurmountable barriers. The demand for racial justice on the part of American Negroes is balanced by an almost equal psychological reality of the fear of the removal of racial barriers.

* * * *

The hopes and beliefs of the Negro that racial equality and democracy could be obtained through litigation, legislation, executive action, and negotiation, and through strong alliances with various white liberal groups, were supplanted by disillusionment, bitterness, and anger which erupted under the anguished cry of "Black Power" which pathetically sought to disguise the understandable desperation and impotence with bombast and rhetoric.

A critical danger—and probably a difference without a pragmatic distinction—between the determinants of retrogression in the first post-Reconstruction period and the present is that whereas the promises of racial progress were reversed in the nineteenth century by the fanaticism, irrationality, and cruel strength of white segregationists—the impending racial retrogression of today might come about largely through self-hatred leading to the fanaticism, dogmatism, rigidity, and self-destructive cruelty of black separatists. If this comes about, it will not be enough to excuse this monstrous perpetuation of the lie of racism and postponement of the goals of democracy and humanity by asserting that the frustrations and bitterness of the victimized Negro account for his present irrationality and rigidity. A similar and equally valid psychological explanation could be offered to explain the racial cruelties of desperate and miserable poor whites of the past and present. Understanding is not acceptance.

White segregationists were able to inflict and perpetuate racial injustices upon Negroes because rational, sophisticated, and moderate whites were silent in the face of barbarities. They permitted themselves to be intimidated and bullied by white extremists until they were morally and almost functionally indistinguishable from their worst and most ignorant elements. A similar threat and dilemma face the rational, thoughtful Negro today. If he permits himself to be cowed into silence by unrealistic Negro racists, he will be an active partner in fastening the yoke of impossible racial separatism more tightly around the neck of America. He—you, through your silence, will permit the difficult goals of a racially nonsegregated society to be lost by default. You would have given to black racists what you, your fathers and grandfathers fought and died to prevent giving to white racists. The victories which white segregationists, in spite of all their material and political power, could not have won for themselves, black separatists would have won for them—and we through our silence would make this possible.

To prevent the repetition of the tragedy of racial retrogression and a return to the "nadir" of race relations in America, we must be realistic in our appraisal of the present state of race relations in America. . . . We must analyze as tough-mindedly as possible the dynamics and symptoms of our times if we are to develop effective and realistic remedies.

During the past few years it became excruciatingly clear for the Negro that the more things changed the more they remained the same—or worsened. The promises and hope for progress became a relentless quagmire of words.

The drama of direct action, non-violent confrontation of the more obvious signs of Southern racial injustice became trite, and was not particularly relevant or effective in dealing with the persistent, pervasive, and subtle problems of racism which afflicted the Northern Negro. More appropriate and effective methods have not yet been found to deal with Northern racism.

The guilt and indignation of some Northern whites against Southern forms of racism turned into white backlash or mutism when the Northern Negro began to take seriously the claims of civil rights progress and sought some observable signs of them in Northern cities.

The anguish and desperation of the Northern Negro have been expressed in the latest series of ghetto eruptions which started in the Harlem riot of the summer of 1964, reached a crescendo in the Watts riot of 1965 and continued through the current series of riots in Newark and Detroit of this past summer. Another significant expression of the Northern Negro's "no-win" fatalism is found in the rise of the "Black Power" slogan and momentum which skyrocketed at the time of the Meredith shooting in Mississippi in June of 1966 and continues as an obbligato to the sounds of ghetto violence and futility.

It is important to keep in mind the date (June, 1966) when the "Black Power" slogan became nationally advertised—in order not to be confused about the cause and effect relationship between "Black Power" and "white backlash."

Whatever may be its tactical, strategic, and rational shortcomings and ambiguity, "Black Power" did not cause "white backlash" . . . The existence of "white backlash," the unwillingness of whites to be serious in meeting the demands of Negroes for the same rights and responsibilities granted as a matter of course to all other Americans—including the newest refugee from European, Latin American, or Asiatic oppression—caused the outbursts of hysterical bitterness and random hostility inherent in the cry of "Black Power."

"Black Power" emerged as a response to the following facts:

- a recognition of the fact that the center of gravity of the civil rights movement had moved to the Northern urban racial ghettos where it was now immobilized by ambiguous intensified white resistance to any meaningful change in the predicament of Negroes;

- the recognition of the fact that successful litigation, strong legislation, free access to public accommodations, open housing laws, strong pronouncements on the part of the President, governors or mayors, and even the right to vote or to hold office were not relevant to the overriding fact that the masses of Negroes were still confined to poverty and to the dehumanizing conditions of the ghetto;

● and that in spite of the promises of a Great Society and the activity of the war on poverty, the Negro's children were still doomed to criminally inferior schools and his youth and males the victims of unemployment, underemployment and stagnation.

"Black Power" is the cry of defiance of what its advocates have come to see as the hoax of racial progress—of the cynicism of the appeals to the Negro to be patient and to be lawful as his needs are continually subordinated to more important national and international issues and to the needs, desires, and conveniences of more privileged groups.

Whites, by virtue of their numerical, military, and economic superiority, reinforced by historical American racism which grants higher status to whites by virtue of skin color alone, do have the power to decide whether the future of Negroes—the Negro masses, the Negro middle class, or the Negro elected official—will be positive, negative, or stagnant.

This core reality of the dynamics of power is not likely to be influenced by sentimental and idealistic appeals for justice, by smiles or promises or by emotional sloganeering.

"Black Power," in spite of its ambiguity, its "no-win" premise, its programmatic emptiness and its pragmatic futility does have tremendous psychological appeal for the masses of Negroes who have "nothing to lose" and some middle class Negroes who are revolted by the empty promises and the moral dry-rot of affluent America.

"Black Power" is a bitter retreat from the possibility of the attainment of the goals of any serious racial integration in America. . . .

It is an attempt to make a verbal virtue of involuntary racial segregation. . . .

It is the sour grapes phenomenon on the American racial scene. . . .

"Black Power" is the contemporary form of the Booker T. Washington accommodation to white America's resistance to making democracy real for Negro Americans. While Booker T. made his adjustment to and acceptance of white racism under the guise of conservatism, many if not all of the "Black Power" advocates are seeking to sell the same shoddy moral product disguised in the gaudy package of racial militance.

Nonetheless, today "Black Power" is a reality in the Negro ghettos of America—increasing in emotional intensity, if not in rational clarity. And we, if we are to be realistic, cannot afford to pretend that it does not exist. Even in its most irrational and illusory formulations—and particularly when it is presented as a vague and incoherent basis upon which the deprived Negro can project his own pathetic wishes for a pride and an assertiveness which white America continues mockingly or piously to deny him—"Black Power" is a powerful political reality which cannot be ignored by realistic Negro or white political officials.

It is all too clear that among the casualties of the present phase of American race relations are reason, clarity, consistence and realism. Some "Black Power" spokesmen, like their white segregationist counterparts, demand the subjugation of rational and realistic thought and planning to dogmaticism and fanaticism. By their threats and name calling, they seek to intimidate others into silence or a mindless mouthing of their slogans.

To be effective and to increase his chances of survival in the face of name-calling verbal racial militants, the trained Negro must demonstrate that he is concerned and can bring about some positive changes in the following intolerable areas of ghetto life:

1. criminally inefficient and racially segregated public schools;
2. dehumanizingly poor housing;
3. pervasive job discrimination and joblessness;
4. shoddy quality of goods and high prices in local stores;
5. the dirt, filth, and stultifying drabness of ghetto streets and neighborhoods;
6. the adversary relationship between police and the residents of the ghettos.

This requires the mobilization and use of human intelligence to define the problems, to study and analyze them and to develop practical and implementable solutions to them. This cannot be done on the basis of race—whites and Negroes must join together in an experiment to determine whether systematic and empathic use of human intelligence and training can be a form of power which can be used constructively in the quest for solutions of long standing urban and racial problems. This is the rationale of The Metropolitan Applied Research Center. We are under no illusions that this will be easy. . . . We know that power confrontation brings risks not found in the cloistered halls of academia. We know that we cannot expect the protections and safety of the detached isolated scholars. But we believe that human intelligence is a social trust and that the stakes are worth the risks.

Another dilemma, not related to the dilemmas and inconsistencies of "Black Power," is the fact that in the present doldrums of the civil rights movement the cleavage between the masses of Negroes and the middle class has become more clear and exacerbating. The masses of Negroes are now starkly aware of the fact that recent civil rights victories benefited primarily a very small percentage of middle class Negroes while their predicament remained the same or worsened. Added to Ralph Bunche and our traditional civil rights leaders who are invited to Washington, we now have Thurgood Marshall, Robert Weaver, Walter Washington as the appointed Mayor of Washington, D.C., a few vice presidents in private industry, a few more Negroes in New England prep schools and Ivy League colleges, and more white colleges and universities are looking for one or two "qualified Negroes" for their faculties. These and other tokens of "racial progress" are not only rejected by the masses of Negroes but seem to have resulted in their increased and more openly expressed hostility toward middle class Negroes. They see the advances of the middle class Negroes as being at their expense, at worst, or obscuring their plight or, at best, not being in any way relevant to their being condemned indefinitely to their dehumanizing predicament. There are some clues which suggest that the recent ghetto implosions were not only antiwhite, but also involved vague stirrings of anti-Negro middle class sentiment among the rioters.

The present dilemma of the Negro is focused for the trained Negro intellectual. He must now choose sides. He must now clarify the nature of the enemy. He must dare to say that the enemy was never to be understood in terms of color . . . but in the more difficult and abstract terms of human irrationality, ignorance, superstition, rigidity, and arbitrary cruelty.

These are the common enemies which underlie all forms of tyranny—racism, authoritarianism, McCarthyism. . . .

They are no less enemies when being sold or offered as truth or salvation by blacks, yellows or whites. . . .

If Negroes and whites who understand this can make it clear, we can help to save America. We will use the power of disciplined intelligence combined with respect for moral values and humanity to save Negroes from the destructive possibilities of white and black dilemmas and thereby contribute to the survival of America. . . . For America cannot survive if Negroes do not. . . . And Negroes and no other group of human beings are likely to survive if America does not.

NATHAN HARE, JR.,

Scholar, Publisher, Activist

Nathan Hare was born in Slick, Oklahoma, April 9, 1934. He received an A.B. degree from Langston University in Oklahoma in 1954, where he had established an excellent reputation, academically as well as in sports. He was awarded the novice welterweight Golden Gloves championship in 1954.

Hare received both his master's and his Ph.D. degrees from the University of Chicago and subsequently taught at Howard University and San Francisco State. At both institutions, his vigorous support of academic freedom and active support of student groups contributed to his leaving. At San Francisco State, Hare was largely responsible for the establishment of one of the first black studies departments and served as its chairman during his tenure there.

In addition to numerous contributions to black periodicals and scholarly journals, Hare has written a book called The Black Anglo-Saxons. *He has been selected for* Who's Who in American Education, *and is currently the publisher of the sucessful journal,* The Black Scholar. *In this journal, Hare seeks to unite the black intellectuals and the brothers on the street. He also hopes to point out to the masses the importance of black scholarship and scientific analysis.*

"IN THE SEARCH FOR EDUCATIONAL RELEVANCE, BLACK TODAY IS REVOLUTIONARY AND NATIONALISTIC."

"Black Power"—Its Goals and Methods*

Interview with Dr. Nathan Hare, Jr.

Q: Dr. Hare, what do you mean by "black power"?

A: "Power" is the ability to influence another person—even against his will, if necessary. We know what "black" is. So "black power" means the exercise by black people of influence on the forces which oppress us. Those forces happen to be white, for the most part.

Q: How do you intend to exercise this influence?

A: The philosophy of black power is to bring about equality—not just equality of opportunity; we want equality *and* opportunity.

The Declaration of Independence declares the right to life, liberty and the pursuit of happiness. The catch is that it doesn't give you the chance to catch up with happiness. We don't want the pursuit. We want the happiness.

We want equality, not equality of opportunity.

This is what we seek, by whatever means seem necessary as we go along. Our ways will be revealed as the time comes.

Q: Is this black-power movement a basic change in Negro tactics—a new approach to Negro problems?

A: At least I feel—and I sense that black-power people feel—that we have been using the wrong tactics in the past, that our old tactics have not worked. Assimilation has not worked. Indeed, it has hampered our struggle.

We've been singing when we should be swinging, maybe. As Malcolm X [the late Black Muslim leader] said, we've been praying when we should have been preying, or playing when we should be flaying—you know, skinning alive.

* Reprinted from *U.S. News and World Report*, LXII (May, 1967), pp. 64-68. Copyright © 1967 U.S. News and World Report, Inc.

But certainly we are going to work on new means and new tactics for bringing about this equality—not equality of opportunity, but equality.

Q: Can you give us an idea of the direction in which the black-power movement is heading?

A: Well, it seems to be moving toward self-assertion, self-sufficiency by the black people. It is a product of the failure of assimilation and the quest for assimilation, which has been a long struggle. We have come to see, we feel, that assimilation won't work, partly because it mortifies the ego or the self-respect of the black person who feels that the only way he can get salvation is by being mingled among white persons. So he chases white persons into one neighborhood after another, into one school after another, making very little physical progress either place.

There has been some token integration—which some of us have refused. But statistics show there has been no real progress, occupationally or what not.

So we have realized that integration and equalization are not synonymous. Moreover, equality is not synonymous with sameness. There is no necessity for us to take over all of the culture norms and values of the white society, and we are going to begin to test them and to pick out those that we regard as desirable, and reject those—such as the Viet Nam slaughter—which we deem to be undesirable.

Q: Is this a turning from individual effort to a group effort by Negroes?

A: Look—suppose you have a wall, and imagine that the persons on this side are mainly black and the persons on the other side are mainly white, and the blacks are trying to get over the wall because it's better over there.

As each one climbs up he steps on the heads and backs of the others. Then as they get up they are pushed back, one by one—or maybe a few individual blacks are let across so they can help push the others back.

So—as I said way back in 1964, when Stokely Carmichael [Chairman of the Student Nonviolent Coordinating Committee] was a student of mine, even though he already had his ideas then—maybe the best thing that black people should do is to turn back upon themselves for a little while, get their *esprit de corps* together and build a big ramrod, then all of them together rush and batter the wall down. This seems better than the idea of individualistic assimilation—of trying to act like people on the other side, trying to take over their clothing, manners, hair styles, color or what not, and trying to get up there one by one.

Q: Does this mean you are abandoning integration?

A: Yes, as an end in itself. I'm sure that there is no effort to reject all white persons. Some white persons—even though they are few, like one half of 1 per cent—are blacker than most black persons in their thinking.

On the other hand, you have a majority of black persons who think white—although that majority is decreasing rapidly. So we can't just put it on the basis of skin color any more. But we have, of course, to watch the white person. Basically we take a person at his word. Then when he falls back on his word you handle him as you handle any other traitor of any color.

So therefore we don't see integration as anything which is a desirable end in itself. I can imagine a utopian world in which everybody would be integrated. But this does not seem to be possible under the present thinking and structure.

Therefore, we at least want the chance to develop on our own—not pray to the white establishment for equal rights, but become self-sufficient and assert ourselves and build our own communities. Maybe we'll have to decide whether we want to let white persons into our institutions, and so forth.

Q: Have you abandoned integration as a means, as well as an end?

A: We're giving up on it as a means to an end. We don't see it as a means to an end. It started as at least an idealistic means to an end, but it had become an end in itself, until this sort of Black Muslim, black-power type of push began.

White people thought that we could not have any institutions which were basically black which were of good quality. This has the effect of a self-fulfilling prophecy, because if you think that black persons cannot possibly have a good bank, then you don't put your money in it. All the best professors leave black universities to go to white universities as soon as they get the chance. The blacks even do the same thing. And this makes your prediction, which wasn't true in the beginning, come out to be true.

Q: You say you want more than equality of opportunity—

A: Equality of opportunity is more than just the right to go to school. A colleague of mine has proposed that every Negro child be given scholarships through the Ph.D. level, if he desires. Of course, there has to be some catching up, and even equal opportunity at the present time would be putting us at a disadvantage, still.

Yet, we don't ask any special favors. We just want to get

people off our backs, stop whacking us down every time we rise up, and let us go by ourselves.

We have depended on the white "liberal" reform for centuries, and it has made too little progress. We want to go mainly by ourselves—try our own way.

Q: How do Negroes—who are only about 12 per cent of the population—expect to gain power all by themselves, apart from whites?

A: Well, there are white allies. But I'd like to point out that the white man rules all over the world, even though he's in the minority in the world scene. The white man is in the minority in Rhodesia and South Africa, here in the District of Columbia, and in certain parts of Mississippi and Alabama. Yet he rules. This is something which we have to get rid of.

The blacks outnumber the whites 23 to 1 in Rhodesia. But they grumble in the dark, and then when a white person passes by they tuck their tails and fall silent. Why, they could have taken each a finger—10 of them a finger apiece, 10 a toe apiece, and 3 could take any other appendages which they desired—and pulled each white man apart, if they had been organized and determined.

Q: But here in the United States, where you are outnumbered 8 or 9 to 1, how do you expect to gain power?

A: It's sort of ludicrous for an enemy group to come here with microphones and cameras expecting their opponents to tell them what they intend to do. It's not wise for a group to reveal its plans to its enemy.

Q: Do you consider whites your enemy?

A: I'm an enemy of those whites who are enemies of mine, who are enemies of justice.

Q: How do you differentiate?

A: We take them at their word until they're proven to be traitors, and then we purge them from our midst.

Q: Is black power an anti-white movement?

A: No. It is an anti-antiblack movement.

Q: Do you think most Negroes hate whites?

A: No. I think most white persons hate Negroes.

Q: So you will not reveal your plans for black power to white people—

A: No, I wouldn't—not to many of them, and certainly not to strangers, and not to the whites as a whole.

Q: Do you actually have secret plans to seize black power?

A: I would say "no comments" on that. We're working on that problem. I think people will find out when the time comes.

Q: Would you say, then, that white people are in for some surprises?

A: I would suppose that they are. In fact, I used to go around predicting a black blitzkrieg.

Q: How would you define a black blitzkrieg?

A: It's sort of like a thousand giant Watts riots sweeping the country. [Watts was the 1965 riot area in Los Angeles.]

Q: Do you still think that's a possibility?

A: Not a thousand Watts—that's exaggerating. But I think a great number of them. I still feel that it's possible, though I don't feel that it's wise or necessarily desirable to predict it.

Q: What is the attitude of the black-power movement toward violence?

A: They feel that, whenever attacked, American law and mores dictate that a person fights back. And it eventually has become acceptable to do so.

Q: You talk about fighting back when attacked. But what if you are not attacked? Do you consider violence a justifiable means to gain what you call black power?

A: No. I don't think we need violence for that. We have our ways, which we aren't revealing to the whites.

Q: What is behind these riots that have been erupting in so many cities of this country?

A: They are trying to say to the power structure that they aren't getting what they feel they deserve.

Q: Is this considered by the black-power movement an acceptable means of expressing their feelings?

A: We don't have any judgments about that. We try to withhold judgments. Killing is not bad or good in itself. It can be bad if you kill a person for no cause, but it gets you a Medal of Honor if you kill a person in a situation in which the establishment finds killing desirable. So it's a matter of cultural definition as to what is desirable or good.

Q: If it came to what you call a black blitzkrieg, do you think the Negroes could possibly win in this country?

A: I don't have any idea. I'm not a military strategist. But I understand that the Viet Cong have done a pretty good job while being outnumbered. Even in conventional warfare, we have great weapons such as atomic bombs that we don't use now. I don't think the United States can afford to be dropping atom bombs on its major cities. But this is a possibility.

Q: Do you think there is a serious possibility of guerrilla civil war between whites and blacks in this country?

A: I don't see why it is so impossible in this country. What's so different about this country? And what's so different about the blacks, as compared to other groups, that they would never come around to that if other means were not successful?

Of course, civil war would probably be harder here than anywhere else. But I don't think it's impossible.

Q: Where would you draw the line? Where would you stop in this battle for equality?

A: I'm not waging a civil war. I don't want you to get that impression.

Q: But you talk about it as a possibility—

A: As a sociologist, sure. As a sociologist I'm obliged to discern and communicate the truth, and these are things which I see, sociologically speaking. It's not something which I'm calling for. It's just an unfortunate fact.

Q: Would you personally advocate going as far as civil war, if necessary?

A: I would not want to make any comment in that regard, because I would not want to be regarded as advocating it on the one hand—but, on the other hand, I do not want to be an enemy of the civil-war people, the guerrillas, if they start. I don't want them to get me. So I'm not taking any stand. I'm just trying to be a sociologist.

Q: How real do you regard the possibility of civil war—and how soon?

A: I regard it as very real. But it would not happen all at once. There has to be so much organization—and, before that, so much discontent and loss of faith by so many persons. So, if it's comforting to you, it's going to be quite a while off yet—though not so far off as to be outside of our life span.

Q: Suppose that, by whatever means, you do succeed in achieving black power. What would you do with it?

A: Black power does not mean the overthrow of white power. It is not a matter of replacing white power with black power. We'd set up institutions or even emerge as an important, significant part of the existent white institutions.

We would hope that it would not come to pass that black power would turn around and do the same thing that white power has done. Of course, if that *should* come to pass, we would have to admit that turn about is fair play. But we don't envision that or desire it. We do not strive to take over. We just want to be right up there on an equal plane—either separately or integrated or by any means.

Autonomy for Negroes

Q: Does the idea of a separate State for Negroes enter into your thinking?

A: Well, the District of Columbia is two-thirds black, and pretty soon we're going to have what amounts to a separate State here, if we gain some autonomy through home rule. So, I think we'll start with the District of Columbia and see how it works out.

Q: If you took over the District of Columbia, would you tell the Federal Government to move out?

A: We could let them stay here, if the Government is willing to operate in a black city—a black State.

The Federal Government could still have its White House. Now, there are some persons who want to move it to Howard University and call it the "Black House." But I think we could let it stay the White House.

Of course, we'd have to start charging people tolls, like other cities do, to come in here.

Q: Charge tolls to outsiders coming into the capital?

A: Yes, such as commuters coming in here to work. Because all the streets are made to their advantage—one way going out during rush hours at night, one way coming in during rush hours in the morning, parking here—and we can't even get in to use our own facilities. Yet they pay their taxes to another State. So we'll have to start charging tolls after we have got this.

Q: Would you charge the Government rent for the land that it uses?

A: All these things would have to be worked out by the administrative elements of the black-power movement.

Q: In Washington and a few other communities where Negroes are a majority they could, of course, take political power. Is that what you have in mind as black power?

A: No. As I said, power by any means available. Political power would be one thing. We also want some economic power. We want some social power.

Q: Can you take economic power by the vote?

A: No, not much.

Q: Then how would you get economic power?

A: We must insist that we have not abandoned such things as voting and legal remedies and things of that kind. On the other hand, we must insist on keeping our means to ourselves.

Q: As a minority, don't you worry about hurting your chances by antagonizing the majority?

A: We don't worry about that. We worried too long about what white folks think about us—about the white backlash. What we need to do is lash the white backlash with the blacklash. So we're going to stop caring about what white

people think. We've tried to change white hearts and souls.
We failed. It is desirable, of course, to have mass sympathy on our side. But we can't depend on that too much,
especially since we are fighting tradition, and traditions are
very hard to eradicate by appealing to people by reason. So
there has to be some alteration of methods. You know, there's
always this hang-up on numbers—the idea that you need the
whole world with you to do anything. I understand that only
30,000 persons were actively involved in the Russian Revolution. I don't know how many persons Castro had in the
hills with him in Cuba, but not a great many.

Some persons have all kinds of theories—such as, say, get
a few pounds of this drug, LSD, and drop it in the water
supply of each major city and disorient the city.

You don't need the whole world on your side any more,
and people are coming to see that.

Q: You say you have found it hard to appeal to reason. What
are you appealing to now? Fear?

A: No, no. We don't intend to scare anybody. But we want
to indicate that we're not scared any more.

Q: This black-power philosophy that you have described—is
it growing or spreading fast?

A: Yes.

Q: Where is it growing fastest?

A: On black college campuses.

Q: Is this the result of Stokely Carmichael's activities—his
speaking and organizing tour from campus to campus?

A: Recently he has been doing that. I think that it's a good
thing, because the people in the slums don't really understand
things, or they can't articulate.

Q: Is it your idea that campus leaders will become the leaders
of the people in the slums?

A: Yes. All of them will not be picketing or marching in the
streets. But once black universities have become part of the
new trend, then everybody that comes through those universities will be touched.

Q: If black universities become known as centers of black
power, how long do you think black universities will last?

A: I don't know. But the way they exist now, we want to
give them to the white folks, anyway. If they are going to
continue as they have, as brainwashing factories, putting out
freak persons with black faces and white minds, then maybe
they should be closed.

Q: Is Stokely Carmichael really the formulator of black-
power philosophy?

A: There was an "organization for black power" formed in

1963 by Jesse Gray in New York. And Adam Clayton Powell, when he spoke at Howard University about a year ago, proposed what he called "audacious power." Then Stokely Carmichael made the phrase "black power" famous during the Meredith march in Georgia last summer.

Q: So Mr. Carmichael did not originate black power—

A: He is the most famous advocate of it.

Q: Do you see Stokely Carmichael as the Negro leader of the future?

A: Yes, for the near future, at least. You see, revolutionary change occurs in stages, and types of leaders accord with the various stages. So leaders change. And the Rev. Dr. Martin Luther King—some of the leaders are reluctant to retire, like fighters who hang on too long. When leaders have fulfilled their function, it's time for them to retire.

"Contempt for Uncle Toms"

Q. Do you think the Negro movement is coming into an era of leadership by college professors, such as yourself?

A: They increasingly are going to have to do that. Otherwise they will not be able to teach black students very well, because the students at most black colleges have great contempt for their professors—regard them as Uncle Toms, or, rather, as "Dr. Thomases."

Professors won't be able to communicate with black students if they don't start taking an active role in black power. And many of them are beginning to do that.

DICK GREGORY,

Comedian, Civil Rights Activist

Richard Claxton Gregory was born a welfare case in St. Louis in 1932. He attended Southern Illinois University intermittently from 1951 to 1956 where he was an outstanding athlete. While in the armed forces, his talent as a comedian first became recognized. In recent years, however, he has devoted less time to his career as a television and night club entertainer to allow full-time involvement in civil rights efforts. In 1967 he ran against Mayor Daley of Chicago and in 1968 as a write-in candidate for President on the Peace and Freedom Party ticket. Both of these efforts failed by large margins, but they pointed out to his people his sincere desire to help them achieve more political independence.

As one of America's best known entertainers, Gregory has used his singular talent for racial humor to educate the American public to the culture and thoughts of the black man. In addition to his political aspirations and the use he makes of his wit and wry humor, Gregory has earned a place among the annals of black leadership through his participation in numerous protest marches, demonstrations, and rallies. During many crucial moments such as the Watts riot of 1966, the Chicago disturbances in 1968, and the voter-registration drive in Selma, he has helped alleviate the tensions of racial hatred and misunderstanding.

"A DIVINE LIBEL SUIT WOULD SURELY 'HATE AND DESPISE' A RELIGIOUS ESTABLISHMENT WHICH CAN CONTINUE TO BUILD AND DECORATE BUILDINGS WHILE HUMAN BEINGS STARVE TO DEATH DAILY."

112

One Less Door*

A scared Negro is one thing. A mad Negro is something else. I had always gone down South scared. But in September, when I went down to Selma, Alabama, Whitey had a mad Negro on his hands.

Those brave, beautiful kids from SNCC had started their big voter registration drive in Selma, and had asked me to help them. I was too sick to travel, but I didn't want to let them down. I sent Lillian in my place. She was pregnant again. We didn't know it at the time, but she was carrying twin girls. Lillian was in jail a week before I was able to get to Selma.

It was a Friday night. I talked to Lillian through a jail-house window, and she said everything was all right. Then I went to speak at a rally. I walked through a deputized posse of 200 red necks, into a church that had been tear-gassed a few days before. I got up on stage in front of a crowd of scared Negroes. They needed some courage. Courage to go out and buck the system, courage to stand up and be counted in a town where the front row of their church was filled that night with white policemen pretending to be newspaper reporters and taking notes. I directed my speech at those cops in the front row. I was mad. I told that audience how surprised I was to see a dumb Southern cop who knew how to write. The crowd was nervous. They had never heard such talk in front of a white man before.

It always amazes me to see how the Southern white folks will knock themselves out, pose as all kinds of things to slip into a Negro meeting, and we haven't gotten around to wanting to slip into a Ku Klux Klan meeting. I think that speaks for itself. The whole world wants to slip in and be around

* Reprinted from *Nigger: An Autobiography*, 1964, by Dick Gregory with Robert Lipsyte. By permission of E. P. Dutton and the author.

113

right and good and Godliness, but only fools want to be around filth.

They looked at each other and giggled nervously, but they sat up a little straighter.

A Southern white man. Only thing he has to be able to identify with is a drinking fountain, a toilet, and the right to call me nigger.

They liked that. A few people clapped, and somebody yelled: "You tell 'em, brother."

Every white man in America knows we are Americans, knows we are Negroes, and some of them know us by our names. So when he calls us a nigger, he's calling us something we are not, something that exists only in his mind. So if nigger exists only in his mind, who's the nigger?

They laughed and they clapped.

Now let's take it one step further. This is a Bible here. We know it's a book. Now if I sat here and called it a bicycle, I have called it something it is not. So where does the bicycle exist? In my mind. I'm the sick one, right?

And they were cheering now, and screaming and laughing and the white cops up front looked pale. The crowd wasn't afraid of them.

I talked for about an hour that Friday night. I told them how important it was for them to get out and support the voter registration drive on Monday. If they registered, they could vote, and if they voted the politicians would represent their interests, too.

Saturday, Lillian came out of jail, and Saturday night I went back to the church to speak again. Before I began, I asked the audience to sing, "Were You There When They Crucified the Lord?" Then I started, and I wasn't mad any more, and I laid it down to them.

It's amazing how we come to this church every Sunday and cry over the crucifixion of Christ, and we don't cry over these things that are going on around and among us. If He was here now and saw these things, He would cry. And He would take those nails again. For us. For this problem.

It just so happened that in His day and time, religion was the big problem. Today, it is color.

What do you think would happen to Christ tonight if He arrived in this town a black man and wanted to register to vote on Monday? What do you think would happen? Would you be there? You would? Then how come you're not out there with these kids, because He said that whatever happens to the least, happens to us all. . . .

Let's analyze the situation.

We're not saying, "Let's go downtown and take over City Hall."

We're not saying, "Let's stand on the rooftops and throw bricks at the white folks."

We're not saying, "Let's get some butcher knives and some guns and make them pay for what they've done."

We're talking to the white man, and this is what we're saying.

We're saying, "We want what you said belongs to us. You have a constitution. I'm a black man, and you make me sit down in a black school and take a test on the United States Constitution, a constitution that hasn't worked for anyone but you. And you expect me to learn it from front to back. So I learned it.

"You made me stand up as a little kid and sing 'God Bless America,' and 'America the Beautiful,' and all those songs the white kids were singing. I Pledge Allegiance to the Flag. That's all I'm asking you for today."

Something important happened in 1963, and the sooner we wake up and realize it, the better off this whole world is going to be. Because for some reason God has put in your hands the salvation of not just America—this thing is bigger than just this country—but the salvation of the whole world. . . .

The Negro in America has the highest standard of living, the highest educational standard, the highest medical standard of any black man the world over and of most white men outside America. And yet there are backward countries getting more respect from this American white man than you people could ever command. Do you know why?

It's because we grinned when he wanted us to grin. We cried when he wanted us to cry We've spent money when he wanted us to spend money. And we've done without when he said do without.

He owns all the missiles in the world, and when he talks to you about owning a switchblade you become ashamed.

He started all the wars, and when he talks to you about cutting somebody on Saturday night you become ashamed.

He makes me feel small. He calls me everything on the job but my name, so I'm aggravated before I get home.

Then he tells me about my education. Well, if it takes education his-style to produce a clown that would throw dynamite in a church, I hope we never get that.

I have a newspaper and I wish I brought it tonight. It embarrasses me just to look at it. It's a newspaper from 1848, a New Orleans newspaper.

On the back page are ads offering rewards for the return of runaway slaves. Can you believe in 1848 we were running away, rebelling, and we didn't have any place to run to? 1848. Slaves were running away.

Can you imagine what this old Negro had to go through? Can you imagine the day a Negro woman went to a black man and said: "Honey, I'm pregnant," and both of them fell on their knees and prayed that their baby would be born deformed? Can you imagine what this Negro went through, hoping his baby is born crippled?

Because if he was born crippled, he would have less chance of being a slave and more chance of having freedom.

Think about that. Think about the woman you love coming to you and saying she's pregnant with your baby and you both pray the baby is born crippled.

This is what the slaves went through. And a hundred years later, we have parallels.

A hundred years later and you people are worrying about your kids being in jail overnight, being in jail because they demonstrated for freedom. So many parents who don't even know where their kids are, for the first time they'll know where their kids are twenty-four hours a day. In jail. And know that they're there for a good cause and a good reason.

How many mothers let their sons play football, and all he can get from that is a chance to help his team win a victory. A victory that will be forgotten tomorrow. So can't you let your son fight for freedom, something that the whole world will profit from, forever?

Sometimes I wonder how much this system has corrupted us. Sometimes I wonder when we will wake up to see that the day is over when we can say: "I'm not involved."

Those four kids who were killed in that church in Birmingham, they weren't demonstrating.

You don't have to participate. Just be black. Or be white, and for our cause. When the bomb is thrown, somebody has to die.

And do you know that 50 per cent of the killings are our fault? That's right. We let this white man go crazy on us, instead of straightening him out when we should have.

Each one of us scratched our heads five years too long.

Sure, tomming was good once upon a time. That's how we got here. The old folks knew that was the only way they could raise you. What we call Uncle Tomism today was nothing but finesse and tact then. The old folks had to scratch their heads and grin their ways into a white man's heart. A white man who wouldn't accept them any other way.

But at what point do we stop tomming?

A Negro is better off going to a foreign country fighting for America than he is coming to the South fighting for the Negro cause. When he's in a foreign country, fighting to give those people rights he doesn't even get, the whole of America is behind him. When he comes down here, there are only a few behind him.

So it's coming down to this. You have to commit. You're going through the same thing today that the folks went through when the Lord was crucified.

"Who else is with Christ?" the Romans asked.

And everybody just stood there. And prayed silently. And they went back and said: "I prayed."

No, sister, I didn't even see your lips move.

Were you there when they crucified the Lord? It's a nice song to sing. But this time, you have an opportunity to be there.

Sure would be a heck of a thing, twenty, thirty years from now when they're singing a song about these days, and your grandkids and great-grandkids can stand up and say: "Yeah, baby, he was there, my grandfather was there."

And when they ask you, you can nod your head and say: "Yeah, I was there."

I'd like to tell you a story before I leave. I talked to the father of one of the kids who died in that church in Birmingham. He said to me: "You know, Gregory, my daughter begged me to let her demonstrate, and I told her no. I told her she was too young. And she looked at me, and she said: 'Then you do it, Daddy.' ". . .

And that's what that man will have to live with for the rest of his life. Because if Birmingham had had enough Negroes behind them, there wouldn't have been a bombing. . . .

These kids here in Selma aren't doing anything just for themselves. There's nothing selfish about what they're doing here. Freedom will run all over this town. But you have to get behind them. Because there are too many white folks in front of them.

Get behind your kids in this town.

Good-by and God Bless You and Good Night.

They burst into my hotel room, a dozen of them, laughing and screaming and singing, and for a moment all I saw were the flickering flames the first one was carrying in his hands. I jumped up and my stomach turned over and then I was angry because they had scared me, and then I cried. It was a cake with candles. It was my first birthday party. I was thirty-one.

Jim Sanders was there, and his new wife, Jackie, and my managers and agents and writers and some of the other performers from the night club. We drank and we talked and they didn't believe this was my first real party. And I told them about Richard, the kid I once knew in St. Louis who used to buy himself a Twinkie Cupcake and steal a little pink candle and pretend he was having a party.

Oh, Momma, I wish you could see your little Richard now. He's all right. I didn't lie to you, Momma, about people buying me birthday presents, about people inviting me over their houses. It's true now, so it's no lie any more. And you know, Momma, that old lady who saw a star in the middle of my forehead, she was right. We thought I was going to be a great athlete, and we were wrong, and I thought I was going to be a great entertainer, and that wasn't it, either. I'm going to be an American citizen. First-class.

Hot damn, we're going to bust this thing. I feel it when I stand in front of a crowd of people hungry for freedom, and I feel it when we march down a street for our rights. Hot water seeping up into a cold body, that dry taste in my mouth. The monster. But it's not content to beat some mother's son in a foot race, any more, and it's not satisfied to make people laugh and love me. Now it wants some respect and dignity, and it wants freedom. It's willing to die for freedom.

It's getting stronger every day. It would frighten you, Momma. But now it has truth and justice and the Constitution of the greatest country in the world on its side.

It's not just a Negro monster. I saw it in a Northern white boy who marched with us for freedom through the snow in Georgia. He had no soles on his shoes, and his feet were blue and he never said a word. I asked him why he didn't go home and take that big engineering job he had been offered. He said that there would nothing to build on unless every American citizen got his rights first.

When I saw him, Momma, I laughed at every Northern liberal who ever said: "Slow down, you people, don't alienate your friends." Yeah, baby, were you there when they crucified the Lord? Or were you just singing?

Yeah, that monster's growing stronger, Momma. I saw it in New York where we marched against school segregation, Northern-style, marched to give little black kids a chance for a better education and college and good jobs. And a chance for little white kids to sit with us and know us and learn to love and hate us as individuals, not just fear and hate us as a color like their parents do.

I saw it in Chester, Pennsylvania, with Stanley Branche, where we marched for equal opportunities, a chance to be ordinary if we wanted, to be great if we could. Just a chance to be Americans.

I saw it in Atlanta where we marched against segregation in restaurants. I was in my first sit-in there, and I did my first official negotiating. I learned that when honesty sits around a conference table, black men and white men can understand and feel each other's problems, and help each other.

I saw the monster in Mississippi where we marched for voter registration, so a Negro can cast his ballot for the government he lives under and supports with his tax money, and dies for in wars.

I saw it in San Francisco where white doctors and lawyers marched on the lines with us and went to jail with us and showed the world that this isn't a revolution of black against white, this is a revolution of right against wrong. And right has never lost.

This is a revolution. It started long before I came into it, and I may die before it's over, but we'll bust this thing and cut out this cancer. America will be as strong and beautiful as it should be, for black folks and white folks. We'll all be free then, free from a system that makes a man less than a man, that teaches hate and fear and ignorance.

You didn't die a slave for nothing, Momma. You brought us up. You and all those Negro mothers who gave their kids the strength to go on, to take that thimble to the well while the whites were taking buckets. Those of us who weren't destroyed got stronger, got calluses on our souls. And now we're ready to change a system, a system where a white man can destroy a black man with a single word. Nigger.

When we're through, Momma, there won't be any niggers any more.

MALCOLM X,

Orator, Organizer

A proud black spokesman before his assassination on February 21, 1965, Malcolm X was born in Omaha, Nebraska, on May 19, 1925, as Malcolm Little. He lost both parents tragically during his childhood and at the age of fifteen he left school, went to New York, took several menial jobs, sold marijuana, and turned to burglary after becoming addicted to drugs. After being sent to prison at the age of twenty-one for burglary, Malcolm became acquainted with the Black Muslim sect and later became its most outspoken advocate. He was an assistant minister of an Islamic temple in Detroit and, as he rose to prominence in the hierarchy, became second only to Elijah Muhammad.

In 1964, however, he withdrew from the Black Muslims because of increasing conflict with its leader and formed his own group, the Organization of Afro-American Unity, and organized an Islamic religious center, the Muslim Mosque, Inc. He took the name, Al Hajj Malik Al-Shabazz in 1964 after a holy pilgrimage to Mecca and two trips to Africa. His death at the age of thirty-nine cut short the life of a man whose uncompromising self-assertiveness and unwillingness to retreat in the face of hostility have become important symbols in the struggle of black Americans for equality and racial dignity.

"THE ONLY PERSON WHO CAN ORGANIZE THE MAN IN THE STREET IS THE ONE WHO IS UNACCEPTABLE TO THE WHITE COMMUNITY."

Message to the Grass Roots*

We want to have just an off-the-cuff chat between you and me, us. We want to talk right down to earth in a language that everybody here can easily understand. We all agree tonight, all of the speakers have agreed, that America has a very serious problem. Not only does America have a very serious problem, but our people have a very serious problem. America's problem is us. We're her problem. The only reason she has a problem is she doesn't want us here. And every time you look at yourself, be you black, brown, red or yellow, a so-called Negro, you represent a person who poses such a serious problem for America because you're not wanted. Once you face this as a fact, then you can start plotting a course that will make you appear intelligent, instead of unintelligent.

What you and I need to do is learn to forget our differences. When we come together, we don't come together as Baptists or Methodists. You don't catch hell because you're Baptist, and you don't catch hell because you're a Methodist. You don't catch hell because you're a Methodist or Baptist, you don't catch hell because you're a Democrat or a Republican, you don't catch hell because you're a Mason or an Elk, and you sure don't catch hell because you're an American; because if you were an American, you wouldn't catch hell. You catch hell because you're a black man. You catch hell, all of us catch hell, for the same reason.

So we're all black people, so-called Negroes, second-class citizens, ex-slaves. You're nothing but an ex-slave. You don't like to be told that. But what else are you? You are ex-slaves. You didn't come here on the "Mayflower." You came here on a slave ship. In chains, like a horse, or a cow, or a chicken. And you were brought here by the people who came here on

* Reprinted from *Malcolm X Speaks,* 1965. By permission of Merit Publishers and Mrs. Betty Shabazz.

the "Mayflower," you were brought here by the so-called Pilgrims, or Founding Fathers. They were the ones who brought you here.

We have a common enemy. We have this in common: We have a common oppressor, a common exploiter, and a common discriminator. But once we all realize that we have a common enemy, then we unite—on the basis of what we have in common. And what we have foremost in common is that enemy—the white man. He's an enemy to all of us. I know some of you all think that some of them aren't enemies. Time will tell.

In Bandung back in, I think, 1954, was the first unity meeting in centuries of black people. And once you study what happened at the Bandung conference, and the results of the Bandung conference, it actually serves as a model for the same procedure you and I can use to get our problems solved. At Bandung all the nations came together, the dark nations from Africa and Asia. Some of them were Buddhists, some of them were Muslims, some of them were Christians, some were Confucianists, some were atheists. Despite their religious differences, they came together. Some were communists, some were socialists, some were capitalists—despite their economic and political differences, they came together. All of them were black, brown, red or yellow.

The number-one thing that was not allowed to attend the Bandung conference was the white man. He couldn't come. Once they excluded the white man, they found that they could get together. Once they kept him out, everybody else fell right in and fell in line. This is the thing that you and I have to understand. And these people who came together didn't have nuclear weapons, they didn't have jet planes, they didn't have all of the heavy armaments that the white man has. But they had unity.

They were able to submerge their little petty differences and agree on one thing: That there one African came from Kenya and was being colonized by the Englishman, and another African came from the Congo and was being colonized by the Belgian, and another African came from Guinea and was being colonized by the French, and another came from Angola and was being colonized by the Portuguese. When they came to the Bandung conference, they looked at the Portuguese, and the Frenchman, and the Englishman, and at the Dutchman, and learned or realized the one thing that all of them had in common—they were all from Europe, they were all Europeans, blond, blue-eyed and white skins. They began to recognize who their enemy was. The same man that was colonizing our people in Kenya was colonizing our people in the Congo. The same one in the Congo was colonizing our people in South Africa, and in Southern Rhodesia, and in Burma, and in India, and in Afghanistan, and in Pakistan. They realized all over the world where the dark man was being oppressed, he was being oppressed by the white man; where the dark man was being exploited, he was being exploited by the white man. So they got together on this basis— that they had a common enemy.

And when you and I here in Detroit and in Michigan and in America who have been awakened today look around us, we too realize here in America we all have a common enemy, whether he's in Georgia or Michigan, whether he's in California or New York. He's the same man—blue eyes and blond hair and pale skin—the same man. So what we have to do is what they did. They agreed to stop quarreling among themselves. Any little spat that they had, they'd settle it among themselves, go into a huddle—don't let the enemy know that you've got a disagreement.

Instead of airing our differences in public, we have to realize we're all the same family. And when you have a family squabble, you don't get out on the sidewalk. If you do, everybody calls you uncouth, unrefined, uncivilized, savage. If you don't make it at home, you settle it at home, you get in the closet, argue it out behind closed doors, and then when you come out on the street, you pose a common front, a united front. And this is what we need to do in the community, and in the city, and in the state. We need to stop airing our differences in front of the white man, put the white man out of our meetings, and then sit down and talk shop with each other. That's what we've got to do.

I would like to make a few comments concerning the difference between the black revolution and the Negro revolution. Are they both the same? And if they're not, what is the difference? What is the difference between a black revolution and a Negro revolution? First, what is a revolution? Sometimes I'm inclined to believe that many of our people are using this word "revolution" loosely, without taking careful consideration of what this word actually means, and what its historic characteristics are. When you study the historic nature of revolutions, the motive of a revolution, the objective of a revolution, the result of a revolution, and the methods used in a revolution, you may change words. You may devise another program, and you may change your goal and you may change your mind.

Look at the American Revolution in 1776. That revolution

was for what? For land. Why did they want land? Independence. How was it carried out? Bloodshed. Number one, it was based on land, the basis of independence. And the only way they could get it was bloodshed. The French Revolution—what was it based on? The landless against the landlord. What was it for? Land. How did they get it? Bloodshed. Was no love lost, was no compromise, was no negotiation. I'm telling you—you don't know what a revolution is. Because when you find out what it is, you'll get back in the alley, you'll get out of the way.

The Russian Revolution—what was it based on? Land; the landless against the landlord. How did they bring it about? Bloodshed. You haven't got a revolution that doesn't involve bloodshed. And you're afraid to bleed. I said, you're afraid to bleed.

As long as the white man sent you to Korea, you bled. He sent you to Germany, you bled. He sent you to the South Pacific to fight the Japanese, you bled. You bleed for white people, but when it comes to seeing your own churches being bombed and little black girls murdered, you haven't got any blood. You bleed when the white man says bleed; you bite when the white man says bite; and you bark when the white man says bark. I hate to say this about us, but it's true. How are you going to be nonviolent in Mississippi, as violent as you were in Korea? How can you justify being nonviolent in Mississippi and Alabama, when your churches are being bombed, and your little girls are being murdered, and at the same time you are going to get violent with Hitler, and Tojo, and somebody else you don't even know?

If violence is wrong in America, violence is wrong abroad. If it is wrong to be violent defending black women and black children and black babies and black men, then it is wrong for America to draft us and make us violent abroad in defense of her. And if it is right for America to draft us, and teach us how to be violent in defense of her, then it is right for you and me to do whatever is necessary to defend our own people right here in this country.

The Chinese Revolution—they wanted land. They threw the British out, along with the Uncle Tom Chinese. Yes, they did. They set a good example. When I was in prison, I read an article—don't be shocked when I say that I was in prison. You're still in prison. That's what America means: prison. When I was in prison, I read an article in *Life* magazine showing a little Chinese girl, nine years old; her father was on his hands and knees and she was pulling the trigger because he was an Uncle Tom Chinaman. When they had the revolution over there, they took a whole generation of Uncle Toms and just wiped them out. And within ten years that little girl became a full-grown woman. No more Toms in China. And today it's one of the toughest, roughest, most feared countries on this earth—by the white man. Because there are no Uncle Toms over there.

Of all our studies, history is best qualified to reward our research. And when you see that you've got problems, all you have to do is examine the historic method used all over the world by others who have problems similar to yours. Once you see how they got theirs straight, then you know how you can get yours straight. There's been a revolution, a black revolution, going on in Africa. In Kenya, the Mau Mau were revolutionary; they were the ones who brought the word "Uhuru" to the fore. The Mau Mau, they were revolutionary, they believed in scorched earth, they knocked everything aside that got in their way, and their revolution also was based on land, a desire for land. In Algeria, the northern part of Africa, a revolution took place. The Algerians were revolutionists, they wanted land. France offered to let them be integrated into France. They told France, to hell with France, they wanted some land, not some France. And they engaged in a bloody battle.

So I cite these various revolutions, brothers and sisters, to show you that you don't have a peaceful revolution. You don't have a turn-the-other-cheek revolution. There's no such thing as a nonviolent revolution. The only kind of revolution that is nonviolent is the Negro revolution. The only revolution in which the goal is loving your enemy is the Negro revolution. It's the only revolution in which the goal is a desegregated lunch counter, a desegregated theater, a desegregated park, and a desegregated public toilet; you can sit down next to white folks—on the toilet. That's no revolution. Revolution is based on land. Land is the basis of all independence. Land is the basis of freedom, justice, and equality.

The white man knows what a revolution is. He knows that the black revolution is world-wide in scope and in nature. The black revolution is sweeping Asia, is sweeping Africa, is rearing its head in Latin America. The Cuban Revolution—that's a revolution. They overturned the system. Revolution is in Asia, revolution is in Africa, and the white man is screaming because he sees revolution in Latin America. How do you think he'll react to you when you learn what a real revolution is? You don't know what a revolution is. If you did, you wouldn't use that word.

Revolution is bloody, revolution is hostile, revolution knows no compromise, revolution overturns and destroys everything that gets in its way. And you, sitting around here like a knot on the wall, saying, "I'm going to love these folks no matter how much they hate me." No, you need a revolution. Whoever heard of a revolution where they lock arms, as Rev. Cleage was pointing out beautifully, singing "We Shall Overcome"? You don't do that in a revolution. You don't do any singing, you're too busy swinging. It's based on land. A revolutionary wants land so he can set up his own nation, an independent nation. These Negroes aren't asking for any nation—they're trying to crawl back on the plantation.

When you want a nation, that's called nationalism. When the white man became involved in a revolution in this country against England, what was it for? He wanted this land so he could set up another white nation. That's white nationalism. The American Revolution was white nationalism. The French Revolution was white nationalism. The Russian Revolution too—yes, it was—white nationalism. You don't think so? Why do you think Khrushchev and Mao can't get their heads together? White nationalism. All the revolutions that are going on in Asia and Africa today are based on what?—black nationalism. A revolutionary is a black nationalist. He wants a nation. I was reading some beautiful words by Rev. Cleage, pointing out why he couldn't get together with someone else in the city because all of them were afraid of being identified with black nationalism. If you're afraid of black nationalism, you're afraid of revolution. And if you love revolution, you love black nationalism.

To understand this, you have to go back to what the young brother here referred to as the house Negro and the field Negro back during slavery. There were two kinds of slaves, the house Negro and the field Negro. The house Negroes—they lived in the house with master, they dressed pretty good, they ate good because they ate his food—what he left. They lived in the attic or the basement, but still they lived near the master; and they loved the master more than the master loved himself. They would give their life to save the master's house—quicker than the master would. If the master said, "We got a good house here," the house Negro would say, "Yeah, we got a good house here." Whenever the master said "we," he said "we." That's how you can tell a house Negro.

If the master's house caught on fire, the house Negro would fight harder to put the blaze out than the master would. If the master got sick, the house Negro would say, "What's the matter, boss, we sick?" We sick! He identified himself with his master, more than his master identified with himself. And if you come to the house Negro and said, "Let's run away, let's escape, let's separate," the house Negro would look at you and say, "Man, you crazy. What you mean, separate? Where is there a better house than this? Where can I wear better clothes than this? Where can I eat better food than this?" That was that house Negro. In those days he was called a "house nigger." And that's what we call them today, because we've still got some house niggers running around here.

This modern house Negro loves his master. He wants to live near him. He'll pay three times as much as the house is worth just to live near his master, and then brag about "I'm the only Negro out here." "I'm the only one on my job." "I'm the only one in this school." You're nothing but a house Negro. And if someone comes to you right now and says, "Let's separate," you say the same thing that the house Negro said on the plantation. "What you mean, separate? From America, this good white man? Where you going to get a better job than you get here?" I mean, this is what you say. "I ain't left nothing in Africa," that's what you say. Why, you left your mind in Africa.

On that same plantation, there was the field Negro. The field Negroes—those were the masses. There were always more Negroes in the field than there were Negroes in the house. The Negro in the field caught hell. He ate leftovers. In the house they ate high up on the hog. The Negro in the field didn't get anything but what was left of the insides of the hog. They call it "chitt'lings" nowadays. In those days they called them what they were—guts. That's what you were—gut-eaters. And some of you are still gut-eaters.

The field Negro was beaten from morning to night; he lived in a shack, in a hut; he wore old, castoff clothes. He hated his master. I say he hated his master. He was intelligent. That house Negro loved his master, but that field Negro—remember, they were in the majority, and they hated the master. When the house caught on fire, he didn't try to put it out; that field Negro prayed for a wind, for a breeze. When the master got sick, the field Negro prayed that he'd die. If someone came to the field Negro and said, "Let's separate, let's run," he didn't say "Where we going?" He'd say, "Any place is better than here." You've got field Negroes in America today, I'm a field Negro. The masses are the field Negroes. When they see this man's house on fire, you don't hear the little Negroes talking about "our government is in trouble." They say, "The government is in trouble." Imagine a Negro: "Our government"! I even heard one say "our astronauts." They won't even let him near the plant—and "our astronauts"! "*Our* Navy"—that's a Negro that is out of his mind, a Negro that is out of his mind.

Just as the slavemaster of that day used Tom, the house Negro, to keep the field Negroes in check, the same old slavemaster today has Negroes who are nothing but modern Uncle Toms, twentieth-century Uncle Toms, to keep you and me in check, to keep us under control, keep us passive and peaceful and nonviolent. That's Tom making you nonviolent. It's like when you go to the dentist, and the man's going to take your tooth. You're going to fight him when he starts pulling. So he squirts some stuff in your jaw called novocaine, to make you think they're not doing anything to you. So you sit there and because you've got all of that novocaine in your jaw, you suffer—peacefully. Blood running all down your jaw, and you don't know what's happening. Because someone has taught you to suffer—peacefully.

The white man does the same thing to you in the street, when he wants to put knots on your head and take advantage of you and not have to be afraid of your fighting back. To keep you from fighting back, he gets these old religious Uncle Toms to teach you and me, just like novocaine, to suffer peacefully. Don't stop suffering—just suffer peacefully. As Rev. Cleage pointed out, they say you should let your blood flow in the streets. This is a shame. You know he's a Christian preacher. If it's a shame to him, you know what it is to me.

There is nothing in our book, the Koran, that teaches us to suffer peacefully. Our religion teaches us to be intelligent. Be peaceful, be courteous, obey the law, respect everyone; but if someone puts his hand on you, send him to the cemetery. That's a good religion. In fact, that's that old-time religion. That's the one that Ma and Pa used to talk about: an eye for an eye, and a tooth for a tooth, and a head for a head, and a life for a life. That's a good religion. And nobody resents that kind of religion being taught but a wolf, who intends to make you his meal.

This is the way it is with the white man in America. He's a wolf—and you're sheep. Any time a shepherd, a pastor, teaches you and me not to run from the white man and, at the same time, teaches us not to fight the white man, he's a traitor to you and me. Don't lay down a life all by itself. No, preserve your life, it's the best thing you've got. And if you've got to give it up, let it be even-steven.

The slavemaster took Tom and dressed him well, fed him well and even gave him a little education—a *little* education; gave him a long coat and a top hat and made all the other slaves look up to him. Then he used Tom to control them.

The same strategy that was used in those days is used today, by the same white man. He takes a Negro, a so-called Negro, and makes him prominent, builds him up, publicizes him, makes him a celebrity. And then he becomes a spokesman for Negroes—and a Negro leader.

I would like to mention just one other thing quickly, and that is the method that the white man uses, how the white man uses the "big guns," or Negro leaders, against the Negro revolution. They are not a part of the Negro revolution. They are used against the Negro revolution.

When Martin Luther King failed to desegregate Albany, Georgia, the civil-rights struggle in America reached its low point. King became bankrupt almost, as a leader. The Southern Christian Leadership Conference was in financial trouble; and it was in trouble, period, with the people when they failed to desegregate Albany, Georgia. Other Negro civil-rights leaders of so-called national stature became fallen idols. As they became fallen idols, began to lose their prestige and influence, local Negro leaders began to stir up the masses. In Cambridge, Maryland, Gloria Richardson; in Danville, Virginia, and other parts of the country, local leaders began to stir up our people at the grass-roots level. This was never done by these Negroes of national stature. They control you, but they have never incited you or excited you. They control you, they contain you, they have kept you on the plantation.

As soon as King failed in Birmingham, Negroes took to the streets. King went out to California to a big rally and raised I don't know how many thousands of dollars. He came to Detroit and had a march and raised some more thousands of dollars. And recall, right after that Roy Wilkins attacked King. He accused King and CORE (Congress of Racial Equality) of starting trouble everywhere and then making the NAACP (National Association for the Advancement of Colored People) get them out of jail and spend a lot of money; they accused King and CORE of raising all the money and not paying it back. This happened; I've got it in documented evidence in the newspaper. Roy started attacking King, and King started attacking Roy, and Farmer started attacking both of them. And as these Negroes of national stature began to attack each other, they began to lose their control of the Negro masses.

The Negroes were out there in the streets. They were talking about how they were going to march on Washington. Right at that time Birmingham had exploded, and the Negroes in Birmingham—remember, they also exploded. They began to stab the crackers in the back and bust them up 'side their head—yes, they did. That's when Kennedy sent in the troops, down in Birmingham. After that, Kennedy got on the television and said "this is a moral issue." That's when he said he was going to put out a civil-rights bill and the Southern crackers started talking about how they were going to boycott or filibuster it, then the Negroes started talking—about what? That they were going to march on Washington, march on the Senate, march on the White House, march on the Congress, and tie it up, bring it to a halt, not let the government proceed. They even said they were going out to the airport and lay down on the runway and not let any airplanes land. I'm telling you what they said. That was revolution. That was revolution. That was the black revolution.

It was the grass roots out there in the street. It scared the white man to death, scared the white power structure in Washington, D.C., to death; I was there. When they found out that this black steamroller was going to come down on the capital, they called in Wilkins, they called in Randolph, they called in these national Negro leaders that you respect and told them, "Call it off." Kennedy said, "Look, you all are letting this thing go too far." And Old Tom said, "Boss, I can't stop it, because I didn't start it." I'm telling you what they said. They said, "I'm not even in it, much less at the head of it." They said, "These Negroes are doing things on their own. They're running ahead of us." And that old shrewd fox, he said, "If you all aren't in it, I'll put you in it. I'll put you at the head of it. I'll endorse it. I'll welcome it. I'll help it. I'll join it."

A matter of hours went by. They had a meeting at the Carlyle Hotel in New York City. The Carlyle Hotel is owned by the Kennedy family; that's the hotel Kennedy spent the night at, two nights ago; it belongs to his family. A philanthropic society headed by a white man named Stephen Currier called all the top civil-rights leaders together at the Carlyle Hotel. And he told them, "By you all fighting each other, you are destroying the civil-rights movement. And since you're fighting over money from white liberals, let us set up what is known as the Council for United Civil Rights Leadership. Let's form this council, and all the civil-rights organizations will belong to it, and we'll use it for fund-raising purposes." Let me show you how tricky the white man is. As soon as they got it formed, they elected Whitney Young as its chairman, and who do you think became the co-chairman? Stephen Currier, the white man, a millionaire. Powell was talking about it down at Cobo Hall today. This is what he was talking about. Powell knows it happened. Randolph knows it happened.

Wilkins knows it happened. King knows it happened. Every one of that Big Six—they know it happened.

Once they formed it, with the white man over it, he promised them and gave them $800,000 to split up among the Big Six; and told them that after the march was over they'd give them $700,000 more. A million and a half dollars—split up between leaders that you have been following, going to jail for, crying crocodile tears for. And they're nothing but Frank James and Jesse James and the what-do-you-call-'em brothers.

As soon as they got the set-up organized, the white man made available to them top public-relations experts; opened the news media across the country at their disposal, which then began to project these Big Six as the leaders of the march. Originally they weren't even in the march. You were talking this march talk on Hastings Street, you were talking march talk on Lenox Avenue, and on Fillmore Street, and on Central Avenue, and 32nd Street and 63rd Street. That's where the march talk was being talked. But the white man put the Big Six at the head of it; made them the march. They became the march. They took it over. And the first move they made after they took it over, they invited Walter Reuther, a white man; they invited a priest, a rabbi, and an old white preacher, yes, an old white preacher. The same white element that put Kennedy into power—labor, the Catholics, the Jews, and liberal Protestants; the same clique that put Kennedy in power, joined the march on Washington.

It's just like when you've got some coffee that's too black, which means it's too strong. What do you do? You integrate it with cream, you make it weak. But if you pour too much cream in it, you won't even know you ever had coffee. It used to be hot, it becomes cool. It used to be strong, it becomes weak. It used to wake you up, now it puts you to sleep. This is what they did with the march on Washington. They joined it. They didn't integrate it, they infiltrated it. They joined it, became a part of it, took it over. And as they took it over, it lost its militancy. It ceased to be angry, it ceased to be hot, it ceased to be uncompromising. Why, it even ceased to be a march. It became a picnic, a circus. Nothing but a circus, with clowns and all. You had one right here in Detroit—I saw it on television—with clowns leading it, white clowns and black clowns. I know you don't like what I'm saying, but I'm going to tell you anyway. Because I can prove what I'm saying. If you think I'm telling you wrong, you bring me Martin Luther King and A. Philip Randolph and James Farmer and those other three, and see if they'll deny it over a microphone.

No, it was a sellout. It was a takeover. When James Baldwin

came in from Paris, they wouldn't let him talk, because they couldn't make him go by the script. Burt Lancaster read the speech that Baldwin was supposed to make; they wouldn't let Baldwin get up there, because they know Baldwin is liable to say anything. They controlled it so tight, they told those Negroes what time to hit town, how to come, where to stop, what signs to carry, what song to sing, what speech they could make, and what speech they couldn't make; and then told them to get out of town by sundown. And every one of those Toms was out of town by sundown. Now I know you don't like my saying this. But I can back it up. It was a circus, a performance that beat anything Hollywood could ever do, the performance of the year. Reuther and those other three devils should get an Academy Award for the best actors because they acted like they really loved Negroes and fooled a whole lot of Negroes. And the six Negro leaders should get an award too, for the best supporting cast.

Last Answers and Interviews*

On Racism

Malcolm was asked the difference between white racism and black racism.

MALCOLM: Usually the black racist has been produced by the white racist. In most cases where you see it, it is the reaction to white racism, and if you analyze it closely, it's not really black racism. I think black people have shown less racist tendencies than any people since the beginning of history. . . .

If we react to white racism with a violent reaction, to me that's not black racism. If you come to put a rope around my neck and I hang you for it, to me that's not racism. Yours is racism, but my reaction has nothing to do with racism. My reaction is the reaction of a human being, reacting to defend himself and protect himself. This is what our people haven't done, and some of them, at least at the high academic level, don't want to. But most of us aren't at that level.

Answer to question, Harvard Law School Forum, December 16, 1964

QUESTION: What do you think is responsible for race prejudice in the U.S.?

MALCOLM: Ignorance and greed. And a skilfully designed program of miseducation that goes right along with the American system of exploitation and oppression.

If the entire American population were properly educated— by properly educated, I mean given a true picture of the history and contributions of the black man—I think many whites would be less racist in their feelings. They would have more

* Reprinted from *Malcolm X Speaks*, 1965. By permission of Merit Publishers and Mrs. Betty Shabazz.

respect for the black man as a human being. Knowing what the black man's contributions to science and civilization have been in the past, the white man's feelings of superiority would be at least partially negated. Also, the feeling of inferiority that the black man has would be replaced by a balanced knowledge of himself. He'd feel more like a human being. He'd function more like a human being, in a society of human beings.

So it takes education to eliminate it. And just because you have colleges and universities, doesn't mean you have education. The colleges and universities in the American educational system are skilfully used to miseducate.

> *From interview on January 18, 1965, printed in* Young Socialist, *March-April, 1965*

Intermarriage and a Black State

PIERRE BERTON: Now before you left Elijah Muhammad and went to Mecca and saw the original world of Islam, you believed in complete segregation of the whites and the Negroes. You were opposed both to integration and to intermarriage. Have you changed your views there?

MALCOLM: I believe in recognizing every human being as a human being—neither white, black, brown or red; and when you are dealing with humanity as a family there's no question of integration or intermarriage. It's just one human being marrying another human being, or one human being living around and with another human being.

I may say, though, that I don't think it should ever be put upon a black man, I don't think the burden to defend any position should ever be put upon the black man, because it is the white man collectively who has shown that he is hostile toward integration and toward intermarriage and toward these other strides toward oneness.

So as a black man and especially as a black American, any stand that I formerly took, I don't think that I would have to defend it, because it's still a reaction to the society, and it's a reaction that was produced by the society; and I think that it is the society that produced this that should be attacked, not the reaction that develops among the people who are the victims of that negative society.

BERTON: But you no longer believe in a black state?

MALCOLM: No.

BERTON: In North America?

MALCOLM: No, I believe in a society in which people can live like human beings on the basis of equality.

> *From the Pierre Berton Show, taped at Station CFTO-TV in Toronto, January 19, 1965*

How to Organize the People

MALCOLM: The only person who can organize the man in the street is the one who is unacceptable to the white community. They don't trust the other kind. They don't know who controls his actions. . . .

(Marlene Nadle asked if he planned to use hate to organize the people.)

MALCOLM: I won't permit you to call it hate. Let's say I'm going to create an awareness of what has been done to them. This awareness will produce an abundance of energy, both negative and positive, that can then be channeled constructively. . . .

The greatest mistake of the movement has been trying to organize a sleeping people around specific goals. You have to wake the people up first, then you'll get action.

MISS NADLE: Wake them up to their exploitation?

MALCOLM: No, to their humanity, to their own worth, and to their heritage. The biggest difference between the parallel oppression of the Jew and the Negro is that the Jew never lost his pride in being a Jew. He never ceased to be a man. He knew he had made a significant contribution to the world, and his sense of his own value gave him the courage to fight back. It enabled him to act and think independently, unlike our people and our leaders.

> *From Marlene Nadle's article,* Village Voice, *February 25, 1965*

Dollarism and Capitalism

MALCOLM: It is true that most of your South American countries are satellites of the United States. But they don't have to feel bad. This country made a satellite out of Khrushchev, made him lose his job. Everybody becomes a satellite nowadays.

They did—go and study the relations between the United States and Russia during the past four or five years and you'll find this country maneuvered Russia into almost becoming a satellite. They had to get rid of Khrushchev in order to get some of their independence back.

I say that as objectively as I can. I'm not trying to jump into anybody's camp, I don't have any axes to grind. This is just my own opinion from observations that I've made traveling around the world and listening with big ears.

It's easy to become a satellite today without even being aware of it. This country can seduce God. Yes, it has that seductive power—the power of dollarism. You can cuss out colonialism, imperialism and all other kinds of isms, but it's hard for you to cuss that dollarism. When they drop those dollars on you, your soul goes.

Answer to question, Militant Labor
Forum, January 7, 1965

QUESTION: What is your opinion of the world-wide struggle now going on between capitalism and socialism?

MALCOLM: It is impossible for capitalism to survive, primarily because the system of capitalism needs some blood to suck. Capitalism used to be like an eagle, but now it's more like a vulture. It used to be strong enough to go and suck anybody's blood whether they were strong or not. But now it has become more cowardly, like the vulture, and it can only suck the blood of the helpless. As the nations of the world free themselves, then capitalism has less victims, less to suck, and it becomes weaker and weaker. It's only a matter of time in my opinion before it will collapse completely.

From interview, Young Socialist,
March–April, 1965

On Going Back to Africa

Malcolm was asked how he thought Afro-Americans would be received by the Africans if they should go back to Africa.

MALCOLM: After lengthy discussions with many Africans at all levels, I would say some would be welcome and some wouldn't be welcome. Those that have a contribution to make would be welcome, but those that have no contribution to make would not be welcome; I don't think any of us, if we look at it objectively, could find fault with that.

And I believe this, that if we migrated back to Africa culturally, philosophically and psychologically, while remaining here physically, the spiritual bond that would develop between us and Africa through this cultural, philosophical and psychological migration, so-called migration, would enhance our position here, because we would have our contacts with them acting as roots or foundations behind us. You never will have a foundation in America. You're out of your mind if you think that *this* government is ever going to back you and me up in the same way that it backed others up. They'll never do it. It's not in them.

As an example, take the Chinese. You asked me about Red China. The Chinese used to be disrespected. They used to use that expression in this country: "You don't have a Chinaman's chance." You remember that? You don't hear it lately. Because a Chinaman's got more chance than they have now. Why? Because China is strong. Since China became strong and independent, she's respected, she's recognized. So that wherever a Chinese person goes, he is respected and recognized because he has a country behind him, a continent behind him. He has some power behind him. They don't respect him, they respect what's behind him.

By the same token, when the African continent in its independence is able to create the unity that's necessary to increase its strength and its position on this earth, so that Africa too becomes respected as other huge continents are respected, then, wherever people of African origin, African heritage or African blood go, they will be respected—but only when and because they have something much larger that looks like them behind them. With that behind you, you will get some respect. Without it behind you, you can do almost anything under the sun in this society—pass any kind of law that Washington can think of—and you and I will still be trying to get them to enforce that law. We'll be like that Chinaman [about whom] they used to say, "He doesn't have a Chinaman's chance." Now you don't have a Negro's chance. But with Africa getting its independence, you and I will have more of a chance. I believe that 100 per cent.

And this is what I mean by a migration or going back to Africa—going back in the sense that we reach out to them and they reach out to us. Our mutual understanding and our mutual effort toward a mutual objective will bring mutual benefit to the African as well as to the Afro-American. But you will never get it just relying on Uncle Sam alone. You are looking to the wrong direction. Because the wrong people are in Washington, D.C., and I mean from the White House right on down. I hope I don't step on anybody's toes by saying that. I didn't vote for him, so I can say it.

> *Answer to question, HARYOU-ACT forum for Domestic Peace Corps members, Harlem, December 12, 1964*

FLOYD B. McKISSICK,

Lawyer, Community Land Developer

The militant with gentle eyes, Floyd McKissick has not changed much since his days of marching with CORE and with Martin Luther King. For him black power is attainable through economic development. Moreover, a harmonious relationship between blacks and whites will exist only when blacks are given a piece of the action.

McKissick received his degree from North Carolina Law School. He soon began handling large numbers of civil rights cases and became a well-known constitutional lawyer. In 1966 he was appointed national director of CORE. An intense, uninhibited man, he provided effective leadership of the organization until 1965, when he established F. B. McKissick Enterprises, a firm created to promote black economic development.

In January, 1969, he began launching a major program, "Soul City," which is a new town in Warren County, North Carolina, to be built and occupied primarily by blacks with low and moderate incomes and the poor of other races. Soul City, North Carolina, is an experiment in integrated living. It is an attempt to alleviate the conditions that have led thousands of unskilled Negroes and others who have been shortchanged by industrialism to migrate to urban ghettos in the North. Soul City, McKissick hopes, will lure them back and enable blacks and whites to live and work together as equals.

"A MAN'S COLOR, IF IT IS BLACK, IS MOST FREQUENTLY USED AS A MEANS OF ENFORCING ECONOMIC LIMITATION. IT IS USED AS A VISIBLE TOOL OF OPPRESSION."

Excerpts From Three-Fifths of a Man*

The inevitable is happening. History is catching up with America. For the first time since the American system of racism, exploitation, and oppression was developed, it is seriously being threatened.

The Man has been warned. As in the case of other world civilizations, there have been si ns of impending doom. Rome, Carthage, Athens—all highly developed civilizations—ignored the warnings of history, only to fall from power and then to decay.

Vietnam and Detroit, Cuba and Watts, Cambodia and Newark, all sound the cry that warns America to change—or be destroyed.

But it does not appear that America or the capitalist system that America dominates has the ability to change. Capitalism is a system that preaches the maintenance of the status quo at all costs. It is a system dependent for its very existence upon the rigid standards of class and caste—no matter how vehemently its proponents profess equality of man.

The capitalist system by nature has demanded cheap labor upon which to feed. It has required an inferior, dependent people to create the wealth that is reinvested for the benefit of the few.

In most of the world, particularly Latin America, Africa, and Asia, cheap labor is still very much a necessity for the feudal economies still dependent upon the United States. However, within the boundaries of the United States, automation has made such a labor force all but obsolete.

In the time that automation has been taking over America, few steps have been taken for the retraining and education of

*Reprinted from *Three-Fifths of a Man*, 1969. By permission of The Macmillan Company and the author.

the displaced Black People who historically have provided cheap labor. No steps have been taken to facilitate the redistribution of the nation's wealth.

The poor have been ignored. They have been isolated from the rest of the society—without adequate nourishment, medical services, education, or housing. Lacking these tools, they have been ill equipped to compete in this complex society. They have been trapped in the bonds of their own poverty.

White America has refused to accept its responsibilities to the Black poor—the products of a brutal system of slavery, blocked every step of the way from participating in the economy, prevented even from being "homesteaders," left landless, moneyless, and uneducated after the Civil War. At no time did America offer opportunity to the Black masses; at no time did the Black population receive the chances offered every other group of immigrants—the Irish, the Italians, the Jews, the Poles.

In America caste is defined by color, class by economic status. A man's color, if it is Black, is most frequently used as a means of enforcing economic limitations. It is used as a visible tool of oppression. Morality is a nonexistent force in America. Religion has deteriorated to the point where it merely reinforces the system. Churches have become a haven for the oppressor and a shield for his crimes.

In the same short speech, the President of the United States announced that federal paratroopers had been sent to Detroit and called for a national day of prayer. That speech symbolized for many American Black People the hypocrisy and cruelty of the present system and its leaders.

Religion can be valid only when it is addressed to the needs of the people—not to the whims of the masters. No valid religion can uphold a system that subjugates and exploits more than one-half of the world's population. Yet the policies of every major religious institution, Protestant, Catholic, and Jewish, are in some way affected by what is economically expedient. This expediency has led religious institutions into many secular fields of endeavor, such as real estate speculation and the manufacture of such miscellaneous items as wines and jellies—all tax-exempt capitalist enterprises.

These commitments have served to unite further the religious community with the business community, consequently obscuring the supposed primary moral commitments of the church. (Even the Pope of the Roman Catholic Church is subject to political and secular pressures. Capitulation to such pressure was evident in the disregard of the heir apparent to Cardinal Spellman of New York in the appointing of the

Cardinal's successor. In his place the present Archbishop of New York, Terence Cooke, a comparatively conservative prelate, was appointed.)

Ironically, that which has been done, said, and taught by American religious leaders in their attempts to keep their churches solvent and viable is that which has cost the church its right to moral leadership and every vestige of clerical independence—creating a vacuum that has never been filled and providing unprincipled politicians with a chance to exploit the vacuum.

The result of this moral irresponsibility has been a racist system, reinforced by many of its religious institutions and beliefs. And the result of this system has been a white man without morality. Any man who really believes in his own superiority cannot deal morally with those he considers inferior. It is not possible for a racist white man to judge a crime committed against Blacks as he would judge one committed against whites—and since the white man controls the administration of justice, Black Men cannot possibly be treated with fairness.

In the minds of whites, distinctions exist even between genocides. World-wide horror greeted the revelations of Nazi Germany's extermination of innocent Jews. Little attention was paid to the systematic mutilation and extermination of Congolese by the Belgians. White Europeans and Americans seemed unmoved by pictures and reports of Black Congolese by the thousands having their heads cut off as punishment for not working fast enough. They were indifferent to the wanton murders of hundreds of thousands of Blacks, but they responded with indignation and alarm when white missionaries lost their lives.

The duplicity of standards is clear. White Americans are dismayed by the mass murder of whites by other whites, as indicated by their bitter reaction to the slaughter of Jews by the Nazis. They are indifferent to the mass murder of colored people by other colored people, even when such murders are financed and inspired by white foreigners. In Indonesia approximately four million nonwhite people died as a result of mass executions by a regime supported by the American CIA. White Americans tacitly condone the mass murder of nonwhite people by whites—as in the Congo, Algeria, Vietnam, India, South Africa, Rhodesia, and Kenya. Their acceptance of the murder and torture of nonwhites by whites is clearly established historically in their own land. It is in America that the Indian was exterminated and that the lives of Blacks were made cheap. But the horror and outrage of white

Americans is reserved for the few occasions when whites are killed by Blacks.

The inconsistencies and cruelties of America make it unlikely for the Black Man to be reconciled with the system. When a system minimizes the worth of a Black life, it is not likely that a Black Man who is truly free will elect to continue that kind of degradation.

The English—once the greatest colonialist power in the world—had the good sense to withdraw from Kenya when the Mau Mau relayed the message that they were no longer welcome.

Not America. Black People in Harlem, Watts, Detroit, Newark, Tampa, Miami, Syracuse, Plainfield, and dozens of other American cities have given the message that the white cops, white storekeepers, and white national guardsmen are not welcome. But white America has had neither the grace nor the foresight to withdraw.

America's mayors and governors have shown an amazing lack of perception and astounding shortsightedness. White Americans seem to feel that rebellions born of anger and oppression can be squelched by an Anti-Riot Bill—a bill that addresses itself not to the causes of the rebellions but to restricting the free speech and travel of Black leaders. But with each Black Man who is jailed or killed in the quest for his freedom, another revolutionary hero is created. For each Black leader who is silenced, another Black Man, even more militant, will take his place. For each atrocity committed against Black People, revolutionary zeal increases and the task of policing the ghetto becomes more costly—and more dangerous.

There is no need for Americans, Black or white, to live through such hell. There is no reason to subject humanity to yet another holocaust. If Americans take advantage of trends already existing in this country, pending catastrophe can be converted to a national awakening.

In many counties of Mississippi and South Carolina, as well as other southern states, Black People are already in the majority. In these counties, rudimentary Black institutions already exist. If the electoral system in these areas is carefully safeguarded by the federal government, more Black Men will be elected to high office. There will be more Black sheriffs and more Black tax collectors. This development will no doubt result in large numbers of white people moving elsewhere—those whites who refuse to live and work with Blacks. It should also result in the counter migration of urban Blacks to these areas in numbers at least sufficient to meet the manpower needs of the area. Within one generation there could well be two or three states that are Black led, Black controlled, and predominantly Black populated. Those whites who elected to stay would be welcome—they would be the whites willing to work together with Blacks for mutual progress.

During Reconstruction, Black Men wrote good laws and adopted them. They did not use their new-found power vindictively. It is likely that Black Men today would also pass good laws, but this time, with Black Men in charge of their enforcement, the laws would also be enforced.

In these predominantly Black states, Blacks must own and control the large part of the economy. Political control without economic power is insufficient. The federal government could reimburse white southern businessmen who would relinquish their holdings to the Black Community. A Corporation Act could provide for the transfer of such property to Black shareholders and justly facilitate such transactions.

When Black People are in control of at least a few American states, they will be able to exert enough influence within the federal system to affect the treatment of their Black brothers in America's urban centers, as well as the exercise of American foreign policy. Of course, as we have said earlier, other radical changes will have to be made in order to facilitate such events.

It now remains to be seen if Americans will heed the warning. W. E. D. Du Bois understood, in 1935, the only alternatives still available today.

Such mental frustration cannot indefinitely continue. Some day it may burst in fire and blood. Who will be to blame? And where the greatest cost? Black folk, after all, have little to lose, but Civilization has all.

This the American Black Man knows; his fight here is a fight to the finish. Either he dies or wins. If he wins it will be by no subterfuge or evasion of amalgamation. He will enter modern civilization here in America as a Black Man on terms of perfect and unlimited equality with any white man, or he will enter not at all. Either extermination root and branch, or absolute equality. There can be no compromise. This is the last great battle of the West.

To Develop Soul City*

There is an urgent requirement to make multiple attacks on the problems facing the poor—both Black and white, rural and urban. There is also the incontrovertible realization that the rural poor will continue to pour into our vast metropolitan areas. The cities are unprepared to receive them. Lack of planning, foresight and concern relegate these new migrants to the crime and disease ridden slums and to menial, meaningless jobs, if they are able to find work at all.

The decay of America's cities is self-perpetuating. Poverty, racism and inadequate, demeaning welfare systems guarantee the continuation of chaotic conditions in America's urban centers.

Most American cities have been built haphazardly; they have been randomly expanded to meet the ever-increasing demands of burgeoning populations. No effective means have been found to coordinate their growth. No well planned, large scale effort has been made to provide services commensurate with the need.

Black people suffer more from these conditions than do others. If we are to achieve our national domestic goals and avoid further alienation of the Black community, we must mount massive programs to rehabilitate our cities. There must be equally intensive movement to improve rural life; and simultaneously there must be increased efforts to build new towns.

One of the main problems existing in cities across the United

*Reprinted from "A Proposal for Planning Funds to Develop Soul City, a New Town in North Carolina," August, 1969, pp. 2–5, 10–11. By permission of the author.

States is that of overcrowding. Overcrowding, resulting in hazardous, unsanitary conditions as well as increased crime and inadequate public services, is most acute in the ghetto areas inhabited by Black Americans. This is true primarily because Blacks have historically been excluded from the American economy, resulting in political powerlessness. Consequently, when city governments are faced with fiscal difficulties, the first to feel the pinch are generally the ghetto residents. In many instances, following the failure of peaceful demonstrations, the only way Black people have known to call attention to their plight is destruction and violence. As a result there have been the abundance of urban rebellions in recent years. The comparatively meager resources allocated for the ghetto as a result of these rebellions have been accompanied by more strenuous police action and increased hostility and resentment from surrounding white communities. The end result has been perpetuation of racial tensions and fears, themselves one of the root causes of urban blight.

America's cities are currently so overburdened that new cities are needed. Such a concept is not unprecedented and is in line with current federal policy. European countries have been experimenting with new cities for a relatively long period of time. In the United States, there are scores of attempts to build new communities.

Building new towns, with their own industries, commercial and civic services and residential areas may prove to be the most important innovation to help relieve the problem of the present—or future—urban dweller. Black people, however, will benefit little by current efforts. Few of the new towns will achieve economic integration. The small numbers of Blacks who will live in these communities will be lost in a sea of white suburbanites and may find themselves even further from the ability to determine their own affairs.

There has never been a serious attempt on the part of Blacks to build new towns: new planned communities which can accommodate large populations; which can provide new opportunities for youth; which can provide homes for families who desire to live in a truly open society; new locations for industry. Further expansion of cities already overburdened is not the answer. Decentralization of political and economic power within existing cities would offer a partial solution, but Blacks have been struggling for years to effect such a transfer, to no avail.

New towns built by Black people would provide an opportunity for the establishment of meaningful economic and political power without challenge to those already in control of existing cities. New towns could present a chance to use the experience of urban America to avoid repetition of the problems now facing our cities. They would provide an opportunity to develop educational systems truly responsive to the needs of disadvantaged minority group children.

A new urban center, carefully designed and coordinated by a competent central organization, could provide a model for other urban areas and could channel valuable energies and resources which are now wasted or being spent in anti-social means. Building a new city would provide needed work for many unemployed and underemployed. It would provide opportunities for creative young Black architects and planners. Perhaps even more important, it would contribute to a necessary sense of optimism among America's minorities. The tangible evidence of a new city conceived of, planned and built primarily by Black people could bring hope to the depressed areas of the nation.

The new town will incorporate all aspects of urban life in such a fashion as to provide maximum opportunities for individual growth and civic life. The town will include commercial and industrial development as well as residences. It will incorporate all other institutions and services which are integral to modern life, i.e., schools, churches, recreation, sanitation, and adult education and training.

The town, to be called Soul City, is to be located in Warren County, North Carolina. 1810.8 acres of land have been purchased and McKissick Enterprises holds option on additional adjacent land. It is projected that between 4500 and 5000 acres will be required. The site is in the Black belt of North Carolina. A southern site should be extremely attractive to the rural poor who might otherwise migrate to the major metropolitan areas.

North Carolina offers particular advantages since it has a political climate which is conducive to official cooperation, and has an active statewide program to develop new industry.

Soul City will not be limited to members of one race. It will, in fact, provide an opportunity for Blacks to welcome whites on a basis of full equality. It will also provide the opportunity to demonstrate the capacity for innovation, administration and productive work of Black Americans working along with whites.

Soul City will not further segregation. It will provide a source of inspiration to Blacks and other disadvantaged groups throughout the country. It will become living proof to members of all races that the Black man can succeed and prosper within the existing economy and can, in fact, exercise a role of leadership for the entire nation. The talent and the industry which will be attracted to Soul City will be progressive and varied.

While Soul City is to be developed by a predominantly Black company, and while the concept of this new town has grown out of concern for the plight of racial minorities, it will not be a totally "Black town." It is a Black inspired community, in the sense that most American communities are "white inspired."

Extensive, honest and in-depth effort will be made to insure that Soul City affords full citizenship and equality to every person. People happen to have been born with varying colors, sizes and shapes. As a result, they have been exposed to differing experiences and sub-cultures. Soul City will take these differences into consideration and will be concerned first with the situation of those persons who have been disadvantaged as a result of racism, prejudice or segregation. It is recognized, however, that we live in a multi-racial and multi-ethnic society and that progress for any segment of the nation is dependent on progress for all. Furthermore, a community does not exist in a vacuum, but exists as part of a pattern of inter-dependencies with other communities, other political and governmental units, and with the economy of the region and the country.

McKissick Enterprises' stated purposes of developing "Black Economic Power" is viewed by the company as a means toward developing a society of equals and a society where Black and white are brothers. Most cities and towns in America are far from achieving equality of opportunity. Soul City will be an attempt to move into the future—a future where Black people welcome white people as equals. It is hoped that this venture can succeed in developing an atmosphere of mutual respect based on achievement and acceptance of differences.

We know that this future of equality of opportunity and freedom of choice will not be realized through rhetoric or by the written word. We do believe that we can build Soul City so that it will, in fact, attract and hold substantial numbers of non-Black persons as residents, as workers and as businessmen.

This will be accomplished through the following, and other actions:

1. Creation of an atmosphere in Soul City in which persons of any background feel welcome.
2. Establishing true equality of opportunity.
3. Efforts to recruit residents from the Indian, Jewish,

Spanish-speaking, Oriental communities, and from all elements of the general population.

4. Creating an economically integrated pattern of housing.
5. Offering job training, decent jobs and good living conditions to all poor persons.
6. Designing Soul City to reflect a multi-ethnic society.
7. Developing a broad scope of cultural and social programs which appeal to many classes of persons.
8. Involving non-Blacks in the planning and development of Soul City.

ELIJAH MUHAMMAD,

Spiritual Leader of the Black Muslims

On July 4, 1930, a man appeared in the black ghetto of Detroit. He called himself W. C. Farad Muhammad. He had come to lead the blacks toward a new self-image through an organization later called the Black Muslims. When he disappeared sometime after June 30, 1934, he left as his prophet, Elijah Poole, the son of a Baptist minister. Born in Sandersville, Georgia, in 1897, Elijah Poole migrated to Detroit with his family in the 1920s. He became Farad's First Minister of Islam and directed the Muslims' training school for ministers and the highly secret Fruit of Islam—a leadership training corps for the battles of Armageddon. Poole also founded Temple No. 2 in Chicago, presently the headquarters of the Muslim Movement. At that time, his "slave" name, Poole, was dropped and he became Elijah Muhammad.

In 1942 he was jailed for encouraging resistance to the draft as he had been earlier for refusing to send his child to a public school. Elijah Muhammad and the Muslims believe that this country will never grant equality to Negroes. They therefore reject interracial cooperation. As a result of this basic belief, the Muslims direct their attention to the development of their own culture and their own economic institutions. They have purchased land in rural areas and have established restaurants, cleaners, barbershops, and meat, grocery, and department stores in various cities across the country.

In terms of culture, they emphasize group solidarity and encourage their thousands of members to live respectably and provide for their families. They are forbidden to gamble, smoke, drink liquor, overeat, buy on credit, or be idle.

*An ultimate goal of this group seems to be an entirely sepa-
rate black colony, for steps are being taken in that direction.
In the meantime, they are among the best organized and best
disciplined of the current black movements.*

**"INTEGRATION MEANS SELF-DESTRUCTION . . . —DEATH
AND NOTHING ELSE."**

Message to the Blackman*

Help Self:

What Must Be Done with the Negroes?

Since our being brought in chains to the shores of America, our brain power, labor, skills, talent and wealth have been taken, given and spent toward building and adding to the civilization of another people. It is time for you and me, the so-called Negroes, to start doing for ourselves. We must not let our children be as are we, beggars of another man for his home, facilities, clothing, food and the means of providing a living. Man depends on land for the necessities, food, clothing and shelter for survival. A prime requisite for freedom and independence is having one's own land. There can be no freedom without a people having their own land.

The acquisition of land has been the factor for more wars than any other cause. Economists agree that in order for any type of nation or system, capitalism or communism, democracy or totalitarian or what have you, to exist and have a degree of independence there must be ownership of land. The so-called Negroes are without a state they can call their own. We have nothing to show for our more than 310 years of forced slave labor and more than 100 years of our free servitude to our slave-masters' children.

We were brought here to work. We have worked! We are still the workers. Some of us say, "What will we do if we do not work for the whiteman? How will we live?" I say, when

* Reprinted from *Message to the Blackman*, 1965. By permission of Islam No. 2 and the author.

you are free and independent you have a job! You have a tremendous task of doing something for self. You have the job of building a civilization for yourself as other free and independent people are doing for themselves.

As a people, we must become producers and not remain consumers and employees. We must be able to extract raw materials from the earth and manufacture them into something useful for ourselves. This would create jobs in production. We must remember that without land there is no production. The surplus of what we produce we would sell. This would develop a field of commerce and trade as other free and independent people whose population is less than that of the 20 million so-called Negroes who are dependent in America.

We must begin at the cradle and teach our babies that they must do something for self. They must not be like we, their fathers, who look to the slave-makers' and slave-masters' children for all. We must teach our children now with an enthusiasm exceeding that which our slave-masters used in having our forefathers imbed the seed of dependency within us. We must stop the process of giving our brain power, labor and wealth to our slave-masters' children. We must eliminate the master-slave relationship.

We must educate ourselves and our children into the rich power of knowledge which has elevated every people who have sought and used it. We must give the benefit of our knowledge to the elevation of our own people.

Presently in this country, in almost all of the major universities and colleges, there are thousands of young students from Africa and Asia. Yet, as young, primitive and backward as we say these countries of Africa and Asia might be, their students here are returning to their shores. Their intent and purpose is to give their people the benefit of their learning. All civilized people give the benefit of their knowledge, skill and wealth to their own people. Those who do not are called traitors, defectors, spies, tools and Toms.

Why should we spend 12 and 16 years seeking an education only to give the benefit of our knowledge back to the one we sought it from? It is time for us to wake up! Why should we work to give the meager earnings of our labor back to our slave-masters' children? Why can't we have our own? Why can't we do for our own? Why can't we strive toward keeping our brain power, labor and wealth within and among and elevating our own?

We must have that which will make us want to do for ourselves as other people want and do for themselves. You ask, "How can this be done?" The so-called Negroes must be taught and given Islam. Why Islam? Islam, because it teaches first the knowledge of self. It gives us the knowledge of our own. Then and only then are we able to understand that which surrounds us. "Know thyself" is the doctrine Socrates espoused, and this is the base of the educational system in America. The religion of Islam makes the so-called Negroes think in terms of self and their own kind. Thus, this kind of thinking produces an industrious people who are self-independent. Islam is actually our religion by nature. Allah is the proper name for God. Islam is not a European-organized white man's religion. It is time for the so-called Negroes to help their own kind and be benefited by Islam.

Land of Our Own and Qualifications
The Unity of 22 Million

The unity of 22 million so-called Negroes up from slavery is the answer to our salvation.

We are suffering untold torture and murder at the hands of our enemies (the children of our slave-master) because of the lack of unity. The cause of this lack of unity among us is due to the work and teaching of our enemies, the slave-masters' children. Our slave-masters' children have reared our fathers and mothers to be enemies of each other. They have destroyed our love of self and kind. They have educated us to hate and refuse all that goes for black people.

This lack of love for self and kind keeps us divided, and being divided we are a nation of prey at the hands of our ever open enemies. Whatever the amount of education we receive from our enemies we are still the slaves of our enemies due to this lack of knowledge of self, God and the devil; the true religion; self-pride; self-interest; and self-independence and the desire of a country and of a government of our own under the law of justice and righteousness for every one of our poor black people throughout the earth.

But let us start first here in America where we are the victims of no freedom, justice, and equality and we know the pains of being divided.

At present, we have hundreds of clubs and organizations; thousands of teachers; hundreds of educators, scholars, scientists, technicians, doctors, lawyers, judges, congressmen, ambassadors, professors, tradesmen of all kinds and engineers of most every kind. We have all kinds of religious believers, teachers, preachers by the thousands, agriculturists, herdsmen and cattlemen and fisherman and hundreds of hunters of wild game.

What more do we need but unity of the whole for the whole? What actually is preventing this unity of 22 million or more of us is the ignorance and foolish love and fear of our enemies in the professional and leadership class of this nation of 22 million black people up from slavery.

There are disgraceful "Uncle Toms" in a world of freedom, learning and advanced science in every branch of study. How long shall we seek the white men's education to become their servants instead of becoming builders of a progressive nation of our own on some of this earth that we can call our own?

Why are you so foolish to think it cannot be done? I have Allah (God) and the world of the righteous on my side to accomplish this.

There is no hope for us in Christianity; it is a religion organized by the enemies (the white race) of the Black Nation to enslave us to the white race's rule. But our unity under the crescent with our Allah's guidance can get us anything we desire in the way of help and some of this earth that we can call our own.

By the help of Allah, I have and I will still prove to you that Allah (God) has given me the only solution to our problem here under this race of merciless devils. If you can prove to me that you have a better solution for the future of our Nation I will bring my followers and myself and join you. And if the solution given to me from Almighty Allah is best, come you and your followers and join with me.

How Can We Unite?

So you say that we cannot unite and produce our own necessities? We are 22 million or more people depending on the white American citizens to produce food, clothes, shelter, transportation, employment and our educational training.

And if they (white Americans) do not share equally with us, we charge them with discriminating; some of us will go to the extreme of disregarding ourselves in trying to force the white American citizens to give equal respect. The love of self and self-respect along with the will to do something for self, if given a chance, will get you the respect of all civilized nations.

It is a shame and disgrace to the intelligence of any people to lie at the feet and doorsteps of another nation, asking, praying to be cared for. Love and unity of self and kind is the key to our salvation.

If you say we cannot unite, you are wrong. We can unite! Before your very eyes you see the Believers in Allah (God) and his religion. Islam uniting and this Divine power from Allah working among us, uniting us into a nation of brotherly love, disapproves the lie of that "old saying" that the Negroes cannot unite.

I agree with you who are in the Christian churches, lovers and followers of white Christians, that you cannot enjoy love and unity among yourselves. The basic aim and purposes of the religion, Christianity, was to deceive other races, namely, the black, brown, yellow and red, to make an easy prey for the white race.

But today, you and I both see the powerless forces of Christianity unable to bring about peace among those who profess it.

Since Christian Europe and America cannot bring peace to their troubled world with all their satellite nations as helpers, what kind of peace can they make for us?

Their religion divides one against the other. This I am sure we all can agree upon. We must know self to gain self-respect. This will remove that old slave idea that the so-called Negroes cannot unite and build an independent nation on some of this good earth that we can call our own. Stop looking for others to help you in that in which you can help yourself.

The white man has made the black man lazy that he may rule and enslave him by producing and selling to him that which he can produce himself. But the white man knows that he has destroyed the black man's unity, and as long as the black man thinks he cannot love and unite with black, the white man knows that he has a permanent slave.

Come and let us unite under the crescent and do something for ourselves in the way of supporting our own needs. Go after some of this earth for our nation of 22 million here in North America. If it cannot be had here, there is plenty of earth elsewhere.

We want nothing short of a home on this earth that we can call our own—not to be servants and slaves for other free nations.

Let us capture the market of our people by producing their needs. We cannot produce our needs on the soil of another.

Of Land and a Nation

What we must understand today is the importance of acquiring land of our own. We are no longer a mere handful of people. We are a little better than 22 million in population and still increasing.

We cannot forever continue to depend upon America to give us a job, send us to school, build our houses and sell us her food and give nothing in return.

America was not established and chartered with constitutional guarantees for the Black man but for the white man.

America was not founded to guarantee the freedom and equality of the Black man and woman, and, indeed, she is not seeking to grant these privileges to our people today.

In what other country on this earth will you find 22 million people within the framework of another people's government seeking to become qualified citizens joyously singing the song of integration? Our people are the fools of the nations. Integration means self-destruction, and the means to this end is exactly that—death and nothing less.

The Black people throughout the earth are seeking independence for their own, not integration into white society What do we look like trying to integrate with our 400-year-old enemies? The average so-called Negro wants to change his own flesh color and blood for a strange blood and flesh.

In order to build a nation you must first have some land. From our first generation of slaves to the present generation of our people, we have been unable to unite and acquire some land of our own due to the mental poisoning of our former slave-masters, who destroyed in us the desire to think and do for self and kind.

Do you as educated and professional men and women desire to be recognized forever as the mental slaves, beggars of white America?

Today, the international conception of honor, pride and dignity is not concerned with individuals within a country but is rather concerned with your work and value as a part of an established nation.

In order to be recognized today you must represent your nation. We must understand the importance of land to our nation.

The first and most important reason that the individual countries of Europe, Africa and Asia are recognized as nations is because they occupy a specific area of the earth. Second, they are recognized because of the effectiveness of their internal unity and policies and then by their enactment of international policies and agreements with other established nations. The black man has been actually worthless when it comes to exercising the rights as human beings in an ever-advancing civilization. So remember, we cannot demand recognition until we have some land that we can call our own.

You might argue that this is impossible, but I say to you, with Almighty Allah (God) on my side this is not only possible but is in the working for our people and will manifest itself soon!

ROY INNIS,

Activist, Tactician

Roy Innis is an outspoken young man and a principal advocate of neo-black nationalism—within a community framework. He was born June 6, 1934, at St. Croix, Virgin Islands, but, at the age of twelve, he moved with his family to the United States, where they settled in Harlem. He left New York's Stuyvesant High Shool to join the army at an early age, but before becoming involved in the Black Movement, he had attended the City College of New York and worked briefly in chemistry and research.

In 1965 Innis was elected chairman of the Harlem chapter of CORE. He served in this position until 1968, when he became CORE's national associate director. In this capacity Innis has been largely responsible for redirecting the ideology of CORE toward self-determination and black power. As a result of his efforts, CORE became a predominantly black organization.

"WE ARE PAST THE STAGE WHERE WE CAN TALK SERIOUSLY OF WHITES ACTING TOWARDS BLACKS OUT OF MORAL IMPERATIVES."

Separatist Economics:
A New Social Contract*

There exists today a crisis of immense proportions within the boundaries of the United States of America. This crisis is the direct result of the breakdown of the relationship between black and white people in our society. It was scarcely a good relationship to begin with. For blacks it has been degrading and dehumanizing; for whites, it has been abrasive, guilt-ridden, and a perpetual thorn. Over the decades, the problem has festered and spread to the point where it now threatens to destroy the entire political organism in which it is rooted.

Even at this late date, we can provide an alternative to the collision course of whites and blacks in this country. But to do so, we must develop entirely new solutions to the massive problems of the past. The present programs and plans offered by well-meaning agencies, groups, and individuals are entirely insufficient. Aside from the fundamental lack of understanding in the past of the nature and degree of racism in this country, there has been a failure to coordinate the multiplicity of suggested "solutions." Such solutions, in any case, have never been structured by black people. They have always been structured by whites who interpreted our needs and in many cases designed these solutions to accommodate their own needs.

Where the collision of black and white is concerned, we have falsely assumed in America that a contract or constitution designed for a dominant majority, with distinct attributes, self-interests, and needs, could simply be adapted, by minor modifications, to fit the needs of a significant minority with different attributes, interests, and needs. Obviously, this has not worked. A crucial weakness has been the lack of control by black people over the institutions that surround them: institutions that

* Reprinted from *Black Economic Development*, 1969. By permission of Prentice-Hall, Inc. and the author.

not only establish imposed values for them but also control the flow of goods and services within their communities, thereby shaping the quality of their lives. The black community sees these institutions in the hands of people with interests too often at odds with their own. Thus, schools in black neighborhoods too often do not teach, sanitation departments do not protect, employment departments do not find jobs, welfare departments do not give adequate relief, housing departments do not give decent housing. Most ironic of all, human rights departments do not guarantee human rights.

The obvious solution, then, is a *new social contract,* to be drawn in the mutual interest of both parties. This contract must redefine the relationship between blacks and whites, to the extent that black people are recognized as a major interest group. While this redefinition is in progress, there are palpable changes to be implemented.

Large, densely populated black areas, especially in urban centers, must have a change in status. They must become political sub-divisions of the state, instead of sub-colonial appendages of the cities. Blacks must manage and control the institutions that service their areas, as has always been the case for other interest groups. There is an immediate need in the institutions of education, health, social service, sanitation, housing, protection, etc. Black people must be able to control basic societal instruments in the social, political, and economic arenas.

Definitions

In short, black people must see liberation from the dominance and control of white society. Nothing less than this liberation will allow black people to determine their own destinies.

Perhaps, at this point, a few definitions are in order. There is always a controversy as to whether our tactics, our objectives, are reformist or revolutionary. In my own view, black people at this stage of their development are not and should not be talking about some romantic thing called revolution, but rather a more pragmatic and necessary step called liberation. There is a difference between the two. A revolution, of course, occurs where one class of a national group rebels against another class of that same group, as in the Russia of 1917, the France of the late Eighteenth Century. Liberation comes about in a setting of two distinct groups, where one is suppressing the other. Jews caught in Egypt in the time of the Pharaohs did not talk about revolution against what was the most powerful and formidable military machine of the time. They talked about liberation—separating themselves from Egyptians.

We black nationalists, too, must speak of separating ourselves. We live in a setting where one group—not our own—controls the institutions, and the flow of goods and services. We can change our condition by liberating ourselves and placing these vital instruments of social and economic destiny in our own hands. This is what we mean by separation—quite a different matter from segregation, which is the condition that now exists, in fact, throughout the United States.

Separation is a more equitable way of organizing the society. The important distinction is that in such a society the control of goods and services flowing through a distinct geographical area inhabited by a distinct population group would be in the hands of those indigenous to the area. In other words, if we have a clearly defined sociological unit called Harlem, New York City, the people of Harlem will control the flow of goods and services there. The same would hold true for the white areas of New York City: the white would control their own "action."

In the struggle toward self-determination, there has been a great deal of argument about the order of steps to be taken. Should we be talking first about politics, about culture, or should we be talking about economics? Let me suggest that we can resolve this dilemma by understanding first of all that these three stages of liberation are virtually inseparable. There must be some sort of socio-cultural renaissance if there is to be movement in any other direction. There must be some sort of politico-economic development if the cultural movement is to have any base on which to acquire significance.

My feeling is that we have already begun part of this movement. That is, black people have begun revitalizing their culture, recreating their values. We must now phase in the element of economic growth. The failure of many of the past economic measures—community action, training and hiring programs, and the like—is that they have been little more than board games, depending on some sort of arithmetic progression. What we need to do now is to find the geometric factor that can speed up this process. And that is why we turn to the control of institutions. But some further definition is needed.

Capitalism or Development

In the new focus on economic control, there has been much talk about something called "black capitalism." Many of our people have been deluded into endless debates centered around this term. There is no such animal. Capitalism, like socialism, is an economic and political philosophy that describes the experience of Europeans and their descendants—Americans. Blacks must innovate, must create a new ideology. It may include elements of capitalism, elements of socialism, or elements of neither: that is immaterial. What matters is that it will be created to fit our needs.

So then black people are not talking about black capitalism. Black people are talking about economic development. We are talking about the creation and the acquisition of capital instruments by means of which we can maximize our economic interests. We do not particularly try to define styles of ownership; we say that we are willing to operate pragmatically and let the style of ownership fit the style of the area or its inhabitants.

The question of autonomy is critical. Any reliable sociological analysis will indicate that we live in natural units called communities. Where whites are concerned, these natural sociological units then become natural political units—political subdivisions of county, state, or federal government. This does not happen with black communities, so that extensive areas like Harlem in New York, Roxbury in Boston, Watts in Los Angeles, exist as colonial appendages of the urban center. In fact, government programs almost always deal with us as part of urban centers, and in terms of the overall condition of those centers. This is something we must resist strenuously, for there is a fundamental conflict of interest between our communities—the so-called ghettos—and the urban centers in which they are situated. The urban centers are managed by political and institutional barons who include our piece of "turf" in their domain. And we see that whenever we make any attempt to change that relationship—political, social, or economic—we meet the massive resistance of these barons. This sort of frustration has led and will continue to lead to disastrous confrontations between blacks and whites.

We understand also that the urban setting, throughout history, has been the energizer of mankind, thus the cradle of change. It is there that blacks, too, will have to find their solutions. We cannot go off to conduct a masquerade of change in newly created little rural centers. But if we are to develop in the urban centers, our position must be newly understood.

There is a very striking similarity between the so-called underdeveloped countries and our underdeveloped black communities. Both have always been oppressed; almost always there is an unfavorable balance of trade with the oppressors or exploiters; both suffer from high unemployment, low income, scarce capital, and we can point to a series of other similarities. But let me point to at least one vital difference. In every so-called underdeveloped country, the people have a measure of sovereignty. They have a vastly greater amount of autonomy compared with the black communities across this country. It seems to me, then, that a natural impetus for our communities is to move to gain that missing ingredient—sovereignty, or at least a greater degree of autonomy and self-determination.

In other words, I am saying there is no way we can divorce economic development from political imperatives. You cannot have economic development unless you have certain supportive political realities, one of which is some degree of self-determination.

The Dividends

What economic gratuities would flow from self-determination? Let us consider the massive budgets provided to pay for the goods and services of a single black community (which are then almost always poorly distributed in that community). Take the schools, for example. In a community like Harlem, close to a hundred million dollars is spent yearly for goods and services to supply the schools. We must assume, in fact we know, that in almost every instance those goods and services are purchased from sources outside the community. Now we in the black community pay taxes that are intended to be used to pay for these commodities, so that nominally, all tax monies are returned to us in this form. But what really happens is that our tax monies are returned to agents of the urban centers—the mayor and his commissioners and department heads —who will then use that money to enhance the economic interest of the white-dominated urban center by buying goods and services outside the black communities they are meant to serve.

That same hundred million dollars could have gone, let us say, to a corporation in Harlem put together by two or three black entrepreneurs and awarded a contract to supply books for the Harlem schools. It is immaterial that this hypothetical corporation does not own a publishing house or a printing plant. Neither do the white corporations that presently supply books to the public school system in Cleveland, or New York, or any place else across this country. They are merely middlemen. They buy from someone else and sell to the schools. They move paper from one side of their desk to the other and turn a handsome profit. That kind of profit could be turned just as easily within the black community, to increase its income by the millions. Multiply the massive budgets for the schools by the massive budgets in health and hospital services, sanitation, and all the other urban services, and you get a massive amount of money that represents a guaranteed market.

The name of this in economics is guaranteed market. That is what you have when you are selling to your own institutions: there will always be a demand for your goods and services. If you have control of these institutions you are able to determine who will get the contracts, and you can direct them back to your own people.

So here we see at least one route by which the black people can get a running start in economic development without huge investments in machinery, materials, technical expertise, and without most of the other impediments that are immediately cited when we talk about economic development. And it is a way in which we could secure a maximum return to our community from those precious tax dollars that we pay year after year.

Of course, this same division of interest and diversion of profit has social as well as economic consequences. We must control our schools if we are to upgrade education and pass on positive values to our children. We must control health facilities if we are to cut down our mortality rate. We must control the law enforcement in our areas if the police are to serve their proper function—which is protection, not oppression. In short, we must control every single institution that takes our tax monies and is supposed to distribute goods and service equitably for us.

Vehicles for Self-Determination

The Congress of Racial Equality has been working to develop vehicles and instruments for black self-determination at both the local and national levels.

The Harlem Commonwealth Council

The first group in America to formalize the advance of black business beyond the "Mom-and-Pop" stage was the Harlem Commonwealth Council in New York. With a controversial grant from the Demonstration Office of the Office of Economic Opportunity, the HCC was organized as a nonprofit, tax exempt corporation which invests in profitmaking businesses and uses the accumulated income to re-invest in other businesses. The National Association of Manufacturers and McKinsey and Company agreed to provide help, along with two universities.

The HCC's first brochure notes that Harlem's half million people can spend half a billion dollars for consumer goods every year—a sum larger than the gross national product of many underdeveloped nations. Yet, says the brochure, "the economic sickness of Harlem" is that most of this capital is siphoned off from the community by the outsiders who own 80 per cent of Harlem's business volume. "One root problem of Harlem is that almost no one who lives there owns anything."

Accordingly, the goal of HCC is to "bring back to Harlem that internal economic vitality which is essential to social development. . . . It is not enough to attract white-owned industry. Finding jobs for blacks is not enough either, critical as that is. Both of these become enough only if we can also develop Harlem's capital."

To implement its plans, HCC set up a community-based Board of Directors who, with help from the outside consultants, quickly developed their own ability to pick and choose among business opportunities. As objectives they selected those businesses which would meet community needs (e.g., a 24-hour pharmacy selling prescription medicines by their generic names, thus permitting prices considerably lower than those for brand name medicines), and modern businesses which capitalize on Harlem's strategic location in Manhattan (e.g., an Automotive Diagnostic Center near the Triborough Bridge which feeds in traffic from two other boroughs).

The HCC is not looking for yesterday's businesses but tomorrow's opportunities. They are utilizing the most modern market instruments to determine markets and potentials; helping locate business opportunities in Harlem and then finding the potential businessmen to run them; designing training and apprenticeship programs to prepare a black man to run his own business; and providing the technical services to train managers.

The Cleveland Plan

In Cleveland, Ohio, CORE has projected the development of a consortium of black economic institutions designed to significantly broaden the base of ownership by the black community of productive capital instruments. The Cleveland program is seeking $10 million of funding for a two-year operational budget, to establish sustaining economic institutions through which black residents could be both owners of capital instruments and wage earners. An excerpt from the formal summary of the proposal* states this general concept:

> CORENCO (CORE Enterprises Corporation) contends that the way to correct (the economic imbalance between black and white communities) is to effect institutional changes which increase the productive power of underproductive households and individuals so that they may legitimately receive enough income to satisfy their reasonable needs and desires. Although it is a method which would tend to protect existing private property, it would also tend to build a "New Black Economy" in the black community, so financed that it becomes owned in moderately-sized holdings by the great majority of households and individuals who own no productive capital in the existing economy. . . .
>
> New financing techniques can enable the man without capital to buy it, and to pay for it out of the wealth it produces, and therefore to enjoy a new stream of income, if there is a demand for his employment—and the only full employment possible in our advanced industrial economy must result from the building and operation of a second economy producing humanly useful and desirable goods—he will then have two sources of income with which, on the one hand, to erase his poverty and, on the other hand, to provide the market—the effective market —for the expanded output by industry and business.

CORENCO will establish research and development teams to promote a wide range of economic projects aimed at creating a black economic infrastructure and increasing black ownership and employment in the institutions that purchase and distribute goods and services in the black community.

The Federal Bill

Most of the problems we have discussed in this chapter we have tried to deal with, to some degree, in the Community Self-Determination Bill. This bill, created by CORE with a wide spectrum of expert assistance, was introduced before the

*A copy of this proposal can be obtained from the Congress of Racial Equality, 200 West 135th Street, New York, New York 10030.

Congress of the United States in July of 1968, receiving support from all political corners. (Ironically, but not surprisingly, most of the opposition came from labor, from the leadership of the AFL–CIO, which used to proclaim itself the great friend of the black man. In the current history of the civil rights movement and the black power movement, we have had to fight our biggest and toughest battles against the labor unions. More recently, the AFL–CIO has declared itself opposed to so-called black capitalism and thus, by implication, to black self-determination. Meanwhile, of course, they continue to endorse programs advocating jobs for blacks—jobs that the unions themselves consistently prevent us from getting.)

The Community Self-Determination Bill can serve as a social, political, and economic tool by means of which the black communities can make giant strides. Through it, we can create community instruments that can in themselves create community industries; these in turn would produce jobs for men. It would provide for a variety of types of ownership, for community boards in black areas to coordinate economic development and the control of indigenous institutions.

These community boards would be the sole agencies in the black community responsible for both social welfare and economic development. They would give contracts to community industries and raise sound financing for them with the help of a new banking system—community development banks.

As projected, the program will provide incentive for broad-based community ownership. It will contain provisions for research, development, and training, for the development of innovations in health, welfare, education, and other community services. It will provide performance bond guarantees to enable existing industries that cannot now meet bonding requirements to compete for a fair share of contracts for the black communities. It contemplates providing incentives for outside industry to come into our areas—though not to stay. Unlike other programs, we do not want to bring white industries into the black community to create jobs. We want industries to come into the community to create *instruments*, to sell them to us, and then move out.

Will It Work?

So what we are talking about, in the final analysis, is not jobs, but instruments that create jobs. We are not talking about bringing white businesses into black communities, but about building economic instruments that themselves can hire blacks. Nor are we talking merely, as some people seem to construe it, of substituting black ownership of a pants-pressing business for white ownership of a pants-pressing business, for that is looking at the economics of the community on the lowest scale. We are talking about the acquisition of capital instruments on a major scale, to maximize the flow of money in the community and begin that geometric progression toward economic well-being.

This separatist economics, as I choose to call it, is not essentially different from the basic principles of developmental economics employed by any people—for example, the Americans of the post-Revolutionary period. It is the manipulation of the economy of black areas in a preferential way to obtain an edge and protect the interests of the community; to place a membrane around the community that allows full commercial intercourse with outside business interests while setting preconditions and guidelines advantageous to the community for those who may seek to operate within the community. This principle is known by many names, one of the more familiar being *tariff*.

Will whites go along with this? I must be honest—I do not have an unshakeable faith in white people; I have no experience that would support such a faith.

But the underlying assumption of all I have said here is that whites who have the most power (real power) and the most to lose from chaos *will* go along with it; that the Community Self-Determination Bill will become the high-powered vehicle of the new black economy. What I assume is that an enlightened self-interest will head off the impending collision in this country—and I am talking about the enlightened self-interest of black people and white.

For we are past the stage where we can talk seriously of whites acting toward blacks out of moral imperatives. That does not work. Yet we can still talk of change coming about through enlightened self-interest, the prime motivator of orderly change in society throughout the history of mankind. That is the only thing that works without destroying what it seeks to save.

STOKELY CARMICHAEL,

Organizer, Author, Orator

Stokely Carmichael has a long history of active participation in the Black Movement. Although he was born in Port-of-Spain, Trinidad, he received much of his early education in New York City and Washington, D. C. While a student at Howard University, he was very active in student government and such civil rights efforts as freedom rides, picketing with CORE, and marches through Mississippi. With the beginning of the Student Non-violent Coordinating Committee in 1960, Carmichael moved to a more active and outspoken role in the South's racial conflicts. He helped found the Lowndes County Freedom Organization in Alabama and helped to direct the SNCC Mississippi Summer Project for civil rights. In 1966 after his graduation from Howard with a B.A. in philosophy, he was elected chairman of SNCC and has since played a leading role in civil rights protests throughout the United States. As a result he has been jailed more than twenty-five times. It was Carmichael who was credited with popularizing the concept of Black Power. In order to further elaborate this concept, he and Charles V. Hamilton have written a successful book entitled Black Power.

After his break with SNCC in 1967, he became a member of the Black Panther Party for a short time, but apparently could not reconcile himself to their alliance with white groups. He has presently all but relinquished his active leadership in the Black Movement. Perhaps his greatest accomplishment was that his fiery rhetoric allowed many blacks to entertain thoughts of pride and dignity and to act out many of their repressed feelings, thereby paving the way for the development of self-pride. Carmichael has recently been studying in Africa

*and elsewhere, in an effort to prepare himself for the next
stage of the movement.*

**"A 'NON-VIOLENT' APPROACH TO CIVIL RIGHTS IS AN
APPROACH BLACK PEOPLE CANNOT AFFORD AND A LUX-
URY WHITE PEOPLE DO NOT DESERVE."**

Excerpts from

Black Power: Its Needs and Substance*

By STOKELY CARMICHAEL and
CHARLES V. HAMILTON**

Today, the American educational system continues to reinforce the entrenched values of the society through the use of
words. Few people in this country question that this is "the
land of the free and the home of the brave." They have had
these words drummed into them from childhood. Few people
question that this is the "Great Society" or that this country
is fighting "Communist aggression" around the world. We
mouth these things over and over, and they become truisms
not to be questioned. In a similar way, black people have been
saddled with epithets.

"Integration" is another current example of a word which
has been defined according to the way white Americans see it.
To many of them it means black men wanting to marry white
daughters; it means "race-mixing"—implying bed or dance
partners. To black people, it has meant a way to improve their
lives—economically and politically. But the predominant white
definition has stuck in the minds of too many people.

Black people must redefine themselves, and only *they* can
do that. Throughout this country, vast segments of the black

*Reprinted from *Black Power*, 1967. By permission of Random
House, Inc. and the authors.

**Carmichael's co-author, Charles V. Hamilton, is a political scien-
tist and a college professor. He too has spoken widely on the black
movement and has several enlightening articles on the subject.

communities are beginning to recognize the need to assert their own definitions, to reclaim their history, their culture; to create their own sense of community and togetherness. There is a growing resentment of the word "Negro," for example, because this term is the invention of our oppressor; it is *his* image of us that he describes. Many blacks are now calling themselves African-Americans, Afro-Americans or black people because that is *our* image of ourselves. When we begin to define our own image, the stereotypes—that is, lies—that our oppressor has developed will begin in the white community and end there. The black community will have a positive image of itself that *it* has created. This means we will no longer call ourselves lazy, apathetic, dumb, good-timers, shiftless, etc. Those are words used by white America to define us. If we accept these adjectives, as some of us have in the past, then we see ourselves only in a negative way, precisely the way white America wants us to see ourselves. Our incentive is broken and our will to fight is surrendered. From now on we shall view ourselves as African-Americans and as black people who are in fact energetic, determined, intelligent, beautiful and peace-loving.

There is a terminology and ethos peculiar to the black community of which black people are beginning to be no longer ashamed. Black communities are the only large segments of this society where people refer to each other as brother—soul-brother, soul-sister. Some people may look upon this as *ersatz,* as make-believe, but it is not that. It is real. It is a growing sense of community. It is a growing realization that black Americans have a common bond not only among themselves, but with their African brothers.

More and more black Americans are developing this feeling. They are becoming aware that they have a history which predates their forced introduction to this country. African-American history means a long history beginning on the continent of Africa, a history not taught in the standard textbooks of this country. It is absolutely essential that black people know this history, that they know their roots, that they develop an awareness of their cultural heritage. Too long have they been kept in submission by being told that they had no culture, no manifest heritage, before they landed on the slave auction blocks in this country. If black people are to know themselves as a vibrant, valiant people, they must know their roots. And they will soon learn that the Hollywood image of man-eating cannibals waiting for, and waiting on, the Great White Hunter is a lie.

With redefinition will come a clearer notion of the role black Americans can play in this world. This role will emerge clearly out of the unique, common experiences of Afro-Asians. Only when black people fully develop this sense of community, of themselves, can they begin to deal effectively with the problems of racism in *this* country. This is what we mean by new consciousness; this is the vital first step.

The next step is what we shall call the process of political modernization—a process which must take place if the society is to be rid of racism. "Political modernization" includes many things, but we mean by it three major concepts: (1) questioning old values and institutions of the society; (2) searching for new and different forms of political structure to solve political and economic problems; and (3) broadening the base of political participation to include more people in the decision-making process.

The values of this society support a racist system; we find it incongruous to ask black people to adopt and support most of those values. We also reject the assumption that the basic institutions of this society must be preserved. The goal of black people must *not* be to assimilate into middle-class America, for that class—as a whole—is without a viable conscience as regards humanity. The values of the middle class permit the perpetuation of the ravages of the black community. The values of that class are based on material aggrandizement, not the expansion of humanity. The values of that class ultimately support cloistered little closed societies tucked away neatly in tree-lined suburbia. The values of that class do *not* lead to the creation of an open society. That class *mouths* its preference for a free, competitive society, while at the same time forcefully and even viciously denying to black people as a group the opportunity to compete.

Thus we reject the goal of assimilation into middle-class America because the values of that class are in themselves anti-humanist and because that class as a social force perpetuates racism. We must face the fact that, in the past, what we have called the movement has not really questioned the middle-class values and institutions of this country. If anything, it has accepted those values and institutions without fully realizing their racist nature. Reorientation means an emphasis on the dignity of man, not on the sanctity of property. It means the creation of a society where human misery and poverty are repugnant to that society, not an indication of laziness or lack of initiative. The creation of new values means the establishment of a society based, as Killens expresses it in *Black Man's Burden*,* on "free people," not "free enterprise" (p. 167). To do this means to modernize—*indeed, to civilize*—this country.

Supporting the old values are old political and economic structures; these must also be "modernized." We should at this point distinguish between "structures" and "system." By system, we have in mind the entire American complex of basic institutions, values, beliefs, etc. By structures, we mean the specific institutions (political parties, interest groups, bureaucratic administrations) which exist to conduct the business of that system. Obviously, the first is broader than the second. Also, the second assumes the legitimacy of the first. Our view is that, given the illegitimacy of the system, we cannot then proceed to transform that system with existing structures.

Black people have seen the city planning commissions, the urban renewal commissions, the boards of education and the police departments fail to speak to their needs in a meaningful way. We must devise new structures, new institutions to replace those forms or to make them responsive. There is nothing sacred or inevitable about old institutions; the focus must be on people, not forms.

Existing structures and established ways of doing things have a way of perpetuating themselves and for this reason, the modernizing process will be difficult. Therefore, timidity in calling into question the boards of education or the police departments will not do. They must be challenged forcefully and clearly. If this means the creation of parallel community institutions, then that must be the solution. If this means that black parents must gain control over the operation of the schools in the black community, then that must be the solution. The search for new forms means the search for institutions that will, for once, make decisions in the interest of black people. It means, for example, a building inspection department that neither winks at violations of building codes by absentee slumlords nor imposes meaningless fines which permit them to continue their exploitation of the black community.

Essential to the modernization of structures is a broadened base of political participation. More and more people must become politically sensitive and active (we have already seen this happening in some areas of the South). People must no longer be tied, by small incentives or handouts, to a corrupting

---

* John Oliver Killens, *Black Man's Burden*. New York: Trident Press, 1965. Killens has also written other books on blacks, including *'Sippi* (1967).

and corruptible white machine. Black people will choose their own leaders and hold those leaders responsible to *them*. A broadened base means an end to the condition described by James Wilson in *Negro Politics,* whereby "Negroes tended to be the objects rather than the subjects of civic action. Things are often done for, or about, or to, or because of Negroes, but they are less frequently done *by* Negroes" (p. 133). Broadening the base of political participation, then, has as much to do with the quality of black participation as with the quantity. We are fully aware that the black vote, especially in the North, has been pulled out of white pockets and "delivered" whenever it was in the interest of white politicians to do so. That vote must no longer be controllable by those who have neither the interests nor the demonstrated concern of black people in mind.

As the base broadens, as more and more black people become activated, they will perceive more clearly the special disadvantages heaped upon them as a group. They will perceive that the larger society is growing more affluent while the black society is retrogressing. Black people will become increasingly active as they notice that their retrogressive status exists in large measure because of values and institutions arraigned against them. They will begin to stress and strain and call the entire system into question. Political modernization will be in motion. We believe that it is now in motion. One form of that motion is Black Power.

The adoption of the concept of Black Power is one of the most legitimate and healthy developments in American politics and race relations in our time. The concept of Black Power speaks to all the needs mentioned in this chapter. It is a call for black people in this country to unite, to recognize their heritage, to build a sense of community. It is a call for black people to begin to define their own goals, to lead their own organizations and to support those organizations. It is a call to reject the racist institutions and values of this society.

The concept of Black Power rests on a fundamental premise: *Before a group can enter the open society, it must first close ranks.* By this we mean that group solidarity is necessary before a group can operate effectively from a bargaining position of strength in a pluralistic society. Traditionally, each new ethnic group in this society has found the route to social and political viability through the organization of its own institutions with which to represent its needs within the larger society. Studies in voting behavior specifically, and political behavior generally, have made it clear that politically the

American pot has not melted. Italians vote for Rubino over O'Brien; Irish for Murphy over Goldberg, etc. This phenomenon may seem distasteful to some, but it has been and remains today a central fact of the American political system.

Black people must lead and run their own organizations. Only black people can convey the revolutionary idea—and it is a revolutionary idea—that black people are able to do things themselves. Only they can help create in the community an aroused and continuing black consciousness that will provide the basis for political strength. In the past, white allies have often furthered white supremacy without the whites involved realizing it, or even wanting to do so. Black people must come together and do things for themselves. They must achieve self-identity and self-determination in order to have their daily needs met.

Black Power means, for example, that in Lowndes County, Alabama, a black sheriff can end police brutality. A black tax assessor and tax collector and county board of revenue can lay, collect, and channel tax monies for the building of better roads and schools serving black people. In such areas as Lowndes, where black people have a majority, they will attempt to use power to exercise control. This is what they seek: control. When black people lack a majority, Black Power means proper representation and sharing of control. It means the creation of power bases, of strength, from which black people can press to change local or nation-wide patterns of oppression—instead of from weakness.

It does not mean *merely* putting black faces into office. Black visibility is not Black Power. Most of the black politicians around the country today are not examples of Black Power. The power must be that of a community, and emanate from there. The black politicians must stop being representatives of "downtown" machines, whatever the cost might be in terms of lost patronage and holiday handouts.

Black Power recognizes—it must recognize—the ethnic basis of American politics as well as the power-oriented nature of American politics. Black Power therefore calls for black people to consolidate behind their own, so that they can bargain from a position of strength. But while we endorse the *procedure* of group solidarity and identity for the purpose of attaining certain goals in the body politic, this does not mean that black people should strive for the same kind of rewards (i.e., end results) obtained by the white society. The ultimate values and goals are not domination or exploitation of other groups, but rather an effective share in the total power of the society.

Nevertheless, some observers have labeled those who advocate Black Power as racists; they have said that the call for self-identification and self-determination is "racism in reverse" or "black supremacy." This is a deliberate and absurd lie. There is no analogy—by any stretch of definition or imagination—between the advocates of Black Power and white racists. Racism is not merely exclusion on the basis of race but exclusion for the purpose of subjugating or maintaining subjugation. The goal of the racists is to keep black people on the bottom, arbitrarily and dictatorially, as they have done in this country for over three hundred years. The goal of black self-determination and black self-identity—Black Power—is full participation in the decision-making processes affecting the lives of black people, and recognition of the virtues in themselves as black people. The black people of this country have not lynched whites, bombed their churches, murdered their children and manipulated laws and institutions to maintain oppression. White racists have. Congressional laws, one after the other, have not been necessary to stop black people from oppressing others and denying others the full enjoyment of their rights. White racists have made such laws necessary. The goal of Black Power is positive and functional to a free and viable society. No white racist can make this claim.

It is a commentary on the fundamentally racist nature of this society that the concept of group strength for black people must be articulated—not to mention defended. No other group would submit to being led by others. Italians do not run the Anti-Defamation League of B'nai B'rith. Irish do not chair Christopher Columbus Societies. Yet when black people call for black-run and all-black organizations, they are immediately classed in a category with the Ku Klux Klan. This is interesting and ironic, but by no means surprising: the society does not expect black people to be able to take care of their business, and there are many who prefer it precisely that way.

In the end, we cannot and shall not offer any guarantees that Black Power, if achieved, would be non-racist. No one can predict human behavior. Social change always has unanticipated consequences. If black racism is what the larger society fears, we cannot help them. We can only state what we hope will be the result, given the fact that the present situation is unacceptable and that we have no real alternative but to work for Black Power. The final truth is that the white society is not entitled to reassurances, even if it were possible to offer them.

When the concept of Black Power is set forth, many people

immediately conjure up notions of violence. The country's reaction to the Deacons for Defense and Justice, which originated in Louisiana, is instructive. Here is a group which realized that the "law" and law enforcement agencies would not protect people, so they had to do it themselves. If a nation fails to protect its citizens, then that nation cannot condemn those who take up the task themselves. The Deacons and all other blacks who resort to self-defense represent a simple answer to a simple question: what man would not defend his family and home from attack?

But this frightened some white people, because they knew that black would now fight back. They knew that this was precisely what *they* would have long since done if *they* were subjected to the injustices and oppression heaped on blacks. Those of us who advocate Black Power are quite clear in our own minds that a "non-violent" approach to civil rights is an approach black people cannot afford and a luxury white people do not deserve. It is crystal clear to us—and it must become so with the white society—*that there can be no social order without social justice*. White people must be made to understand that they must stop messing with black people, or the blacks *will* fight back.

Next, we must deal with the term "integration." According to its advocates, social justice will be accomplished by "integrating the Negro into the mainstream institutions of the society from which he has been traditionally excluded." This concept is based on the assumption that there is nothing of value in the black community and that little of value could be created among black people. The thing to do is siphon off the "acceptable" black people into the surrounding middle-class white community.

The goals of integrationists are middle-class goals, articulated primarily by a small group of Negroes with middle-class aspirations or status. Their kind of integration has meant that a few blacks "make it," leaving the black community, sapping it of leadership potential and know-how. As we noted in Chapter I, those token Negroes—absorbed into a white mass—are of no value to the remaining black masses. They become meaningless show-pieces for a conscience-soothed white society. Such people will state that they would prefer to be treated "only as individuals, not as Negroes"; that they "are not and should not be preoccupied with race." This is a totally unrealistic position. In the first place, black people have not suffered as individuals but as members of a group; therefore, their liberation lies in group action. This is why SNCC—and the concept of Black Power—affirms that helping *individual* black people to solve their problems on an *individual* basis does little to alleviate the mass of black people. Secondly, while color blindness *may* be a sound goal ultimately, we must realize that race is an overwhelming fact of life in this historical period. There is no black man in this country who can live "simply as a man." His blackness is an ever-present fact of this racist society, whether he recognizes it or not. It is unlikely that this or the next generation will witness the time when race will no longer be relevant in the conduct of public affairs and in public policy decision-making. To realize this and to attempt to deal with it does not make one a racist or overly preoccupied with race; it puts one in the forefront of a significant *struggle*. If there is no intense struggle today, there will be no meaningful results tomorrow.

"Integration" as a goal today speaks to the problem of blackness not only in an unrealistic way but also in a despicable way. It is based on complete acceptance of the fact that in order to have a decent house or education, black people must move into a white neighborhood or send their children to a white school. This reinforces, among both black and white, the idea that "white" is automatically superior and "black" is by definition inferior. For this reason, "integration" is a subterfuge for the maintenance of white supremacy. It allows the nation to focus on a handful of Southern black children who get into white schools at a great price, and to ignore the ninety-four percent who are left in unimproved all-black schools. Such situations will not change until black people become equal in a way that means something, and integration ceases to be a one-way street. Then integration does not mean draining skill and energies from the black ghetto into white neighborhoods. To sprinkle black children among white pupils in outlying schools is at best a stop-gap measure. The goal is not to take black children out of the black community and expose them to white middle-class values; the goal is to build and strengthen the black community.

"Integration" also means that black people must give up their identity, deny their heritage. We recall the conclusion of Killian and Grigg: "At the present time, integration as a solution to the race problem demands that the Negro foreswear his identity as a Negro." The fact is that integration, as traditionally articulated, would abolish the black community. The fact is that what must be abolished is not the black community, but the dependent colonial status that has been inflicted upon it.

The racial and cultural personality of the black community

must be preserved and that community must win its freedom while preserving its cultural integrity. Integrity includes a pride—in the sense of self-acceptance, not chauvinism—in being black, in the historical attainments and contributions of black people. No person can be healthy, complete and mature if he must deny a part of himself; this is what "integration" has required thus far. This is the essential difference between integration as it is currently practiced and the concept of Black Power.

Discussion and Study Questions

1. Why does liberation, according to Carmichael, lie in group action rather than in individual achievement? How workable, in your opinion, are the "power bases" which Carmichael advocates for black communities?

2. On what basis does Clark feel the concept of black power is fatalistic and generally self-defeating? How would Carmichael disagree with Clark on the racist implications of black power?

3. According to Jones, how have the black bourgeois contributed to tokenism?

4. Discuss the relationship between the views of Jones and Farmer with regard to white liberals.

5. Why is the acquisition of land so important to the development of black national consciousness for McKissick, Elijah Muhammad, and others? Why does Innis reject the return to rural centers advocated by some in favor of development in urban centers or ghettos?

6. What are Elijah Muhammad's objections to Christianity? How does Jones' idea of white Christianity's role in early black enslavement concur with Elijah Muhammad's point of view?

7. Compare and contrast the self-help concept as discussed by Elijah Muhammad and Washington.

8. What is the position of Malcolm X with regard to a black-white coalition?

9. "Message to the Grass Roots" was Malcolm's last speech before leaving the Muslims. Can you see any evidence of

his increasing estrangement from them? For example, how does his approach to the land question differ from Elijah Muhammad's?

10. In light of these essays, why should one consider self-awareness a prerequisite to self-determination?

Education

Education

One of the underlying factors in the second-class status of the Black Man is his inferior education, for in any enslaved people ignorance is a prerequisite for their oppression. For this reason, education is the focal point of emphasis for the spokesmen and essays included in this section. While most realize that education is not the sole solution to the plight of black people, they perceive it as being fundamental to combating the evils of injustice encountered by Blacks in their daily lives. Consequently, these essays reflect much concern about the relevancy of the education to which Blacks are subjected. In some essays, the emphasis is on abolishing discriminatory education through integrated schools; others suggest that a truly meaningful education is attainable only through separate, black-controlled community schools. In almost all of the essays there is a call for a redirection of education. It should be transformed by black people and from a black perspective to combat the severe deprivation which is being inflicted upon the masses of black people. On the whole, the essays reflect a dire need for an education which is more oriented to the total reality of black life.

In addition to recognizing the importance of acquiring basic educational skills, the more militant spokesmen are concerned about the process of learning and the quality of thinking that is being developed. Many of them also see education as being intimately related to the political realities of black life. Thus, while the concern about black education is consensual, the analysis of this dilemma and the programs espoused are varied.

Clark's essay, for example, points out that the civil rights legislation of 1954 has led to faulty rationalization and procedures for educating Blacks. The essays by Wilkins and Hare offer contrasting notions of black academic separatism in terms of the proper perspective from which black studies curricula should be viewed. Farmer acknowledges the inferior quality of education for blacks in the inner cities and calls for greater community control and participation in school affairs. Karenga proposes specific programs and strategies for black students in white colleges. He, as Hare, sees the need for attaining psychological independence through separate black curricula within white universities. Powell's essay is significant in this section because it is an appeal to college students to use their education to work for the betterment of black people. He urges them to serve as a vanguard unit in the enlightenment and education of the black masses.

Fifteen Years of Deliberate Speed*

By KENNETH B. CLARK

The history of civil rights litigation in state and federal courts up to the *Brown* decision of 1954 can be understood in terms of a basic struggle, dating back to the *Dred Scott* decision of 1857, to determine the social and judicial perception of the Negro, to determine how the Negro is to be perceived and treated in relation to the treatment of other human beings within the framework of American democracy.

The underlying problem was that the Negro was regarded as semi-human or in some subtle way as sub-human; and as not only different, but different and inferior. The common denominator of *Dred Scott, Plessy vs. Ferguson,* and almost all related court decisions up to *Brown* was that the Negro in some way was special and inherently unworthy of the rights white American citizens would be expected to have without question and without litigation. Indeed, the fact that the Negro was required to persist in seeking judicial determination of his rights was, in itself, indicative of the basic racist reality of the society of which he was a part.

Therefore, the May 31, 1955, implementing decision of the Supreme Court in *Brown,* which enunciated a policy of guidance to the states for carrying out the *Brown* mandate to desegregate public schools "with all deliberate speed," was a conscious effort to make fundamental social change less disruptive. The court, in seeking to facilitate a rational and orderly transition from a system of segregation to one of nonsegregated schools, asked that such criteria as "local conditions" be considered. It was clear that in this decision the court was stepping outside the limited role of determining the constitutionality of segregation and was assuming the

*Reprinted from *Saturday Review,* LII (December, 1969), pp. 59–61. By permission of Saturday Review, Inc., and the author.

more complex role of establishing guidelines for administrative and social change.

Some observers interpreted this decision—with some justification—as the court's accepting the gradualist approach as means for effective desegregation. In retrospect, the "deliberate speed" formula seems a serious error to many, including Supreme Court Justice Hugo Black, who criticized the court in a 1968 statement. In practice it seems to have led to more rather than to less disruption. Here, court reliance on social science evidence would have been useful, for students of social change have observed that prompt, decisive action on the part of recognized authorities usually results in less anxiety and less resistance in cases where the public is opposed to the action than does a more hesitant and gradual procedure. It is similar to the effect of quickly pulling off adhesive tape—the pain is sharper but briefer, and hence more tolerable.

The essential questions faced by the Supreme Court were not questions of legal precedent, historical in nature, but questions relating to the social consequences of legally imposed segregation. Without such evidence, the court could only speculate about the probable damage caused by the violation of Constitutional rights implicit in segregated education. The social scientists testified concerning the damage inherent in the total pattern of segregation on the human personality. On the basis of their testimony, the court held that separate educational facilities are inherently unequal by virtue of being separate. By providing such evidence, the social scientists made it possible to avoid the need to obtain proof of individual damage, and to avoid assessment of the equality of facilities in each individual school situation. The assumption of inequality could now be made wherever segregation existed.

However, in doing so, the court, which appeared to rely on the findings of social scientists in the 1954 decision, rejected the findings in handing down the 1955 implementation decision. An empirical study of various forms and techniques of desegregation suggested that the gradual approach to desegregation did not increase its chances of success or effectiveness. The findings further suggested that forthright, direct desegregation within the minimum time required for the necessary administrative changes tended to facilitate the process. Gradualism or any form of ambiguity and equivocation on the part of those with the power of decision was interpreted by the segregationists as indecision, provided them with the basis for increasing resistance, and gave them time to organize, intensify, and prolong their opposition. The pattern of massive resistance and sporadic, violent opposition to desegregation occurred after the 1955 decision. There is no evidence that a more direct, specific, and concrete implementation decree would have resulted in any more tension, procrastination, or evasion than the seemingly rational, statesmanlike deliberate speed decision of the court. It does not seem likely that the pace of public school desegregation could have been slower.

The results of "all deliberate speed" have been ironic and tragic. In the South, where, admittedly, American racism was most violent, primitive, and deeply rooted, progress could be substantial and still leave a racist society fundamentally untouched. After *Brown,* a number of Southern states developed and tested strategies of resistance to the court decision. Massive resistance of interposition was resorted to in defiance of the court, and the degree of integration in elementary and secondary schools has been minimal. Nevertheless, the South has accepted or initiated more overt changes than the North. In fact, the South can look at the North with a certain ironic condescension in terms of the acceptance of rapid change toward a non-racist society.

The North, for its part, did not think the *Brown* decision applied to its schools. The North had joined earlier in the Negro reaction against Southern resistance to change. Now it became clear that racism was also virulent in the North, all the more insidious for its having been long unrecognized. Even Negroes had not consciously acknowledged the depth of racism inherent in Northern society. And when the North discovered its racism, it tended to provide justification for it. In addition, in the academic community, it began to be clear in the 1960s that apparently sophisticated and compassionate theories used to explain slow Negro student performance might themselves be tainted with racist condescension. Some of the theories of "cultural deprivation," "the disadvantaged," and the like, popular in educational circles and in high governmental spheres until recently and in fact still prevalent, were backed for the most part by inconclusive and fragmentary research and much speculation. The eagerness with which such theories were greeted was itself a subtly racist symptom.

The cultural deprivation theory rejects explanations of inherent racial or biological inferiority, and asserts that the total pattern of racial prejudice, discrimination, and segregation found in a racist society blocks the capacity of school personnel to teach minority group children with the same observable efficiency as that given other children. These children may, therefore, be expected to remain academically retarded no matter how well they are taught. Among the specific barriers emphasized by different writers in varying degrees are: environmentally determined sensory deficiencies; withdrawn or hyperactive behavior; low attention span; peculiar or bizarre language patterns; lack of verbal stimulation; absence of father or stable male figure in the home; and lack of books in the home.

In spite of the fact that these factors have dominated the literature and have been frequently repeated and generally accepted as explanations of the academic retardation of lower status children, they have not been verified as causal factors through any precise and systematic research reported in the published literature. The evidence, or indeed lack of evidence, suggests, therefore, that this concept has gained acceptance through intuition, general impressions, and repetition.

Nevertheless, cultural deprivation theorists have not only provided the public school educational establishment with a respectable rationalization for maintaining the status quo of educational inefficiency for low status children, but the related technology of this theory—compensatory or educational enrichment programs—appears to provide the basis for inherent contradictions in its premises and assumptions.

An uncritical acceptance of this theory and explanation seems to be contradicted by:

(1) the concretely demonstrated psychological fact of the normal curve in the distribution of human intellectual potential, personality characteristics, motivation, and other personal characteristics believed to be related to academic performance;

(2) the modifiableness of human beings;

(3) the fact that normal human beings who are taught, motivated to learn, expected to learn, and provided with conditions conducive to learning, will learn up to or near the limits of their capacity.

Furthermore, the cultural deprivation theories are clear violations of the law of parsimony, since they seek more complex explanations without determining that simpler explanations are not adequate. Cultural deprivation theories appear to by-pass more direct and specific educational variables such as quality of teaching and supervision, acceptance or rejection of the students by teachers, and educational methods and facilities.

Given the history of educational rejection of Negro children, it would seem obvious to one trained in the methods of science that much more direct variables would have to be held constant and checked out with more precision and more sensitive instruments than the Colemen report [*Equality of Educational Opportunity,* by James Coleman]* does before one could resort to the more elaborate, ambiguous, and seemingly uncontrollable catchall variable of cultural deprivation. In this regard it is significant that the literature, while eloquent and repetitive in its expansion of the cultural deprivation hypothesis, is almost totally silent on discussions or research that seek to determine the relationship between subtle or flagrant rejection of a child by his teachers because of race, color, economic status and family income, and the level of his academic performance. These social, psychological, and educational variables seem worthy of a serious attention and research that they have not as yet received.

Theories of cultural deprivation are often regarded as liberal, because they posit environmental inadequacy rather than genetic inferiority, and because they are often used to support demands for integration. The problem with this approach, exemplified by the Coleman report, is that it concludes that the environmentally caused characteristics of white children are the positive component of integrated schools, and that Negro children educationally gain primarily from association with white children.

Further research is necessary to determine whether correlation and causal factors have been confused in this important study. But perhaps most important, it is necessary to study the majority white school as a total unit as compared to the majority Negro school, to determine what happens in the school itself *because* white children are present. Sensitive instruments must be sought to measure teacher and administrative expectations, counseling attitudes, quality of curriculum, and the like, but beyond the assessment of these individual factors it is necessary to evaluate the total pattern of advantage or deprivation.

On the basis of years of observation and research of ghetto education, I would advance the proposition that one would find a significantly high correlation between a pattern of deprivation and ghetto schools, and a pattern of advantage and white urban and suburban schools. It is not the presence of the white child per se that leads to higher achievement for the Negro child who associates with him in class; it is the quality of the education provided because the white child is there that

* The Coleman report is a survey carried out by The National Center for Educational Statistics of the U.S. Office of Education, published in 1966.

makes the difference, or so I believe the empirical evidence indicates. To argue, without irrefutable proof, that this is not the case is to lend support to a racially defined environmental theory of academic achievement that is no less callous in its consequences than a genetic theory of racial inferiority would be.

Perhaps the most ironic development since the 1954 *Brown* decision, however, has not been the continuation of white racism in the South, nor the acknowledgment of the more subtle white racism of the North, but the emergence and growth of black racism. In 1954, when the *Brown* decision was handed down, desegregation and integration were the priority of the civil rights movement and Negroes generally. Fifteen years later, many militants have proclaimed the death of the civil rights movement and have denied the value of integration itself, and specifically have questioned the significance of the *Brown* decision and the truth of the social science findings on which it rested. One must thus look at the decision and its social science foundation for a new perspective, and inquire whether these charges are justified.

During the period since 1954, black nationalism has experienced a sharp rise in support from young Negro militants and from many whites. This represents in some forms the continuation of the nationalism of the Garvey movement of the 1920s, identifiable in degree by the black nationalism of Malcolm X. In other, and more serious, manifestations it has gained support among Negro students and youth. The seeming common denomination of both is the repudiation of integration and the apparent repudiation of the struggle for desegregation, the rejection of the *Brown* decision, and the implicit rejection of the whole rationale and psychological approach to the meaning of racism. This would logically include a denial of the social science explanation of the inevitability of inferiority in segregated systems, on which the *Brown* decision depended.

Under the guise of assuming a positive identity, black nationalism has adopted an imitation of white racism with its hallowing of race, its attempt to make a virtue out of color, its racist mystique. This rationale argues that the detrimental consequences of a bi-racial society are neutralized or transformed into positive consequences by virtue of the fact that Negroes themselves are now asserting the value of racism. This argument would give primary weight to voluntarism, that is, that racism would lead to affirmative not negative results if it were voluntarily accepted or sought by the previous victims, as it was voluntarily maintained by the oppressors.

The character of racism would depend on the attitude one had toward it; it would have no objective reality of its own.

The paranoia of racism, whether imposed or sought, must rest on insecurity. It is the verification of the psychological interpretation of the negative consequences of segregation. Racism does produce doubts and insecurities in the victims as well as in the perpetrators. It increases hostility and aggression and self-hatred.

The Lorelei quest for identity through racism is based on superstition. Despite the verbal transformation from self-contempt to apparent pride, the conditions of injustice remain. We are asked to obscure them by the rhetorical posturing of pride. In a strikingly similar analogy, it is psychologically obvious that any man who proclaims how irresistible and potent and virile he is must have deep doubts about it. He would clearly be regarded as preoccupied with sexual anxiety. Such self-pretense conceals—or attempts to conceal—deep, poignant, and tragic insecurity. Given the fact that the realities of racism in America have not changed, that the Negro is still condemned to segregated schools, to segregated and deteriorated residential areas, and to an economic role that is not competitive with the white society, the cult of blackness must be recognized as what it is—a ritualized denial of anguished despair and resentment of the failure of society to meet its promises.

Separatism is an attempt to create verbal realities as substitutes for social, political, and economic realities. It is another and intense symptom of the psychological damage a racist society inflicts on its victims.

A specific indication of the damage of separatism is that the victims internalize racism. Some forms of black separatism involve genuine and deep self-destructive, suicidal dynamics. They reflect the most cruel, barbaric, tragic, dehumanizing consequences of white oppression—the wish of the oppressed to die—and in dying to destroy others in a similar predicament. The white racists who so damage their fellow human beings must be prepared to face the same judgment the Nazis, who sent millions to death camps, must face.

Responding to a button reading "Being Black Is Not Enough," some Negroes have said, "Well, being white has always been enough." But if one looks at the moral decay, the instability, and the unresolved problems of white society, one perceives that being white is not enough, that it is effective only in terms of self-aggrandizement and at the expense of exploitation of those who are not white. Its success depends on victimization, for racism is not only subjective, it also demands an object. Positive racism has the necessary obverse of rejection of all those who do not happen to meet the chosen racial criteria.

So, rather than refute the social science assumptions that led to the *Brown* decision, the present cult of black separatism intensely verifies it. Black separatism can be seen as a "sour-grapes-and-sweet-lemon" reaction against the failure of the society to implement and enforce the findings of *Brown*.

The vocal, well-publicized, well-endowed cult has to be understood for what it is, for otherwise it can be cynically manipulated and used by white racists who are now the often silent allies of the separatists. The rationale of the sophisticated white intellectual who endorses black separatism in his university, his church, his political party, his academic or professional society, while continuing to live in a restricted suburb and continuing to support the institutional relegation of Negroes to inferior status, must be seen by Negroes for what it is: an attempt to handle racial antiviolence, to deal with guilt.

The basic standard for such understanding is that which functioned in the *Brown* decision, namely that racism and segregation are a reflection of superstition, institutionalized untruth, cruelty, and injustice, and that race is irrelevant as a criterion for preference or rejection. The poignant tragedy is that the society is using the victimized groups as the agent for the perpetuation of irreconcilable injustice and racial irrelevance. Any white or black intellectual who denies this must be more comfortable with superstition and rationalization. One cannot deal with the reorganization of society on a nonracial basis by intensifying racist symptoms.

Nor can one build a solid pride on the quicksands of emotion, anger, rage, hatred—no matter how justifiable. Genuine pride—the pride that makes life worth the struggle with some hope of serenity—must come from solid personal achievement, from sensitivity and concern and respect for one's fellow man, from compassion and willingness to struggle to give some substance to one's own life by trying to help others live with confidence in the possibility of positives. Pride, like humility, is destroyed by one's insistence that he possesses it.

Racism in any form is dangerous, but particularly, as is now true among many whites and Negroes, when it is intellectually supported. Such supporters often fail to follow the implication of their rhetoric to its logical conclusion: that, if segregation and separatism are desirable and good as a phase and as a means, they are even more to be desired as ends in themselves.

All the implications of the *Brown* decision and all the social science arguments in its support point to the inherent dangers of racism. The latest surge toward self-imposed separatism is the greatest verification of all. I read into the separatist movement among Negroes a more severe symptom than those described in *Brown*. It convinces me even more persuasively that we must redouble our efforts to obliterate racism, whatever its manifestations, wherever it appears.

ROY WILKINS,

NAACP Executive Director

One measure of the black man's progress in the face of discrimination can be seen in Roy Wilkins' movement from his birth in St. Louis, as the grandson of a Mississippi slave, to a childhood in an integrated neighborhood of working class people in St. Paul, Minnesota, to his present position of executive director of NAACP and a leading spokesman and writer for that faction of the black movement which advocates nonviolent approaches to fighting racism.

Having worked his way through the University of Minnesota with numerous jobs, Wilkins became a reporter, upon graduation in 1923, for the Kansas City Call, a Negro weekly. From this vantage point, he was able to see first hand many of the conditions of poor housing, Jim Crow laws, police brutality, and other injustices that he and the NAACP have fought so vigorously through the years. Under Wilkins, NAACP has achieved many victories for the blacks. Wilkins' first campaigns were against lynching in the 1950s, against school segregation in the Brown case of 1954, and the March on Washington in 1963. A commanding though soft-spoken man, Wilkins has used as his chief weapons, boycotts, publicizing injustices through news media, and fighting through the Senate and the courts.

"NO MATTER HOW ENDLESSLY THEY TRY TO EXPLAIN IT, THE TERM 'BLACK POWER' MEANS ANTI-WHITE POWER."

The Case Against Separatism: "Black Jim Crow"*

In the 1920s in Kansas City, Missouri, I learned a lesson that I never forgot. It has come home to me forcibly these past twelve months in the demands of 1968–69 college students for autonomous black units on some of their campuses. A Kansas City school-bond issue for the then racially segregated town provided $985,000 to build an athletic plant and field for a junior high school for white students—and $27,500 to convert a factory building into an elementary school for black children.

This was the ugly face of segregated education. The system must not be revived. It must not be invited back at the request, nay, the ultimatum of black students themselves.

No person who has watched the halting march of Negro civil rights through the years can fail to sympathize with the frustrations and anger of today's black students. In their hurt pride in themselves and in their outrage, they have called retreat from the tough and trying battle of a minority for dignity and equality. They don't call it a retreat, of course. They renounce "white middle class values" so they can refuse logically to be judged by the standards of the times and of the place they live in. Every black dissenter is an Uncle Tom and every white one a racist. Vituperation, not reason, is invoked.

Racial Breast-Beating

They say they need to get together in their own dormitories to build a common strength. After they are strong and sure of

* Reprinted from *Newsweek*, LXXIII (February 10, 1969). By permission of Newsweek, Inc., and the author

themselves they will be able to meet other groups as true equals.

Who can declare them completely wrong? Certainly, they are right about the strength that comes from being with their brothers. Certainly they are right about the usefulness of a study of Afro-American history and culture. They are right, also, in calling for increased enrollment of Negro students and in requesting more black faculty members. But in demanding a black Jim Crow studies building within a campus and exclusively black dormitories or wings of dormitories, they are opening the door to a dungeon. They do not see that no black history becomes significant and meaningful unless it is taught in the context of world and national history. In its sealed-off, black-studies centers, it will be simply another exercise in racial breast-beating.

Abdication

To oppose black academic separatism is not to ignore black youth or to be unmindful of the spirit displayed by so many of them. They must be heard and they are heard; I have talked on numerous occasions with student groups, some members of which were not Wilkins cheerleaders. But it would be an abdication of responsibility, to them and to those who will follow us both, to acquiesce in a course which we know to be wrong, solely to avoid their criticism.

The key word in the current spate of similarly worded demands of black students is "autonomous." No university administration faithful to its trust can grant this. There is substantial informed opinion that tax money cannot be used to set up racial enclaves within campuses. I am sure that sooner or later a court test would arise. And all this is apart from the practical difficulty that it costs more money to establish real studies centers than most colleges can afford and that the qualified personnel—black or white—is simply not available at this time.

The demanding students might well find themselves saddled with a poor substitute for a center, foisted on them by an administration ready to buy peace at any price. Thus would segregated education once more run true to form.

An alternative with good chances of success would be to concentrate as a beginning on two centers of genuine stature, one on the East Coast and one on the West. The financing and staffing of two such university-based institutes would not be an impossible task, and they would draw not only on their own resident scholars but on exchange and visiting personnel as well. Meanwhile, valid courses in Afro-American history and culture should be established at all good colleges and universities to the extent that qualified faculty, black or white, can be found. Also, it should be the immediate task of every school claiming to be a school to provide an extensive library on the Negro past and present, in Africa, and in the New World.

Incidentally, the familiar "reading course" should not be disdained; after all, my generation had no "black-studies" curriculum—but we found ways to learn about ourselves and our past.

The Case for Separatism: "Black Perspective"*

By NATHAN HARE, Jr.

"Appalling" is the only word I know that begins to describe the sneaky way in which critics like Roy Wilkins accuse us of "separatism." Our cries for more black professors and black students have padded white colleges with more blacks in two years than decades of whimpering for "integration" ever did.

We blacks at white colleges remain associated with racists physically, although we seek social and psychological independence from their oppression. The Amos 'n' Andy administrators at Negro colleges, by contrast, are physically separated but accommodated to their dependence on white racism as well as the establishment's remote control of their black destiny.

Blacks who teach at white colleges have argued long and bitterly over course content and instructor assignments with white departmental chairmen of various shades of racist persuasions. They would rather have a white moderate professor with a Ph.D. teaching a history sequence starkly barren of blackness than a black man without a degree who has spent long hours in research on the subject. They hold up the white Ph.D.'s publications in learned journals, unmindful of the fact that a black man doing research, for example, on the slavery era in "learned journals" is obliged to footnote slave-master historians or historians acceptable to a society which then condoned black slavery. Second-rate colleges require black persons with functionally white minds, using the Ph.D. as one

* Reprinted from *Newsweek*, LXXIII (February 10, 1969). By permission of Newsweek, Inc., and the author.

tested means of policing that policy, yet at the same time, first-class universities think nothing of hiring an unschooled Eric Hoffer, who now holds forth at Berkeley.

With regard to course content, the white aim is mainly to black out the black perspective. White professors at universities such as Yale will dust off old courses in race relations and African tribalism for what might be called a polkadot studies program, while Negro professors will trot out their old courses in Negro history and Negro music for Negro-studies courses which they cynically call black. If all a black-studies program needs is a professor with a black skin to prattle about Negro subject matter, then our Negro schools would never have failed so painfully as they have.

In the search for educational relevance, black today is revolutionary and nationalistic. A black-studies program which is not revolutionary and nationalistic is, accordingly, quite profoundly irrelevant. The black revolutionary nationalist, aware and proud of his blackness, demands the right to exist as a distinct category, to be elevated as such by any means necessary. The Negro, contrarily, would just as soon be white. He longs to escape his blackness and, in the search for integration achieves disintegration.

Thus, the key to the difference between a black-studies program and a Negro-studies program is a black perspective. Black students are descendants of a people cut off from their attachment to land, culture and nation (or people-hood). This condition is aggravated further by a whitewashed education. The expressive phase of the black-studies program is designed to regenerate the mortified ego of the black child. For instance, a proud black history can restore and construct a sense of pastness, of collective destiny, as a springboard to the quest for a new collective future. For black children crippled by defeatist attitudes, hardened by generations of exclusion, this is potentially therapeutic.

Pragmatic Component

At the same time, we must resist the white perspective which seeks to restrict black studies to the stereotyped study of art and religion predominantly. Black studies should comprise a comprehensive, integrated body of interdisciplinary courses just as in the case of long-established departments of social science and American studies. There is a desperate need for a pragmatic component which focuses on the applied fields of knowledge such as economics.

Many will argue that science and mathematics are "pure" subjects; though that may be true in a sense, the uses of science may be directed toward atomic weapons of destruction or, in the case of a community-oriented black studies, devoted to such matters as rat control.

I can visualize, for instance, a reading problem in "black" mathematics that would not be saturated with middle-class referents such as stocks and bonds. Rather, the teacher might ask in order to whet the ghetto child's appetite for math: "If you loot one store and burn two, how many do you have left?" The example might be improved; but there is no substitute for a black perspective based on the principle of self-control.

Education Is the Answer*

By JAMES L. FARMER

No issue confronting the nation today is more critical than the problem of improving the quality of education in our inner cities, particularly the quality of education we offer our ghetto youngsters, the poor and the deprived.

In the decade between 1954 and 1964, we in the civil rights movement won what appeared at the time to be many significant victories. Despite all the drama of the years following the U.S. Supreme Court decision on school desegregation, however, the life condition of the average black person or, for that matter, of the average poor person has not changed.

The original focus of our movement was to get rid of segregation. We succeeded in breaking down some barriers: The lot of blacks lucky enough to be in the middle classes has now improved, and the black college graduate has an infinitely easier time getting a good job now than he had a few years ago. But for every 10 of the educated blacks who walk through the front doors to new, untraditional jobs, more than 100 undereducated ones are running out the back. Segregation itself has actually been increasing as more whites have fled to the suburbs, leaving the inner cities blacker than ever.

Our efforts at desegregation have provided, at best, only a partial solution. Many of us realize now that we didn't focus on the real problem, but others do not.

"I am absolutely baffled," an old friend, a black man, said to me the other day. "A few years ago you so-called civil rights leaders told us that the most militant and progressive and meaningful thing we could do was to integrate the lily white suburbs. My wife and I took the bull by the horns and bought a split-level house in Gorgeous Gardens. We mowed the lawn

* Reprinted from *Today's Education*, LVIII (April, 1969), pp. 25-26. By permission of NEA and the author.

and we faced all the gaff—the burning crosses and the isolation—and now we have overcome. We are accepted by our neighbors. They invite us for cocktails and we have them over for tea. And so now our old friends call us Uncle Toms for living out there with all those white folks."

What put my friend into his predicament is that what we thought to be adequate answers to our problems several years ago have now proved to be obsolete and archaic. The real problem that confronts us today is that the poor are not being educated, and without education, any talk about political or economic power is idiocy.

At Bedford-Stuyvesant in Brooklyn, for example, only one-third of the youngsters who start to high school graduate, and 87 percent of that one-third come out with a meaningless piece of paper called the general diploma. A kid grabs his general diploma thinking, I've served my time and now I'm going to make it. Then he goes downtown to get a job and isn't even capable of filling out an application blank.

I believe that examples of this kind of horrifying waste are proof that inner-city education must change. Our responsibility in education is not merely to provide access to knowledge. It is not merely to provide the package of learning and put it before the youngsters. The real job is to see that they take the package and come out educated people. We are not doing the job. The methods, materials, and curriculums that are geared to educate middle-class white youngsters simply do not work with those who are neither white nor middle-class.

Teachers need to be specially trained to work in ghetto schools. Many teachers going into such schools today are lost. They recognize that Johnny is insolent, but not that he may be insolent because he had no breakfast. If Suzy falls asleep, they think it is because she is dull, never dreaming that her home is a one-room flat where she can't get enough rest. I think that it is essential for teachers to be familiar with the life style of their students and with their home conditions. I suggest that as part of a teacher's education he should have to spend an internship in the community where he is going to teach, learning ghetto ways and ghetto language.

Not only do ghetto schools need specially trained teachers, they need special curriculums; those planned for middle-class white youngsters lack relevance in the inner city. The children of the poor need to develop pride and dignity and self-esteem in the course of becoming educated.

As one means to this end, the schools need to introduce programs of ethnic studies. As another, I believe that textbooks should be revised to include discussion of the contributions minorities have made and that special courses should teach the histories of minorities. One tragedy of the minorities is that history courses have generally ignored their history. Black and white students alike should have the chance to see black men as a proud and equal cultural entity, fitting in with other ethnic entities that go to make up the American pluralistic culture.

Finally, I believe that the schools have the responsibility to try to make up for some of the deficiencies in the community and the home. For instance, the schools should provide study space and study hours for children who have no place to do schoolwork at home. They should put in as many compensatory facilities as possible to make up for things that are missing at home.

Thanks to the antipoverty program, the poor, formerly silent and invisible, have gained voice and visibility. These people have reached the point where they consider the education of their children the most vital issue affecting them. They are determined to have their youngsters receive a better start in life and better training to cope with the problems of living in our society than they, the parents, have had. This determination is responsible for the most significant social thrust in this country at the present time—the demand that control of inner-city schools be in the hands of inner-city residents.

The demand is reasonable—suburban communities have this kind of control—and I urge the nation's educators to respect it and to help these people share constructively in educational decision making for their children.

In the past, school-related decisions have been made primarily by two parties—management, as represented by the boards of educations, and employees, as represented by teachers. Now a third party, consumers, as represented by community residents, is asking to participate in decision making. Since the consumers' prime interest is in the quality of the product, I believe that it is in the teacher organizations' own best interest to help community residents to organize and participate in decision making.

If proper guidelines are established to protect the rights of teachers as employees, I believe that community participation in decision making will speed the day when the relationship between school and community will not be a hostile, adversary one, but a happy, cooperative partnership in the exciting adventure of educating youngsters.

MAULANA RON KARENGA,

Organizer, Teacher

Ron Karenga is a man of many talents. He is intelligent, witty, and he has the ability to communicate truly to blacks.
Karenga was born July 14, 1941, in Maryland. He now lives in Los Angeles with his wife and children.

He attended the University of California, Los Angeles, and was graduated cum laude. He has a master's degree and is working toward a doctorate in political science. In addition to these educational accomplishments, he has been employed as a social worker and has lectured on numerous topics such as urban problems and African history. He has also served as an instructor of Swahili. He also reads Spanish and French and is studying other languages. In 1965, shortly after the Watts riot, he founded US, a black nationalist cultural organization. One of Karenga's primary concerns is achieving unity among black people.

"TO CIVILIZE IS THE UNIVERSITY'S FIRST REAL DUTY...."

The Black Community and the University: A Community Organizer's Perspective*

I would like to start off by saying something that is not as academic as it is relevant, and that is: *All praise is due to black people.*

I came here in the dark, in a sense, because I didn't know who I was going to be talking to. But whether I talk to blacks or whites, somehow whites always tend to get the message. Now, when I say that all praise is due to black people, that suggests the scope and content of what I'm going to say tonight. I'm not as impressed with academic distinctions as I am with concrete programs that might better the lives of black people in this country. My first commitment emotionally is to black people; everything that I do, think, or say is intended for their benefit; and I would sacrifice the discussion of philosophy for the satisfaction of any concrete need.

Now, my title is a bit long—I've almost forgotten what it was—but I suppose the question really is whether or not white universities have anything to offer black communities. That's a good question. If they do have something to offer, what is their role? That is also a good question. I see no difference between white universities and white people; and we have three roles for white people as well as for white universities. For the sake of academic courtesy I suppose I should offer them as a "syndrome." There are three things: nonintervention, foreign aid, and civilizing committees.

What is nonintervention? What you have to understand is that you cannot intervene in the black community. You don't

*Reprinted from *Black Studies in the University*, 1969. By permission of Yale University Press and the author.

really have any role in the community; your basic role is outside the community, external to it. And you also have to understand that the university is not basically an educational institution—it's a *political* institution. Everything moves in terms of political power, because without that power nothing is accomplished. The educational institution has traditionally been, and is now, one of the institutions that the power structure maintains, in order to reinforce its own position. One learns to be a "better American," I assume, by going to an American university; where else could one learn to be a better American than in a university? What you have to understand is that you should not fool yourselves by thinking that education is an academic thing; it is basically a political thing, and it provides identity, purpose, and direction within an American context.

If you are a white institution, for example, and blacks come in here, then the blacks come out "white," too, unless they have some different identity, purpose, and direction to shield them from all of this. The only relevance I see for a white institution in terms of blacks is for learning technical skills; there is little else that whites can teach them. As far as the humanities and the social sciences are concerned, white people have little or nothing to offer.

I suppose I should like to be challenged—I prefer a debate to assertions in situations like this, if for no other reason than the convenience of conversation—so let me briefly recapitulate what I was saying. It can be summed up in a sentence: the white university is not primarily an educational institution but a political one, and it seeks to maintain the power base of American society. All those people who go to work for the CIA, for the government at large, for big industry (which is government, in a sense) come from the universities. What you are doing here, really, is trying to find out how you can stop intervening in black people's affairs.

The experiment of Columbia University in terms of black people's affairs is very relevant here. That was an intervention in the community. We say that we are another country—you have to accept that. We are a colony ruled by a mother country—that's the outside world—we live in another world. What we have to do, then, is to try desperately to keep the outside world from imposing its authority and its value system upon us. Its values are communicated best through its university system. And again, the first thing I would propose for a university is nonintervention—nonintervention in terms of political intervention, that is—not taking over things in the black community, tearing down buildings and putting up your things.

Now, of course, when I say these things I am not petitioning you and asking you. I am doing this simply for the sake of conversation—because I suppose I owe it. I don't believe we should ask you not to do this; I believe that we should build enough power to *stop* you from doing this. But I am just identifying your actions now; I am not dealing with the matter of how we should *curtail* them.

Nonintervention also means that you should not try to control those bodies in the black communities that would create for black people what similar bodies in white communities create for white people. You have to realize that you cannot make decisions for us any more. If we are going to be a free people and gain the identity, purpose, and direction which will let us be black people, we cannot be under external influences from white people.

The second thing that you could do—and I suppose must do—is to provide "foreign aid." If we are "another country," then certainly you are "foreigners." Now, that aid should be broken down into two parts: financial aid, which is self-explanatory; and technical aid, which might need some explanation. Financial aid has to do with the money that you have collected. The university is a financial institution of sorts; it has access to money that other people don't have. Now, if one is really going to do something for his country—not for us, but for his community, for the community around him, which is closing in on him, he thinks—then it would seem politically expedient, not out of love of humanity or black people, *not* to take a tape recorder, put on tennis shoes, grow a beard, and go into a community to "investigate," and produce another study that only bores you by its length, and does not inform you by its content. *Stop* things like that, and *make* those financial contributions—contributions that are really reparations. Such a relationship would involve our having the financial institutions to receive that money—and there's that first point again, of nonintervention. What white universities usually do is "set up projects." By controlling the finances of such projects they control at the same time the political allegiances of the people in the institution. Again, I repeat, universities are political institutions. They would not *exist* unless they went along with the political climate in the country or in the region where they are functioning. So the first thing under "foreign aid" is financial aid, without strings.

The second thing is technical aid—technical aid in terms of research. White people have an affinity for research. Research bores me—statistics and collecting. I don't have the "pack rat mentality" that I've noticed in others. Yet the university has always been a framework in which people could do this type of thing, do research. Do your research and produce your research—so that black people can take it and use it to their own advantage. But the research should be done without interpretation. Data should be collected and turned over. It should not be interpreted, for when it is interpreted, it becomes of use to you only. But it could be technical aid, in terms of the ways and means that black people might better themselves, if they had certain data not available to them now.

The last thing—and this is really the most important thing, because white people are not going to give up anything that is not to their own advantage—is a civilizing committee. Perhaps that's a harsh word, but I didn't come here to please people; I came to inform them. We have witnessed the phenomenal way in which white people have tried to civilize us for 450 years when it was they, I suppose—and the "I suppose" is for social courtesy—who were uncivilized. To civilize is the university's first real duty, and the strength of your duty would depend on how you communicated a *new* ideology to the people outside of the university, or perhaps even to some instructors and administrators within the university.

Actually, I was trying to keep you university people out of this, so that you could just do the "humanitarian" thing that I suppose you believe you would like to do. Universities always like to think of themselves as liberal institutions, humanitarian institutions; they even teach subjects under what they call "humanities," which I suppose has something to do with "liberalism" and "humanitarianism." So I would say that those universities that have the money, personnel, equipment, and technical know-how ought to figure out some way to inform those white people in this country who don't have the views that they're supposed to have—that is, humanitarian views.

I see that as a major project, and I think that if white universities would spearhead this effort, it would be much more successful than it is now. Not that it's going to meet with overwhelming success, I assure you, because there are political considerations, and there is going to be political pressure on you to stop this nonsense. Nonetheless, you owe it to your tradition, at least your avowed tradition, to make some effort in this direction. It is needed, and I think that perhaps you would provide the best source of it.

Let me recapitulate—and I was brief intentionally so that you could argue with me. There are three things I see the university as needing to do. First, nonintervention with regard to the black community: stop imposing yourself through projects that only benefit you and the white community, or the business community. Stop trying to make political decisions about what we do. Do not pass value judgments on what we do. Second, afford us foreign aid—financial and technical. As I said before, the university is one of the largest financial institutions in the country, and as a matter of reparations perhaps some kind of transaction could be made so that we could be repaid for some of the efforts that our forefathers made. Technical aid should be given in terms of universities having the facilities and personnel to collect data that we can interpret and use to our own benefit. Third, and the most important thing, create a civilizing movement in this country among whites. I think that if you don't have any social content in this educational thing, then the academic institution is of no importance at all. That is why we concluded long ago that we use reason too well to be overly impressed by other people's use of it. We are more interested in living life than in discussing it. I would suggest that the civilizing movement start from the university—this on the very basis that the university has always had an avowed tradition of liberalism, humanitarianism, and a few other "isms" that are related, but should not be mentioned, lest you be bored by the long list of complimentary adjectives, and forget what else I have said.

Question Period

QUESTION

Mr. Karenga, given the fact that there are black people in predominantly white institutions, and following up your line of thought, that one of the things that happens very often to black people who attend such institutions is that they come out so white that they are of very little value to the black community, do you feel that there is anything these predominantly white institutions could do to provide a kind of *positive* nonintervention, to provide a countervailing force to the conditioning of black people which takes place in such institutions, given the value system under which they operate and their political nature? What specific things might they do to prevent that?

KARENGA

That's a very good question. I suppose I should answer that in terms of the foreign aid thing—that would be on the educational level, which I didn't discuss because I was sure that it would come up. Something very profound has happened; whites really don't understand it, and some blacks have a very

difficult time understanding it too. Black people want three
basic things, identity, purpose, and direction, and unless black
people can be provided with this they will not be able to function as black people but will end up always as servants to
white people. In the end they will bore you, even at your
"conversation parties," because they will have nothing to say
except a poorly selected quotation from one of your writers,
not from their own. The black studies curricula that universities have should be supervised by blacks; you should import
black teachers.

QUESTION

I'm asking what I hope is a methodological question. The
bulk of what you said revolves around attitudes, values, what
you've classified under "inspiration" as contrasted in your
methodological point with "information." One point of "information," as I picked it up, that one might necessarily include
as a cover to the black experience—assuming that my attitude
is partly right, that I can get to the values—as Marcus Garvey.
Now, is there more "information" of a specific sort that you
would want to mention as appropriate to a black curriculum?
Or is the black attitude, value, etc., the information itself?
[KARENGA: What you're looking for is "subject matter"?]
Well, assuming that I can live up to your expectations of the
understanding of attitude, value, etc., let me go on to the
question whether there is any specific "information" that I
ought to add to the curriculum?

KARENGA

Of course. The first thing that we think of is black history.
That's the most accessible subject and that's really the place
where one is "inspired" and "informed." One is inspired by
the images that are projected and one is informed by the processes that these images went through, whether they succeeded
or didn't in the real world. Now, we have developed another
type of interpretation in which we say that none of our black
heroes fail. We believe in progressive perfection: they did as
much as they could given the time and circumstance. I would
never expect Garvey to do as much as I am doing, if for no
other reason than that he didn't have this mike or tape. So, let's
say black history.

QUESTION

Let us assume that the white community in this country
heeds your advice: does not intervene, provides foreign aid,
and performs a civilizing function among some groups, as it

should. What then do you see for the future? What is it that we're going to? What kind of society will we then achieve? What is the result?

KARENGA

One could have two visions, but as I'm not a prophet, I shall deal with only one. I could see a balance of power. The whole question is a question of power. Simply stated, power is the ability to realize one's will. I think that the reason why whites are having this discussion and why we have to meet and organize is because we like power—and because if we had power, these questions would become irrelevant and we would realize our will as we saw it. I can see a balance of power. I don't see us co-existing until that power balance is achieved. I can say that now, but the intensity and quality of the struggle will really determine the relationship: you've got to understand that. That is why the civilizing or—let's change it, let me use a euphemism—the "humanizing" movement is so important. If it works, the intensity and quality of the struggle will be different than if it fails. The make-up of the future depends upon the struggle itself. For example, me: I am really only interested in love and study; I'm not really interested in violence and stuff like that, but here we are. This is a violent world, and I can't pretend I don't live in it. That should be considered.

Let me recapitulate and sum up all this by saying that I have no answer as to how things will come out. As for me, I am only interested in the balance of power—that no one have the power to determine my destiny except me, that I live in a place where I can realize and fulfill all my desires and needs according to my own determination. I have no real desire to enforce my will on anybody: we make a distinction between nationalism, which we practice, and racism, which others practice. Racism says, What I have is not only good for me, it's good for you and I'm going to enforce it on you. Nationalism says, What I have is good for me, it is not necessarily good for others. So, I would like to see just a balance of power. The struggle, however, will answer your question.

QUESTION

Let me push you a little bit further, if I may. You've played academic games, you've got a feel and an ear for the street people, you know what's happening. What in the way of courses would you recommend? You talked about history, you talked about some other things; but if you were in charge of the Yale curriculum committee, how would you handle it?

In terms of developing specific courses or sets of studies, not in terms of rhetoric.

KARENGA

One should not dismiss the word; in the beginning was the word. And even if I discuss the curriculum, I shall have to use words. So, don't discourage me.

I didn't bring a list of courses with me. I suppose I could be creative on the spot—we're impulsive anyhow. Let's go down it again. One, I would have black history; black history in two things: Afro-American history and African history. Second, I would have Swahili, because I am interested in psycholinguistically moving black people to a language which can communicate collective values. We're against individualism. We're for personality, not individuality. We say that personality is that which is me in relation to everyone else—individuality is me in *spite* of everyone else. What white people have developed in terms of individualism is good for them; I would not attack it—it's an "American" thing, and one should not attack "American" things.

If we move from African and Afro-American history to Swahili, then the next thing that I would teach is cultural philosophy. There, I would develop a syndrome of seven basic values black people should have and give substance to all of those. Those are mythology (that's black), a value for history in terms of the frame of reference I gave you earlier, a model for social organization, a model for economic organization (which, of course, would be cooperative economics), a model for political organization (which would give black people a model of how to gain, maintain, and use power), a creative motif (which we've developed also in terms of functional, collective, and committed art, like LeRoi Jones'), and finally, an ethos that would be based on achievement of the other six.

I would move from cultural philosophy in terms of values to political philosophy in terms of the political trends we've gone through—from the early nationalism of David Walker to the abolitionist philosophy of Frederick Douglass to the father of black nationalism, Marcus Garvey, to religious nationalism in the form of Islam under the Honorable Elijah Muhammad to religio-political nationalism that US has produced and developed. These are political trends. I suppose I could go on indefinitely in terms of things I would like to see done, but if you pay me and give me a consulting job I could come back . . .

QUESTION

On the language thing, why particularly Swahili as opposed to other African languages or a combination of other African languages?

KARENGA

That's a very good question. We use Swahili for our organization, and we chose it on the basis of two things: (1) Swahili is a Pan-African language, that is, it is non-tribal, it is the only language in Africa that is non-tribal; (2) we cannot claim any tribe, we can only claim Africa itself, so we are the first Pan-Africans, of a sort. If we choose Hausa, there's a Hausa tribe. If we choose Zulu, there's a Zulu tribe. So, then, where should we go but to Swahili, which has no tribe? And because, also, linguistically Swahili adjusts better to the conversations of modern day: it has been able to absorb at a more rapid pace those technical terms that are necessary in terms of communicating modern events. I would suppose there are no challenges to that.

ADAM CLAYTON POWELL, JR.,

Minister, Politician

During the late 30's, a young activist minister, Adam Clayton Powell, Jr., was seen at the front of many successful picket lines and boycotts against unfair employment practices in New York. Although in 1937 he had succeeded his father as pastor of one of the world's largest Protestant congregations, Harlem's Abyssinian Baptist Church, Powell's interest in political leadership persisted. He was elected as a United States Representative to Congress from New York in 1941. In 1961 Representative Powell became chairman of the Education and Labor Committee. He was the first Negro to hold a congressional committee chairmanship. Despite criticism of his controversial private life, his years as chairman were marked by dedication and success in passing important legislation. Among the most significant are the act denying federal funds to any project where discrimination exists, the Minimum Wage Bill of 1961, the Anti-Poverty Bill, and the Manpower Development Training Act. Although his fighting a defamation suit from 1960 to 1963, and his being stripped of his chairmanship in 1966 and denied his Congressional seat from 1967 to 1969 have certainly not left his reputation undamaged, he has remained one of the most powerful black politicians of our time. His philosophy, which places great emphasis on black education, voting power, and increased involvement for blacks in all phases of life, continues to influence and motivate large numbers of black Americans.

"HUMAN RIGHTS ARE GOD-GIVEN. CIVIL RIGHTS ARE MAN-MADE."

"Can There Any Good Thing Come Out of Nazareth?"*

Almost 2,000 years ago, that question was a contemptuous inquiry in the book of John.

"And Nathanael said unto Philip, 'Can there any good thing come out of Nazareth?' Philip saith, 'Come and see.'"

Nazareth was the Mississippi of Galilee. There were no great artists or philosopher-kings or musicians. There was no center of learning such as Howard University.

In this commencement of your life, the world will ask: Can there any good thing come out of Howard?

As black students educated at America's finest black institution of higher learning, you are still second-class citizens.

A mere 100 years in the spectrum of time separates us from the history of slavery and a lifetime of indignities.

Next year, on March 2, 1967, Howard will celebrate the centennial of its founding. Next year, on March 21, 1967, the Committee on Education and Labor of which I am the Chairman will also celebrate its one hundredth anniversary.

How ironic that the Committee on Education and Labor which was formed immediately after the Civil War to help black slaves make the transition into freedom should have a black man 100 years later as its Chairman.

One of the purposes of the Committee's founding was to take care of Howard University. It is too late for you who are graduating to know this unless you plan to pursue graduate work here, but it is not too late for the faculty to know it: the Education and Labor Committee is in charge of Howard University. Howard, along with other Federal institutions such as St. Elizabeth's and Gallaudet College, is under the jurisdiction of my Committee.

*Reprinted from a baccalaureate address at Howard University, Washington, D.C., May 29, 1966. By permission of the author.

While both Howard and I as Chairman of this Committee will celebrate our 100 years together, joy of our success is tempered by the sobering fact that our status as black people has been denied first-class acceptance.

Keith E. Baird, writing in the spring edition of *Freedomways,* gives eloquent voice to these thoughts in his poem, "Nemesis":

> You snatched me from my land,
> Branded my body with your irons
> And my soul with the slave-name, "Negro"
> (How devilish clever to spell it upper case
> And keep me always lower!)

To possess a black skin today in America means that if you are in Los Angeles driving your pregnant wife to a hospital, you'll be shot to death by a white policeman.

A black skin means that if your family lives in Webster County, Mississippi, your average family income will be $846 a year—$16.30 a week for an entire family.

A black skin today is an unemployment rate twice that of whites, despite a skyrocketing gross national product of $714 billion dollars and an unprecedented level of employment.

A black skin means you are still a child, that all the white liberals who have helped you to take your first steps toward freedom and manhood now believe they own your soul, can manage your lives and control your civil rights organizations. Only SNICK [Student Nonviolent Coordinating Committee] has been able to resist the seductive blandishments of white liberals.

So beware not only of Greeks bearing gifts, but colored men seeking loans and Northern white liberals!

At this graduation today, this is the reality of self you must face. Your graduation comes at a particularly critical period of the black man's searching re-assessment of who he is, what he should become and how he should become IT.

The history of the last 25 years of the freedom struggle has been capsuled in only two concepts: integration and civil rights.

During those years, our leaders—and black people are the only people who have "leaders"—other groups have politicians, statesmen, educators, financiers and businessmen—but during those years, our leaders drugged us with the LSD of integration. Instead of telling us to seek audacious power—more black power—instead of leading us in the pursuit of excellence, our leaders led us in the sterile chase of integration as an end in itself in the debasing notion that a few white skins sprinkled amongst us would somehow elevate the genetics of our development.

As a result, ours was an integration of intellectual mediocrity, economic inferiority and political subservience.

Like frightened children, we were afraid to eat the strong meat of human rights and instead sucked the milk of civil rights from the breasts of white liberals, black Uncle Toms and Aunt Jemimas.

From the book of Hebrews, a diet of courage is offered to black people:

> For every one that useth milk is unskillful in the word of righteousness: for he is a babe. But strong meat belongeth to them that are of full age, even those who by reason of use have their senses exercised to discern both good and evil.

Historically, strong meat was too risky for most black people for it would have enabled them to discern both good and evil, the difference between civil rights and human rights.

– I –

Human rights are God-given. Civil rights are man-made. Civil rights has been that grand deception practiced by those who have not placed God first, who have not believed that God-given rights can empower the black man with superiority as well as equality.

– II –

Our life must be purposed to implement human rights:
- the right to be secure in one's person from the excessive abuses of the state and its law-enforcing officials.
- the right to freedom of choice of a job to feed one's family.
- the right to freedom of mobility of residence.
- the right to the finest education man's social order can provide.
- and most importantly, the right to share fully in the governing councils of the state as equal members of the body politic.

– III –

To demand these God-given human rights is to seek black power, what I call audacious power—the power to build black institutions of splendid achievement.

Howard University was once well on its way toward becoming a lasting black institution of splendid achievement when it struggled to contain the intellectual excitement and dynamic creativity of such black scholars as Alain Locke, Sterling Brown, E. Franklin Frazier, Sam Dorsey, Eugene Holmes, James Nabrit and Rayford Logan—all on the campus at the same time. What glorious symbols they were of black creativity!

But where are the black symbols of creativity of 1966? Where is the greatness of our yesteryears? Where are the sonnets black poets once sung of the black man's agony of life? Can any good thing come out of Howard today?

– IV –

There can and there must. I call today for a black renaissance at Howard University. Resurrect black creativity, not only in literature, history, law, poetry and English, but more so in mathematics, engineering, aerodynamics and nuclear physics.

Like Nicodemus, Howard must be born again—born again in the image of black greatness gone before.

Will one black woman here today dare to come forth as a pilgrim of God, a Sojourner Truth—as a black Moses, Harriet Tubman, or a Nannie Burroughs?

Will one black man here today dare be a Demark Vesey, a Nat Turner, a Frederick Douglass, a Marcus Garvey, a W. E. B. Du Bois or a Malcolm X?

One with God is a majority.

This divine oneness can restore Howard to the Glory of Charlie Houston whose classrooms were the womb of the civil rights movement—a womb that birthed a Thurgood Marshall.

But the womb has aborted and the good thing which must come out of Howard must also come out of black people.

– V –

Ask yourselves that higher question: Can any good thing come of black people?

We are the last revolutionaries in America—the last trans-fusion of freedom into the blood stream of democracy.

Because we are, we must mobilize our wintry discontent to transform the cold heart and white face of this nation.

Indeed, we must "drop our buckets" where we are. We must stop blaming "Whitey" for all our sins and oppressions and deal from situations with strength. Why sit down at the bargaining table with the white man when you have nothing with which to bargain? Why permit social workers and vari-ous Leagues and Associations to represent us when they are representing the decadent white power structure which pays their salaries, their rent and tells them what to say? Such men cannot possess the noble arrogance of power that in-spires men, moves nations and decides the fate of mankind.

— vi —

I call for more arrogance of power among black people, but an arrogance of power that is God-inspired, God-led and God-daring.

As Cassius said: "The fault, dear Brutus, is not in our stars, but in ourselves, that we are underlings."

"So every bondman in his own hand bears the power to cancel his captivity."

We can cancel the captivity of our souls and destroy the enslavement of our minds by refusing to compromise any of our human rights.

The era of compromise for the black man is gone!

Birmingham, Harlem and Watts have proved this. You cannot compromise man's right to be free, nor can you sit down and "reason together" whether man should have some rights today and full rights tomorrow.

Let somebody reason with Mrs. Barbara Deadwyler in Los Angeles that a white policeman really did not intend to kill her black husband.

Black children of Howard, take up thy beds and walk into the new era of excellence.

Arise, and walk into a new spirit of black pride.

"Can there any good thing come out of Nazareth? Come and see, said Philip."

Nathanael came and saw Jesus and the world felt, as he did, the power of his love and the beauty of his words.

Can there any good thing come out of Howard University here today?

"Come and see," you Howard graduates must say.

"Come and see" us erect skyscrapers of economic accomplishment, scale mountains of educational excellence and live among the stars of audacious political power.

"Come and see" us labor for the black masses—not the black leaders—but the black masses who have yearned for audacious leadership.

Discussion and Study Questions

1. Why does Clark feel that cultural deprivation has been an exaggerated hypothesis in justifying unequal education for blacks in northern cities? What other variables are more likely responsible for their inferior education?

2. What modifications in school practices and curricula does Farmer suggest in his essay?

3. According to Hare, what is the difference between black and Negro, between a black-studies program and a Negro-studies program?

4. Contrast the positions taken by Hare and Wilkins on black studies curricula.

5. In what sense is the university a political institution from Karenga's point of view?

6. How does Karenga's project for "foreign aid" compare to Young's "domestic Marshall Plan," and Forman's "black reparations" (see pages 287 and 394)?

7. How does Hare's concept of the black professor's role in the movement compare to Du Bois' idea concerning the "Talented Tenth"?

8. Why is the distinction which Powell makes between human rights and civil rights essential to his concept of "audacious" power? In his baccalaureate address, what future role does he espouse for the college-educated black?

Black-White
Coalition

Black-White Coalition

The essays and men represented in this part tend to emphasize the necessity of a black-white partnership in the fight for freedom and social justice. In many cases such a coalition between peoples is considered to be essential to the acquisition of real power and influence for black people. The existing "system" is thought to be such that numbers, that is, people who have common concerns and grievances, must come together in order to wield more powerful influence. It can be said, therefore, that many of the ideas presented herein rise above the question of skin color to see the essence of the Black man's plight as being intimately related to the struggle between the haves and the have-nots or between the powerful and the powerless. In these essays the black-white coalition is not always considered to be synonymous with integration. In some cases, integration is viewed as an ultimate goal of such an alliance, while in others such a partnership is often merely a temporary alliance based on expediency.

King's letter is a justification for the nonviolent demonstrations of the early 1960s and a call for negotiations between Blacks and whites to speed justice. Brooke suggests that Negroes continue to work with white allies and use persuasion in their struggle, largely because of their minority status. Cleaver discusses the fact that America has been perpetuated on lies and myths. He implies that both blacks and whites who recognize this may find a coalition possible. Young urges white officials to utilize their institutions and facilities to initiate programs which help the people they officially serve. Evers calls for Blacks and whites to work together as brothers of humanity by helping each other meet basic needs and solve common problems. Rustin develops the idea that black people can maintain their dignity through economic advancement and participation in the democratic process.

MARTIN LUTHER KING, JR.,

Minister, Nobel Peace Prize Winner

Martin Luther King began his career as the undisputed leader of the nonviolent faction of the civil rights movement as a young minister in Montgomery, Alabama.

Between the famous Montgomery bus boycott of 1955-56 and the Memphis demonstrations for striking garbage collectors, King was jailed more than twelve times, stabbed by a deranged woman in Harlem, and kicked and beaten by a member of the National States Rights Party; his home was also bombed. Through it all, however, he preached and practiced the nonviolent approach to combating discrimination against the poor and the blacks of America.

Born in Atlanta on January 15, 1929, King has an impressive number of degrees and awards for scholarship and leadership. After graduating from Morehouse College in Atlanta at the age of nineteen, he attended Crozer Theological Seminary in Chester, Pennsylvania, on a scholarship and graduated as valedictorian in 1951. He was awarded his Ph.D. in systematic theology from Boston University in 1955. In 1947 he was ordained and elected copastor with his father at Ebenezer Baptist Church in Atlanta. He married Coretta Scott on June 18, 1953, and returned to the South to become pastor of the Dexter Avenue Baptist Church in Montgomery, Alabama. In 1957 he organized the Southern Christian Leadership Conference and served as its president until his death. In 1964 he was awarded the Nobel Peace Prize for his efforts on behalf of peace and mankind in general. He is the only Negro who has received this honor.

To a nation already in the midst of examining its policies of racism and violence, King's murder by a white assassin in Memphis, Tennessee, on April 4, 1968, came as a great shock and resulted in a noticeable setback for passive protest in America.

"NONVIOLENCE WAS A CREATIVE DOCTRINE IN THE
SOUTH BECAUSE IT CHECKED THE RABID SEGREGATION-
ISTS WHO WERE THIRSTING FOR AN OPPORTUNITY TO
PHYSICALLY CRUSH NEGROES."

The Negro Is Your Brother*

While confined here in the Birmingham city jail, I came across your recent statement calling our present activities "unwise and untimely." Seldom, if ever, do I pause to answer criticism of my work and ideas. If I sought to answer all of the criticisms that cross my desk, my secretaries would be engaged in little else in the course of the day, and I would have no time for constructive work. But since I feel that you are men of genuine good will and your criticisms are sincerely set forth, I would like to answer your statement in what I hope will be patient and reasonable terms.

I think I should give the reason for my being in Birmingham, since you have been influenced by the argument of "outsiders coming in." I have the honor of serving as president of the Southern Christian Leadership Conference, an organization operating in every Southern state, with headquarters in Atlanta, Georgia. We have some eighty-five affiliate organizations all across the South, one being the Alabama Christian Movement for Human Rights. Whenever necessary and possible, we share staff, educational and financial resources with our affiliates. Several months ago our local affiliate here in Birmingham invited us to be on call to engage in a nonviolent direct-action program if such were deemed necessary. We readily consented, and when the hour came we lived up to our promises. So I am here, along with several members of my staff, because we were invited here. I am here because I have basic organizational ties here.

Beyond this, I am in Birmingham because injustice is here. Just as the eighth-century prophets left their little villages and carried there "thus saith the Lord" far beyond the boundaries of their hometowns; and just as the Apostle Paul left his little village of Tarsus and carried the gospel of Jesus Christ to

* Reprinted from a letter written in the Birmingham jail in 1963. By permission of Joan Daves and the Martin Luther King, Jr. Estate.

practically every hamlet and city of the Greco-Roman world, I too am compelled to carry the gospel of freedom beyond my particular hometown. Like Paul, I must constantly respond to the Macedonian call for aid.

Moreover, I am cognizant of the interrelatedness of all communities and states. I cannot sit idly by in Atlanta and not be concerned about what happens in Birmingham. Injustice anywhere is a threat to justice everywhere. We are caught in an inescapable network of mutuality, tied in a single garment of destiny. Whatever affects one directly affects all indirectly. Never again can we afford to live with the narrow, provincial "outside agitator" idea. Anyone who lives inside the United States can never be considered an outsider.

You deplore the demonstrations that are presently taking place in Birmingham. But I am sorry that your statement did not express a similar concern for the conditions that brought the demonstrations into being. I am sure that each of you would want to go beyond the superficial social analyst who looks merely at effects and does not grapple with underlying causes. I would not hesitate to say that it is unfortunate that so-called demonstrations are taking place in Birmingham at this time, but I would say in more emphatic terms that it is even more unfortunate that the white power structure of this city left the Negro community with no other alternative.

In any nonviolent campaign there are four basic steps: collection of the facts to determine whether injustices are alive, negotiation, self-purification, and direct action. We have gone through all of these steps in Birmingham. There can be no gainsaying of the fact that racial injustice engulfs this community. Birmingham is probably the most thoroughly segregated city in the United States. Its ugly record of police brutality is known in every section of this country. Its unjust treatment of Negroes in the courts is a notorious reality. There have been more unsolved bombings of Negro homes and churches in Birmingham than in any other city in this nation. These are the hard, brutal, and unbelievable facts. On the basis of them, Negro leaders sought to negotiate with the city fathers. But the political leaders consistently refused to engage in good-faith negotiation.

Then came the opportunity last September to talk with some of the leaders of the economic community. In these negotiating sessions certain promises were made by the merchants, such as the promise to remove the humiliating racial signs from the stores. On the basis of these promises, Reverend Shuttlesworth and the leaders of the Alabama Christian Movement for Human Rights agreed to call a moratorium on any type of demonstration. As the weeks and months unfolded, we realized that we were the victims of a broken promise. The signs remained. As in so many experiences of the past, we were confronted with blasted hopes, and the dark shadow of a deep disappointment settled upon us. So we had no alternative except that of preparing for direct action, whereby we would present our very bodies as a means of laying our case before the conscience of the local and national community. We were not unmindful of the difficulties involved. So we decided to go through a process of self-purification. We started having workshops on nonviolence and repeatedly asked ourselves the questions, "Are you able to accept blows without retaliating?" and "Are you able to endure the ordeals of jail?" We decided to set our direct-action program around the Easter season, realizing that, with the exception of Christmas, this was the largest shopping period of the year. Knowing that a strong economic withdrawal program would be the by-product of direct action, we felt that this was the best time to bring pressure on the merchants for the needed changes. Then it occurred to us that the March election was ahead, and so we speedily decided to postpone action until after election day. When we discovered that Mr. Conner was in the runoff, we decided again to postpone action so that the demonstration could not be used to cloud the issues. At this time we agreed to begin our nonviolent witness the day after the runoff.

This reveals that we did not move irresponsibly into direct action. We, too, wanted to see Mr. Conner defeated, so we went through postponement to aid in this community need. After this we felt that direct action could be delayed no longer.

You may well ask, "Why direct action, why sit-ins, marches, and so forth? Isn't negotiation a better path?" You are exactly right in your call for negotiation. Indeed, this is the purpose of direct action. Nonviolent direct action seeks to create such a crisis and establish such creative tension that a community that has consistently refused to negotiate is forced to confront the issue. It seeks so to dramatize the issue that it can no longer be ignored. I just referred to the creation of tension as a part of the work of the nonviolent resister. This may sound rather shocking. But I must confess that I am not afraid of the word "tension." I have earnestly worked and preached against violent tension, but there is a type of constructive nonviolent tension that is necessary for growth. Just as Socrates felt that it was necessary to create a tension in the mind so that individuals could rise from the bondage of myths and half-truths to the unfettered realm of creative analysis and objective appraisal, we must see the need of having nonviolent gadflies to create the kind of tension in society that will help men to rise from the dark depths of prejudice and racism to the majestic heights of understanding and brotherhood. So, the purpose of direct action is to create a situation so crisis-packed that it will inevitably open the door to negotiation. We therefore concur with you in your call for negotiation. Too long has our beloved Southland been bogged down in the tragic attempt to live in monologue rather than dialogue.

One of the basic points in your statement is that our acts are untimely. Some have asked, "Why didn't you give the new administration time to act?" The only answer that I can give to this inquiry is that the new administration must be prodded about as much as the outgoing one before it acts. We will be sadly mistaken if we feel that the election of Mr. Boutwell will bring the millennium to Birmingham. While Mr. Boutwell is much more articulate and gentle than Mr. Conner, they are both segregationists, dedicated to the task of maintaining the status quo. The hope I see in Mr. Boutwell is that he will be reasonable enough to see the futility of massive resistance to desegregation. But he will not see this without pressure from the devotees of civil rights. My friends, I must say to you that we have not made a single gain in civil rights without determined legal and nonviolent pressure. History is the long and tragic story of the fact that privileged groups seldom give up their privileges voluntarily. Individuals may see the moral light and voluntarily give up their unjust posture; but, as Reinhold Niebuhr has reminded us, groups are more immoral than individuals.

We know through painful experience that freedom is never voluntarily given by the oppressor; it must be demanded by the oppressed. Frankly, I have never yet engaged in a direct-action movement that was "well-timed" according to the time-table of those who have not suffered unduly from the disease of segregation. For years now I have heard the word "wait." It rings in the ear of every Negro with a piercing familiarity. This "wait" has almost always meant "never." It has been a tranquilizing thalidomide, relieving the emotional stress for a moment, only to give birth to an ill-formed infant of frustration. We must come to see with the distinguished jurist of yesterday that "justice too long delayed is justice denied." We have waited for more than three hundred and forty years for our God-given and constitutional rights. The nations of Asia and Africa are moving with jetlike speed toward the goal of political independence, and we still creep at horse-and-buggy pace toward the gaining of a cup of coffee at a lunch counter. I guess it is easy for those who have never felt the stinging darts of segregation to say "wait." But when you have seen vicious mobs lynch your mothers and fathers at will and drown your sisters and brothers at whim; when you have seen hate-filled policemen curse, kick, brutalize, and even kill your black brothers and sisters with impunity; when you see the vast majority of your twenty million Negro brothers smothering in an airtight cage of poverty in the midst of an affluent society; when you suddenly find your tongue twisted and your speech stammering as you seek to explain to your six-year-old daughter why she cannot go to the public amusement park that has just been advertised on television, and see tears welling up in her little eyes when she is told that Funtown is closed to colored children, and see the depressing clouds of inferiority begin to form in her little mental sky, and see her begin to distort her little personality by unconsciously developing a bitterness toward white people; when you have to concoct an answer for a five-year-old son asking in agonizing pathos, "Daddy, why do white people treat colored people so mean?"; when you take a cross-country drive and find it necessary to sleep night after night in the uncomfortable corners of your automobile because no motel will accept you; when you are humiliated day in and day out by nagging signs reading "white" and "colored"; when your first name becomes "nigger" and your middle name becomes "boy" (however old you are) and your last name becomes "John," and when your wife and mother are never given the respected title "Mrs."; when you are harried by day and haunted by night by the fact that you are a Negro, living constantly at tiptoe stance, never quite knowing what to expect next, and plagued with inner fears and outer resentments; when you are forever fighting a degenerating sense of "nobodyness"—then you will understand why we find it difficult to wait. There comes a time when the cup of endurance runs over and men are no longer willing to be plunged into an abyss of injustice where they experience the bleakness of corroding despair. I hope, sirs, you can understand our legitimate and unavoidable impatience.

You express a great deal of anxiety over our willingness to break laws. This is certainly a legitimate concern. Since we so diligently urge people to obey the Supreme Court's decision of 1954 outlawing segregation in the public schools it is rather strange and paradoxical to find us consciously breaking laws. One may well ask, "How can you advocate

breaking some laws and obeying others?" The answer is found
in the fact that there are two types of laws: there are just
laws and there are unjust laws. I would agree with St. Augus-
tine that "An unjust law is no law at all."

Now, what is the difference between the two? How does one
determine when a law is just or unjust? A just law is a man-
made code that squares with the moral law, or the law of
God. An unjust law is a code that is out of harmony with the
moral law. To put it in the terms of St. Thomas Aquinas, an
unjust law is a human law that is not rooted in eternal and
natural law. Any law that uplifts human personality is just.
Any law that degrades human personality is unjust. All segregation statutes are unjust because segregation distorts the soul
and damages the personality. It gives the segregator a false
sense of superiority and the segregated a false sense of inferiority. To use the words of Martin Buber, the great Jewish
philosopher, segregation substitutes an "I–it" relationship for
the "I–thou" relationship and ends up relegating persons to the
status of things. So segregation is not only politically, economically, and sociologically unsound, but it is morally wrong
and sinful. Paul Tillich has said that sin is separation. Isn't
segregation an existential expression of man's tragic separation,
an expression of his awful estrangement, his terrible sinful-
ness? So I can urge men to obey the 1954 decision of the
Supreme Court because it is morally right, and I can urge
them to disobey segregation ordinances because they are
morally wrong.

Let us turn to a more concrete example of just and unjust
laws. An unjust law is a code that a majority inflicts on a
minority that is not binding on itself. This is difference made
legal. On the other hand, a just law is a code that a majority
compels a minority to follow, and that it is willing to follow
itself. This is sameness made legal.

Let me give another explanation. An unjust law is a code
inflicted upon a minority which that minority had no part in
enacting or creating because it did not have the unhampered
right to vote. Who can say that the legislature of Alabama
which set up the segregation laws was democratically elected?
Throughout the state of Alabama all types of conniving methods are used to prevent Negroes from becoming registered
voters, and there are some counties without a single Negro
registered to vote, despite the fact that the Negroes constitute
a majority of the population. Can any law set up in such a
state be considered democratically structured?

These are just a few examples of unjust and just laws.
There are some instances when a law is just on its face and

unjust in its application. For instance, I was arrested Friday on a charge of parading without a permit. Now, there is nothing wrong with an ordinance which requires a permit for a parade, but when the ordinance is used to preserve segregation and to deny citizens the First Amendment privilege of peaceful assembly and peaceful protest, then it becomes unjust.

Of course, there is nothing new about this kind of civil disobedience. It was seen sublimely in the refusal of Shadrach, Meshach, and Abednego to obey the laws of Nebuchadnezzar because a high moral law was involved. It was practiced superbly by the early Christians, who were willing to face hungry lions and excruciating pain of chopping blocks before submitting to certain unjust laws of the Roman Empire. To a degree, academic freedom is a reality today because Socrates practiced civil disobedience.

We can never forget that everything Hitler did in Germany was "legal" and everything the Hungarian freedom fighters did in Hungary was "illegal." It was "illegal" to aid and comfort a Jew in Hitler's Germany. But I am sure if I had lived in Germany during that time, I would have aided and comforted my Jewish brothers even though it was illegal. If I lived in a Communist country today where certain principles dear to the Christian faith are suppressed, I believe I would openly advocate disobeying these anti-religious laws.

I must make two honest confessions to you, my Christian and Jewish brothers. First, I must confess that over the last few years I have been gravely disappointed with the white moderate. I have almost reached the regrettable conclusion that the Negro's great stumbling block in the stride toward freedom is not the White Citizens Councillor or the Ku Klux Klanner but the white moderate who is more devoted to order than to justice; who prefers a negative peace which is the presence of injustice; who constantly says, "I agree with you in the goal you seek, but I can't agree with your methods of direct action"; who paternalistically feels that he can set the timetable for another man's freedom; who lives by the myth of time; and who constantly advises the Negro to wait until a "more convenient season." Shallow understanding from people of good will is more frustrating than absolute misunderstanding from people of ill will. Lukewarm acceptance is much more bewildering than outright rejection.

In your statement you asserted that our actions, even though peaceful, must be condemned because they precipitate violence. But can this assertion be logically made? Isn't this like condemning the robbed man because his possession of money precipitated the evil act of robbery? Isn't this like condemning

Socrates because his unswerving commitment to truth and his philosophical delvings precipitated the misguided popular mind to make him drink the hemlock? Isn't this like condemning Jesus because His unique God-consciousness and never-ceasing devotion to His will precipitated the evil act of crucifixion? We must come to see, as federal courts have consistently affirmed, that it is immoral to urge an individual to withdraw his efforts to gain his basic constitutional rights because the quest precipitates violence. Society must protect the robbed and punish the robber.

I had also hoped that the white moderate would reject the myth of time. I received a letter this morning from a white brother in Texas which said, "All Christians know that the colored people will receive equal rights eventually, but is it possible that you are in too great of a religious hurry? It has taken Christianity almost 2000 years to accomplish what it has. The teachings of Christ take time to come to earth." All that is said here grows out of a tragic misconception of time. It is the strangely irrational notion that there is something in the very flow of time that will inevitably cure all ills. Actually, time is neutral. It can be used either destructively or constructively. I am coming to feel that the people of ill will have used time much more effectively than the people of good will. We will have to repent in this generation not merely for the vitriolic words and actions of the bad people but for the appalling silence of the good people. We must come to see that human progress never rolls in on wheels of inevitability. It comes through the tireless efforts and persistent work of men willing to be coworkers and God, and without this hard work time itself becomes an ally of the forces of social stagnation.

You spoke of our activity in Birmingham as extreme. At first I was rather disappointed that fellow clergymen would see my nonviolent efforts as those of an extremist. I started thinking about the fact that I stand in the middle of two opposing forces in the Negro community. One is a force of complacency made up of Negroes who, as a result of long years of oppression, have been so completely drained of self-respect and a sense of "somebodyness" that they have adjusted to segregation, and, on the other hand, of a few Negroes in the middle class who, because of a degree of academic and economic security and because at points they profit by segregation, have unconsciously become insensitive to the problems of the masses. The other force is one of bitterness and hatred and comes perilously close to advocating violence. It is expressed in the various black nationalist groups that are springing up over the nation, the largest and best known being Elijah

Muhammad's Muslim movement. This movement is nourished by the contemporary frustration over the continued existence of racial discrimination. It is made up of people who have lost faith in America, who have absolutely repudiated Christianity, and who have concluded that the white man is an incurable devil. I have tried to stand between these two forces, saying that we need not follow the do-nothingism of the complacent or the hatred and despair of the black nationalist. There is a more excellent way, of love and nonviolent protest. I'm grateful to God that, through the Negro church, the dimension of nonviolence entered our struggle. If this philosophy had not emerged, I am convinced that by now many streets of the South would be flowing with floods of blood. And I am further convinced that if our white brothers dismiss as "rabble-rousers" and "outside agitators" those of us who are working through the channels of nonviolent direct action and refuse to support our nonviolent efforts, millions of Negroes, out of frustration and despair, will seek solace and security in black nationalist ideologies, a development that will lead inevitably to a frightening racial nightmare.

Oppressed people cannot remain oppressed forever. The urge for freedom will eventually come. This is what has happened to the American Negro. Something within has reminded him of his birthright of freedom; something without has reminded him that he can gain it. Consciously and unconsciously, he has been swept in by what the Germans call the Zeitgeist, and with his black brothers of Africa and his brown and yellow brothers of Asia, South America, and the Caribbean, he is moving with a sense of cosmic urgency toward the promised land of racial justice. Recognizing this vital urge that has engulfed the Negro community, one should readily understand public demonstrations. The Negro has many pent-up resentments and latent frustrations. He has to get them out. So let him march sometime; let him have his prayer pilgrimages to the city hall; understand why he must have sit-ins and freedom rides. If his repressed emotions do not come out in these nonviolent ways, they will come out in ominous expressions of violence. This is not a threat; it is a fact of history. So I have not said to my people, "Get rid of your discontent." But I have tried to say that this normal and healthy discontent can be channeled through the creative outlet of nonviolent direct action. Now this approach is being dismissed as extremist. I must admit that I was initially disappointed in being so categorized.

But as I continued to think about the matter, I gradually gained a bit of satisfaction from being considered an extremist.

Was not Jesus an extremist in love?—"Love your enemies, bless them that curse you, pray for them that despitefully use you." Was not Amos an extremist for justice?—"Let justice roll down like waters and righteousness like a mighty stream." Was not Paul an extremist for the gospel of Jesus Christ?— "I bear in my body the marks of the Lord Jesus." Was not Martin Luther an extremist?—"Here I stand; I can do no other so help me God." Was not John Bunyan an extremist?— "I will stay in jail to the end of my days before I make a mockery of my conscience." Was not Abraham Lincoln an extremist?—"This nation cannot survive half slave and half free." Was not Thomas Jefferson an extremist?—"We hold these truths to be self-evident, that all men are created equal." So the question is not whether we will be extremist, but what kind of extremists we will be. Will we be extremists for hate, or will we be extremists for love? Will we be extremists for the preservation of injustice, or will we be extremists for the cause of justice.

I had hoped that the white moderate would see this. Maybe I was too optimistic. Maybe I expected too much. I guess I should have realized that few members of a race that has oppressed another race can understand or appreciate the deep groans and passionate yearnings of those that have been oppressed, and still fewer have the vision to see that injustice must be rooted out by strong, persistent, and determined action. I am thankful, however, that some of our white brothers have grasped the meaning of this social revolution and committed themselves to it. They are still all too small in quantity, but they are big in quality. Some, like Ralph McGill, Lillian Smith, Harry Golden, and James Dabbs, have written about our struggle in eloquent, prophetic, and understanding terms. Others have marched with us down nameless streets of the South. They sat in with us at lunch counters and rode in with us on the freedom rides. They have languished in filthy roach-infested jails, suffering the abuse and brutality of angry policemen who see them as "dirty nigger lovers." They, unlike many of their moderate brothers, have recognized the urgency of the moment and sensed the need for powerful "action" antidotes to combat the disease of segregation.

Let me rush on to mention my other disappointment. I have been disappointed with the white church and its leadership. Of course, there are some notable exceptions. I am not unmindful of the fact that each of you has taken some significant stands on this issue. I commend you, Reverend Stallings, for your Christian stand this past Sunday in welcoming Negroes to your Baptist Church worship service on a nonsegregated basis. I commend the Catholic leaders of this state for integrating Springhill College several years ago.

But despite these notable exceptions, I must honestly reiterate that I have been disappointed with the church. I do not say that as one of those negative critics who can always find something wrong with the church. I say it as a minister of the gospel who loves the church, who was nurtured in its bosom, who has been sustained by its spiritual blessings, and who will remain true to it as long as the cord of life shall lengthen.

I had the strange feeling when I was suddenly catapulted into the leadership of the bus protest in Montgomery several years ago that we would have the support of the white church. I felt that the white ministers, priests, and rabbis of the South would be some of our strongest allies. Instead, some few have been outright opponents, refusing to understand the freedom movement and misrepresenting its leaders; all too many others have been more cautious than courageous and have remained silent behind the anesthetizing security of stained-glass windows.

In spite of my shattered dreams of the past, I came to Birmingham with the hope that the white religious leadership of this community would see the justice of our cause and with deep moral concern serve as the channel through which our just grievances could get to the power structure. I had hoped that each of you would understand. But again I have been disappointed.

I have heard numerous religious leaders of the South call upon their worshipers to comply with a desegregation decision because it is the law, but I have longed to hear white ministers say, follow this decree because integration is morally right and the Negro is your brother. In the midst of blatant injustices inflicted upon the Negro, I have watched white churches stand on the sidelines and merely mouth pious irrelevancies and sanctimonious trivialities. In the midst of a mighty struggle to rid our nation of racial and economic injustice, I have heard so many ministers say, "Those are social issues which the gospel has nothing to do with," and I have watched so many churches commit themselves to a completely otherworldly religion which made a strange distinction between bodies and souls, the sacred and the secular.

There was a time when the church was very powerful. It was during that period that the early Christians rejoiced when they were deemed worthy to suffer for what they believed. In those days the church was not merely a thermometer that recorded the ideas and principles of popular opinion; it was the thermostat that transformed the mores of society. Wherever the early Christians entered a town the power structure got disturbed and immediately sought to convict them for being "disturbers of the peace" and "outside agitators." But they went on with the conviction that they were "a colony of heaven" and had to obey God rather than man. They were small in number but big in commitment. They were too God-intoxicated to be "astronomically intimidated." They brought an end to such ancient evils as infanticide and gladiatorial contests.

Things are different now. The contemporary church is so often a weak, ineffectual voice with an uncertain sound. It is so often the arch supporter of the status quo. Far from being disturbed by the presence of the church, the power structure of the average community is consoled by the church's often vocal sanction of things as they are.

But the judgment of God is upon the church as never before. If the church of today does not recapture the sacrificial spirit of the early church, it will lose its authentic ring, forfeit the loyalty of millions, and be dismissed as an irrelevant social club with no meaning for the twentieth century. I meet young people every day whose disappointment with the church has risen to outright disgust.

I hope the church as a whole will meet the challenge of this decisive hour. But even if the church does not come to the aid of justice, I have no despair about the future. I have no fear about the outcome of our struggle in Birmingham, even if our motives are presently misunderstood. We will reach the goal of freedom in Birmingham and all over the nation, because the goal of America is freedom. Abused and scorned though we may be, our destiny is tied up with the destiny of America. Before the Pilgrims landed at Plymouth, we were here. Before the pen of Jefferson scratched across the pages of history the majestic words of the Declaration of Independence, we were here. For more than two centuries our foreparents labored here without wages; they made cotton king; and they built the homes of their masters in the midst of brutal injustice and shameful humiliation—and yet out of a bottomless vitality our people continue to thrive and develop. If the inexpressible cruelties of slavery could not stop us, the opposition we now face will surely fail. We will win our freedom because the sacred heritage of our nation and the eternal will of God are embodied in our echoing demands.

I must close now, but before closing I am impelled to mention one other point in your statement that troubled me profoundly. You warmly commended the Birmingham police force for keeping "order" and "preventing violence." I don't believe you would have so warmly commended the police force if you had seen its angry violent dogs literally biting six unarmed, nonviolent Negroes. I don't believe you would so quickly commend the policemen if you would observe their ugly and inhuman treatment of Negroes here in the city jail; if you would watch them push and curse old Negro women and young Negro girls; if you would see them slap and kick old Negro men and young boys; if you would observe them, as they did on two occasions, refusing to give us food because we wanted to sing our grace together. I'm sorry that I can't join you in your praise for the police department.

It is true that they have been rather disciplined in their public handling of the demonstrators. In this sense they have been publicly "nonviolent." But for what purpose? To preserve the evil system of segregation. Over the last few years I have consistently preached that nonviolence demands that the means we use must be as pure as the ends we seek. So I have tried to make it clear that it is wrong to use immoral means to attain moral ends. But now I must affirm that it is just as wrong, or even more, to use moral means to preserve immoral ends.

I wish you had commended the Negro demonstrators of Birmingham for their sublime courage, their willingness to suffer, and their amazing discipline in the midst of the most inhuman provocation. One day the South will recognize its real heroes. They will be the James Merediths, courageously and with a majestic sense of purpose facing jeering and hostile mobs and the agonizing loneliness that characterizes the life of the pioneer. They will be old, oppressed, battered Negro women, symbolized in a seventy-two-year-old woman of Montgomery, Alabama, who rose up with a sense of dignity and with her people decided not to ride the segregated buses, and responded to one who inquired about her tiredness with ungrammatical profundity, "My feets is tired, but my soul is rested." They will be young high school and college students, young ministers of the gospel and a host of their elders courageously and nonviolently sitting in at lunch counters and willingly going to jail for conscience's sake. One day the South will know that when these disinherited children of God sat down at lunch counters they were in reality standing up for the best in the American dream and the most sacred values in the Judeo-Christian heritage.

Never before have I written a letter this long—or should I say a book? I'm afraid that it is much too long to take your precious time. I can assure you that it would have been much shorter if I had been writing from a comfortable desk, but what else is there to do when you are alone for days in the dull monotony of a narrow jail cell other than write long letters, think strange thoughts, and pray long prayers?

If I have said anything in this letter that is an understatement of the truth and is indicative of an unreasonable impatience, I beg you to forgive me. If I have said anything in this letter that is an overstatement of the truth and is indicative of my having a patience that makes me patient with anything less than brotherhood, I beg God to forgive me.

Yours for the cause of Peace and Brotherhood,

MARTIN LUTHER KING, JR.

EDWARD W. BROOKE,

United States Senator

Born in Washington, D.C., October 26, 1919, Edward W. Brooke grew up in a solid middle-class environment. After graduating from Howard University in 1941 and serving as an army captain with an all-black unit in Italy during World War II, in which he received a Bronze Star for bravery, he entered Boston University and earned the degrees of LL.B. in 1948 and LL.M. in 1950.

As the editor of the Boston University Law Review, Brooke had already begun a distinguished career when he became attorney general of Massachusetts in 1962. After two terms in this office, he was elected to the United States Senate, becoming its first Negro member since 1881 and the days of Reconstruction. At that time Senator Brooke said, "I do not intend to become a national leader of the Negro people; I intend to do my job as a Senator from Massachusetts." Accordingly, he has deemphasized race in his political ascendency and has directed most of his legislative efforts toward other aspects of good government through the Armed Services and the Banking and Currency Committees of which he is a member. Senator Brooke, however, has served on the National Advisory Committee on Civil Disorders and as chairman of the Ad Hoc Congressional Committee on the Poor People's Campaign, and, more recently, has refused to support many Republican party views and nominations which would be harmful to black Americans.

Senator Brooke is included in this text not primarily because of his deeds and assistance to black people, but because of the position he holds and its symbolic significance to blacks.

"THE AMERICAN NEGRO MUST WIN ALLIES, NOT CONQUER ADVERSARIES."

The Problem of Civil Rights*

In the twenty years since World War II, America has taken great strides toward eliminating some forms of racial injustice. This could not have been achieved without a remarkable moral awakening by great numbers of white Americans. But more than anyone else, Negro Americans—especially those in the civil rights movement—are responsible for those great strides.

Nothing I might say about the civil rights movement would give it the recognition and praise it deserves. It is a magnificent crusade that expresses the very essence of American—and human—ideals. The courage, endurance, common sense and tactical genius of its leaders, such as A. Philip Randolph and Martin Luther King, are superb. Wedding restraint with action, they have achieved remarkable success against seemingly impossible odds.

How have the civil rights leaders managed to keep the movement nonviolent despite the violence endured by civil rights workers? They have been accused of radicalism, but their only radical action has been exposing the radicalism of others. They have developed superb techniques of protest, grounded in high legal and moral principles. They have moved millions of Negroes—and millions more whites—to feel a sense of personal involvement. The sit-ins and demonstrations, marches and boycotts, lawsuits and voter registration drives—these programs have been brilliantly executed. And who can claim that without these vast labors a hundredth of the progress of the last decade would have been achieved? The debt of Americans to the men and women, black and white, who are active in the struggle is incalculable. Here is a peaceful crusade that is going to remake America in the image of her constitutional principles at last, and when the history of this century is written, the movement may well be singled out as its most important social transformation.

* Reprinted from *The Challenge of Change*, 1966. By permission of Little, Brown and Company and Edward W. Brooke.

The American Negro must win allies, not conquer adversaries. For the harsh reality is that we are a small minority. We are not only a minority in terms of population. The disproportion in our material resources is far more overwhelming. There are few Negroes of great wealth. Negro votes have become significant in pivotal elections, but relative to the white vote, they are still a small percentage. Ownership of industry and the means of communication; control of local, state and federal government; membership in what is called the "power elite"—these are securely in the possession of white Americans. Even if there were a revolutionary tradition in America, Negroes would be foolhardy to resort to revolution. A hot war against whites would be, on strategic grounds alone, pure madness. And Negro leaders and civil rights organizations have never advocated violence. In Watts and in the few other places where violence has flared, it has not been caused by the civil rights movement but by the eruption of the social and economic volcano which smolders in the ghettos and slums of America. The Negro realizes that for victory we need allies. And we need all of the moral, legal, economic and political assistance that allies can offer. To those who oppose us, our strategy must be based on influence and inducement, on altering thought patterns and old standards—on appeal to hearts and minds. For the best way to defeat an enemy is to make of him a friend. Not the sword, but persuasion. And this fortunately has been recognized by those civil rights leaders who are genuinely dedicated to the cause of civil rights.

The Negro wants to live in an integrated society with all that that implies. He no longer is willing to live on the outside looking in. He wants his children to attend good schools. But he also wants them to attend integrated schools. He wants school bussing as necessary but temporary relief in the establishment of integrated schools. But he also wants the destruction of the Negro ghetto which, among other benefits, will establish permanent school integration. He wants equal job opportunities and equal pay for equal skills and equal services. For he knows that with equal job opportunities he can improve his skills and services, which in turn will increase his income, thereby improving his standard of living.

In competitive America, skills, training, ambition, knowledge and acquaintances are what count—these are the products of investment and development over many generations. There is, I think, no other meaningful way to examine the "Negro" problem. And it is here that the Negro's needs are greatest. The ability to compete—man to man, skill for skill, degree for degree—will not be bestowed upon Negroes magically. Mere passage of time will solve nothing—indeed, the gap, as I have mentioned, is widening.

The solution will not be easy. It will require much more than passing and enforcing laws dealing with the surface aspects of equality of opportunity. It will require working with the human stuff which is the real measurement of equality. And yet the task, however massive, must be faced. Racial inequality permeates every aspect of our national life; no domestic or foreign issue is more important. Now that the pretense of "equal opportunity for all" has been exposed, the course of action we pursue to make the slogan real will determine the nature and content of American democracy for the remainder of this century.

ELDRIDGE CLEAVER,

Black Panther, Author

Leroy Eldridge Cleaver was born in 1935 in Wabbaseka, Arkansas. From there and later from Phoenix, Arizona, he moved to the Watts section of Los Angeles with his family.

While still in junior high school he began a series of arrests and convictions for bicycle theft, drug hustling, rape, and assault. Having therefore spent most of his adult life in jails ranging from a Whittier, California, reformatory to San Quentin, Cleaver is largely self-educated.

Like Frederick Douglass, his self-education has served him well, for he is the author of many forceful essays on the Black Panther ideology and the explosive conditions of black ghettos. Many of his writings, notably Soul on Ice *and* Post-Prison Writings and Speeches, *are searingly honest memoirs of his life in the ghetto, his continuous conflicts with law enforcement authorities, and his movement from ghetto origins to the Black Muslims to the Black Panther Party. As minister of information to this political revolutionary group, Cleaver has gained the support of numerous young whites and blacks who endorse his contempt for the establishment and his programs for ending American racism and imperialism.*

A man of unquestioned intellectualism, Cleaver is senior editor of Ramparts *magazine, and has been a candidate for President on the Peace and Freedom Party ticket—a predominantly white group. Like those of many less controversial spokesmen represented in this book, Cleaver's words are marked with determination and brilliant insight. Although he is in political exile in Algeria, Cleaver is totally committed to black liberation and social justice on an international scale.*

"WHAT THE BLACK MAN IN BABYLON NEEDS IS ORGAN-
IZED BLACK POWER, AND WITH THAT POLITICAL POWER
HE CAN CARVE OUT HIS PLACE IN THE SUN—AND IT
WON'T BE ON A RESERVATION OR IN THE GAS CHAM-
BERS. . . . "

The White Race and Its Heroes*

From the beginning, America has been a schizophrenic nation. Its two conflicting images of itself were never reconciled, because never before has the survival of its most cherished myths made a reconciliation mandatory. Once before during the bitter struggle between North and South climaxed by the Civil War, the two images of America came into conflict, although whites North and South scarcely understood it. The image of America held by its most alienated citizens was advanced neither by the North nor by the South; it was perhaps best expressed by Frederick Douglass, who was born into slavery in 1817, escaped to the North, and became the greatest leader-spokesman for the blacks of his era.

This most alienated view of America was preached by the Abolitionists, and by Harriet Beecher Stowe in her *Uncle Tom's Cabin*. But such a view of America was too distasteful to receive wide attention, and serious debate about America's image and her reality was engaged in only on the fringes of society. Even when confronted with overwhelming evidence to the contrary, most white Americans have found it possible, after steadying their rattled nerves, to settle comfortably back into their vaunted belief that America is dedicated to the proposition that all men are created equal and endowed by their Creator with certain inalienable rights—life, liberty and the pursuit of happiness. With the Constitution for a rudder and the Declaration of Independence as its guiding star, the ship of state is sailing always toward a brighter vision of freedom and justice for all.

Because there is no common ground between these two contradictory images of America, they had to be kept apart. But the moment the blacks were let into the white world—let out of the voiceless and faceless cages of their ghettos

* Reprinted from *Soul on Ice*, 1968. By permission of McGraw-Hill Book Company and the author.

singing, walking, talking, dancing, writing, and orating *their* image of America and of Americans—the white world was suddenly challenged to match its practice to its preachments. And this is why those whites who abandon the *white* image of America and adopt the *black* are greeted with such unmitigated hostility by their elders.

For all these years whites have been taught to believe in the myth they preached, while Negroes have had to face the bitter reality of what America practiced. But without the lies and distortions, white Americans would not have been able to do the things they have done. When whites are forced to look honestly upon the objective proof of their deeds, the cement of mendacity holding white society together swiftly disintegrates. On the other hand, the core of the black world's vision remains intact, and in fact begins to expand and spread into the psychological territory vacated by the non-viable white lies, i.e., into the minds of young whites. It is remarkable how the system worked for so many years, how the majority of whites remained effectively unaware of any contradiction between their view of the world and the world itself. The mechanism by which this was rendered possible requires examination at this point.

Let us recall that the white man, in order to justify slavery and, later on, to justify segregation, elaborated a complex, all-pervasive myth which at one time classified the black man as a subhuman beast of burden. The myth was progressively modified, gradually elevating the blacks on the scale of evolution, following their slowly changing status, until the plateau of separate-but-equal was reached at the close of the nineteenth century. During slavery, the black was seen as a mindless Supermasculine Menial. Forced to do the backbreaking work, he was conceived in terms of his ability to do such work —"field niggers," etc. The white man administered the plantation, doing all the thinking, exercising omnipotent power over the slaves. He had little difficulty dissociating himself from the black slaves, and he could not conceive of their positions being reversed or even reversible.

Blacks and whites being conceived as mutually exclusive types, those attributes imputed to the blacks could not also be imputed to the whites—at least not in equal degree—without blurring the line separating the races. These images were based upon the social function of the two races, the work they performed. The ideal white man was one who knew how to use his head, who knew how to manage and control things and get things done. Those whites who were not in a position to perform these functions nevertheless aspired to them. The ideal black man was one who did exactly as he was told, and did it efficiently and cheerfully. "Slaves," said Frederick Douglass, "are generally expected to sing as well as to work." As the black man's position and function became more varied, the images of white and black, having become stereotypes, lagged behind.

The separate-but-equal doctrine was promulgated by the Supreme Court in 1896. It had the same purpose domestically as the Open Door Policy toward China in the international arena: to stabilize a situation and subordinate a non-white population so that racist exploiters could manipulate those people according to their own selfish interests. These doctrines were foisted off as *the epitome of enlightened justice, the highest expression of morality*. Sanctified by religion, justified by philosophy and legalized by the Supreme Court, separate-but-equal was enforced by day by agencies of the law, and by the KKK & Co. under cover of night. Booker T. Washington, the Martin Luther King of his day, accepted separate-but-equal in the name of all Negroes. W. E. B. Du Bois denounced it.

Separate-but-equal marked the last stage of the white man's flight into cultural neurosis, and the beginning of the black man's frantic striving to assert his humanity and equalize his position with the white. Blacks ventured into all fields of endeavor to which they could gain entrance. Their goal was to present in all fields a performance that would equal or surpass that of the whites. It was long axiomatic among blacks that a black had to be twice as competent as a white in any field in order to win grudging recognition from the whites. This produced a pathological motivation in the blacks to equal or surpass the whites, and a pathological motivation in the whites to maintain a distance from the blacks. This is the rack on which black and white Americans receive their delicious torture. At first there was the color bar, flatly denying the blacks entrance to certain spheres of activity. When this no longer worked, and blacks invaded sector after sector of American life and economy, the whites evolved other methods of keeping their distance. The illusion of the Negro's inferior nature had to be maintained.

One device evolved by the whites was to tab whatever the blacks did with the prefix "Negro." We had *Negro* literature, *Negro* music, *Negro* doctors, *Negro* politicians, *Negro* workers. The malignant ingeniousness of this device is that although it accurately describes an objective biological fact—or, at least, a sociological fact in America—it concealed the paramount psychological fact: that to the white mind, prefixing anything with "Negro" automatically consigned it to an inferior category. A well-known example of the white necessity to deny due credit to blacks is in the realm of music. White musicians were famous for going to Harlem and other Negro cultural centers literally to steal the black man's music, carrying it back across the color line into the Great White World and passing off the watered-down loot as their own original creations. Blacks, meanwhile, were ridiculed as *Negro* musicians playing inferior coon music.

The Negro revolution at home and national liberation movements abroad have unceremoniously shattered the world of fantasy in which the whites have been living. It is painful that many do not yet see that their fantasy world has been rendered uninhabitable in the last half of the twentieth century. But it is away from this world that the white youth of today are turning.

The white youth of today have begun to react to the fact that the "American Way of Life" is a fossil of history. What do they care if their old baldheaded and crew-cut elders don't dig their caveman mops? They couldn't care less about the old, stiffassed honkies who don't like their new dances: Frug, Monkey, Jerk, Swim, Watusi. All they know is that it feels good to swing to way-out body-rhythms instead of dragassing across the dance floor like zombies to the dead beat of mind-smothered Mickey Mouse music. Is it any wonder that the youth have lost all respect for their elders, for law and order, when for as long as they can remember all they've witnessed is a monumental bickering over the Negro's place in American society and the right of people around the world to be left alone by outside powers? They have witnessed the law, both domestic and international, being spat upon by those who do not like its terms. Is it any wonder, then, that they feel justified, by sitting-in and freedom riding, in breaking laws made by lawless men? Old funny-styled, zipper-mouthed political night riders know nothing but to haul out an investigating committee *to look into the disturbance* to find the cause of the unrest among the youth. Look into a mirror. The cause is you, Mr. and Mrs. Yesterday, you with your forked tongues.

A young white today cannot help but recoil from the base deeds of his people. On every side, on every continent, he sees racial arrogance, savage brutality toward the conquered and subjugated people, genocide; he sees the human cargo of the slave trade; he sees the systematic extermination of American Indians; he sees the civilized nations of Europe fighting in imperial depravity over the lands of other people—and over possession of the very people themselves. There seems to be no end to the ghastly deeds of which his people are guilty.

GUILTY. The slaughter of the Jews by the Germans, the dropping of atomic bombs on the Japanese people—these deeds weigh heavily upon the prostrate souls and tumultuous consciences of the white youth. The white heroes, their hands dripping with blood, are dead.

The young whites know that the colored people of the world, Afro-Americans included, do not seek revenge for their suffering. They seek the same things the white rebel wants: an end to war and exploitation. Black and white, the young rebels are free people, free in a way that Americans have never been before in the history of their country. And they are outraged.

There is in America today a generation of white youth that is truly worthy of a black man's respect, and this is a rare event in the foul annals of American history. From the beginning of the contact between blacks and whites, there has been very little reason for a black man to respect a white, with such exceptions as John Brown and others lesser known. But respect commands itself and it can neither be given nor withheld when it is due. If a man like Malcolm X could change and repudiate racism, if I myself and other Muslims can change, if young whites can change, then there is hope for America. It was certainly strange to find yourself, while steeped in the doctrine that all whites were devils by nature, commanded by the heart to applaud and acknowledge respect for these young whites—despite the fact that they are descendants of the masters and I the descendant of slaves. The sins of the fathers are visited upon the heads of the children—but only if the children continue in the evil deeds of the fathers.

WHITNEY M. YOUNG, JR.,

Urban League Executive

As did his contemporaries, Brooke and Wilkins, Whitney Young grew up in a biracial community and has since held the steadfast conviction that an integrated society can and must exist. He was born July 31, 1921, in Lincoln Ridge, Kentucky. After graduating from high school at fourteen, he continued his education at Kentucky State College, Massachusetts Institute of Technology, and the University of Minnesota.

Young resigned as dean of the Atlanta University School of Social Work to become executive director of the Urban League in 1961. A biracial organization with more than sixty-five branches in predominantly black communities, the Urban League believes that cooperation between the races is essential to the black civil rights movement. It emphasizes economic activities to overcome racial discrimination and to relieve poverty and inadequate education.

Although Young has shifted somewhat from his "Marshall Plan" reprinted here, this essay reflects his primary concern for the poor blacks of America and his emphasis on better economic and educational opportunities to raise the inferior level of poverty-stricken people all over the nation.

"THE EFFECTS OF MORE THAN THREE CENTURIES OF OPPRESSION CANNOT BE OBLITERATED BY DOING BUSINESS AS USUAL."

Crisis — Challenge — Change*

To many black people "leisure" is not a very cheerful word. All too often their leisure has been enforced by unemployment. Those who have found work have often had to supplement meager earnings by taking a second job, leaving no time for other activities. In some cases, they were too tired, because their work was so arduous, and "leisure" was not included in their vocabulary.

Only in recent years have we been welcome in many of the parks—even those financed by the state or federal governments. Consequently, even today parks are a fairly new experience for many black people. They are a resource few of us have been able to enjoy, since, in many cases, they were not accessible and warmth and a welcome were lacking.

Many parks within the cities were segregated. White parks, parks for white people, were lovely places that we could drive past, noting the beauty and facilities—before driving on. As a youngster in Kentucky, I would drive past Cherokee Park, which was a white park, and then go on to Chickasaw Park—for black people. The contrast was amazing. Those who needed it most often had the least. The poor didn't have the private facilities—the golf courses, etc.—that are available to the more affluent. So, quite frankly, I haven't had much opportunity to gain a knowledge of your field. However, I do know that you now have some youngsters in your ranks who were better trained and are more sensitive to human needs, and that there is now a desire to change and to place greater priority on what can be achieved in the inner city.

A Real Crisis in the City

It is important that as you move in this direction you under-

*Reprinted from *Parks and Recreation*, IV (April, 1969), pp. 42-43, 61-67. By permission of *Parks and Recreation* and the author.

stand that there is a real crisis in the city—one in which we are all involved. We may have traveled to America on different ships, but we are in the same boat now, and that boat is not sailing on a calm sea.

The poor are not an unusual phenomenon in our society. But what is different is the growing awareness of the poor that they are considered to be of a different and inferior status. They are no longer hidden in the rural South but, for the most part, live in urban communities. They are exposed to more sophisticated media. They see affluence on their television screens and they live next door to it. Today's poor people are more determined than ever before to change their status. This is not a phenomenon of the moment. Rather it is continuing, sustaining and ever-increasing and it is coupled with impatience. The poor have had enough education to know how other groups have effected change in our society. Women marched and demonstrated and were disorderly until they got suffrage. Working men rioted and engaged in sit-ins, boycotts, picketing, and violence until they won their rights through the Wagner Act. The poor know how Americans freed themselves from the domination of Britain by engaging in civil disobedience like the Boston Tea Party. They know how the Irish, Italians and Jews and other minority groups have thrown off the yoke of oppression through a variety of techniques—some of them quite violent.

The Young Are at Best Contemptuous

The poor today are also unique in that they have strong new allies in young people. I am not speaking of the hippies or the yippies; I am speaking of your daughters and sons and mine. Young people today are aware of the gap between what we as a society practice and what we preach. They are at best contemptuous; at worst, violently in turmoil about the fact that we live in a society with a gross national product of some one trillion dollars and yet at least 15 percent of our people live in squalor and poverty. These young allies are not likely—as some of you may wish and hope—to follow the example of past generations who were radical in their teens, liberal in their twenties, conservative in their thirties, and reactionary in their forties. They will not follow that course because, for the most part, they have never known poverty and, therefore, are not as preoccupied with economic security as was our generation. Today's young people will continue to confront and to challenge American society and to keep not only the establishment, but also mom and daddy up against the wall. Those of you who do not yet have teenage children may just as well prepare for it.

What Democracy Is All About

The first thing that I would challenge you with is the recognition that the National Recreation and Park Association, as one of the institutions of American society, has to look at the attitudes of the people to see whether they have forgotten what democracy is all about. There are far too many Americans who perceive democracy as simply a combination of institutions that makes it possible for one to have more television sets, two cars, refrigerators and a home in the suburbs. I think there are very few Americans who really understand the obligations of democracy and what it should mean to be an American. This was documented recently by a pollster who attempted to get the people in a town to sign a petition stating that they agreed with the first 10 articles of the Constitution. Nine out of 10 refused to sign and resisted the pollster on the grounds that he must be a communist! It is amazing how few of our young people know what the Constitution of America is. I would like to see you dedicate yourselves not just to the improvement of the physical body and the recreational needs of our citizens, but to the utilization of your institutions to aid a rebirth of the American dream and to make the melting pot concept of America reality.

Kerner Commission Cites Racism

I make no pretense that it will be easy to enter into this challenge. You will have to acknowledge as human beings and as an institution that injustice exists in this society. The Kerner Commission, composed of responsible, mostly conservative, white men from all over the country, after studying this situation, decided that the problem was white racism. This was an indictment that most white people talked about and strongly resisted. But, if you read the report, you will understand that racism does not mean that one wants to engage in a lynching party or send black people back to Africa. It means that white Americans consider themselves superior to other human beings of a darker hue. We knew it anyway because until 1964 people were denied entrance into restaurants, hotels, and many other public places as well as certain schools purely on the basis of the color of their skin. If we did not believe that certain people were destined to occupy a status different from others we could not have done those things while at the same time going to church, mouthing clichés about brotherhood, and standing up on the Fourth of July uttering patriotic clichés.

So, the first step is to admit that our society has been unfair to some of its members on the basis of color. Secondly, we must not develop rationalizations and excuses to explain a lack of involvement. I hear people saying that they have lost sympathy with our cause because of the shouts of "black power" and because of the riots.

So Great a Loss

After I had talked to the American Home Builders' Association—that I should be invited to speak there is revolutionary in itself—one man approached me. He told me that he had been a great friend of our people. He loved my people very much in the past and had been a great liberal, he said. He had now lost sympathy with our cause because of the riots and the black power movement. I told him that I would prefer not to debate the merit of indicting the group because of the excesses of a few, but that I would like to find out the extent of our loss. I took a piece of paper and a pencil and asked him if he would tell me, before he lost sympathy, how many integrated subdivisions he had built; how many black people he had employed; how many black people he had helped to get into his neighborhood, his schools, his clubs, even his church? I said: "Please say it slowly so that I can document it for posterity." I wanted to know our great loss. He hadn't done any of these things, he said. My only response was that nothing from nothing leaves nothing. It never occurred to him that if he had been doing these things when he loved my people so much and had so much sympathy for them that we wouldn't have had the riots in the South, or the black power movement.

No Need for Black Cities and States

So, let us not lose sympathy, let us not get caught up with excuses to cop-out because there are some people talking about separatism and moving into a separate state or a separate country. Just keep this in mind, that nobody who is talking about separatism today—and there are about a handful—has availed himself of the opportunity to move into the seven all black cities which we have in this country. There is no need to set up a separate city or state, we already have them. Nobody has moved into them even though I understand they have been offered transportation. I think you ought to know also that you can count on one hand the number of people who have incomes that permit them to move out of the slums, who remain. They act like all other human beings. When they get a chance to move out where there is some grass and trees—they do it.

You have to distinguish the rhetoric from the substance. There are many, many things that people are saying today that are more symbolic than real. As a group you have not yet done a good enough job of recruiting and employing black people; and if you lose all the white people from the recreation and park area, you wouldn't have anybody there. So, I want you to hang in there and not run out because there are cries of "separatism" and "we want all black this and all black that," because they don't really always mean it.

I went into one of our street academies the other day in Harlem, where we take young dropouts whom the schools have called uneducable and we train them and put them into a private high school we started. Of the 60 graduates, all 60 are now in college—this year's graduates. The *New York Times* headlined one of the stories, "From Learning in Harlem to the Halls of Harvard." While I was at a street academy, not so long ago, one of the youngsters was telling me about how we have to have all black schools and teachers and neighborhoods and everything; and I said, "Well, how can you say this? I just saw you talking to this white teacher and you were showing mutual respect and affection for each other." And he said, "Oh, Mr. Young, she ain't white, she is nice."

I think it is awfully important to remember that. So many ghetto youngsters' experiences with white people—whether it was the merchants, police or the landlord—have been negative; that white becomes a description of evil and mistreatment, and not a description of color. Because in that little boy's mind, this woman was not white, she was nice. Many of you can be nice and therefore lose the relevance of color.

A Cry of Desperation

I would hope that you, more than anyone else, will begin to try to interpret the real constructive meaning of "black power."

Like most Americans, I think I would like to have seen the term disappear the day after it was introduced; but thanks to a sensation-seeking press it didn't and it became a popular chant in the ghetto. Black power is less a cry of violence than a cry of desperation. What it says, in effect, is: "I am somebody. I want to be acknowledged as a human being. I have roots. I have pride. I have made a contribution. I want to participate in the affairs of my destiny and my children's destiny. I want to mobilize my strength and resources to reward my friends and punish my enemies as all other groups have done."

I think that when you strip black power of its overtones of violence and separatism, it becomes a very positive force that people in the recreation field can utilize. I think it is very healthy for black people today to want to be involved, to want to engage in self-help, to participate in various community institutions after years of being criticized for being apathetic and indifferent and not coming to PTA meetings. It seems that we are now being criticized for being too pushy. You can't win in this business. Now it is said we want to take over everything. We say, no, not everything, but we do want to take over those institutions which have not succeeded in our communities. Even in an advanced city like New York black children in the twelfth grade of the Ocean Hill-Brownsville School District are three to four years behind on achievement tests. In the fifth grade they are already one to three years behind in reading comprehension. Other institutions have an equal gap. Less than 2 percent of ghetto youngsters are eligible to go to college as compared to 60 percent in white districts.

Blacks Want Some Control in Their Communities

White people have had control of the institutions in black communities—the economic, the educational, the health, the welfare, and the police departments—and these institutions haven't succeeded. The problem has been one of absentee control with those in charge not knowing the community and the people they served.

We are not asking for all black workers, all black teachers, and all black administrators; we are asking for some control. I think that the head of an institution in an all black neighborhood ought to be black to give an incentive and to provide a model for black students by showing that if they stay in school they can get ahead and be boss. But I want to see whites in those institutions, too, so that these youngsters can see there are some whites who are willing to work with, and even under, a black person. That would be a new experience for many of our children. But most of all I want good people—people who have soul. I think, as you try to interpret these terms, you will render a real service.

Welfare Recipients Get Less

A popular slogan these days is—"We made it, why can't they?" This has always disturbed me. It is usually said by people who themselves were beneficiaries. Their families were products of WPA, NYA, CCC and FERA. The government had given them land and provided them with farm agents to help them develop it. They are now getting money not to farm anything. The same thing is said by people who have received great subsidies through defense contracts. It is amazing to me how many people think that the only people who get federal subsidies are welfare clients. They just get less. It would be interesting to look at the federal monies that go into private industries today, or universities, or most of our institutions. These people take a lot more money from the federal government than welfare clients.

But we need to point out to them that the Negro has been unique. He came to this country, not as a volunteer but an involuntary immigrant. His family life was destroyed through a system of conscious deliberate splitting off. The institution of slavery emasculated the family and demoralized the human being. In addition there was the matter of color, and in America this made a difference. Unlike other white Americans with other than wasp backgrounds—black people couldn't hide behind new names and churches. We couldn't have a little operation or something to change our facial features. We tried it—called "Black-No-More." That didn't work. So we have to make black beautiful. And that is why "Mantan" is selling so well. We now have white people rushing to the Caribbean. Nobody likes to be white any more.

Some Basic Changes Needed

Now, as you get ready to launch what I understand is your major outreach into the ghetto, I must warn you that there are some immediate changes that you will have to make—not just in your own attitudes and the realization that this is a great potential that you are tapping. You will have to make some basic changes in your board and staff makeup. If you really are to reach the people who need your services most, then you can't just talk about your concern with the inner city and its people; you have to teach by example. They have to look at you and see that you are a truly democratic institution.

You have to do a better job of recruiting. First, board members, and there are plenty of people around today. Don't go to the old known names of the same people who serve on all the other boards—the Negroes that you have heard about. There are many young people you can bring on your boards who will work. They will be very useful and honest with you. Don't worry too much about their vocabulary—whether they have college degrees. It is better to say "I is rich" than "I am poor."

The Credibility Gap

There are many people who may not have perfect English but who could be invaluable in helping you reach the people you want to. You do suffer a credibility gap. There are not enough black people on the staffs of park or recreation commissions and agencies; but they can be found although it is not easy. I know when I took over the Urban League seven years ago, only 1 percent of our staff was white and I had to go through this special effort to attract, to recruit, to give special training to the whites because they didn't really meet our standards They hadn't had the necessary experiences and backgrounds. They didn't know the psychology of the poor, or the language of the ghetto; and we had to put them—these Phi Beta Kappa's from Harvard and Radcliffe—through a provisional training period where we gave them special remedial experiences in education to bring them to our standards. But we did these things because we were anxious to integrate our staff and to take advantage of the many skills these people could bring. Now 30 percent of our staff is white. We didn't take the easy way out and say "Nobody applies," or "They don't meet our standards," or "What about our Christmas party?" We didn't take any of these courses of action.

Now, when you employ black people . . . when you really

get into it . . . remember you can't apply the old missionary attitude of: "Here I am, you know, to help you poor natives. Here I am to bring you salvation. Here I am, the great white father who has come to lead you to the promised land by helping you to adopt the white people's way of life."

Blacks Can Bring Strength to Society

Black people today are not impressed with the white community. It is not quite that moral; and its value is questionable. We observe some of your youngsters' reaction to white society today—they flee Greenwich, Connecticut, for Greenwich Village. It becomes clear that maybe what we are looking for is not cultural absorption, but cultural exchange. You must see the strength that black people can bring into this society. While they may not have the money, technology and know-how, they do bring the compassion, faith, patience, style, grace and soul that many of our white institutions and white people can certainly use. So, tell them that you recognize this strength.

We have spent too much time talking about the pathology of black America and too little time talking about the pathology of white America. We have spent too much time talking about the weaknesses rather than the strengths of black people, who through resilience and ingenuity have survived a hostile society—not the 25 percent whose families are socially disorganized but the 75 percent who, in spite of everything, have stable families. We need to say to these people, "We recognize that you have these strengths and we are reaching out so you can help us. We are not here just to be nice little missionaries to help you."

There are some ingenious things being done by commissioners today. I am very impressed with some of the things they are doing in New York—some of the things Tom Hoving has done, and some of the things that Augie Heckscher has done in the ghetto; taking different mobile units, jazzmobiles, dancemobiles; bringing the culture of that community, its background, its history, to it; the vest-pocket parks. There is great talk these days about mini-swimming pools. There are things that creative and imaginative people can do, and they are finding that this community is starved for these facilities.

Fight for Community Needs

Finally, I urge you to take a position on some national issues that affect the people that you are talking about serving. This is the way of getting credibility. Nothing would be more heart-warming and convincing to a little black boy than to see his park supervisor join in the fight for better housing and for model cities and for rent supplements and for educational programs. Then he could really say, "He cares about me, he doesn't care whether I bounce a basketball or whether I swim well, but he is concerned about my total body, my mind and my soul and my spirit."

I should not really end without speaking of the causes of the tragedy of the inner city . . . We should look at the major legislation that this country has passed which is now being sabotaged by not giving the appropriations needed to implement the programs. Who knows better than the people in this profession what it means to these people to be poor, to be ignored, to be anonymous. You have seen it in the ghetto and you know it better than the people who never get into them. You should not be merely treating the symptoms of the society and its injustice but you should be standing up to fight for the things that will stop this occurring in another generation. You ought to be taking positions on legislative measures. The nice people in this society are too quiet and, therefore, Congress responds and reacts only to the kooks, the conservatives, and the reactionaries who are constantly taking issue. Certainly you can take some position without jeopardizing your tax-exempt status and you do it best through your association.

The Greatest Hypocrites

Now, there are a lot of things at stake in what I have been trying to say to you. Your country is at stake; our country. Whether we go down in history as the greatest hypocrites that ever lived or whether we make the world believe that we are just, civilized human beings, or whether we come to be known as—as someone put it the other day—a nation under guard, with invectives and guns for all, remains to be seen. I think our cities are also at stake. They may become dungeons of violence and despair, or, conversely they may become havens of hope, and a symbol of our great creative skill to do anything we really want to do.

But, I think what is most important is that the individual himself is at stake. This issue more than any other separates the wheat from the chaff; the decent human being from the human vegetable with clothes on. If you cannot identify with the impoverished of our society, then you are in worse shape than the victim. You have benefited from America but you have not been an American. Most of all, the persons who will realize your limitations will be your own children. They are the ones who look at you and decide whether you are for real or not. They are the ones who today believe that their fathers and their mothers are phonies and that they have a double standard of values. The one kind of value they try to impart to their children concerns standing up for what you believe in and not conforming, and yet children see their parents conforming all the time.

A Communication's Story

One story, and I will close. Mel Batton, who is the chairman of J. C. Penney, and a member of our board of directors, told me of a breakfast conversation he had had with his children, a boy 21 and a girl 23. They asked him "Where are you going this week, Dad?" and he said "I am going out with Whitney Young of the Urban League. We are holding lunches for businessmen in three cities to try to expand employment opportunities for Negro citizens and to raise some money for the Urban League." His son almost fell off the stool. He said, "You are going to do what?" And his father explained again to him, and the girl said, "You mean you aren't going out this week to maximize the profits of J. C. Penney and figure out some way you can undercut Woolworth or to find some product from which you can get a greater margin of profit?" And he replied, "No" and he explained again what he was going to do. There was complete silence for a moment, and then his daughter, with tears in her eyes, jumped off her stool and came over and hugged him and kissed him. And he said to me, "You know, Whitney, I have given my children everything in terms of cars, allowances, clothes and tuition, but I have never gotten as much genuine respect and affection as I got in that one moment." And he said, "I want to thank you and the Urban League for making this possible." Now he is communicating with his kids. And so that's what is at stake far more than what happens to black people, it's what happens to you as a man, as a decent human being; as a father and as a husband.

As Tennyson once said: "In a boundless universe let us this thought rehearse; we can be boundless better or we can be boundless worse."

By your invitation to me I am convinced of your desire and hope to be boundless better.

CHARLES EVERS,

Civil Rights Worker, Southern Political Leader

When Charles Evers played in the dirt roads of Decatur, Mississippi, with his brother, Medgar, during the thirties, he surely never dreamed he would one day become mayor of a biracial southern town, but on July 7, 1969, he was inaugurated as mayor of Fayette, Mississippi.

Born on September 11, 1922, James Charles Evers interrupted his education in 1941 to volunteer for army duty in the Pacific during World War II. He eventually finished high school and received a degree in social science from Alcorn College, Mississippi. He has since received two honorary doctorate degrees from Luther College, Decorah, Iowa, and Washington University in St. Louis.

Having played a major role in establishing NAACP bases all over Mississippi, Evers found the transition from civil rights activities to politics natural and inevitable. He helped form the Loyal Democratic Party to challenge the segregated Mississippi State delegation in 1964. A straightforward, plain-spoken man, he points out, "We in Mississippi, black and white, are going to have to work out our own problems." That the solutions to racial strife will be achieved through working together is implicit in Mayor Evers' entire attitude.

"I COULD NEVER GO AROUND PREACHING AGAINST THE WHITES WHAT THEY HAVE PREACHED AGAINST US."

Notes and Comments*

Late last month, Charles Evers came to New York and made a speech. Mr. Evers is the man who on the seventh of July, will become the first black mayor of the town of Fayette, Mississippi. He made a speech at a party given for him by some friends of ours, Arthur and Marian Logan, and listening to it gave us a great deal of pleasure. Mr. Evers did not prepare his remarks. He did not have to. We think what he said is the best speech we have ever heard by anyone running for or elected to the office of mayor. Mr. Evers said:

"All of us have won a victory in Mississippi. All the poor blacks, and all the concerned, scared whites. I'm not going to belittle the whites, because they need help, just as we need help. Whatever we have done was made possible by men like Medgar, John, Dr. King, and Bobby. Their lives made it possible not for Charles Evers to get elected but for all Americans in the state of Mississippi to have the right to go to the polls. They wanted to end hate and destruction in our country. This past Tuesday, part of their hope became a reality. Others came and helped us, too. John Lewis came, and he'd just got married. Paul O'Dwyer came all the way from New York just to be there. And many others helped us with their work and their prayers. This is not a celebration for Charles Evers but for all of us—the lesser-known and the better-known. I did nothing special. I don't deserve a pat on the back. It's my duty to do it. Everyone did it—doctors, mothers, fathers, pool sharks, and cabdrivers. I pray every day that I never become anything special. We've also got to mention Governor Rockefeller. He's one of the few whites who over the years has done something for the poor folks. We know that whatever happens in Mississippi affects the people in New York, and that whatever happens in New York affects the people in Mississippi.

*Reprinted from *The New Yorker*, XLV (June 14, 1969), pp. 29-30. By permission of Charles Evers and *The New Yorker* Magazine.

We're all God's children. He brought us all here. And those of us who are more affluent have something special to do. I don't mean being braggadocios. But He equipped us to go out and help our brothers. We're going to show the whites down there—the whites who have done so much to hurt us—that it's so easy to do good. We're going to say to all the blacks: Don't get mad, get smart. Don't shoot your brother, and don't bomb him. Just vote him out of office. Because the right will prevail. All the mean folks in this country will someday be gone. And then the country will belong to the good folks.

"You can't blame the kids for what is happening in this country, and you can't blame the blacks. It is the system which has kept *us* in the corner. But the black mayor and the black aldermen of Fayette are going to behave the same to everyone: young, in-between, old; black, white; rich, poor. We're going to prove this to white America. When you whites come to Fayette, you'll be able to drive there. And if you speed, we'll charge you the same amount we charge anyone. White and black, in our time, will pay the same cost of speeding—a dollar a mile per hour. Now, the mayor gets his salary from traffic fines. And when you win, I lose. I hope they put me out of business. When you get arrested in Fayette, you're not going to be abused. No policeman is going to strike anyone. If I ever hear of any policeman hitting any man, he will be fired in a moment. We are not going to tolerate any brutality. We need industry in Fayette. We got no jobs down there. We're 75 per cent of the population of the town, and 65 per cent of us blacks are on welfare. Twenty per cent of us are unemployed. The average level of education is less than the fifth grade. The average income is under a thousand dollars. There is not a single playground or swimming pool in town. It's not just the black folks who don't have these things. Nobody does. There are shack houses and no sewers. This is what white America has done to us. But we twelve blacks are going to make it better for blacks and whites. My dad always said, 'Don't ever destroy anything or anybody.' So we're all going to live and struggle together to make it a decent town. There are thirty-nine million poor folks in this country, and we blacks are only twenty-two million. That means there are a lot of poor Mexicans, poor Indians, poor Puerto Ricans, and poor whites—millions of all of us. That's why we're going to be mayor and aldermen for all our citizens. On July the seventh, we take office. On July the eighth, we are going to enact a law that will read something like this: 'Anyone found carrying a gun in this town will be sent to jail for six months.' There ain't nobody going to practice violence in our town.

Then we'll issue an order saying that there will be no more discrimination in this town. And any contractor or shop-keeper—anyone—who doesn't comply is going to be prose-cuted. Our schools will be open to everybody. There will be one school system, and that's all. Maybe what we do in Mississippi will help our black brothers and our white brothers all over the country. I'm only here to say: Let's help ourselves. Let's not cast anybody off, and let's not hate anybody. I'm not even going to hate that old chief of police, whom I'm going to fire on July the eighth.

"It can be done. It's got to be done. We got no choice. Please, any of you here who are sitting on the fence, get down off it on the right side. Thank you so much. Come visit us in Fayette. Have no fear."

BAYARD RUSTIN,

Pacifist, Civil Rights Leader

Bayard Rustin has had a long career of civil rights activity, beginning as youth organizer for the A. Philip Randolph-led March on Washington in 1941 and continuing now as executive secretary of the A. Philip Randolph Institute, an organization committed to improving the conditions of all America's oppressed and forgotten people.

Rustin was born in Westchester, Pennsylvania, in 1910. After high school in Westchester, he attended college at Wilberforce University in Ohio, Cheyney State Teachers College in Pennsylvania, and City College of New York. Following his participation in the 1941 March on Washington, he became field secretary for CORE, served as an advisor to King between 1955 and 1960, and was the chief organizer of the 1963 civil rights March on Washington. He was jailed as a conscientious objector during World War II, and served a thirty-day sentence on a North Carolina chain gang for his participation in the first freedom ride in 1947. As executive secretary of the War Resisters' League, his primary interest has been in overall social reform; he is also vitally concerned about racial injustice, however, and consistently speaks out for internal educational and political reforms by blacks. For Rustin, the key to racial progress is not direct, violent action, but political action and social reform with all Americans working together for a common goal.

"IF THERE IS ANYTHING POSITIVE IN THE SPREAD OF THE GHETTO, IT IS THE POTENTIAL POLITICAL POWER BASE THUS CREATED . . ."

Towards Integration as a Goal*

The proposition that separation may be the best solution of America's racial problems has been recurrent in American Negro history. Let us look at the syndrome that has given rise to it.

Separation, in one form or another, has been proposed and widely discussed among American Negroes in three different periods. Each time, it was put forward in response to an identical combination of economic and social factors that induced despair among Negroes. The syndrome consists of three elements: great expectations, followed by dashed hopes, followed by despair and discussion of separation.

The first serious suggestion that Negroes should separate came in the aftermath of the Civil War. During that war many Negroes had not only been strongly in favor of freedom but had fought for the Union. It was a period of tremendous expectations. Great numbers of Negroes left the farms and followed the Union Army as General Sherman marched across Georgia to the sea; they believed that when he got to the sea they would be not only free but also given land—"forty acres and a mule." However, the compromise of 1876 and the withdrawal of the Union Army from the South dashed those expectations. Instead of forty acres and a mule, all they got was a new form of slavery.

Out of the ruins of those hopes emerged Booker T. Washington, saying in essence to Negroes: "There is no hope in your attempting to vote, no hope in attempting to play any part in the political or social processes of the nation. Separate yourself from all that and give your attention to your innards: that you are men, that you maintain dignity, that you drop your buckets where they are, that you become excellent of character."

*Reprinted from *The American Federationist*, LXXVI (January, 1969), pp. 5-7. By permission of AFL–CIO *American Federationist* and the author.

Of course, it did not work. It could not work. Because human beings have stomachs, as well as minds and hearts, and equate dignity, first of all, not with caste but with class. I preached the dignity of black skin color and wore my hair Afro style long before it became popular; I taught Negro history in the old Benjamin Franklin High School, where I first got my teaching experience, long before it became popular.

But in spite of all that, it is my conviction that there are three fundamental ways in which a group of people can maintain their dignity: one, by gradual advancement in the economic order; two, by being a participating element of the democratic process; and three, through the sense of dignity that emerges from their struggle. For instance, Negroes never had more dignity than when Martin Luther King won the boycott in Montgomery or at the bridge in Selma.

This is not to say that all the values of self-image and identification are not important and should not be stimulated; but they should be given secondary or tertiary emphasis for, unless they rest on a sound economic and social base, they are likely only to create more frustration by raising expectations or hopes with no ability truly to follow through.

The second period of frustration and the call for separation came after World War I. During that war, 300,000 Negro troops went to France—not for the reason Mr. Wilson thought he was sending them, but because they felt that if they fought for their country they would be able to return and say: "We have fought and fought well. Now give us at home what we fought for abroad."

Again, this great expectation collapsed in total despair as a result of postwar developments: Lynchings in the United States reached their height in the early twenties; the Palmer raids did not affect Negroes directly but had such a terrifying effect on civil liberties that no one paid any attention to what was happening to Negroes; the Ku Klux Klan moved its headquarters from Georgia to Indianapolis, the heart of the so-called North; and unemployment among Negroes was higher at that period than it had ever been before. It was at that time, too, that Negroes began their great migration to the North, not from choice but because they were being driven off the land in the South by changed economic conditions.

The war having created great expectations, and the conditions following the war having shattered them, a really great movement for separation ensued—a much more significant movement than the current one. Marcus Garvey organized over 2 million Negroes, four times the number the NAACP has ever organized, to pay dues to buy ships to return to Africa.

Today, we are experiencing the familiar syndrome again. The Civil Rights Acts of 1964 and 1965 and the Supreme Court decisions all led people seriously to believe that progress was forthcoming, as they believed the day Martin Luther King said, "I have a dream." What made the March on Washington in 1963 great was the fact that it was the culmination of a period of great hope and anticipation.

But what has happened since? The ghettos are fuller than they have ever been, with 500,000 people moving into them each year and only some 40,000 moving out. They are the same old Bedford-Stuyvesant, Harlem, Detroit, and Watts, only they are much bigger, with more rats, more roaches and more despair.

There are more Negro youngsters in segregated schoolrooms than there were in 1954—not all due to segregation or discrimination, perhaps, but a fact. The number of youngsters who have fallen back in their reading, writing and arithmetic since 1954 has increased, not decreased, and unemployment for Negro young women is up to 35, 40 and 50 percent in the ghettos. For young men in the ghettos, it is up to 20 percent and this is a conservative figure. For family men, the unemployment is twice that of whites. Having built up hopes, and suffered the despair which followed, we are again in a period where separation is being discussed.

I maintain that, in all three periods, the turn to separation has been a frustration reaction to objective political, social and economic circumstances. I believe that it is fully justified, for it would be the most egregious wishful thinking to suppose that people can be subjected to deep frustration and yet not act in a frustrated manner.

But however justified and inevitable the frustration, it is totally unrealistic to divert the attention of young Negroes at this time either to the idea of a separate state in the United States, or to going back to Africa, or to setting up a black capitalism (as Mr. Nixon and CORE are now advocating), or to talk about any other possibility of economic separation, when those Negroes who are well off are the 2 million Negroes who are integrated into the trade union movement.

This is not to belittle in any way the desirability of fostering a sense of ethnic unity or racial pride among Negroes or relationships to other black people around the world. This is all to the good, but the ability to do this in a healthy rather than a frustrated way will depend upon the economic viability of the Negro community, the degree to which it can participate in the democratic process here rather than separate from it, and the degree to which it accepts methods of struggle that are productive.

I would not want to leave this subject without observing that, while social and economic conditions have precipitated thoughts of separation, it would be an oversimplification to attribute the present agitation of that idea exclusively to those causes. A good deal of the talk about separation today reflects a class problem within the Negro community.

I submit that it is not the lumpen-proletariat, the Negro working classes, the Negro working poor, who are proclaiming: "We want Negro principals, we want Negro supervisors, we want Negro teachers in our schools." It is the educated Negroes. If you name a leader of that movement, you will put your finger on a man with a master's or a Ph.D. degree. Being blocked from moving up, he becomes not only interested in Negro children, but in getting those teaching jobs, supervisory jobs and principal jobs for his own economic interest. While this is understandable, it is not true that only teachers who are of the same color can teach pupils effectively. Two teachers had an effect upon me; one was black and the other was white, and it was the white teacher who had the most profound effect, not because she was white but because she was who she was.

Negroes have been taught that we are inferior and many Negroes believe that themselves and have believed it for a long time. That is to say, sociologically we were made children. What is now evident is that the entire black community is rebelling against that concept in behalf of manhood and dignity. This process of rebellion will have as many ugly things in it as beautiful things.

Also, while rebelling there is rejection of those who used to be loved most. Every teenager has to go through hating mother and father, precisely because he loves them. Now he's got to make it on his own. Thus, Martin Luther King and A. Philip Randolph and Roy Wilkins and Bayard Rustin and all the people who marched in the streets are all "finks" now. And the liberals, and the Jews who have done most among the liberals, are also told to get the hell out of the way.

The mythology involved here can be very confusing. Jews may want now to tell their children that they lifted themselves in this society by their bootstraps. And when Negroes have made it, they will preach that ridiculous mythology, too. That kind of foolishness is only good after the fact. It is not a dynamism by which the struggle can take place.

But to return to separation and nationalism. We must distinguish within this movement that which is unsound from that which is sound, for ultimately no propaganda can work for social change which is not based on absolute psychological truth.

There is an aspect of the present thrust toward black nationalism that I call reverse-ism. This is dangerous. Black people now want to argue that their hair is beautiful. All right. It is truthful and useful. But, to the degree that the nationalist movement takes concepts of reaction and turns them upside down and paints them glorious for no other reason than that they are black, we're in trouble—morally and politically. The Ku Klux Klan used to say: "If you're white, you're right; if you're black, no matter who you are, you're no good." And there are those among us who are now saying the opposite of the Ku Klux Klan: "He's a whitey, he's no good."

The Ku Klux Klan said: "You know, we can't have black people teaching" and they put up a big fight when the first Negro was hired in a white school in North Carolina. Now, for all kinds of "glorious" reasons, we're turning that old idea upside down and saying: "Well, somehow or other, there's soul involved and only black teachers can teach black children." But it is not true. Good teachers can teach children.

The Ku Klux Klan said: "We don't want you in our community; get out." Now there are blacks saying: "We will be violent as a means of impressing our will on the situation." And now, in conference after conference, a small number of black people use violence and threats to attempt to obstruct the democratic process.

What is essential and what we must not lose sight of is that true self-respect and a true sense of image are the results of a social process and not merely a psychological state of mind.

It is utterly unrealistic to expect the Negro middle class to behave on the basis alone of color. They will behave, first of all, as middle-class people. The minute Jews got enough money to move off Allen Street, they went to West End Avenue. As soon as the Irish could get out of Hell's Kitchen, they beat it to what is now Harlem. Who thinks the Negro middle classes are going to stay in Harlem? I believe that the fundamental mistake of the nationalist movement is that it does not comprehend that class ultimately is a more driving force than color and that any effort to build a society for American Negroes that is based on color alone is doomed to failure.

Now, there are several possibilities. One possibility is that we can stay here and continue the struggle; sometimes things will be better, sometimes they will be worse. Another is to separate ourselves into our own state in America. But I reject that because I do not believe that the American government will ever accept it. Thirdly, there is a possibility of going back to Africa and that is out for me, because I've had enough experience with the Africans to know that they will not accept that.

There is a kind of in-between position—stay here and try to separate and yet not separate. I tend to believe that both have to go on simultaneously. That is to say, there has to be a move on the part of Negroes to develop black institutions and a black image, and all this has to go on while they are going downtown into integrated work situations, while they are trying to get into the suburbs if they can, while they are doing what all other Americans do in their economic and social grasshopping. That is precisely what the Jew has done. He has held on to that which is Jewish, and nobody has made a better effort at integrating out there and making sure that he's out there where the action is. It makes for tensions, but I don't believe there's any other viable reality.

Furthermore, I believe that the most important thing for those of us in the trade union movement, in the religious communities and in the universities is not to be taken in by methods that appeal to people's viscera but do not in fact solve the problems that stimulated their viscera.

We must fight and work for a social and economic program which will lift America's poor, whereby the Negro who is most grievously poor will be lifted to that position where he will be able to have dignity.

Secondly, we must fight vigorously for Negroes to engage in the political process, since there is only one way to have maximum feasible participation—and that is not by silly little committees deciding what they're going to do with a half million dollars, but by getting out into the real world of politics and making their weight felt. The most important thing that we have to do is to restore a sense of dignity to the Negro people.

If that can happen, the intense frustration around the problem of separation will decrease as equal opportunities—economic, political and social—increase. And that is the choice before us.

Discussion and Study Questions

1. What exactly is the white man's myth which is at the core of Cleaver's essay?

2. Of what value can young whites be in Cleaver's coalition plan? How does his view on this issue relate to Farmer's in "Are White Liberals Obsolete?" (p. 85). Why does he seem to feel such a coalition is essential to revolutionary action in this country?

3. What similarities do you note between the style of Evers and Washington? What factors might account for these similarities?

4. Explain how King considers nonviolence both as a strategy and as a philosophy of life.

5. Compare and contrast King (232), Gregory (401), Elijah Muhammad (152), and Forman (394) in terms of their views on the white church.

6. What does Rustin suggest as the reasons for the past and present interest in separatism?

7. Discuss the differences and similarities between Cleaver and the other spokesmen of this section in relation to their attitude toward black-white cooperation.

Government,
Politics, and Courts

Government, Politics, and Courts

The use of these terms, "Government, Politics, and Courts," indicates that the persons and essays included here feel that the existing institutional mechanisms comprised of governmental agencies and programs, judicial action, and political operations are workable for improving the lot of the black American. For the most part, these essays are not primarily concerned with drastic institutional change, but rather with finding ways to use these systems more effectively for the Black man's betterment.

Often, the ideas and philosophies expressed in these essays point toward individual achievement and accomplishment as symbols of the real and significant progress which is possible for the masses of black people. It is felt that the masses can be motivated and inspired to greater achievements by the example of others who have risen above certain obstacles. In those essays where the emphasis is on mass or group progress, the basic premise remains that existing institutions are workable. Advocates of such a viewpoint find it possible to work within the system to publicize grievances and injustices, to institute programs, and to test invalid implementation of laws through court action.

For example, governmental action is urged through poverty programs, voting rights bills and other civil rights legislation. The use of peaceful protest marches, demonstrations and lobby action is also favored. In addition, political appointments and increased use of the ballot are thought to be viable strategies.

Young and Wright use economic statistics to point out the need for extensive governmental intervention and support to improve the quality of life for large numbers of Blacks. Wilkins' essay answers current challenges to nonviolent strategies by delineating the progress made by civil rights groups and organizations through concerted agitation in the areas of housing, employment, and education. The King and Brooke essays call for governmental action which takes significant steps to prevent violence and destruction by alleviating some of their underlying causes. The interviews with Innis, Wilkins, and Young suggest, in different ways, particular strategies that the Nixon and succeeding administrations might use to implement platform promises and additional programs. Whatever strategy or program is advocated, however, the idea which seems consistent in this group of essays is that true equality and justice are attainable within the existing institutional framework.

Needed Now: A Special Effort*

By WHITNEY M. YOUNG, JR.

The scales of justice have been heavily weighted against the Negro for over three hundred years and will not suddenly in 1964 balance themselves by applying equal weights. In this sense, the Negro is educationally and economically malnourished and anemic. It is not "preferential treatment" but simple decency to provide him for a brief period with special vitamins, additional food, and blood transfusions.

This is a situation which clearly calls for emergency action on a broad scale in urban communities across the land. Fact-finding committees, pilot projects, tokenism and halfhearted, one-dimensional small-scale efforts will not suffice. This nation and the world need a demonstration that we can bridge the social, economic and educational gap that separates American Negroes from their fellow citizens. It is mandatory that a broad-spectrum, intensive program be launched in the United States, a program that will bring the majority of American Negroes to the point at which they can compete on an equal basis in the nation's increasingly complex and fast-moving industrial economy.

That is why the National Urban League and I, together, have called for an unprecedented domestic "Marshall Plan" approach to these problems. We urgently recommend co-operative *special efforts* by private, public, and voluntary organizations in a massive "crash" attack on the complete range of economic and social ills involved.

Once before, a century ago, this nation focused the attention of the world on its effort to change the status of the Negro. The hopes and expectations of that time were cynically bartered away in political and economic deals. The

* Reprinted from *To Be Equal*, 1964. By permission of McGraw-Hill Book Company and the author.

world, with other events to occupy its attention, took little notice. Negroes, with no education, no economic power, few leaders equipped to cope with the conditions, were powerless to prevent their exploitation.

Today, conditions are radically different. The justified impatience of the Negro must be met with responsible action from the entire white community.

This *special effort* program that we recommend should phase out as need for it diminishes over the next decade. It will not be cheap. But it will prove to be an invaluable investment that will reap great returns. Its cost must be viewed in the same terms as programs of preventive medicine. What were the savings from small-pox vaccine? From polio shots? Or from economic infusions such as the Marshall Plan and our other foreign aid projects? Although the Marshall Plan cost us more than $17 billion, what price can we honestly put on saving Western Europe from being overrun by Communism, on building healthy economies across a war-ravaged continent and strengthening nations in other corners of the world?

We have long given special emergency aid to the oppressed, the sick, the handicapped and the deprived. In recent years we have seen this concept applied through our aid—in employment, education, and welfare—to Hungarian and Cuban refugees. We see it annually carried out in the form of emergency help to "depressed" and "disaster" areas, suffering from joblessness or devastation by hurricanes, drought, and other misfortunes.

The "GI Bill of Rights" after World War II and the Korean War was a comprehensive approach to meeting the special needs of our veterans who had been out of the mainstream of American life during their military service. The Servicemen's Readjustment Act of 1944 helped construct needed hospital facilities, established regional, branch, and local veterans' facilities to prevent GIs from throwing their money away on overpriced housing, made available loan guarantees for purchase of farmland, buildings, livestock, machinery, and business needs, established a veterans' placement service that put a representative in each state and provided readjustment allowances for unemployed vets.

The American Negro has been out of the mainstream for more than three centuries and a special effort must be made to bring him into the central action of our society. The effects of more than three centuries of oppression cannot be obliterated by doing business as usual. In today's complex, technological society, a sound mind, a strong back, and a will to succeed are no longer sufficient to break the bonds of deprivation as was the case with minority groups in the past.

A comparable effort must also be made for millions of other Americans of minority groups—the Mexican-Americans, Puerto Ricans, and others—so that these millions will also benefit. I am confining my remarks to Negroes, because I am more expert on the problems of my own people, and because their plight is worse than that of any other minority (except perhaps for our seven hundred thousand Indians). However, I ought to make it clear that I do not believe in extraordinary measures to help more Negroes progress and become self-supporting simply because they are Negro. I believe we must receive assistance until we can make use of equal opportunities now opening to us because we are Americans, and no Americans ought to be deprived or disenfranchised economically, politically, or socially.

Thus our call for an immediate, dramatic, and tangible domestic Marshall Plan is aimed at closing the intolerable economic, social, and educational gap that separates the vast majority of us Negro citizens from other Americans. Unless this is done, the results of the current heroic efforts in the civil rights movement will be only an illusion, and the struggle will continue, with perhaps tragic consequences.

In our plea for such a domestic Marshall Plan, we are asking for *special effort*, not for special privileges. Our program is designed to reverse economic and social deterioration of urban families and communities and to help develop the tools and understanding that will prevent such deterioration in the future. Here is the proposed *special effort* program:

1. Our basic definition of equal opportunity must include recognition of the need for special effort to overcome serious disabilities resulting from historic handicaps. When you find a man in the wilderness dying from malnutrition you don't just bring him to civilization and turn him loose with a pat on the back saying, "We've saved you, now you're on your own; lots of luck!" He is on the point of starvation. He requires special attention, careful diet and rest, and psychological and physical aid to readjust to civilization.

The Negro has been starving, not in the wilderness, but in the midst of the world's richest nation in the period of its greatest prosperity in history. He has been sighted, but whether his true condition has been "diagnosed" accurately and will be corrected by the majority is yet to be seen.

2. America must recognize and assess at a higher value than ever before the human potential of its Negro citizens, and then our society must move positively to develop that potential.

It is no accident that the U.S. Department of Labor and economists such as Gunnar Myrdal, Eli Ginzberg and others agree that the Negro population is America's greatest undeveloped natural resource. The extraordinary contributions to America of those Negro citizens who have overcome incredible handicaps merely hint at the tremendous benefits that will be ours when Negroes can participate freely in our society.

3. The best schools and the best teachers are needed:
—to instill in Negro children and other educationally disadvantaged youth a desire for excellence;
—to motivate them to achieve and prepare them to advance up the economic ladder with full understanding of the rewards they will receive.

We do not need more examples of school boards treating ghetto schools as the Siberias of their systems, relegating to them largely the problem teachers, probational teachers, neophyte teachers on a "make or break" basis. We need insight, courage, understanding, and an educational value system which parallels that of the medical profession, where doctors and nurses who selflessly devote themselves to combating an epidemic, for example, earn greater prestige than those who dispense pills for allergies and colds in the suburbs.

4. A conscious, planned effort must be made to bring qualified Negroes into "entrance jobs" in *all* types of employment, to upgrade them and aid them to qualify for advancement, and to place them in positions of responsibility, *including the full range* of management positions. The day is past when token integration and pilot placement of Negroes in business and industry, labor and government can be considered solutions. These devices never were acceptable nor adequate, except to white Americans.

For employers the special effort, domestic Marshall Plan approach means exercising the same creative zeal and imagination to include Negro workers at all levels that management has used throughout the years in excluding them. And incorporating Negroes into the work force will not happen automatically by taking down a sign, pasting up a poster, or autographing the President's

Plans for Progress Program—a statement of fair-hiring practices. It means honest, realistic seeking out of workers, for fillable jobs, not just positions for which industry can't find whites—such as nuclear physicists, or secretaries who look like Lena Horne and can type 120 words per minute.

Special effort means not hiding behind lame excuses. Any employer who does not want to hire can find excuses. This approach suggests that if a business has never hired Negroes in its offices or plants and two equally qualified people apply, it should hire the Negro to redress the injustice previously visited upon him. Such action has double virtue: it gives Negro youth a new role model and promotes the image of a truly American company.

5. Effective, positive action must be taken to destroy the racial ghetto and to open housing opportunities of all types on the basis of need and ability to buy or rent. Too long the cancerous sore of the ghetto has festered in our urban communities, spewing forth human wreckage and the major portion of criminal offenders; draining our body politic of treasure; robbing us of the meaningful contributions of hundreds of thousands of citizens whose lives and ambitions have been thwarted and truncated.

6. Health and welfare agencies, both public and private, must bring to the ghettoized population their best services and most competent personnel. Needed are trained workers who understand the myriad ills that afflict ghetto dwellers—unstable family patterns, illegitimate births, the direct relationship between low socio-economic status and social problems—and how to rehabilitate urban Negro families.

7. Qualified Negroes should be sought and named to all public and private boards and commissions, particularly those that shape policy in the areas of employment, housing, education, and health and welfare services. These are the key areas in which the racial differential is greatest and the need for dramatic change—meaning the inclusion of Negro citizens in decision-making—is most urgent.

To achieve this, strong leadership within the Negro community must be encouraged and developed. This leadership will then be ready to step into the vanguard of the teamwork effort so imperative in resolving the smoldering problems of civil rights. The experiences of 1963 should have made clear, if it was not evident before, that the era of paternalistic handling by whites of the needs and ambitions of Negro citizens is gone. American Negroes are done with being "done *for*"; they demand the right to participate, to do for themselves and determine their own destiny.

8. Every opportunity to acquire education and technical skills must be utilized to the fullest. Every means of strengthening the social and economic fabric of the Negro community must be employed.

Negro citizens, adults as well as young people, must maintain and even accelerate the sense of urgency that now characterizes the drive for first-class citizenship.

9. It is vital that government at all levels, philanthropic foundations, labor, business, and industry reassess their financial support of, and cooperation with, established organizations committed to securing equal opportunity for Negro citizens to share in the fundamental privileges and rights of American democracy.

It is imperative that all of these major sources of support increase substantially their contributions, both financial and non-financial, to the preventive and remedial programs carried on by responsible Negro leadership organizations. These agencies aid Negroes to help themselves by staying in school, registering and voting, making use of adult education classes and retraining centers. For far too long the agencies that have seen the needs and attempted unspectacularly but effectively to meet them have suffered from a crippling anemia of finances, caused by the acute myopia of government, philanthropy, business, and labor.

10. Negro citizens must exert themselves energetically in constructive efforts to carry their full share of responsibilities and to participate in a meaningful way in every phase of community life. It is not enough to man the machinery of protest. Equally important today and twice as important tomorrow is participation in the responsibilities and opportunities of full citizenship in our democracy. This means Negroes moving not only onto the picket lines but also into PTA meetings, moving not only into lunch counters but also into libraries, moving into both community facilities and committee rooms, into both public accommodations and public hearings, and,

finally, moving onto the commissions and boards to exercise their rights and insure their fair share.

The *special effort* program outlined above represents a mature, realistic, broad-front attack on the existing problems, a program through which significant breakthroughs of sufficient scale and extent can be accomplished. The program has a simple, practical aim: to provide the Negro citizen with the leadership, education, jobs, motivation and opportunities which will permit him to help himself. It is not a plea to exempt him from the independence and initiative demanded by our free, competitive society. Just the opposite. It is a program crafted to transform the dependent man into the independent man. It makes practical economic sense as a measure to reduce unemployment and welfare costs and to increase our productivity and national income by including Negro citizens in the benefits of our rich society. The President's economic advisers estimate that our Gross National Product could be raised 2.5 percent if the Negro worker's earnings were commensurate with the nation's average.

This program makes historical sense as a rehabilitation of the damage inflicted upon the Negro by generations of injustice and neglect. He, too, has given his blood, sweat, and tears to build our country. Yet, where the labor and initiative of other minority groups have been rewarded by assimilation into the society, the black American has been isolated and rejected.

There are profound moral and religious justifications in this domestic Marshall Plan. Our country is in sharp jeopardy as long as it has within its body politic a socially and economically deprived group of citizens, whether they are actually enslaved or denied the full benefits of equality and freedom by an insidious economic and psychological slavery. In this sense, the crash program proposed is not an effort to impose the guilt and sins of a past generation on our present white community. This is rather an appeal for all Americans, working together, to rid present-day America of its sickening disease, its moral shame.

Steady As She Goes*

By ROY WILKINS

In the transition period of the civil rights movement, 1966 is developing into a critical year. The fifty-seventh annual convention of our NAACP is thus a gathering of more than ordinary significance.

All about us are alarms and confusions as well as great and challenging developments. Differences of opinion are sharper. For the first time since several organizations began to function where only two had functioned before, there emerges what seems to be a difference in goals.

Heretofore there were some differences in methods and in emphases, but none in ultimate goals. The end was always to be the inclusion of the Negro American, without racial discrimination, as a full-fledged equal in all phases of American citizenship. The targets were whatever barriers, crude or subtle, which blocked the attainment of that goal.

There has now emerged, first, a strident and threatening challenge to a strategy widely employed by civil rights groups, namely, non-violence. One organization, which has been meeting in Baltimore, has passed a resolution declaring for defense of themselves by Negro citizens if they are attacked.

This position is not new as far as the NAACP is concerned. Historically our Association has defended in court those persons who have defended themselves and their homes with firearms. Extradition cases are not as frequent or as fashionable as they once were, but in past years we have fought the extradition of men who had used firearms to defend themselves when attacked.

We freed seventy-nine Arkansas sharecroppers in a four-

* Keynote address at NAACP Fifty-seventh Annual Convention, 1969. Reprinted by permission of the author and NAACP.

year court battle beginning in 1919. They had returned gun-fire directed at a meeting they were holding in a church.

We employed the late Clarence Darrow in 1926 to defend a man and his family when a member of a mob threatening his newly-purchased Detroit home was shot and killed. The NAACP has subscribed to non-violence as a humane as well as a practical necessity in the realities of the American scene, but we have never required this as a deep personal commitment of our members. We never signed a pact either on paper or in our hearts to turn the other cheek forever and ever when we were assaulted.

But neither have we couched a policy of manly resistance in such a way that our members and supporters felt compelled to maintain themselves in an armed state, ready to retaliate instantly and in kind whenever attacked. We venture the observation that such a publicized posture could serve to stir counter-planning, counter-action and possible conflict. If carried out literally as instant retaliation, in cases adjudged by aggrieved persons to have been grossly unjust, this policy could produce—in extreme situations—lynchings, or, in better-sounding phraseology, private, vigilante vengeance.

Moreover, in attempting to substitute for derelict law enforcement machinery, the policy entails the risk of a broader, more indiscriminate crackdown by law officers under the ready-made excuse of restoring law and order.

It seems reasonable to assume that proclaimed protective violence is as likely to encourage counter-violence as it is to discourage violent persecution.

But the more serious division in the civil rights movement is the one posed by a word formulation that implies clearly a difference in goals.

No matter how endlessly they try to explain it, the term "black power" means anti-white power. In a racially pluralistic society, the concept, the formation and the exercise of an ethnically-tagged power, means opposition to other ethnic powers, just as the term "white supremacy" means subjection of all non-white people. In the black-white relationship, it has to mean that every other ethnic power is the rival and the antagonist of "black power." It has to mean "going-it-alone." It has to mean separatism.

Now, separatism, whether on the rarefied debate level of "black power" or on the wishful level of a secessionist Freedom City in Watts, offers a disadvantaged minority little except the chance to shrivel and die.

The only possible dividend of "black power" is embodied in its offer to millions of frustrated and deprived and persecuted black people of a solace, a tremendous psychological lift, quite apart from its political and economic implications.

Idealogically it dictates "up with black and down with white" in precisely the same fashion that South Africa reverses that slogan.

It is a reverse Mississippi, a reverse Hitler, a reverse Ku Klux Klan.

If these were evil in our judgment, what virtue can be claimed for black over white? If, as some proponents claim, this concept instills pride of race, cannot this pride be taught without preaching hatred or supremacy based upon race?

Though it be clarified and clarified again, "black power" in the quick, uncritical and highly emotional adoption it has received from some segments of a beleaguered people can mean in the end only black death. Even if, through some miracle, it should be enthroned briefly in an isolated area, the human spirit, which knows no color or geography or time, would die a little, leaving for wiser and stronger and more compassionate men the painful beating back- to the upward trail.

We of the NAACP will have none of this. We have fought it too long. It is the ranging of race against race on the irrelevant basis of skin color. It is the father of hatred and the mother of violence.

It is the wicked fanaticism which has swelled our tears, broken our bodies, squeezed our hearts and taken the blood of our black and white loved ones. It shall not now poison our forward march.

We seek, therefore, as we have sought these many years, the inclusion of Negro Americans in the nation's life, not their exclusion. This is our land, as much so as it is any American's—every square foot of every city and town and village. The task of winning our share is not the easy one of disengagement and flight, but the hard one of work, of short as well as long jumps, of disappointments, and of sweet successes.

In our fight for Freedom we choose:

1. The power and the majesty of the ballot, the participation of free men in their government, both as voters and as honorable and competent elected and appointed public servants. Year in and year out, the NAACP voter registration work has proceeded. No one except the Federal Government has registered more Negro voters in Mississippi than the NAACP. In six weeks last summer more than twenty thousand new names were added

by our workers alone, with additional thousands during an intensive renewal last winter. That work is continuing under the leadership of our Mississippi state president, Dr. Aaron Henry, and of our state director, Charles Evers. Later this month a summer task force will be at work in Louisiana. Already our South Carolina NAACP is busy on registration, as is our Alabama organization.

We are aware that a Louisiana young man, born along the Mississippi border, has been named and confirmed as one of the seven governors of the Federal Reserve Bank. We know that his extraordinary ability finally tipped the scales, but we know also, that, without ballot power, he would not even have been on the scales ready to be tipped.

2. We choose employment for our people—jobs not hidden by racial labels or euphemisms, not limited by racial restrictions in access and promotion, whether by employers or organized labor. We commend a growing number of corporations for expanding their employment of Negro applicants in technical and professional posts, but we insist that only the surface has been scratched.

We commend the "good guys" among the trade unions for the improvement in opportunities and advancement for the Negro worker, but we condemn the policies of some unions which have either barred or heavily handicapped the Negro worker. Negro employment is in a crisis stage. The rate of unemployment ranges from twice that of whites to four and five times the white rate in some areas. The answer to the complaint of employers that workers are not trained is to institute in-plant training, just as they have in other shortages. The apprentice training stranglehold must be broken, the racially separate seniority lines, the still-persisting segregated local and the remaining crude segregation in plant facilities must be abolished. The demonstrations before the U.S. Steel corporation offices and plants under the cooperative leadership of Dr. John Nixon, our Alabama president, and Henry Smith, our Pennsylvania president, had wide and beneficial impact.

The Negro migrant worker, the forgotten man in the employment picture, must have attention.

In the Watts district of Los Angeles last year the unemployment rate was more than 30 percent, a rate higher than that during the great, nationwide Depression of the Nineteen Thirties. The Negro teenage rate is nearly 25 percent as against 13 percent for white teenagers.

Negro employment is a disaster area demanding the strict enforcement of Title VII of the 1964 Civil Rights Act. The NAACP has filed more than one thousand complaints with the Equal Employment Opportunity Commission and will file more until the law accomplishes what it was enacted to do. As evidence of his continuing concern, Congressman Augustus Hawkins of Los Angeles succeeded in having his bill relating to Federal employment passed by the House as an amendment to Title VII of the 1964 Civil Rights Act.

3. We choose to combat the color line in housing. In one breath our opinion-makers decry the existence of the poverty and filth and crime and degradation of the slums, but in the next they decry low-cost housing and fair housing laws. Here in California the hysteria over whether Negro Americans should live in gullies or be pushed into the sea reached the Proposition 14 stage which the state's highest court has declared unconstitutional. But who cares about the Constitution when a Negro might be enabled to move into the neighborhood? One could think black Americans were men from Mars. Instead, we have been here, side by side with the white folks (some of whom just got here), for 345 years.

They tell us to work hard and save our money, to go to school and prepare ourselves, to be "responsible," to rear and educate our children in a wholesome and directed family atmosphere, to achieve, to "get up in the world."

After we do all this, they look us in the eye and bar us from renting or buying a home that matches our achievements and one in keeping with our aspirations for further advancement.

Some public officials, including mayors of cities, and many candidates for election to public office are not above public double talk and private single talk on this issue. Any candidate who orates about basic Americanism or "the American way," but who hems and haws over fair housing legislation is no friend of the Negro citizen.

The Administration's civil rights bill of 1966 with its vital section barring discrimination in the rental or sale of housing must be enacted with the amendment, already inserted by the committee, providing for administrative redress as well as court action.

Your Congressmen and Senators are at home until July 11 celebrating Independence Day—Freedom Day for the United States. See them or have your branch officers back home see them in person. Urge them to rub some freedom off on twenty million loyal Americans by voting for a strong civil rights bill. Of course the section on punishing in the Federal courts those who attack civil rights workers must pass. And we must have indemnification for victims.

4. Most of all, we choose to secure unsegregated, high quality public education for ourselves and our children. A new report, made public only last week, is a jolt for anyone who thought the 1954 Supreme Court decision or subsequent legislation solved the problem.

The report says officially and professionally what we have contended all along: that predominantly Negro schools are inferior to those attended largely by whites. Also that the achievement gap widens between the first grade and the twelfth. In other words, the longer our children attend racially segregated schools, the farther they fall behind white children.

And, lest the non-Southerners feel smug, the report stated that segregation for both whites and Negroes is more complete in the South, but "is extensive in other regions where the Negro population is concentrated: the urban North, Midwest and West."

The Federal Government, whose Office of Education has made some strong statements, must follow up with a strong enforcement of Title VI of the 1964 law. The empty promises of school officials and the defiance of the whole State of Alabama must not be accepted meekly by Federal officials. The furor over the guidelines issued by HEW is another version of the Dixie bluff on race which has worked so well for so many decades. The guidelines are mild. They are legal and not illegal as Governor Wallace proclaimed to his state's educators. They ask the Southerners to do what is for them a strange thing: obey the school desegregation law. On this point the Federal Government must not yield. The Attorney General and the Department of Justice must back up resolutely the legality of Federal action. There can be no temporizing.

Outside the South the call is for unrelenting activity to wipe out de facto school segregation. Boston, Massachusetts, has proved to be the Mississippi of the North.

In fact, in fairness to Mississippi and in consideration of the starting points and traditions of the two places, Boston is *below* Mississippi on this issue. The details, the traps, the methods and the progress will be covered in workshop discussions, but here it must be said that before we can get jobs to earn increased income to buy and rent better homes, before we can contribute to the enrichment of our nation, we must have free access to quality education.

The man who shoots and burns and drowns us is surely our enemy, but so is he who cripples our children for life with inferior public education.

5. We also choose to wrestle with the complex problems of urban life, all of which include an attitude toward and a treatment of millions of Negro citizens. The solution of urban problems will become the solution of living in the last third of our century since more than 70 percent of Americans now live in urban communities.

If it has been asked once, it has been asked a hundred times: Are we going to have a long, hot summer? The answer has many facets, some extremely complex and difficult. But one quick answer is that the police everywhere can make or break urban racial tensions by their conduct toward minority group citizens.

Last summer you had here an upheaval that shook the world. To many of us who looked from afar, it appeared to be a wild, senseless rampage of hate and destruction. But that was far from the whole truth.

There was powder in Watts, piled up and packed down through the years: wide-scale unemployment, both adult and teenage, slum housing, crowded schools, nonexistent health facilities, inadequate transportation and —the Parker police attitude. Everyone was suspect and everyone was subject to harassment in one form or another. The community smoldered under the peculiar brand that police place upon a whole section with their constant sirens, their contemptuous searches, their rough talk, their ready guns and their general "Godalmightiness."

The lesson they and city officials have learned from last year is to seek not correction and improvement, but still more repression. Mayor Yorty and whoever writes his scripts testified in Sacramento in support of a so-called riot-control bill.

The only thing one has to remember about this bill is that it would allow a policeman to judge whether an utterance or an act is an incitement to riot! On his own judgment he could arrest or club or otherwise deter—or shoot—a person whom he (not the law or the courts) deemed to be an inciter of riot. Down the drain goes freedom of speech and down, too, possibly, goes a life.

The McCone Report on the 1965 riot called for "costly and extreme" remedies for Watts, undertaken with a "revolutionary attitude." The answer of the City of Los Angeles was to vote down a hospital bond issue. The answer of Mayor Yorty and of his man, Chief Parker, is a trampling-tough riot-control bill which, if enacted, would loose the police, almost without restraint, upon a populace sick to death—literally—of race control. To blot out any remaining fitful light, one of the gubernatorial candidates, full of disavowals, is the darling of those ultraconservatives who believe in iron control of what they call "violence in the streets"—their code name for Negroes.

If this is the best that a great city can bring to a hard urban problem, one largely of its own making, then God pity both the whites and the Negroes!

We have no panacea for all these problems. We do not proclaim that what we declare here this week is going to change the course of the whole civil rights movement. We do not know all the answers to the George Wallace problem in Alabama, the James Eastland problem in Mississippi, or to the Boston, Massachusetts, school committee and its Louise Day Hicks problem. We certainly don't know the answers to foreign policy and to tax and interest rate puzzlers.

But in this unsettled time when shifts are the order of the day and when change is in the air, we can sail our NAACP ship "steady as she goes," with more drive to the turbines, more skill at the wheel, but no fancy capers for the sake of capers.

We can follow down into each community the really advanced blueprint of the White House Conference "To Fulfill These Rights," which covered four principal areas: economic security and welfare, education, housing, and the administration of justice.

We can expand and point up the community services of our NAACP branches, each of which is, in reality, a citizenship clinic. Just as medical clinics need specialists to cure physical ills, so our branch clinics should recruit volunteer specialists to diagnose and minister to social ills.

We must involve people in the communities in the solution of our problems—not limiting ourselves to our church or lodge or club group.

We must keep the pressure on our local and state education systems through the employment of every legitimate technique: protests, surveys, discussions, demonstrations, picketing and negotiation. Nothing should be overlooked in fighting for better education. Be persistent and ornery; this will be good for the lethargic educational establishment and will aid the whole cause of public education.

Our branches are at work in their territories. In Baltimore, the NAACP won a case against the police commissioner which the Fourth Circuit Court of Appeals declared revealed the most flagrant police practices ever to come before the court. The Blair County, Pennsylvania, NAACP is busy rooting out the remaining discrimination in public accommodations in Clearfield, Pennsylvania.

The Wilmington, Ohio, NAACP has a program for tutoring adults and dropouts and has recruited college professors and students and textbooks to make the project effective. The Bay City, Michigan, NAACP also has a tutorial program under way as well as continuous work on industrial employment practices and housing. The Stillwater, Oklahoma, NAACP is active on a child care center project and on high school desegregation.

And the Montgomery County, West Virginia, NAACP, bless its heart, is 112 percent above last year in membership and 500 percent above last year in funds raised.

Thirty-one branches found time and funds to be present at the Meredith march rally in Jackson, Mississippi, even though the Association, at the last minute, was insulted by the barring of Charles Evers as an NAACP spokesman.

This is only part of the chronicle of "steady as she goes." In a world where the Mayor of Los Angeles is yelling "riot control," where Rhodesia says "never!" to black representation while in America SNCC raises the chant of black power, where the Federal Government at long last is committed, but both the far right and the far left offer vocal and vicious objection, someone has to drive the long haul toward the group goal of Negro Americans and the larger ideal of our young nation.

Our objective is basically as it was laid down in 1909 by the interracial founders of our NAACP. Back there William Lloyd Garrison expressed the strong feeling that the first

NAACP conference "will utter no uncertain sound on any point affecting the vital subject. No part of it is too delicate for plain speech. The republican experiment is at stake, every tolerated wrong to the Negro reacting with double force upon white citizens guilty of faithlessness to their brothers."

As it was then, so it is today. The republican experiment is at stake in 1966. More than that, the dream of a brotherhood in equality and justice is imperiled.

Our fraternity tonight, as it was then, is the fraternity of man, not the white, or brown, or yellow, or black man, but man.

NATHAN WRIGHT, JR.,

Minister, Educator, Author

Nathan Wright, holder of five college degrees, has been a freedom rider and CORE field secretary. He succeeded Adam Clayton Powell, Jr., as chairman of the Plans Committee for the 1967 National Conference on Black Power and has subsequently played a major role in clarifying the concept of Black Power so that it is understandable to blacks and whites, moderates and liberals. In addition to several books dealing with religion and education, Wright is the author of Black Power and Urban Unrest. *He recently completed* Let's Tackle Racism—a Challenge for a Younger America. *As professor of Urban Affairs and chairman of the Afro-American Studies Department at the State University of New York at Albany, Wright is persuasively articulate on the racial situation in our cities and offers the challenge of truly integrated living to his varied audiences and readers over the country.*

"BOTH OUR RELIGIOUS AND NATIONAL COMMITMENTS ARE TOWARD THE CREATION OF ONE PEOPLE AND NOT SEVERAL WHO LIVE IN HARMONY SIDE BY SIDE."

The Economics of Race*

What Have We Been Doing?

Economics may provide . . . a qualitative yardstick as to the validity of the kinds of commitments which we have been making or which we may plan to make. Here we may ask two crucial questions: What are the economic implications of what we do in regard to race relations? And again, what are the race-relations implications of our nation's economic patterns? These questions may be treated as two sides of the same coin, for their answers are interrelated. A generalization toward which we have been building is that *the economic context of race relations may provide both a fresh understanding of our current situation and a clue to ways leading out of our dilemma.*

In business and government, in education and our social agencies, and in an increasing number of areas of our common life, there is the growing conviction that racial separation and disparity of involvement in American life are both wasteful of our nation's resources and unduly taxing on those who must pay for such waste. Hence such separation and disparity are seen to be immoral, that is, to be contrary to the *mores* or to that which symbolizes the common good.

Several illustrations here may suffice to underscore this point. Among city planners there have for quite some time been discussions as to the implications of the early Roosevelt era's restriction of Building and Loan Associations to home mortgaging. Such restrictions and facilitation as were prompted by the federal government have been seen in retrospect to have largely segregated the suburban communities of America, while leaving the central core of our cities to our

* Reprinted from *The American Journal of Economics and Sociology*, Vol. XXVI (January, 1967), pp. 1-12. By permission of *The American Journal of Economics and Sociology* and the author.

major racial minority. The policy of the federal government was not seen to be based upon bias, but unfortunate consequences for the national good have been brought about.

What are these unfortunate consequences? And just what measures are now being proposed to counteract them? The unfortunate consequences of Negro concentration in large urban areas include such things as:

1. Overcrowded, sub-standard housing, since new housing cannot be built today which would pay for itself and accommodate the poor.

2. As a consequence of the maintenance of large tracts of sub-standard housing, the land tax base of our cities tends to be reduced.

3. The demand for services, meanwhile, is increased, such as fire and police protection, welfare, penal and rehabilitation programs, new forms of education, added sanitation, public works, city planning and redevelopment, public transportation, parking, etc.

4. Demoralization and frustration tend to become major factors in public life and in the community and personal life of those who are caught in our ghettos.

5. Unemployment rates rise, as the physical and psychological gap between employers and potential employees grows through a dispersal of industries to the suburbs and their lessening need for the services of the unskilled.

The implications of what we have been listing here are compounded by the fact that our metropolitan areas are fast becoming the centers around which our national life is focused. The central cities therefore need rejuvenation and rehabilitation, and these are the growing repositories for our nation's Negro poor.

It is estimated that, at the accelerating rate at which Negro migration to our cities has moved in the past decade, Negroes will constitute the majority inhabitants of at least the inner-city areas of most of our nation's major urban centers within ten to twenty years. Even some 1965 projections are said to be sufficiently off in 1966 as to make what was then projected for 1970 true in 1966. Such is the case with Newark which had a projected 1970 Negro population proportion of 46 per cent and even now may have a Negro majority. Its school system's student body at this moment is approximately 80 per cent non-white.

What urban planners have tried to do in recent years is to use the same type of federal economic resource as helped facilitate our post-Roosevelt era residential segregation to desegregate at this time our central cities. With the intention of utilizing massive and calculated government aid, urban planners have been devising plans for the desegregation of our crucial central city areas. Their plans involve at heart the subsidizing of prime demand apartments or other dwelling units at such attractive rates that in the minds of prospective white real estate clients the issue of economy will by far take precedence over any feelings about the avoidance of Negroes. In much this kind of way urban planners hope to desegregate our inner cities, building attractive middle-income government-subsidized housing and providing unpublicized rent subsidies for poor Negro families to be housed comfortably among higher-income groups who pay rents at a level adequate to cover building costs.

That the costs of basic improvement of the Negro's lot are less than policing and servicing costs in our Negro ghettos has prompted the federal government to initiate its rehabilitative programs through the Office of Economic Opportunity and has been a prime factor in recent legislation designed to improve our urban schools. The Demonstration Cities Project conceived by President Johnson also aims at using economic leverages to correct many of our race-relations-oriented problems in our cities.

How we employ economic leverages in our cities is of the utmost importance. The classic programs of the federal government ideally aim at facilitation of basic change in such a way that progress toward rehabilitation and the closing of the physical, psychological, and economic gaps between the Negro and white American will take place. In the VISTA program, for example, the self-help aspect is underscored. In practice, however, the instilling of self-generating mechanisms into programs aimed at the breaking of vicious circles is exceedingly difficult. Nonetheless, if we overlook the possibility of facilitating self-help and fail to keep this as our foremost purpose, then economic aid which initially may be gladly received soon may become an effrontery. Men and women—as well as children—come to hate the hand which too long feeds them. The radio news services carried not long ago what appeared to some to be a tragic-comic story of an appeal by a group of Negro poor for loans from several foreign countries on the stated grounds that they wanted help to help themselves and that in America they could only get a dole. People want to maintain their self-respect. When this is lost, little else of enduring value seems to remain.

Where Do We Go from Here?

One of the shibboleths that have been passed about concerning a resolution of the Negro's predicament as the holder of a substandard certificate of legal tender is that he has an inferior education. The obvious answer that is posed is that the Negro will simply have to be more adequately educated. Then all his problems and disparities will fade away. Table III tests this idea.

Table III

Ratio of Median Money Income of Non-White Families to Median Income of White Families Having the Same Number of Years of Education, March, 1965

Elementary School:	
Less than 8 years	65.91%
8 years	72.99%
High School:	
1 to 3 years	60.30%
4 years	69.06%
College:	
1 to 3 years	71.73%
4 years or more	87.59%

This table suggests several things: (1) Non-whites still earn substantially less than whites, even when they have the same amount of education. (2) That is generally true no matter how much education a non-white obtains. (3) A comparison of the 1965 ratio for non-white vs. white families as a whole (55.98 per cent from the second table above)* with the average of the six ratios in the above table (71.26 per cent) indicates that only about one-fourth (the figure is actually 28.81 per cent) of the disparity between non-white and white family incomes is due to the former, on the average, having less education, while the bulk of the disparity, almost three-fourths, is due to other causes.

*Second table not included in this excerpt. See page 305 for source of original publication.

Education alone, then, is not the answer. Yet a word or two in this regard may be in order. Increasingly the civil rights movement has been taking its sights upon the schools. It has made the claim that both *de facto* segregated education (which is apparently inferior) and otherwise inadequate education (lack of concern, failure to appreciate the real needs of students, etc.) are the inheritance of those who attend schools in our Negro-dominated urban areas. Even though education alone may not be the answer to the Negro's separation from the mainstream of the nation's economic life, it is still true that inferior education will only compound the problem. To the extent that inadequate education prevails in our ghettos, more emphasis must be placed on education, not less. This emphasis should be as monumental as is the task, recognizing all the while that in answering as we must the Negro students' obvious needs, we may obtain handles on the hard-to-pinpoint needs of countless other non-Negro students.

Our civic and religious groups in our cities or with influence in them should take a leadership role in working to bring about better urban education. Such tasks as that of changing age-old school districts into sensible entities and the creation of new formulas for support and responsibility, as between the state and the nation, may prove to be far more economically wise in terms of our attention than our traditional halo-laden lady-bountiful ameliorative stop-gap endeavors.

A massive need for reclamation and for continuing education is a discrete system of community colleges divorced absolutely from the four-year college system and more nearly meshed with the unmet needs within our public schools. Here all adults, nineteen years of age or older—no matter how little education they may have had—should be able to be enrolled for training and retraining vocationally, avocationally, and for cultural enrichment. The drop-out, the relief recipient, the late starter, and all others with adult educational needs not best met in a totally academically-oriented four-year institution should continue their schooling here.

Today everyone in our society should have a minimum of fourteen grades of schooling; and the Department of Labor has been indicating for quite some time that our changing and increasingly technological economy will necessitate on an average for every adult four periods of retraining during their thirty years of employability. Many of our existing community colleges—as the result of undue pressures from and on the four-year college system—have subverted their basic purpose to serve unmet adult needs and have become the first two years of a four-year program. This leaves our urban uneducated Negroes—and countless whites—with little hope for the adult literacy and cultural enrichment outlets they so sorely need. It has been a growing national experience that vocational schools and adult high schools do not attract adults. High schools are for children. College is for adults. We shall not release a growing population of restless and potentially explosive urban poor from their vicious cycle of frustration until truly viable mechanisms for adult fulfillment are created. Private monies—as well as public—should be addressed to this end. Relief monies can be used. The cost-benefit analysis for such programs favors such a creative educational thrust for our urban poor who are, in increasing numbers, Negroes.

The central, overriding economic fact or principle regarding our Negro urban poor is that either they will be trained adequately for life and livelihood and then given opportunity for their due fulfillment, or our poor become liabilities for which our white society must pay a major, geometrically increasing and never-ending relief and policing cost. A reasonable ultimate alternative to provision of full training and full opportunity is genocide. Some feel that—as genocide was possible with a white Christian Germany when extremist feelings held the day—it will be possible in America when white backlash and white lethargy and unwillingness to make the most of American potential meet the deadly monster of a mass of millions of resentful, angry, and untutored Negro poor caught in a vicious cycle of illegitimacy and vice amounting to not much less than total demoralization and almost total outrage.

Along with this overriding economic fact is the clear reality of a failure of past mechanisms for Negro progress in relation to what Negroes see white people of comparable potential as possessing. Obviously new approaches are in order, and for this the best minds that we have should be put to work. In order to do this, several crucial adjustments in our thinking would have to be made. (1) We would have to cease thinking of American race relations, for one thing, as "taking care of itself" or of its problems as being resolved increasingly over a period of some reasonable time. On the contrary, we are creating a monster within our midst, a people being alienated from the mainstream of American life, not by an aggressive and deliberate policy of malicious intent, but by the sedation of ourselves into the feeling that things are not really as they are. (2) A second thing that we would need to do is to cease thinking of race relations as a nice and good thing, as one important national and local task—among many others—to do. American race relations today, like religion and basic ideologies historically, must have an absolute priority . . . or we are as a nation lost!

Now in all of this the civic groups and churches must come to play new and decisive roles. The civic groups and churches of America are representative of America and are so woven into the warp and woof of American life that it might be said with reasonableness that if our civic groups and church people only begin to come to fresh grips with the extremity and scope of the problem in their own personal, corporate, and organizational concerns, a saving shift of focus will have been made in American race relations.

Is Progress Really Possible?

The impetus of all that we have said thus far is in the hope that—in some way—progress in American race relations may replace what amounts to a present state of stagnation or possible retrogression.

Our approaches to possible progress may be seen to consist of four levels of action.

1. *Strategic*. There needs to be developed a major strategy employing the best talent in business and industry and in government and private agencies—including those of education and religion—both on a national and local level. We need to bring to the massive problems of race all the creative leverage of our best minds.

In one community there is the possibility that the major corporate owners of the region's economic life will address themselves in depth to the issues involved, not from the old stance of alleviating a local pressure, but from the point of view of our national survival as the kind of free people which we would believe we are destined to be. It is these men who hopefully will furnish major resources for spurring total community interest and involvement in the pressing concerns and implications of our current race relations patterns.

One major school of business administration some years ago expressed the conviction that Negroes—in the present state of our economic development—could not climb up the economic ladder in new and old areas of employment in the traditional ways with the rapidity that our times demand. The alternative—now tried in a growing number of areas of business and government—is to catapult promising persons to the top echelon. Their presence may thus exert the proper pressure and pull for those in the ranks below to rise.

2. *Symbolic*. Where massive gains cannot be made quickly,

symbolic gains can be made. In our schools and churches and other areas of public and private life—as has been the recent policy of our federal government—Negroes of the greatest potential should be aggressively sought out to take positive and acknowledged leadership positions of both high visibility and influence. A people seemingly without hope may thus be given some measure of promise for the future and so be provided also with a tangible and immediate pledge of our good faith as we set out to put things right. Rules of seniority have no moral basis when privilege has been set up on the base of the past and almost total exclusion of the Negro.

Negroes must be dealt into every American enterprise at least at the point of equity or beyond. If our hearts are in our task, such an endeavor may easily come to pass.

3. *Sympathetic.* In many ways which lead to almost no particular place, but which may serve as a much-needed holding operation, the Negro urban poor especially need our sympathy or sense of involvement with them. Because the hour is late in American race relations, every reasonable means of involvement and presence with our restless and hopeless poor may serve at least an ameliorative purpose.

Such efforts as community organization, summer student projects, and the volunteer services of suburban adults may at the very least postpone the day of violence. This, in our day, is no mean purpose. Hopefully such efforts may do much more in the building of self-respect and confidence. In the days of violence, past and continuing sympathetic involvement may build much-needed bridges of communication. These must be kept open even though the cost may be very great.

The sympathetic hand may be like a two-edged sword. It must be disciplined and should in no wise be mistaken for the strategic thrusts which may or may not have been begun. Too often—and especially with our churches—the ready and needed hand has been mistaken for the capacity on the part of those whom we would help to walk and for our willingness to walk in mutuality every step along the way to the fulfillment of our neighbor's lot. We cannot be true change agents unless we are willing to be changed ourselves, to step aside from our base of privilege and allow and help others to compete with us equitably for the opportunities which we have held for ourselves alone. The giving of white suburban largesse is not the full and final answer but an immediate and highly essential task for our beginning to look toward progress through a total sharing of what we are and have.

4. *Systematic.* We must have the will and determination to

give priority to our race relations concerns. Both our religious and national commitments are toward the creation of one people and not several who live in harmony side by side.

To be open to change calls for such a steady commitment of the will that answers hitherto unknown to us may be both spawned and given recognition and endorsement when they appear upon the horizon of our minds. Without such systematic determination, backed by mechanisms for research, for thoughtful interchange, for creativity, and for the widespread propagation of that which seems essential to the common good, a vital thrust out of the vicious cycle of stagnation cannot be made.

Is progress in American race relations possible? The economics of our current race relations point to the need for progress. The massive placing of our resources on the side of progress may hold the key to hope. Has it not been said by one greater than us all that "Where your treasure is, there shall your heart be also"?

After a Long Hot Summer*

By SENATOR EDWARD W. BROOKE

Our nation has come perilously close to a second civil war. The causes span a century. The consequences are awesome. What a nation sows, it must inevitably reap. In this year of 1967, America reaps a harvest of violence.

Individual and mob acts of violence are deplorable and intolerable. The death and destruction left in a riot's wake are no foundation for progress. They are a bitter monument to the breakdown of order, which is the only foundation upon which progress can be built.

Violence is a sniper's bullet. It is a brick through a store owner's window. But violence can take other forms. It is an act of violence to deny or infringe or violate a man's constitutional rights or his individual dignity. It is an act of violence to deny a man a job because of his race or his religion. It is an act of violence to deny a man the right to live where he chooses because he is Negro.

It is an act of violence to deny children quality education and an opportunity to lead meaningful lives. It is an act of violence to create a spectator population that is not permitted to participate in the nation's progress or its hope for the future.

Such violence betrays the promise and principle upon which this nation was founded. That promise was the issue at stake when the nation engaged in civil war more than a century ago, and it is the issue today. In Lincoln's words: "The promise that . . . the weights would be lifted from the shoulders of all men, and that all should have an equal chance." That is the essence

*Reprinted from *Look* Magazine, XXXI (September 5, 1967), pp. 26-27. By permission of Cowles Communications, Inc., and the author.

of a free society: a profound commitment to an affirmation of the worth and dignity of every individual.

If that is our belief, then we must organize American society in such a way that the blessings of freedom and prosperity may spread to all the people of the United States.

We have achieved neither the promise nor the principle. One-sixth of our total population lives in poverty. One-half of the Negro population lives in poverty. These conditions exist at the price of domestic tranquillity.

No act of injustice, past or present, no conditions of deprivation, no delay in progress can justify or excuse a breakdown in law and order, the indiscriminate killing of people or the wanton destruction of property. Ours is a government of laws, not men. When the hand of any man is raised against a neighbor or a stranger, it is raised against us all. To defy the law subverts and ultimately ruins the only system of government that can protect free men.

It was not so long ago that white violence in Mississippi threatened the admission of a qualified Negro student to a state university. In sending troops to uphold the law in 1962, President Kennedy used words that are just as applicable today: "If this country should ever reach the point where any man or group of men by force or threat of force could long defy [the law], then no law would stand free from doubt, . . . and no citizen would be safe from his neighbors."

When government is called on to respond to an outbreak of violence, its duty is plain. It is to restore law and order. But in performing its duty, government is no less bound to observe the law. Unnecessary violence on the part of government breeds contempt for the law. It gives impetus to further violence.

Violence, be it white or black, can only impede or retard progress. It tears a community apart. It increases bitterness, tension and suspicion. It can destroy the possibility of a dialogue that is essential to the articulation of grievances and effective governmental response.

Violence seriously wounds the community in which it occurs. It brings death and physical destruction. It drains the local treasury. It injures the local economy, making it difficult if not impossible for individuals and businesses to obtain insurance and mortgages. It discourages new investment, crippling future industrial growth.

Government, at every level, has failed to identify and treat the conditions that lead to these tragic consequences. Through indifference, inaction and delay, it has helped to create the atmosphere for violence. The failure of the Federal Government to enforce existing civil-rights legislation and to appropriate funds to finance basic and needed social programs has been a source of frustration and bitterness. The failure of state and local governments to deal with the legitimate grievances of the Negro populations in their communities has contributed to actual and potential riots.

Local and state governments have failed to provide the most elementary services for the Negro communities within their borders. Legitimate grievances are legion. Action to eliminate them lags. A disgruntled and potentially revolutionary class grows at a record pace. Meanwhile, the public officials who most deplore the riots are often their unwitting instigators. Government at all levels must respond to the legitimate requests of responsible Negro leadership. Black Power is a response to white irresponsibility.

State and local governments have a clearly defined choice. They can continue to ignore reasonable requests for governmental action, submitted by responsible members of the Negro community, or, recognizing that their responsibility extends to all parts of the state or municipality, they can enlarge the scope of governmental action to include many who have traditionally been deprived of the most elementary form of public service.

The failure to respond to legitimate complaints promotes militancy. It is an invitation to further violence. Constructive action, on the other hand, can build a society that will end violence.

There is no unanimity of view about the causes of the riots. The likelihood is that there is no single cause. Some believe that there are conspiracies, interstate in character, that have played an important role in some, if not all, of the riots. The House of Representatives has responded to this kind of reasoning by passing a so-called "anti-riot" bill, which prohibits the crossing of state lines for the purpose of inciting riots. A few have also suggested that the riots may even be Communist-inspired, that those who would overthrow our Government are exploiting the misery and resentment of certain segments of the population for their own revolutionary purposes.

In my view, the riots from which the nation suffers are neither Communist-inspired nor the result of an interstate conspiracy. Hunger, bad housing, ill health, lack of work and the absence of law enforcement need no allies to create an atmosphere that breeds violence. However, when we seek the causes of the riots, every hypothesis should be studied and every potential cause examined.

It is for this reason that, immediately after the Detroit riots,

I called for the establishment of a Select Committee on Civil Disorder. I am pleased to heed the President's call and serve on his special advisory commission. This commission can perform a signal service in identifying and in recommending solutions for the causes of the nationwide disturbances that plague us. But it can serve another equally important function. It can be a symbol, a tangible demonstration, that the United States Government is actually and actively concerned. It can relieve the minds of those who fear that government is powerless to act in this crisis. It can give hope to those who have given up hope that their Government can and will help them. It can be a deterrent to further violence.

But no investigation or search for facts need delay congressional action on programs designed to relieve the conditions of poverty in America. Riots must not be used as an excuse to halt the beginning of progress.

Rioters should be prosecuted to the fullest extent of the law. But a "punitive reaction" to the riots, resulting in the refusal of Congress to take positive action, will punish not the rioters but millions of law-abiding people who took no part in and who deplore the riots. A punitive response will spur further violence. It is time to break the vicious cycle of delay, inaction, bitterness and violence.

It is time that the promises made to all Americans generations ago were kept: the promises that life would improve, that jobs would be provided, that schools would be built, that decent housing and health facilities would be available.

In 1949, the Congress promised "a decent home and a suitable living environment for every American family." Franklin D. Roosevelt had already pledged to overcome the disadvantages of one-third of a nation "ill-housed, ill-clad and ill-nourished." We have reaffirmed that pledge to the one-sixth of our population that continues to suffer the disadvantages of poverty. But we are not doing enough to keep that promise.

The entire budget for the poverty program is less than a single month's expenditure in Vietnam. And as one returning veteran remarked, surveying the ashes of his Detroit community, "The war is here." We are not talking about increasing the dole. The vast majority of the nation's 11.5 million poor households receive no public assistance. We are talking about constructive programs to train; to impart skills to the unemployed; to repair the disadvantages of inadequate education; to teach people to read and write; to enable people to own their own homes and businesses. But to reach people under these programs requires more money, wisely spent, than we are now spending.

Government's role in relation to overcoming the problems of poverty in America is in keeping with the traditional concept that government is the people's tool for doing together what cannot be done by people acting alone.

Those who criticize today's poverty program as providing something for nothing, should think back over a century to Lincoln's Homestead Law, which, in giving away the vast lands in the West, opened opportunities for millions of Americans; or land-grant colleges, which have made higher education a reality for millions of Americans.

In more recent years, the development of railroads, airlines, the oil industry and the communications-satellite system were all brought about through vast Government subsidy amounting to billions of dollars.

When I mention adequate Government programs to assist the poor, I am not talking about a giveaway program—I am talking about an investment, the most important investment a government can make: an investment in people, in their future and the nation's future.

Our Government must come to view its responsibility for eliminating poverty and discrimination in America in this positive fashion. It must make this effort as a nation not because there are riots or the threat of riots. It must make this effort because it is legally and morally right. It must make this effort because the nation needs the energy, the commitment and the talent of every American if we are to make progress as a nation and maintain our position as a world leader.

The poor lack power. They are a minority, and they are unorganized. They have no lobby. But the Congress must respond to their needs, even though the impetus to do so does not come through the process of constituency pressure.

The democratic process must be made to work between the majority "haves" and the minority "have nots." If it does not, then the shutting off of the democratic process to the disadvantaged will not allow for peaceful change and progress. Frustration, hopelessness and the lack of a future propel the poor toward violence—which they think brings some results, some attention from the "power structure," some sense of power in the community, be it only the power to destroy. The cost to America of violence is high: in lives, in suffering and in dollars.

We cannot tolerate the consequences of intolerable conditions, so we must change the conditions. A century ago, Lincoln knew that a nation could not endure half-slave and half-free. He did not know what the outcome would be. But he knew the division would cease to exist or the nation would cease to exist.

Today, this nation cannot continue to flourish half-free and half less than free. Our cities will continue to deteriorate, and all progress will be impeded if the full force and attention of government at all levels is not now, finally, mobilized to solve the problems.

It is the voice of the Congress of the United States that has been lacking in this commitment to progress. The image and the action of the Congress have been negative, rather than positive. The reaction of many lawmakers to the riots has been punitive, rather than progressive.

The Congress must assume leadership, must assure the nation that change for the better will take place, and it must take action to secure that change. Once the people of this nation are convinced that the task of securing an equal chance for all our citizens is the primary task on the mind and agenda of Congress, then, I am convinced, we will have taken a major step toward abating the grievances that lead to civil disorder.

The problem of relieving the burdens of poverty, which weigh on many of our citizens, is both simple and complex. Simple because we have the resources to accomplish the task; complex because the forces to put them to use and bring them to bear on the problem effectively are complex. We must want to do it. Action by government at all levels and a personal commitment on the part of every American to fulfill his responsibilities to each other and to his nation are required. Great strides may then be made, the promise of America secured, and the command of Isaiah heeded that "violence shall no more be heard in thy land, wasting nor destruction within thy borders."

When Negro Leaders Look Ahead . . .*

"Appoint a Black Person to Cabinet"

By WHITNEY M. YOUNG, JR.

Q. Mr. Young, do you expect the election of Mr. Nixon to ease or worsen the racial problem in America?

A. Mr. Nixon spent a couple of hours in my office just before his nomination and, from what he said then, I believe he wants to govern—he wants to be a good President. Certainly I think he is intelligent enough for the job, and has shown organizational skill.

I believe that he is going to recognize the need to give Negroes some reassurance of his intentions at an early date through statements on programs and appointments. I think a great deal is going to depend on doing this right away—before he takes office—to allay the fear that many of the black people obviously have that he is insensitive to their problems.

It is no secret that black voters, almost without exception, voted for Hubert Humphrey for President. This reflects their deep concern over the relationship of Mr. Nixon to Senator Strom Thurmond of South Carolina and to Governor Spiro T. Agnew as his vice-presidential candidate.

It also reflects their feeling that he made a sophisticated appeal for the Southern vote in suggesting suppression of dissent and demonstrations. So there was a deep sense of disap-

*Reprinted from *U.S. News and World Report,* LXV (November 25, 1968), pp. 58-61. By permission of U.S. News and World Report, Inc., and the author.

pointment among blacks—even fear over what his election really meant.

That is why a great deal is going to depend on what he does rather quickly by way of appointments and statements and spelling out of tangible programs. I don't mean slogans such as "black capitalism," because I don't think there is any such thing as "black capitalism"—any more than I think there is such a thing as "white capitalism."

Q. What if Mr. Nixon carries out his promise to ease up on federal guidelines to desegregation in the States?

A. It would be a major setback for Negroes. Guidelines have been the most effective tool we have had in progress toward racial equality in schools, and other programs getting federal money.

Q. Is integration losing its popularity with Negroes?

A. No. Too many people have been fooled into thinking that many persons in the black community want segregation. A few loudmouths have said they want it. But all the studies and polls show that 90 per cent of all the Negroes in this country are still aiming toward an open and integrated society.

Our problem now is that the extremists, white and black—who increasingly are forming their own coalitions—say over and over to responsible civil-rights leaders: "It's impossible to work within the system in America. White society is congenitally corrupt and morally bankrupt—so the system must be overthrown."

Now, if Mr. Nixon takes a course of indifference to our problems or of cutting back on implementation of the civil-rights laws that have already been enacted, he will only make prophets of these revolutionists. He will undercut strongly our leadership and weaken the ability of the militant but responsible Negroes to maintain the influence they now have.

We have been able, with great difficulty, to secure the leadership of the masses of black people on the basis of what little has been done for them. If there is any decrease in that, we're in trouble.

Q. Would you regard stiffer handling of riots and other disorders as a setback to your leadership?

A. I think that if there is any move toward suppression simply by force, rather than toward prevention by giving Negroes "a piece of the action" and improving their lot in life, then we will end up in a situation like that of the concentration camp.

The only way to bring about real order is to provide the Negro community—and its responsible leadership—with enough tangible victories so that it can exercise discipline from within. You can achieve order only through internal discipline—not through external forces of guns or armored cars or the National Guard. There can be real stability only when we can say to people, "Look—cool it," and when they ask why, tell them: "Because as of this date we are going to have these jobs and that housing and this health facility."

We need from the new Administration a plan with a timetable so that hopes are not constantly raised, then dashed—for instance, when legislation is sabotaged by the appropriations committees in Congress for things like rent supplements and model cities.

If Mr. Nixon could carry out a definite program, we would have order. We would get order overnight.

Q. What else could build Negro confidence in Mr. Nixon?

A. The most critical thing is his appointments. This would mean the appointment of white people known to be understanding of and sensitive to the problems of the black community, and it would mean the appointment of blacks in whom the black community has confidence—not just some black Republican Mr. Nixon manages to find. There aren't too many black Republicans who are well known, and he will probably have to draw from Democrats.

In any case, he certainly ought to continue the practice of appointment of at least one black person to the Cabinet.

Q. What about the "black capitalism" that Mr. Nixon talked about during the campaign?

A. The concept of encouraging black entrepreneurship—helping black people become managers and stockholders in business—is a sound one. But the term "black capitalism" implies a separateness: a "black" and a "white" economy. That is why it got the applause of both the black extremists and the John Birch Society.

Furthermore, when Mr. Nixon says, "We're going to have to turn this job over to private enterprise," that is a little tricky. Private enterprise is going to have to do the job, but it will have to be undergirded by the Government. You are not going to get private enterprise to remake the "ghettos" and do all the things that have to be done in education on its own —any more than private enterprise would have built an airline without subsidies, or put a man into space.

The Government has to bear part of the initial burden—provide insurance against excessive loss, as well as the tax incentives Mr. Nixon mentions. Otherwise, private enterprise will not do the job.

Q. How do you see your task, and that of other Negro leaders, when Mr. Nixon moves into the Presidency?

A. I think we have the immediate task of placing before the new administration our thoughts on the current situation, and our problems. We should be very candid about those programs that have not been very good, as well as about those that have been very good, and new ideas that ought to be tried.

Then, if Mr. Nixon and his Administration, working with Congress, can respond positively with a plan, it is our job to co-operate. Mr. Nixon is going to be our President, and I am all for making him the best President that we have had. I'm all for offering every bit of co-operation—not just interpreting Negro desires to him, but interpreting to the black community the positive steps he is taking, and trying to get their help.

Mr. Nixon can get valuable help within the black community. For instance, the Urban League has just gotten a 9-million-dollar contract from the Labor Department for on-the-job training because we had a training cost of $550 per person—as compared with $3,500 for the National Alliance of Businessmen and almost $7,000 for the Job Corps—and 85 per cent of the 24,000 people we have trained are working in jobs.

In other words, I hope that Mr. Nixon will help strengthen the black community's responsible and established leadership, instead of experimenting as some of the "community action" projects have done, which only resulted in making them politically motivated projects for the benefit of the extremists.

"We Need to Have a New Constitution"

By ROY INNIS

Q. Mr. Innis, do you look for more racial trouble, or less, when Mr. Nixon takes over the White House?

A. That depends on a couple of factors:

One is that Richard Nixon has a unique opportunity to make a real change in race relations. A couple of key moves and a certain amount of understanding can do that for him. The first thing he should do is to understand clearly that two distinct people—black and white—live in this country, and try to work out a social contract between them for co-existence.

This is important because the Administrations of the past have played games with themselves by trying to deny the existence of blacks as a distinct people. They have tried to suggest that we were just another "ethnic group" in the American melting pot. That kind of thinking led to disastrous programs that have produced the present confrontation between black and white.

Then the next thing would be for the new Administration to join with the black community in putting together meaningful programs—and I do not mean "Mickey Mouse" programs that have been fed to us since the 1930s or even before. I mean serious programs to deal with our unique conditions.

Q. What programs, specifically?

A. First, the Community Self-Determination Act introduced in Congress this year. This is a bill put together by CORE, with the aid of some consultants, and sponsored in the House of Representatives by some Republicans—Charles E. Goodell of New York, who is now Senator, and others.

This bill was set up for so-called poor communities. I say "so-called" because I differ sometimes with others about what a "poor" community is, but basically it certainly applies to black areas of urban centers as well as poor white neighborhoods.

What this bill would do is create community corporations on the business model—serious business corporations that would be responsible for creating and energizing community enterprises. Profits would be converted into social service and thereby act as a stabilizing social, political and economic force in the communities.

It is considered by us to be the most imaginative piece of legislation dealing with this problem in many decades. It is the first one to deal with black people as a people instead of just a segment in over-all programs such as Head Start or the "war on poverty" and other "Mickey Mouse" ideas.

Q. What comes after that?

A. Then we want the transfer of institutions within the black community to the management and control of the people themselves. Nixon should support the concept of community control of schools, welfare, sanitation, fire, police, health and hospitals and all other vital institutions operating in the so-called "ghettos." This kind of move will put those basic instruments of society in our hands so that we can maximize their effect on stability of the community.

Q. How would you finance those institutions?

A. In exactly the same way they are financed now—out of the taxes that we pay. The only difference is that we pay taxes and we never see them again. The money is supposed to come back to us in services, but it is given to some agency which is not our agency. We are saying: "Return our tax moneys to institutions that belong to us so they can function for us."

Q. What other programs do you propose?

A. They are long-range and develop naturally from the ones I've mentioned.

We want a new social contract between blacks and whites—in short, a new Constitution. We need to have a new U.S. Constitution that permits black people to maximize their political interests. It is not possible, at this stage and with this Constitution, to do this. There is no way that we can get a per capita share of political power.

For instance, we have anywhere from 10 to 15 per cent of the population. Even if we used the low number, 10 per cent would mean 10 Senate seats that we are entitled to. But there is no way we can get 10 Senators under the present Constitution. In the House, we should have 43 seats but we have only six now, and a seventh—held by Adam Clayton Powell—was vacated by a majority of the white Republicans and

Democrats in the House, which is a breach of contract in itself.

We will have to have a new Constitution that gives black people, as a people, a per capita share of representation, to be selected and removed by our rules and responsive to our own interests.

Q. Are you no longer interested in integration?

A. The traditional goal of integration is as dead as a doornail. In fact, it never came alive.

Q. Some Negro leaders say that separatism plays into the hands of white segregationists—

A. Unfortunately, they are using sloppy logic. First of all, if separation of the races is good in itself, it wouldn't make any difference to me who else wants it. If another man likes to breathe oxygen and drink water, that is no reason why I shouldn't breathe oxygen and drink water if it serves my functions. Whoever else can be happy or can gain from solutions that are satisfactory to me—so much the better, whether that person be black or white.

The argument against separatism is really fallacious because very few people understand the true nature of separation. Most people think of it as segregation, and we should never confuse the two things.

Segregation is a very obnoxious relationship between two groups in society wherein one group dominates the other and controls its vital institutions, as in America right now.

Separation, however, suggests that we both control our vital institutions and that neither of us dominates the other.

Q. Do you advocate separate schools for the races?

A. There would be two school systems in the urban centers. That operating in the predominantly black area would be predominantly black—managed and controlled by blacks. If one or two whites happen to live in that area—well, they would have full access. We wouldn't segregate them. But clearly it would be our institution, responsive to our interests and our needs.

In the white areas, the same rule would prevail. They would run their institutions to satisfy their needs.

Q. Does a majority of Negroes support separatism?

A. I always answer the question about majority support, or lack of it, in this way:

If you go back in American history to 1770, you could ask the same question of Thomas Jefferson, Ben Franklin, James Madison and Alexander Hamilton. You will find that the solution they were offering for the colonists—which also happened to be a separatist solution—was not widely accepted or understood. And do you know something? Those guys made no attempt to get consensus, because leadership of a people during crisis does not wait for consensus. It projects solutions, and moves to get them implemented. If those solutions succeed, people go along, because their needs are satisfied.

Q. What if Mr. Nixon does not accept the separatist solution of the race problem?

A. Then he will continue on the obvious path to chaos. We will encourage an unfortunate confrontation in which both races must lose.

Q. What kind of confrontation?

A. My reading of the recent past and the present is that there is rising frustration on the part of both blacks and whites. And both peoples are going to react, sometimes very neurotically. This neurotic behavior is going to be expressed in terms of spontaneous outbursts. We are calling them "riots," but actually they are rebellions more than anything else—natural rebellions very similar to the Boston Tea Party.

We are on an escalating path in that direction. In Cleveland this year, the rioting had a Western-style "shoot-out," and we see indications all over the country of more sophisticated versions developing. People have learned from this year's experiences and will try something else next year.

This is a dangerous situation because it has led to a neurotic—you could even call it psychotic—call for "law and order" on the part of whites. We saw three major candidates playing up to that appeal. And we see, more and more, a dangerous social crisis coming about that could only lead to massive destruction on both sides.

Q. Are you optimistic that Mr. Nixon will avert this crisis?

A. I think there are several reasons why, in this very pessimistic world, I might tend to have a certain amount of optimism:

First, I don't think Nixon has the same commitment to past solutions as the Democrats had. He was not a part of the solutions of the 1930s that are being applied to the problems of the 1960s. Therefore he can make a change—right?

Second, the people with whom the blacks have the greatest immediate conflict of interest are the urban whites who manage the politics, the institutions, the unions and so forth. I don't think Nixon has commitments to these whites as the Democrats did. They are not his stronghold, so he is much freer to move against them, even in some kind of momentary association with us.

Third, Nixon lost the black vote by 93 per cent, which is a fantastic number of blacks to be voting against him. I don't think they had much of a reason to vote for him, but they did not have that much of a reason to vote for Humphrey, either. In fact, we had advised them not to vote for either.

In any case, however, as a practical politician—which Nixon is—he has to recognize that it is not good politics to lose 93 per cent of the vote among a people numbering over 25 million. Therefore, I think he will have to do something to change his image with blacks.

Q. Can he do that and still crack down on civil disorders?

A. I hope that he's a brighter man than his campaign rhetoric indicated. He should be astute enough to understand that "law and order" will not suppress the legitimate aspirations of blacks. History has shown that that kind of move can lead only to counterviolence and chaos.

"Peace Is Our No. 1 Domestic Problem"

By ROY WILKINS

Q. Mr. Wilkins, what is the reaction of Negroes to the election of Richard M. Nixon?

A. Most Negro citizens, of course, voted for Hubert Humphrey. In some Negro areas, his support ran beyond 90 per cent. These people do have the feeling that perhaps Mr. Nixon does not appreciate their special problems and may not be willing to make a special effort on their behalf.

Yet once a man gets into the White House, he can change. It is quite possible that a pessimistic estimate of Mr. Nixon today may not be the estimate of him a year from now.

Q. Do you expect him to give the race problem a lower priority than Lyndon B. Johnson did?

A. I don't see how he can. Peace in our domestic scene, and especially in the racial conflict, constitutes our No. 1 domestic problem. He can't very well ignore it. And if I were a candidate who won by less than 400,000 votes out of some 70 million votes, I wouldn't ignore any part of the electorate, no matter how few votes it gave me this year.

Q. What changes in racial policy do you foresee?

A. It is too early to tell precisely. Mr. Nixon has laid stress on the development of "black capitalism" and the luring of white capital into the "ghetto" areas—in housing, employment and development of Negro business. I would hope that there would be genuine encouragement of this program.

One of the first things I would like to see is a positive policy toward Negro business in the Small Business Administration. In the past, the SBA has been tougher than the local banks have been in giving loans and other help to Negro businessmen—retailers, especially.

Q. Mr. Nixon indicated his disapproval of federal guidelines to States on integration. What happens if they are dropped?

A. This is a very important question for us. What the Negro has been trying to escape for 70 years has been local whims in determining his citizenship rights. He wants the Federal Government to tell States and localities: "You can decide within certain limits what you will do, but you cannot violate the basic constitutional guarantees of this man's rights or that group's rights."

Therefore, I'm afraid that if school desegregation is left to localities and States and if Republicans attempt to institute the idea of black grants to States, letting them decide how they will spend the money, then the Negro will simply be returned to a condition that he has spent the last couple of generations trying to escape.

You see, it is theoretically true that the Negro citizens of, say, Indiana could exercise political influence to obtain a fair distribution of federal block grants. But any study of distribution in the past shows that there is not only favoritism between the races but between rich and poor areas. And if you look at the South, where the Negro still lacks real political leverage, the politicians will simply chortle with glee and proceed to do as they please with block grants.

Q. Would Negroes then turn to separatism rather than integration as a solution to their problems?

A. The idea of abandoning integration as a goal is just so much rhetoric so far. Nothing else offers peace and equality as integration does.

The extremists among Negroes would have real influence only if the Nixon Administration turns its back completely on Negroes and gives no encouragement to moderates. Then the Negro people would be inclined to listen more to the cries of extremists than they have so far. I am not saying they would join the extremists. But they certainly would no longer greet them with hostility, because we would have nothing to offer in rebuttal.

Thus you might have more emphasis than before on "black power." I see nothing wrong with "black power" in its basic essentials—such as development of the Negro's economy, of his pride and image and history, of his stake in business and of the whole gamut of things that the Negro has lacked. But the arrogance, the seizure of power, the ignoring of laws, the expediency for the sake of personal or group gains—these are aspects of "black power" that would be harmful.

Q. Do you expect more violence, or less, in times ahead?

A. Hopefully, less violence. Even among some extremists, there is a feeling that, while talking tough, we must concentrate on developing strength within the "ghettos"—better schools, better housing, more Negro business.

I think it is plain that we will be stepping up our political activity. You can see the growth in Negro political power in the results of this year's elections. They show that about 370 Negroes occupy elective offices in the 11 Southern States. We have gained seven seats in State legislatures and hold office as justices of the peace, election commissioners and members of school boards. And we are going to get more men in public office at every level of government throughout the nation, because by 1972 we are going to have an increase of at least one third in the number of Negro votes.

A vast majority of these Negroes are determined to work in the American electoral system peacefully to achieve their ends. If I were President, I would meet them halfway by walking warily on the path of returning powers to the States without some check by the Federal Government to make sure that the Negro rights won in the last few years are not lost to local whims once again.

Showdown for Non-Violence*

By MARTIN LUTHER KING, JR.

The policy of the Federal Government is to play Russian roulette with riots; it is prepared to gamble with another summer of disaster. Despite two consecutive summers of violence, not a single basic cause of riots has been corrected. All of the misery that stoked the flames of rage and rebellion remains undiminished. With unemployment, intolerable housing and discriminatory education a scourge in Negro ghettos, Congress and the Administration still tinker with trivial, half-hearted measures.

Yet only a few years ago, there was discernible, if limited, progress through non-violence. Each year, a wholesome, vibrant Negro self-confidence was taking shape. The fact is inescapable that the tactic of non-violence, which had then dominated the thinking of the civil-rights movement, has in the last two years not been playing its transforming role. Non-violence was a creative doctrine in the South because it checkmated the rabid segregationists who were thirsting for an opportunity to physically crush Negroes. Non-violent direct action enabled the Negro to take to the street in active protest, but it muzzled the guns of the oppressor because even he could not shoot down in daylight unarmed men, women and children. This is the reason there was less loss of life in ten years of Southern protest than in ten days of Northern riots.

Today, the Northern cities have taken on the conditions we faced in the South. Police, national guard and other armed bodies are feverishly preparing for repression. They can be curbed not by unorganized resort to force by desperate Negroes but only by a massive wave of militant non-violence. Non-violence was never more relevant as an effective tactic

*Reprinted from *Look* Magazine, XXXII (April 16, 1968), pp. 23-35. By permission of Joan Daves and the Martin Luther King, Jr. Estate.

than today for the North. It also may be the instrument of our national salvation.

I agree with the President's National Advisory Commission on Civil Disorders that our nation is splitting into two hostile societies and that the chief destructive cutting edge is white racism. We need, above all, effective means to force Congress to act resolutely—but means that do not involve the use of violence. For us in the Southern Christian Leadership Conference, violence is not only morally repugnant, it is pragmatically barren. We feel there is an alternative both to violence and to useless timid supplications for justice. We cannot condone either riots or the equivalent evil of passivity. And we know that non-violent militant action in Selma and Birmingham awakened the conscience of white America and brought a moribund, insensitive Congress to life.

The time has come for a return to mass non-violent protest. Accordingly, we are planning a series of such demonstrations this spring and summer, to begin in Washington, D.C. They will have Negro and white participation, and they will seek to benefit the poor of both races.

We will call on the Government to adopt the measures recommended by its own commission. To avoid, in the Commission's words, the tragedy of "continued polarization of the American community and ultimately the destruction of basic democratic values," we must have "national action—compassionate, massive and sustained, backed by the resources of the most powerful and the richest nation on earth."

The demonstrations we have planned are of deep concern to me, and I want to spell out at length what we will do, try to do, and believe in. My staff and I have worked three months on the planning. We believe that if this campaign succeeds, non-violence will once again be the dominant instrument for social change—and jobs and income will be put in the hands of the tormented poor. If it fails, non-violence will be discredited, and the country may be plunged into holocaust—a tragedy deepened by the awareness that it was avoidable.

We are taking action after sober reflection. We have learned from bitter experience that our Government does not correct a race problem until it is confronted directly and dramatically. We also know, as official Washington may not, that the flash point of Negro rage is close at hand.

Our Washington demonstration will resemble Birmingham and Selma in duration. It will be more than a one-day protest —it can persist for two or three months. In the earlier Alabama actions we set no time limits. We simply said we were going to struggle there until we got a response from the nation on the issues involved. We are saying the same thing about Washington. This will be an attempt to bring a kind of Selma-like movement, Birmingham-like movement, into being, substantially around the economic issues. Just as we dealt with the social problem of segregation through massive demonstrations, and we dealt with the political problem—the denial of the right to vote—through massive demonstrations, we are now trying to deal with the economic problems—the right to live, to have a job and income—through massive protest. It will be a Selma-like movement on economic issues.

We remember that when we began direct action in Birmingham and Selma, there was a thunderous chorus that sought to discourage us. Yet today, our achievements in these cities and the reforms that radiated from them are hailed with pride by all.

We've selected 15 areas—ten cities and five rural districts—from which we have recruited our initial cadre. We will have 200 poor people from each area. That would be about 3,000 to get the protests going and set the pattern. They are important, particularly in terms of maintaining non-violence. They are being trained in this discipline now.

In areas where we are recruiting, we are also stimulating activities in conjunction with the Washington protest. We are planning to have some of these people march to Washington. We may have half the group from Mississippi, for example, go to Washington and begin the protest there, while the other half begins walking. They would flow across the South, joining the Alabama group, the Georgia group, right on up through South and North Carolina and Virginia. We hope that the sound and sight of a growing mass of poor people walking slowly toward Washington will have a positive, dramatic effect on Congress.

Once demonstrations start, we feel, there will be spontaneous supporting activity taking place across the country. This has usually happened in campaigns like this, and I think it will again. I think people will start moving. The reasons we didn't choose California and other areas out West are distance and the problem of transporting marchers that far. But part of our strategy is to have spontaneous demonstrations take place on the West Coast.

A nationwide non-violent movement is very important. We know from past experience that Congress and the President won't do anything until you develop a movement around which people of goodwill can find a way to put pressure on them, because it really means breaking that coalition in Congress. It's still a coalition-dominated, rural-dominated, basically Southern Congress. There are Southerners there with committee chairmanships, and they are going to stand in the way of progress as long as they can. They get enough right-wing Midwestern or Northern Republicans to go along with them.

This really means making the movement powerful enough, dramatic enough, morally appealing enough, so that people of goodwill, the churches, labor, liberals, intellectuals, students, poor people themselves begin to put pressure on congressmen to the point that they can no longer elude our demands.

Our idea is to dramatize the whole economic problem of the poor. We feel there's a great deal that we need to do to appeal to Congress itself. The early demonstrations will be more geared toward educational purposes—to educate the nation on the nature of the problem and the crucial aspects of it, the tragic conditions that we confront in the ghettos.

After that, if we haven't gotten a response from Congress, we will branch out. And we are honest enough to feel that we aren't going to get any instantaneous results from Congress, knowing its recalcitrant nature on this issue, and knowing that so many resources and energies are being used in Vietnam rather than on the domestic situation. So we don't have any illusions about moving Congress in two or three weeks. But we do feel that, by starting in Washington, centering on Congress and departments of the Government, we will be able to do a real educational job.

We call our demonstration a campaign for jobs and income because we feel that the economic question is the most crucial that black people, and poor people generally, are confronting. There is a literal depression in the Negro community. When you have mass unemployment in the Negro community, it's called a social problem; when you have mass unemployment in the white community, it's called a depression. The fact is, there is a major depression in the Negro community. The unemployment rate is extremely high, and among Negro youth, it goes up as high as 40 percent in some cities.

We need an Economic Bill of Rights. This would guarantee a job to all people who want to work and are able to work. It would also guarantee an income for all who are not able to work. Some people are too young, some are too old, some are physically disabled, and yet in order to live, they need income. It would mean creating certain public-service jobs, but that could be done in a few weeks. A program that would really deal with jobs could minimize—I don't say stop—the number of riots that could take place this summer.

Our whole campaign, therefore, will center on the job question, with other demands, like housing, that are closely tied to it. We feel that much more building of housing for low-income people should be done. On the educational front, the ghetto schools are in bad shape in terms of quality, and we feel that a program should be developed to spend at least a thousand dollars per pupil. Often, they are so far behind that they need more and special attention, the best quality education that can be given.

These problems, of course, are overshadowed by the Vietnam war. We'll focus on the domestic problems, but it's inevitable that we've got to bring out the question of the tragic mix-up in priorities. We are spending all of this money for death and destruction, and not nearly enough money for life and constructive development. It's inevitable that the question of the war will come up in this campaign. We hear all this talk about our ability to afford guns and butter, but we have come to see that this is a myth, that when a nation becomes involved in this kind of war, when the guns of war become a national obsession, social needs inevitably suffer. And we hope that as a result of our trying to dramatize this and getting thousands and thousands of people moving around this issue, that our Government will be forced to reevaluate its policy abroad in order to deal with the domestic situation.

The American people are more sensitive than Congress. A Louis Harris poll has revealed that 56 percent of the people feel that some kind of program should come into being to provide jobs to all who want to work. We had the WPA when the nation was on the verge of bankruptcy; we should be able to do something when we're sick with wealth. That poll also showed that 57 percent of the people felt the slums should be eradicated and the communities rebuilt by those who live in them, which would be a massive job program.

We need to put pressure on Congress to get things done. We will do this with First Amendment activity. If Congress is unresponsive, we'll have to escalate in order to keep the issue alive and before it. This action may take on disruptive dimensions, but not violent in the sense of destroying life or property: it will be militant non-violence.

We really feel that riots tend to intensify the fears of the white majority while relieving its guilt, and so open the door to greater repression. We've seen no changes in Watts, no structural changes have taken place as the result of riots. We are trying to find an alternative that will force people to confront issues without destroying life or property. We plan to build a shantytown in Washington, patterned after the bonus marches of the thirties, to dramatize how many people have to live in slums in our nation. But essentially, this will be just like our other non-violent demonstrations. We are not going to tolerate violence. And we are making it very clear that the demonstrators who are not prepared to be non-violent should not participate in this. For the past six weeks, we've had workshops on non-violence with the people who will be going to Washington. They will continue through the spring. These people will form a core of the demonstration and will later be the marshals in the protests. They will be participating themselves in the early stages, but after two or three weeks, when we will begin to call larger numbers in, they will be the marshals, the ones who will control and discipline all of the demonstrations.

We plan to have a march for those who can spend only a day or two in Washington, and that will be toward the culminating point of the campaign. I hope this will be a time when white people will rejoin the ranks of the movement.

Demonstrations have served as unifying forces in the movement; they have brought blacks and whites together in very practical situations, where philosophically they may have been arguing about Black Power. It's a strange thing how demonstrations tend to solve problems. The other thing is that it's little known that crime rates go down in almost every community where you have demonstrations. In Montgomery, Ala., when we had a bus boycott, the crime rate in the Negro community went down 65 percent for a whole year. Anytime we've had demonstrations in a community, people have found a way to slough off their self-hatred, and they have had a channel to express their longings and a way to fight non-violently—to get at the power structure, to know you're doing something, so you don't have to be violent to do it.

We need this movement. We need it to bring about a new kind of togetherness between blacks and whites. We need it to bring allies together and to bring the coalition of conscience together.

A good number of white people have given up on integration too. There are a lot of "White Power" advocates, and I find that people do tend to despair and engage in debates when nothing is going on. But when action is taking place, when there are demonstrations, they have a quality about them that leads to a unity you don't achieve at other times.

I think we have come to the point where there is no longer a choice now between non-violence and riots. It must be militant, massive non-violence, or riots. The discontent is so deep, the anger so ingrained, the despair, the restlessness so wide, that something has to be brought into being to serve as a channel through which these deep emotional feelings, these deep angry feelings, can be funneled. There has to be an outlet, and I see this campaign as a way to transmute the inchoate rage of the ghetto into a constructive and creative channel. It becomes an outlet for anger.

Even if I didn't deal with the moral dimensions and question of violence versus non-violence, from a practical point of view, I don't see riots working. But I am convinced that if rioting continues, it will strengthen the right wing of the country, and we'll end up with a kind of right-wing take-over in the cities and a Fascist development, which will be terribly injurious to the whole nation. I don't think America can stand another summer of Detroit-like riots without a development that could destroy the soul of the nation, and even the democratic possibilities of the nation.

I'm committed to non-violence absolutely. I'm just not going to kill anybody, whether it's in Vietnam or here. I'm not going to burn down any building. If non-violent protest fails this summer, I will continue to preach it and teach it, and we at the Southern Christian Leadership Conference will still do this. I plan to stand by non-violence because I have found it to be a philosophy of life that regulates not only my dealings in the struggle for racial justice but also my dealings with people, with my own self. I will still be faithful to non-violence.

But I'm frank enough to admit that if our non-violent campaign doesn't generate some progress, people are just going to engage in more violent activity, and the discussion of guerrilla warfare will be more extensive.

In any event, we will not have been the ones who will have failed. We will place the problems of the poor at the seat of government of the wealthiest nation in the history of mankind. If that power refuses to acknowledge its debt to the poor, it will have failed to live up to its promise to insure "life, liberty and the pursuit of happiness" to its citizens.

If this society fails, I fear that we will learn very shortly that racism is a sickness unto death.

We welcome help from all civil-rights organizations. There must be a diversified approach to the problem, and I think both the NAACP and the Urban League play a significant role. I also feel that CORE and SNCC have played very significant roles. I think SNCC's recent conclusions are unfortunate. We have not given up on integration. We still believe in black and white together. Some of the Black Power groups have temporarily given up on integration. We have not. So maybe we are the bridge, in the middle, reaching across and connecting both sides.

The fact is, we have not had any insurrection in the United States because an insurrection is planned, organized, violent rebellion. What we have had is a kind of spontaneous explosion of anger. The fact is, people who riot don't want to riot. A study was made recently by some professors at Wayne State University. They interviewed several hundred people who participated in the riot last summer in Detroit, and a majority of these people said they felt that my approach to the problem —non-violence—was the best and most effective.

I don't believe there has been a massive turn to violence. Even the riots have had an element of non-violence to persons. But for a rare exception, they haven't killed any white people, and Negroes could, if they wished, kill by the hundreds. That would be insurrection. But the amazing thing is that the Negro has vented his anger on property, not persons, even in the emotional turbulence of riots.

But I'm convinced that if something isn't done to deal with the very harsh and real economic problems of the ghetto, the talk of guerrilla warfare is going to become much more real. The nation has not yet recognized the seriousness of it. Congress hasn't been willing to do anything about it, and this is what we're trying to face this spring. As committed as I am to non-violence, I have to face this fact: if we do not get a positive response in Washington, many more Negroes will begin to think and act in violent terms.

I hope, instead, that what comes out of these non-violent demonstrations will be an Economic Bill of Rights for the Disadvantaged, requiring about ten or twelve billion dollars. I hope that a specific number of jobs is set forth, that a program will emerge to abolish unemployment, and that there will be another program to supplement the income of those whose earnings are below the poverty level. These would be measures of success in our campaign.

It may be well that all we'll get out of Washington is to keep Congress from getting worse. The problem is to stop it from moving backward. We started out with a poverty bill at 2.4 billion dollars, and now it's back to 1.8 billion. We have a welfare program that's dehumanizing, and then Congress adds a Social Security amendment that will bar literally thousands of children from any welfare. Model cities started out; it's been cut back. Rent subsidy, an excellent program for the poor, cut down to nothing. It may be that because of these demonstrations, we will at least be able to hold on to some of the things we have.

There is an Old Testament prophecy of the "sins of the Fathers being visited upon the third and fourth generations." Nothing could be more applicable to our situation. America is reaping the harvest of hate and shame planted through generations of educational denial, political dis-franchisement and economic exploitation of its black population. Now, almost a century removed from slavery, we find the heritage of oppression and racism erupting in our cities, with volcanic lava of bitterness and frustration pouring down our avenues.

Black Americans have been patient people, and perhaps they could continue patient with but a modicum of hope; but everywhere, "time is winding up," in words of one of our spirituals, "corruption in the land, people take your stand; time is winding up." In spite of years of national progress, the plight of the poor is worsening. Jobs are on the decline as a result of technological change, schools North and South are proving themselves more and more inadequate to the task of providing adequate education and thereby entrance into the mainstream of the society. Medical care is virtually out of reach of millions of black and white poor. They are aware of the great advances of medical science—heart transplants, miracle drugs—but their children still die of preventable diseases, and even suffer brain damage due to protein deficiency.

In Mississippi, children are actually starving, while large landowners have placed their land in the soil bank and receive millions of dollars annually not to plant food and cotton. No provision is made for the life and survival of the hundreds of thousands of sharecroppers who now have no work and no food. Driven off the land, they are forced into tent cities and ghettos of the North, for our Congress is determined not to stifle the initiative of the poor (though they clamor for jobs) through welfare handouts. Handouts to the rich are given more sophisticated nomenclature such as parity, subsidies and incentives to industry.

White America has allowed itself to be indifferent to race prejudice and economic denial. It has treated them as superficial blemishes, but now awakes to the horrifying reality of a potentially fatal disease. The urban outbreaks are "a fire bell in the night," clamorously warning that the seams of our entire social order are weakening under strains of neglect.

The American people are infected with racism—that is the peril. Paradoxically, they are also infected with democratic ideals—that is the hope. While doing wrong, they have the potential to do right. But they do not have a millennium to make changes. Nor have they a choice of continuing in the old way. The future they are asked to inaugurate is not so unpalatable that it justifies the evils that beset the nation. To end poverty, to extirpate prejudice, to free a tormented conscience, to make a tomorrow of justice, fair play and creativity—all these are worthy of the American ideal.

We have, through massive non-violent action, an opportunity to avoid a national disaster and create a new spirit of class and racial harmony. We can write another luminous moral chapter in American history. All of us are on trial in this troubled hour, but time still permits us to meet the future with a clear conscience.

Discussion and Study Questions

1. What is your reaction to Brooke's use of the phrases, "reasonable requests for governmental action" and "responsible members of the Negro community" in "After a Long Hot Summer"?

   What specific governmental actions does Brooke recommend to curb riots?

2. How does Wright propose to close the economic gap between blacks and whites?

   In what way does he indicate that education is not the only answer to the problems of Negroes?

3. What is the psychology behind nonviolent protest, both in terms of those who participate and those against whom it is directed?

   A. What does King mean by *militant* nonviolence?
   B. Did King's philosophy and strategies change between the Birmingham crisis of 1963 and the Memphis crisis of 1968? What differences, if any, are descernible between the two essays? (see p. 232, "The Negro Is Your Brother.")

4. What evidence is there that the governmental programs proposed by Young and Wright have been implemented?

5. What ideological differences can be discerned in the answers offered by Young, Innis, and Wilkins in the interview?

Social and
Institutional Reform

majority in the United States. I speak of the coalition which staged the March on Washington, passed the Civil Rights Act and laid the basis for the Johnson landslide—Negroes, trade unionists, liberals and religious groups.

There are those who argue that a coalition strategy would force the Negro to surrender his political independence to white liberals, that he would be delivered into the camp of

Social and Institutional Reform

The basic theme of the essays in this section is social and institutional reform. In spite of the obvious difficulties of changing the established values of this society, many black spokesmen view such reform as the major tactic for effectively and permanently realizing the goal of complete freedom for all Black Americans. These essays reflect the belief that the core of racial discrimination and injustice lies in the essentially oppressive mores and institutions upon which our society is built. Reforms are therefore needed in institutions such as churches, school systems, news media, banking and finance systems, and health care agencies. The essays indicate a need to reorganize social, political, and economic institutions which tend to function for the benefit of the more privileged members of the society at the cost of the suffering of millions of others—the black and the poor. The rationale, then, is that no matter how many individuals modify their feelings and actions, no fundamental change will occur until basic revisions are made in the institutions upon which Americans depend for their livelihood and social status.

In examining the unjust institutions and social conditions of our country each essay offers some insight into the direction which the Black Movement must take. Most of them do not reject integration as an ultimate goal, and all recognize the importance of a new self-image for the Black American. Some of the spokesmen represented here call for a total restructuring of our political, educational, and economic systems, while others stress the need to reevaluate certain institutions, especially the church.

Mrs. Chisholm's essay points toward economics as the avenue through which America's minority groups can move into the mainstream of society. Jackson's essay expresses the need for the development of economic sustenance in the black communities together with a reform in the church. Bond's emphasis is on political reform through federal programs which can solve the problems of poverty and unemployment. Rustin stresses the use of political machinery to destroy the legal foundations of racism. For him, attaining political power is a primary tactic in the Black man's struggle for equality. Evers discusses the role of the American press in perpetuating racist attitudes and asks for a change in the perspective of news reporting. Forman's demand for reform is directed primarily to the white churches and synagogues of our nation which have profited from and exploited black people through the years. Gregory's essay reinforces Forman's demands for reform with a call for the white religious establishment to reexamine its values and develop a more humanitarian emphasis.

SHIRLEY CHISHOLM,

Teacher, Congresswoman

In 1968 New York City marked a first in American life. Shirley A. Chisholm, in a somewhat surprising victory over James Farmer (p. 84), was sent to Congress as the first black woman to achieve such a national post by election. Born in Brooklyn, New York, November 30, 1924, she has an impressive educational background. With two college degrees and one professional diploma in supervision and administration, the bilingual Mrs. Chisholm has also received two honorary degrees: Doctor of Humane Letters and Doctor of Laws.

Mrs. Chisholm was a teacher, director of a child care center, and an educational consultant before turning to politics as an assemblywoman in the New York State Legislature. Her major concerns have always been centered around our nation's disadvantaged, particularly youth. Her early programs include unemployment insurance for domestic workers and SEEK, a higher education plan designed to enable disadvantaged youth who may not meet entrance requirements but possess academic potential to enter the state universities and receive remedial training. Mrs. Chisholm is emerging not only as a strong agitator for the causes of urban New York, but as a forceful spokesman for legislative and attitudinal changes which will improve the lot of disadvantaged Americans in jobs, housing, and education.

"WE INTEND TO FINISH THE JOURNEY THAT SOMEBODY ELSE SO RUDELY STARTED US ON—AND WE INTEND TO FINISH THE JOB THAT THEY SO FOOLISHLY LEFT UNDONE."

Black Is an Attitude*

One of today's prime problems is the redefinition of old words, terms and goals. Beyond that, we need to use new terms and new words to express new goals when it becomes clear that the old ones can no longer be used—even though we have attempted to redefine them.

In this country so racially divided, so racially conscious and so just plain racist, there is no better place to start than with the terms "black" and "white."

Black, no matter what it once meant, is now first and foremost an attitude. A few weeks ago I spoke in New York about the similarities between the Women's Liberation Movement and the struggle of Black Americans for their freedom. At that time I said:

> Black people have freed themselves from the dead weight of the albatross of blackness that once hung about their neck. They have done it by picking it up in their arms and holding it out with pride for all the world to see. They have done it by embracing it—not in the dark of the moon but in the searing light of the white sun. Thy have said "Yes" to it and found that the skin that was once seen as symbolizing their shame is in reality their badge of honor.

I pointed out that: "Women must come to realize that the superficial symbolisms that surround us as women are negative only when we ourselves perceive and accept them as negative."

This is something that black brothers and sisters in particular must forever keep in mind. Some of you in the audience this evening will be called "Uncle Toms," "Aunt Jemimas"

* Address by Congresswoman Shirley Chisholm to the Student Body of Federal City College, Washington, D.C., 1969. Reprinted by permission of the author.

and other epithets—some of you will deserve it—but many of you will not.

Some of you will be called black militants, black revolutionaries or just plain black—and some of you may deserve the honor.

It is not how you dress, walk or talk, nor is it what you are saying when you are talking by which you should be judged—but fortunately for some and unfortunately for others, that is the present situation. Too often we have fallen into the "bag" of accepting or rejecting people on the superficial basis of what they appear initially to be.

Black is an attitude! It is indicated by actions that show commitment to significant social change even at the possible expense of the loss of personal power and gain. Many of our would-be leaders are running about trying to start and maintain an elitist revolution in the name of social revolution.

Let me tell you here and now that no elitist revolution has ever done a thing for the people—the masses who are truly at the bottom of the economic and political power structure.

Far too often we become cowards when faced with individuals who have strong leadership abilities; individuals who often do not want social revolution as much as they want personal power. Far too often we follow blindly—without questioning their motives—without examining their actions. We follow blindly because what they say that they want to do sounds right. We follow because we are afraid that those around us will mis-understand our questioning and put us down. Too many of us have a need to be accepted no matter what the cost.

Brothers and Sisters—too often that cost is the prostitution of our souls—our spirits—our heritage and our future.

No one man has ever been right about anything—nor has any one group or civilization—nor will they ever be absolutely right.

I am not saying that people who are seeking personal power are not necessary and useful to the revolution. I am far too practical to ever think or say that. What I am saying is don't ever let any one person get into the position of having so much power that ideals can only serve to mask the reality of the situation.

Black is an attitude! It is the acceptance of all things past and all things present for what they are or were but it is also the rejection of ever letting many of those things happen to anyone in the future. The issue is not revenge but freedom. Let our revenge be the freedom from those things that we tend to think are the basis of the white stereotype.

We cannot say that we are committed to the idea of social revolution if our goals are simply to move only Black Americans into the mainstream of American economy. If that is our only goal then we have learned nothing from our unique heritage.

Black is an attitude! We cannot say that we are black if our commitment is only to place ourselves into the dominant positions of society. If we are in truth rejecting the aspects of this culture that make it necessary to have a "nigger" around so that one might feel automatically superior to someone else; if we are in truth rejecting the aspects of our economy that make it necessary to have cheap labor in order that the owners might get rich, a consuming economy that must consume even its source of cheap labor; if we are in truth rejecting a political way of life that promises everything and delivers nothing then we cannot commit ourselves to attain the positions of dominance for the sake of the positions alone and then say that we are black.

How can we say on the one hand that we don't want— have no need to ape the white stereotype and then on the other hand commit ourselves to seeking exactly what it is that has made that stereotype? If what we want is the power to control the way people live, to use them to our own ends, then we are in fact not rejecting what it is that we say that we don't want—we are instead openly and brazenly embracing it.

I am not speaking about morality or idealism. I am talking about practicality and pragmatism. If this country had not tried to hold on to the idea that it needed a "nigger" it wouldn't be in the shape that it is in today— both here at home and abroad. America tried to perpetrate and live a historical lie and now history—reality—and we are catching up to it. There should be a lesson in that for all of us.

America said that it wanted to make the world safe for democracy and then almost immediately tried to colonize and exploit as much of the world as it could.

We claim that what we want is freedom from oppression for all people. Will we too lose sight of the goal when we finish freeing ourselves? Will we too sell-out the freedom of others for our own relative freedom?

Black is an attitude! If we think of ourselves as black because of skin color then I have no doubt that when the skin color becomes acceptable to the majority of America then we will rest easy and try to protect our own reserved position in society—just as every other ethnic group in America has done before us—in the name of protecting themselves from us.

We joke bitterly about the "up-tight Mr. Charlies" who

spend most of their waking hours in fear of black people moving into the neighborhood and causing a drop in realty prices or the "Uncle Tom" whose sole job as assistant personnel manager is to make sure that no other black people get jobs at his company. It seems to me that these people—people of this type—have lost a good portion of what I consider basic to being human. Can we afford the same thing happening to us?

Black Americans must be moved "en masse" into the economic mainstream of this country. For the sake of what is becoming the Social Revolution, this is true. But it is also true that all groups of American poor must be moved into that mainstream—and I am including the white poor whether they like the idea of traveling with us or not.

My reasoning is simple. The majority of the poor cannot—and probably will not—participate in a revolution that is basically cultural—that has at bottom a sophisticated ideological base. A man who has to scuffle to feed himself and his family each and every day has little time left to dream about a better world—not to mention making an active effort toward creating one.

It is partly for this reason that every revolution that has been attempted in the name of bettering life for the total society has produced only a new ruling class. The vast majority of people who were "have-nots" before the revolution were "have-nots" after the revolution precisely because they were in no position, politically, economically or socially, to protect their own interests.

Therefore the most pressing problem of today's society for the majority of Americans—black or white—is how to get into the economic mainstream and remain there.

The majority of America's social activists are young and/or middle-class. By social activists I mean those that are involved in the ideological struggle in America. Few, if any, of the poor and the working lower and lower middle-class are involved at the ideological level—rejecting capitalism and classism or racism.

Many young revolutionaries are aware of this—just as they are aware that rhetoric is not revolution. But too often in this country that is dominated by Madison Avenue and the Mass Media we find that slogans and catch phrases obscure the facts.

The America of politically, socially and economically disenfranchised minority groups' most pressing problem is how to most adequately enfranchise the largest possible numbers of people in the shortest amount of time, at least economically.

Perhaps I should take a minute to clarify what I mean by a Social Revolution. I am talking about the basic reform of social institutions. I am not talking about a "Guaranteed Annual Income" per se but I am talking about fair and equitable economic shares for every man, woman and child.

I am talking about the basic right of everyone to share in the building of a better society than the one we have at present and the right to receive fair and equitable payment for that contribution. In short, "A servant is worthy of his hire."

I believe that at bottom the ideals of democracy are sound but I do not believe that those ideals have ever been practiced—except in terms of an elitist few.

At least a part of the reason that America has drifted farther and farther away from those democratic ideals is because of the economic system that not only allows but forces individuals and groups to seek political power to protect their economic interests; at least a part of what has forced this country to drift farther and farther away from democracy and toward republicanism is a political system that depends so much on "Madison Avenue-type sales appeal," that only the very wealthy, the very influential, or the very lucky can run for—and win—high political office. In case some of you don't know it, I am not wealthy nor have I been until recently very influential. And at the rate that I have been running my mouth around the country I may not be that very long.

But the time has come when every American—black or white—rich or poor—influential or not—must run his mouth. The time has come when all of us must state loudly and clearly what we believe and why we believe it—more than that we must fight for what we believe as if our future—indeed our very lives depended on it. They very well might.

You will note that I have not spoken about specific goals for the Revolution nor have I talked about specific ways in which the Revolution will be waged. I have my reasons—one of which I have already shared with you.

At this stage in the struggle it would be inconsistent for me to attempt to decide for the masses of people what course they should choose. It is far too early for me or for any individual to advance a single over-all plan of action and say that it is the only one that is right.

But there are a few things that I would like to share with you this evening.

Americans, black and white, must be forced to undergo a change of attitude—a change of political attitude—a change of economic attitude—and a change of social attitude.

It is in attitudinal change that Black Studies Courses, the teaching and understanding of Black History and Culture can be helpful—not only to black students but for all Americans—and ultimately not only for black Americans but for all Americans and, in truth, for all people.

But Black Studies Courses aren't enough. No matter what form Social Revolution comes in, one thing about this modern society of ours will remain with us. The technological aspects will still be here. Students must now begin to prepare themselves for that. The number of people to be fed will not allow us to return to an agrarian, land-based society. Many scientists are already predicting great famines as early as the 1980's unless we find some new ways to feed people.

If the world does see massive famine the basic truth behind the American maxim "last-hired, first-fired" will still be true for minority-group Americans. But they will still enjoy the relative wealth they now enjoy when compared with the poor of many other nations of the world.

The social problems that face us are not limited to America; therefore our goals and our solutions cannot be limited to America. Isolationism did not work for white America, it will not work for a black and white America—nor will it work for a black America.

The task that faces us is overwhelming—but it must be done. The road we travel is long, with many pitfalls and there will be many enticing sirens and nymphs along every foot of it—trying to waylay and mislead us—but we must travel it.

Some of us will not make it. Some of us will withdraw whimpering into our own personal wombs—drugs—alcohol—sex—money—bits and pieces of personal power.

Some of us will assault the walls of the citadel alone—dying in an incandescent burst of vainglory—thinking that we died martyrs when in fact we died frustrated cowards and suicidal cop-outs.

Some of us will have our lives snatched from us because our cause and our beliefs threaten anyone and everyone who is seeking personal power.

In spite of these things we will succeed. We have been on this particular (and peculiar) American road for more than 200 years and we intend to finish the journey that somebody else so rudely started us on—and we intend to finish the job that they so foolishly left undone. We will build a democratic America in spite of undemocratic Americans. We have rarely worried about the odds or the obstacles before—we will not start worrying now. We will have both of our goals—Peace and Power!

JESSE L. JACKSON,

Organizer, Minister

Jesse Jackson was born in Greenville, South Carolina, on October 8, 1941. He attended the University of Illinois on a football scholarship, and later transferred to North Carolina Agricultural and Technical College where he was elected student body president. In 1964 he earned his B.S. degree in sociology, and later completed two years at Chicago Theological Seminary. He has subsequently been given honorary D.D. degrees from Lincoln University in Pennsylvania and the Chicago Theological Seminary.

Jackson moved from his civil rights activities as a student to a life-time commitment to pragmatic activism. As one of King's top aides he was literally at his side at the time of the assassination in 1968. Since then Jackson has become the national director of Operation Breadbasket, a community economic self-help program with its headquarters in Chicago. Because of his quick mind, pointed articulation, and activist orientation he has risen to prominence as a black leader, advocating black economic power, pride and dignity for all blacks and all poor people.

"FREEDOM THAT IS MERELY A SLOGAN IS THE MOST DECEPTIVE OF SLAVERIES; THUS THE BLACK COMMUNITY CHOOSES TO BE FREE IN FACT."

Black Power and White Churches*

Whites Should Recognize Their Own Problems

The white church tends to have a certain staleness of form, a kind of spiritual impotence and depletion that attracts its members to a service at which people pour out their guilt feelings, but in which there is not enough concrete significance to affect their behavior.

The long separation of the black and white church is simply a result of the unwillingness of the white church to follow the Christ of universal reconciliation rather than the flag of national patriotism. Thus if the white church is to act in support of the black community it will have to begin by recognizing its own predicament of having pews filled by men who, if challenged, will admit that they glorify their whiteness and who, if pushed, will say that business is business and God is God. Because in their minds Christ does not reign over culture, they have no intention of loving all men as commanded by Christ.

Those who truly believe in reconciliation must capture the initiative in the white church before it will be capable of integrating with those of us in the black church. And the white church, moreover, will have to seize the initiative in the white community. It will have to assume the awesome burden of civilizing the white community, creating the human sensitivity and the willingness to love everybody that are necessary for participation in the human community. Only so can the white church, without profit motive or spiritual exploitation, contribute to the solution of problems plaguing the black community. Our problem is related to the white problem in that the mean spirit of white racism has categorized black

* Reprinted from *Church in Metropolis*, No. 16 (Spring, 1968), pp. 7-9. By permission of the publisher and the author.

people as subhuman. Thus we have been trapped in enforced isolation. Black people have contributed to this problem by submitting to tyranny physically and psychologically. The hearts, the ambitions, the dreams of black people have been geared to imitation and forced assimilation. Black people have not accepted the truth of exploitative separation. Black intellectuals have been tricked into the fear of admitting to the fact of separation and are hence unable to say that much of our identity lies in our state of separation.

The ultimate tragedy of black separation from the mainstream of society is in the dependence of blacks upon whites for everything vital in their lives. Black people have been reduced to being dependent consumers without being allowed to become an independent production force. In the city of Chicago it is estimated that black businesses garner only 15 per cent of the market within the Negro community. As a result, black incomes are submarginal. The adjusted gross income for the city of Chicago is $19.1 billion of which Negroes' adjusted income is $1 billion, compared with an equitable figure of from $4.5 to 6 billion.

Education in the ghetto is bad, not because there is little opportunity to sit by white children but because at graduation black people are prepared only to consume—they are not educationally equipped to produce. The American educational system is structured to help black people as persons (sometimes) but never as "a people."

The simple fact is that until black people have enough power to demand mobility and respect and until white people are willing to participate in the human family and see other people as fully human, social integration will not (and cannot) be realized.

The greatest expression of the cruelties heaped upon us (along with manifestations of racist attitudes as characterized in closed housing policies, police brutality, poor education, political disenfranchisement, etc.) has been the failure of any legislative body to approximate the policy of "forty acres and a mule" (i.e., a capital base for black people). *The Statistical Abstract of the United States Department of Commerce* discloses that Negro per capita income since 1960 has never exceeded 55.9 per cent of that received by whites. Black people were released into legalized freedom without being taken into participation in America. The result of this is that black people caught in the wilderness of capitalism have either died (the death rate is significantly higher among black people than among whites—especially for infant mortality) or have lived in a perverted and distorted way. What is frequently called an "Uncle Tom" is merely a black man deprived of his pride by socio-economic conditions which have driven him to take an expedient philosophy of life. He is biologically black, but culturally and economically compelled to please whites. Such a racist-induced schizophrenia is a human perversion.

We must begin, therefore, by taking our physical separation seriously. Nothing black people did is responsible for it, yet in that separation many vital necessities like health, recreation, education, and meaningful welfare are hardly available. Black money travels out of the ghetto instead of flowing in a circle within it. This is what constitutes the slum character of the ghetto.

How Can Whites and Blacks Help Each Other?

Given the deep spiritual problem plaguing the white church and the material deprivation that has been inflicted upon the black community the real question to deal with is, how can they help each other?

It is important to recognize the fact that the white church must be prepared to take the initiative. For while the black church is open to dialogue, the historical patterns of racism practiced by the white church have created an attitude in the black church of "What's the use?" The black church has now taken the position that it is open to serve and to be servant in the most authentic sense of that term . . . but it will no longer be servile vis-à-vis its relationship to the white church.

What would it mean if at this juncture of history the white church took seriously its call to become servant to man and to society?

Economic Development of the Black Community

There is no more critical priority of mission for the nation than the development of a substantial economic base in the black community. To further this goal, white churches could join black churches in many areas of the nation—in a project that would establish banks and would provide major investment channels for funds that could be deposited in those that already exist. There are approximately twenty-six Negro banks in America. Their combined assets do not equal those of one major bank in the city of Chicago.

One of the major reasons for our status as an "underclass" (to use Myrdal's term) and our consequent posture as a "burden" to the public economy is our lack of a private economy. Black people must develop a private economy. At present we cannot even sustain a workers' market—or a market based upon the demands of persons gainfully employed. Black unemployment reaches a thumping 7 to 9 per cent nationwide but what is even more tragic is the underemployment which blacks suffer. It is 47.4 per cent in the placid community of San Antonio, 45.3 per cent in New Orleans, 38.9 per cent in St. Louis, and 24.2 per cent in Boston. Negroes control less than 25 per cent of the market in the ghetto, and our estimated worth nationwide is only $28 billion at a time when projected GNP will exceed $840 billion in 1968.

Among other things this means that government fiscal policy must be enlisted to assist the Negro community in a more realistic and effective way than direct grants for public assistance or poor relief. Slum clearance will not remove the larger manifestations of slum-shock unless there is a capital base in the black community.

It has been the experience of Operation Breadbasket that one of the most creative channels for immediate investment into Negro businesses is the formation of Small Business Investment Corporations (or SBIC). It is estimated that by 1969 SBIC's throughout the nation will be a $5 billion business. There are at least twenty of these companies with assets exceeding $15 million, at least four with assets that have passed the $30 billion peak. Yet these are white operations at present. It is for black businessmen and white men of good will to work for the extension of these benefits on a more equitable basis into the black community.

Finally, the goal of Operation Breadbasket is not to build a contingent of black capitalists who define their lives by the amount of money they can claim but to build a black community whose members respect themselves and have the economic sustenance to plan for their futures. It is to build a community where men are preoccupied with the privilege of serving rather than postured into the prostitutional attitudes associated with mere survival. Black people must now participate in a reconstruction on their own terms along lines which they themselves establish.

A white church which chooses to live at the intersection of mission and which makes the decision to be *The Church* will not only participate in this reconstruction but will find in the very act of participation the loss of its spurious title "white church." Certain it is that whites can no longer relate to the black community as a board of directors rather than as an authentic bridge of brotherhood and partnership. Freedom that is merely a slogan is the most deceptive of slaveries; thus the black community chooses to be free in fact.

White Church Must Understand Black Consciousness

The emergence of black consciousness is an indispensable force for the development of a black community. Therefore the white church needs to understand and appreciate the propelling and compelling forces of black consciousness and not dismiss it as mere separatism; or a rehash of segregation in new voices. Black consciousness is the psychological foundation for black cooperation, if it is to survive.

Black people see as urgent their control of decisions which directly affect and impinge upon the present and the future of the ghetto.

Operation Breadbasket is only one more sign of the black community's decisions to wed hope to history by hard work and planning. Out of such will come the harvests of abundance from fields where once grew weeds of shame.

The drive to overcome the estrangement between persons and the separation perpetuated by institutions is the thrust of Operation Breadbasket. The white church is challenged to take up the burden with her black brothers. But if the white church is unwilling to share such a load, the black church will stumble on under her heavy yoke that must be borne.

If the truth is not uttered by the anointed, and the seats of government become stools for acts of injustice and impiety, even if the rocks have to cry out, the groanings of the suffering will be heard!

JULIAN BOND,

State Legislator

In 1965, Julian Bond became one of eight blacks elected to Georgia's House of Representatives. However, he was denied his seat because of a statement reflecting opposition to United States involvement in the Vietnam war. After being reendorsed twice by his district, Bond took his case to the Supreme Court which ruled in his favor. He was sworn in as a member of the Georgia House on January 9, 1967.

As an outspoken critic of the Indochinese war and a tenacious fighter for civil liberties, Bond has become well known to the nation's blacks and whites alike. In 1968 he successfully challenged the seating of the Georgia delegation at the Chicago Democratic Convention and became floor leader of those delegates left. In addition, he became the first black man to be nominated from the convention floor for Vice-President. He withdrew shortly after his name was entered, however, for he was too young to meet the age requirement.

Born January 14, 1940, in Nashville, Tennessee, Bond received his early education at the George School in Lincoln, Pennsylvania, where he was reared.

After moving to Atlanta with his family in 1957, Bond matriculated at Morehouse College with a major in English and an avid interest in American history. He has written poetry and worked as a reporter, but was attracted to the civil rights movement very early in life.

While at Morehouse, he organized student sit-ins and similar demonstrations. In the middle of his senior year he left to become communications director of SNCC. After six years with the organization, during which he supervised the information and public relations aspects of the voter registration drives and other campaigns, Bond moved on to politics.

Although Bond seems to personally reject the idea of being

360

a national black spokesman, he is undoubtedly representative of a new breed of politician. He combines a casual grace and courtesy with militancy in seeking to reform existing governmental institutions.

"THE 'COLORED' MINORITIES IN AMERICA MUST RECOGNIZE THE DESPERATE NEED FOR THE CULTIVATION, SINGLY AND COLLECTIVELY, OF THE KIND OF POWER WHITES HAVE MONOPOLIZED SINCE THE AMERICAN EXPERIMENT BEGAN."

Uniting the Races*

This country, which was "discovered" by white men over 400 years ago and "founded" by them in 1776, always was and still is, in the eyes of most of its citizens and rulers, a white man's heaven. In *The Federalist* papers, John Jay wrote, "Providence has been pleased to give this one connected country to one united people . . . a people descended from the same ancestors, speaking the same language, professing the same religion, attached to the same principles of government, very similar in their manners and customs." Under Jay's philosophy, black men were designed by Providence to work for white men; Indians, who were unsuited by Providence to be slaves, had to be exterminated; and Mexicans, being neither Indian nor black, became cultural enemies holding territory that the expansionist white man coveted. America gave birth to the rhetoric of democracy while it breathed life into what became institutionalized racism. European immigrants came here to escape oppression and their young became oppressors.

The record of domestic imperialism waged by white America is matched by a history of varied response from its non-white victims—a history of militant resistance, of separatist movements and of quiet heroic struggle—all aimed at getting the white man's foot off the nonwhite's neck, the white man's noose off the red or black or brown throat. That rebellion has been bloody, as were the uprisings of Denmark Vesey and Nat Turner; and it has been nonviolent—employing oratory, petition, marches, the ballot, the courts and civil disobedience. Now, as we enter the Seventies, it has returned to violence and to blood.

The history of that rebellion is not exclusively black. "Are we not being stripped, day by day, of the little that remains of our ancient liberty?" challenged Tecumseh, a Shawnee

*Reprinted from *Playboy* Magazine, XVII (January, 1970), pp. 128-154. By permission of HMH Publishing Company and the author.

Indian. "Do they not even now kick and strike us as they do their blackfaces? How long will it be before they tie us to a post and whip us and make us work in a cornfield as they do them? Shall we wait for that moment or shall we die fighting before we submit to such?" As usual, a moderate in the crowd answered Tecumseh by saying, "Let us submit our grievances, whatever they may be, to the Congress of the United States." This debate took place in 1812. Whichever side prevailed in that particular dispute, the cause of justice did not—if the present condition of American Indians is an indication.

Today, those same rebels—blacks, Spanish-speaking people, Indians—still fight against white providence. Tecumseh's call to violence still rings out in modern ghettos, barrios and reservations. It is heard because nearly 200 years after the "founding fathers" proposed to dissolve Americans' differences in a melting pot, the only thing that remains unabsorbed is *us*—and our skins. So we no longer wish to melt, to be absorbed, to fit in, to join up, to swim in the mainstream. What black people—and Spanish Americans and the original Americans—*do* want is a share of the goodies they see so abundantly spread around them. We want to have the opportunity to live a decent life. That means a life supported by a family income that is more than barely at the poverty level. It means a life in which education and jobs are guaranteed. It means a life in which police are compassionate public servants, in which storekeepers are not avaricious, in which politicians at least approach honesty.

We have won some small victories. We now have free access to restaurants—which is fine, except that most of us can still afford to eat only at the five-and-ten-cent-store lunch counters where we originally made our stand; and some of us are literally starving. The system conceded to black people the right to sit in the front of the bus—a hollow victory when one's longest trip is likely to be from the feudal South to the mechanized poverty of the North. It has legislated the right to vote for people who seldom see candidates in whom they can put their trust. And this system in 1968 selected as President of the United States a man who, clearly, was not our choice.

Although unemployment and underemployment are among our most crucial problems, this man's Government gives nearly $10,000,000 in Federal contracts to three textile firms in the Carolinas with proven records of discrimination—on the oral promise that they will "do better"; even Nixon's equal-opportunity bureaucrats couldn't stomach that one. Here is a man who cannot help but know that capitalism has yet to solve the problems of white poverty, yet he offers a piti-fully underfinanced public-relations gimmick called black capitalism as an answer to our needs. And while black, brown and red Americans suffer more than whites from the war in Vietnam—in terms of both inductions and deaths—this man has yet to reveal any viable plan for ending the war, the secret plan he said he had more than a year ago. But the war does more, of course, than kill our young men. The 30-billion-dollar annual drain on the Treasury for this conflict and the entire inflated military budget are testimonies to us that America is more interested in killing than in exalting life.

To discuss what could or should be done by any American President or American Congress to include nonwhite Americans as recipients of the supposed benefits of the American way of life is to discuss an endless list of existing but un-enforced Executive orders and Presidential promises. It has been over 15 years, for instance, since the United States Supreme Court, in *Brown vs. Board of Education of Topeka*, declared that segregation in public schools was illegal. The next year, Southern schools were ordered to desegregate with "all deliberate speed." Yet, a decade and a half later, every American city—North, South, East and West—still maintains a racially segregated school system.

Time has demonstrated that cutting off Federal funds has been the single most effective method of enforcing the Court's ruling; yet a combination of racist Southern Federal judges, a policy of appeasement practiced by Democratic and Republican administrations and a lack of national interest in this crucial question have conspired to hold the percentage of integrated black school children in the South to 40 percent. Indeed—until they were stopped in October 1969 by a Supreme Court headed by his own appointee—the Nixon Administration was committing the most bestial sort of political fornication with its political bedfellows, the new Republicans of the South. Together, they instituted court action when other available methods promised to be too speedy. They relaxed Federal pressure at the eleventh hour, giving aid and comfort to every segregation-minded school board and superintendent in the South.

The only just course of action for the Government is to insist that "all deliberate speed" has run its course; to immediately cut off *all* Federal funds to any school district that practices discrimination, whether that district is in Chatham County, Georgia, or Cook County, Illinois; to insist that existing black principals and schoolteachers in integrated settings retain their seniority and job level; to resist the use of culturally biased tests to assign pupils to honors programs or grade levels.

But education alone does not solve problems of poverty and unemployment for a people with high social visibility. Something more revolutionary is required. The Congress should declare that those farmers in the South and Southwest who have built fortunes by collecting Federal monies for not growing crops have forfeited the right to possess that land. The land, in turn, should be redistributed to the landless and frequently jobless people who work it for starvation wages while its owners get rich by harnessing their plows to the Federal wagon. In the South, this type of land reform would mean important progress in property ownership for poor black —and many white—sharecroppers. In the Southwest, it would mean the *chicanos* would have a chance to control the land whose soil their sweat has made fertile over so many years.

President Nixon has begun what no other President in recent years has dared to do—tamper with the outmoded and dependence-fostering welfare system. His proposed reforms, however, would actually work to penalize the large industrial states and would subsidize cheap black labor in the South. And his proposed national floor of $1600 a year for a family of four would be amusing if there were not real people involved with real mouths to feed. The nation ought to establish a workable welfare floor for a family of four of $5500 a year. The Congress ought to insist on retaining the food-stamp and commodities-distribution programs and should abandon the notion of indiscriminately forcing welfare recipients to work. Since no one remains poor by choice in this country, no one should be required to take an unacceptable job simply because he is poor.

A national program enabling land ownership and establishing sustaining welfare standards, if implemented by every state in the union, would begin to halt the flow of poor, unskilled Americans from farm to city. Such a program, if capably administered, would begin to ease, if only temporarily and belatedly, the problems of America's overburdened cities. Federal and state governments, meanwhile, should become the employers of last resort by providing jobs for low-skilled Americans, particularly men, while these same men participate in training programs designed to fit them for today's job market.

If the American minorities—the Mexican, Puerto Rican, Indian and black Americans, and the slowly vanishing poor-white Americans—have the guaranteed opportunity for income, then the pathologies that distort their lives will begin to disappear. At the same time, the "colored" minorities in America must recognize the desperate need for the cultivation, singly and collectively, of the kind of power whites have monopolized since the American experiment began. Each group of us must recognize that evil men and an evil system now crush our every aspiration, that no question of education or job training or integration of jobs and housing can be implemented without a correlated grasp of power by the powerless. One simple way that the Government—if it wanted to—could facilitate this bid for legitimate power would be by dispatching Federal registrars to the numerous Southern counties where voting figures demonstrate that intimidation and fear still prevent black people from voting.

Finally, white America is going to have to accept the judgment of the Kerner Commission report that the fragmentation of the races in this country is *its* problem, and an explosive one. If programs and cures are not advanced and enforced, then no one can hope that life in America will grow less violent or tense, or that other Watts and Detroits and Newarks will not occur again, with greater intensity and greater sophistication. Neither white nor black capitalism is guaranteed by our Constitution, but the fourteenth, fifteenth and sixteenth amendments do guarantee the right of all men to eat, breathe and live. White providence should want it no other way. The nonwhites of America will *struggle* to have it no other way. As an old black abolitionist, Frederick Douglass, said over 100 years ago. "We can be remodified, changed, assimilated, but never extinguished. . . . This is our country. . . . We shall neither die out nor be driven out; but shall go with [white] people, either as a testimony against them or as evidence in their favor, throughout generations."

From Protest to Politics: The Future of the Civil Rights Movement*

By BAYARD RUSTIN

The decade spanned by the 1954 Supreme Court decision on school desegregation and the Civil Rights Act of 1964 will undoubtedly be recorded as the period in which the legal foundations of racism in America were destroyed. To be sure, pockets of resistance remain; but it would be hard to quarrel with the assertion that the elaborate legal structure of segregation and discrimination, particularly in relation to public accommodations, has virtually collapsed. On the other hand, without making light of the human sacrifices involved in the direct-action tactics (sit-ins, freedom rides, and the rest) that were so instrumental to this achievement, we must recognize that in desegregating public accommodations, we affected institutions which are relatively peripheral both to the American socio-economic order and to the fundamental conditions of life of the Negro people. In a highly industrialized, twentieth-century civilization, we hit Jim Crow precisely where it was most anachronistic, dispensable, and vulnerable—in hotels, lunch counters, terminals, libraries, swimming pools, and the like. For in these forms, Jim Crow does impede the flow of commerce in the broadest sense: it is a nuisance in a society on the move (and on the make). Not surprisingly, therefore, it was the most mobility-conscious and relatively liberated groups in the Negro community—lower-middle-class college students—who launched the attack that brought down this imposing but hollow structure.

The term "classical" appears especially apt for this phase of the civil rights movement. But in the few years that have

* Reprinted from *Commentary*, XXXIX (February, 1964), pp. 25–31. By permission of *Commentary* and the author.

passed since the first flush of sits-ins, several developments have taken place that have complicated matters enormously. One is the shifting focus of the movement in the South, symbolized by Birmingham; another is the spread of the revolution to the North; and the third, common to the other two, is the expansion of the movement's base in the Negro community. To attempt to disentangle these three strands is to do violence to reality. David Danzig's perceptive article, "The Meaning of Negro Strategy,"* correctly saw in the Birmingham events the victory of the concept of collective struggle over individual achievement as the road to Negro freedom. And Birmingham remains the unmatched symbol of grassroots protest involving all strata of the black community. It was also in this most industrialized of Southern cities that the single-issue demands of the movement's classical stage gave way to the "package deal." No longer were Negroes satisfied with integrating lunch counters. They now sought advances in employment, housing, school integration, police protection, and so forth.

Thus, the movement in the South began to attack areas of discrimination which were not so remote from the Northern experience as were Jim Crow lunch counters. At the same time, the interrelationship of these apparently distinct areas became increasingly evident. What is the value of winning access to public accommodations for those who lack money to use them? The minute the movement faced this question, it was compelled to expand its vision beyond race relations to economic relations, including the role of education in modern society. And what also became clear is that all these interrelated problems, by their very nature, are not soluble by private, voluntary efforts but require government action—or politics. Already Southern demonstrators had recognized that the most effective way to strike at the police brutality they suffered from was by getting rid of the local sheriff—and that meant political action, which in turn meant, and still means, political action within the Democratic party where the only meaningful primary contests in the South are fought.

And so, in Mississippi, thanks largely to the leadership of Bob Moses, a turn toward political action has been taken. More than voter registration is involved here. A conscious bid for *political power* is being made, and in the course of that effort a tactical shift is being effected: direct-action techniques are being subordinated to a strategy calling for the building of community institutions or power bases. Clearly,

* *Commentary,* February, 1964.

the implications of this shift reach far beyond Mississippi. What began as a protest movement is being challenged to translate itself into a political movement. Is this the right course? And if it is, can the transformaton be accomplished?

The very decade which has witnessed the decline of legal Jim Crow has also seen the rise of *de facto* segregation in our most fundamental socioeconomic institutions. More Negroes are unemployed today than in 1954, and the unemployment gap between the races is wider. The median income of Negroes has dropped from 57 per cent to 54 per cent of that of whites. A higher percentage of Negro workers is now concentrated in jobs vulnerable to automation than was the case ten years ago. More Negroes attend *de facto* segregated schools today than when the Supreme Court handed down its famous decision; while school integration proceeds at a snail's pace in the South, the number of Northern schools with an excessive proportion of minority youth proliferates. And behind this is the continuing growth of racial slums, spreading over our central cities and trapping Negro youth in a milieu which, whatever its legal definition, sows an unimaginable demoralization. Again, legal niceties aside, a resident of a racial ghetto lives in segregated housing, and more Negroes fall into this category than ever before.

These are the facts of life which generate frustration in the Negro community and challenge the civil rights movement. At issue, after all, is not *civil rights,* strictly speaking, but social and economic conditions. Last summer's riots were not race riots; they were outbursts of class aggression in a society where class and color definitions are converging disastrously. How can the (perhaps misnamed) civil rights movement deal with this problem?

Before trying to answer, let me first insist that the task of the movement is vastly complicated by the failure of many whites of good will to understand the nature of our problem. There is a widespread assumption that the removal of artificial racial barriers should result in the automatic integration of the Negro into all aspects of American life. This myth is fostered by facile analogies with the experience of various ethnic immigrant groups, particularly the Jews. But the analogies with the Jews do not hold for three simple but profound reasons. First, Jews have a long history as a literate people, a resource which has afforded them opportunities to advance in the academic and professional worlds, to achieve intellectual status even in the midst of economic hardship, and to evolve sustaining value systems in the context of ghetto life. Negroes, for the greater part of their presence in this country, were forbidden by law to read or write. Second, Jews have a long history of family stability, the importance of which in terms of aspiration and self-image is obvious. The Negro family structure was totally destroyed by slavery and with it the possibility of cultural transmission (the right of Negroes to marry and rear children is barely a century old). Third, Jews are white and have the *option* of relinquishing their cultural-religous identity, intermarrying, passing, etc. Negroes, or at least the overwhelming majority of them, do not have this option. There is also a fourth, vulgar reason. If the Jewish and Negro communities are not comparable in terms of education, family structure, and color, it is also true that their respective economic roles bear little resemblance.

This matter of economic role brings us to the greater problem—the fact that we are moving into an era in which the natural functioning of the market does not by itself ensure every man with will and ambition a place in the productive process. The immigrant who came to this country during the late nineteenth and early twentieth centuries entered a society which was expanding territorially and/or economically. It was then possible to start at the bottom, as an unskilled or semi-skilled worker, and move up the ladder, acquiring new skills along the way. Especially was this true when industrial unionism was burgeoning, giving new dignity and higher wages to organized workers. Today the situation has changed. We are not expanding territorially, the western frontier is settled, labor organizing has leveled off, our rate of economic growth has been stagnant for a decade. And we are in the midst of a technological revolution which is altering the fundamental structure of the labor force, destroying unskilled and semi-skilled jobs—jobs in which Negroes are disproportionately concentrated.

Whatever the pace of this technological revolution may be, the *direction* is clear: the lower rungs of the economic ladder are being lopped off. This means that an individual will no longer be able to start at the bottom and work his way up; he will have to start in the middle or on top, and hold on tight. It will not even be enough to have certain specific skills, for many skilled jobs are also vulnerable to automation. A broad educational background permitting vocational adaptability and flexibility, seems more imperative than ever. We live in a society where, as Secretary of Labor Willard Wirtz puts it, machines have the equivalent of a high school diploma. Yet the average educational attainment of American Negroes is 8.2 years.

Negroes, of course, are not the only people being affected

by these developments. It is reported that there are now 50 per cent fewer unskilled and semi-skilled jobs than there are high school dropouts. Almost one-third of the 26 million young people entering the labor market in the 1960's will be dropouts. But the percentage of Negro dropouts nationally is 57 per cent, and in New York City, among Negroes 25 years of age or over, it is 68 per cent. They are without a future.

To what extent can the kind of self-help campaign recently prescribed by Eric Hoffer in the *New York Times Magazine* cope with such a situation? I would advise those who think that self-help is the answer to familiarize themselves with the long history of such efforts in the Negro community, and to consider why so many foundered on the shoals of ghetto life. It goes without saying that any effort to combat demoralization and apathy is desirable, but we must understand that demoralization in the Negro community is largely a common-sense response to an objective reality. Negro youths have no need of statistics to perceive, fairly accurately, what their odds are in American society. Indeed, from the point of view of motivation, some of the healthiest Negro youngsters I know are juvenile delinquents: vigorously pursuing the American Dream of material acquisition and status, yet finding the conventional means of attaining it blocked off, they do not yield to defeatism but resort to illegal (and often ingenious) methods. They are not alien to American culture. They are, in Gunnar Myrdal's phrase, "exaggerated Americans." To want a Cadillac is not un-American; to push a cart in the garment center is. If Negroes are to be persuaded that the conventional path (school, work, etc.) is superior, we had better provide evidence which is now sorely lacking. It is a double cruelty to harangue Negro youth about education and training when we do not know what jobs will be available for them. When a Negro youth can reasonably foresee a future free of slums, when the prospect of gainful employment is realistic, we will see motivation and self-help in abundant enough quantities.

Meanwhile, there is an ironic similarity between the self-help advocated by many liberals and the doctrines of the Black Muslims. Professional sociologists, psychiatrists, and social workers have expressed amazement at the Muslims' success in transforming prostitutes and dope addicts into respectable citizens. But every prostitute the Muslims convert to a model of Calvinist virtue is replaced by the ghetto with two more. Dedicated as they are to maintenance of the ghetto, the Muslims are powerless to affect substantial moral reform. So too with every other group or program which is not aimed at the destruction of slums, their causes and effects. Self-help efforts, directly or indirectly, must be geared to mobilizing people into power units capable of effecting social change. That is, their goal must be genuine self-help, not merely self-improvement. Obviously, where self-improvement activities succeed in imparting to their participants a feeling of some control over their environment, those involved may find their appetites for change whetted; they may move into the political arena.

Let me sum up what I have thus far been trying to say: the civil rights movement is evolving from a protest movement into a full-fledged *social movement*—an evolution calling its very name into question. It is now concerned not merely with removing the barriers to full *opportunity* but with achieving the fact of *equality*. From sit-ins and freedom rides we have gone into rent strikes, boycotts, community organization, and political action. As a consequence of this natural evolution, the Negro today finds himself stymied by obstacles of far greater magnitude than the legal barriers he was attacking before: automation, urban decay, *de facto* school segregation. These are problems which, while conditioned by Jim Crow, do not vanish upon its demise. They are more deeply rooted in our socio-economic order; they are the result of the total society's failure to meet not only the Negro's needs, but human needs generally.

These propositions have won increasing recognition and acceptance, but with a curious twist. They have formed the common premise of two apparently contradictory lines of thought which simultaneously nourish and antagonize each other. On the one hand, there is the reasoning of the *New York Times* moderate who says that the problems are so enormous and complicated that Negro militancy is a futile irritation, and that the need is for "intelligent moderation." Thus, during the first New York school boycott, the *Times* editorialized that Negro demands, while abstractly just, would necessitate massive reforms, the funds for which could not realistically be anticipated; therefore the just demands were also foolish demands and would only antagonize white people. Moderates of this stripe are often correct in perceiving the difficulty or impossibility of racial progress in the context of present social and economic policies. But they accept the context as fixed. They ignore (or perhaps see all too well) the potentialities inherent in linking Negro demands to broader pressures for radical revision of existing policies. They apparently see nothing strange in the fact that in the last twenty-five years we have spent nearly a trillion dollars fighting or preparing for wars, yet throw up our hands before the need for overhauling our schools, clearing the slums, and really abolishing poverty. My quarrel with these moderates is that they do not even envision radical changes; their admonitions of moderation are, for all practical purposes, admonitions to the Negro to adjust to the status quo, and are therefore immoral.

The more effectively the moderates argue their case, the more they convince Negroes that American society will not or cannot be reorganized for full racial equality. Michael Harrington has said that a successful war on poverty might well require the expenditure of $100 billion. Where, the Negro wonders, are the forces now in motion to compel such a commitment? If the voices of the moderates were raised in an insistence upon a reallocation of national resources at levels that could not be confused with tokenism (that is, if the moderates stopped being moderates), Negroes would have greater grounds for hope. Meanwhile, the Negro movement cannot escape a sense of isolation.

It is precisely this sense of isolation that gives rise to the second line of thought I want to examine—the tendency within the civil rights movement which, despite its militancy, pursues what I call a "no-win" policy. Sharing with many moderates a recognition of the magnitude of the obstacles to freedom, spokesmen for this tendency survey the American scene and find no forces prepared to move toward radical solutions. From this they conclude that the only viable strategy is shock; above all, the hypocrisy of white liberals must be exposed. These spokesmen are often described as the radicals of the movement, but they are really its moralists. They seek to change white hearts—by traumatizing them. Frequently abetted by white self-flagellants, they may gleefully applaud (though not really agreeing with) Malcolm X because, while they admit he has no program, they think he can frighten white people into doing the right thing. To believe this, of course, you must be convinced, even if unconsciously, that at the core of the white man's heart lies a buried affection for Negroes—a proposition one may be permitted to doubt. But in any case, hearts are not relevant to the issue; neither racial affinities nor racial hostilities are rooted there. It is institutions—social, political, and economic institutions—which are the ultimate molders of collective sentiments. Let these institutions be reconstructed *today,* and let the ineluctable gradualism of history govern the formation of a new psychology.

My quarrel with the "no-win" tendency in the civil rights movement (and the reason I have so designated it) parallels my quarrel with the moderates outside the movement. As the latter lack the vision or will for fundamental change, the former lack a realistic strategy for achieving it. For such a strategy they substitute militancy. But militancy is a matter of posture and volume and not of effect.

I believe that the Negro's struggle for equality in America is essentially revolutionary. While most Negroes—in their hearts—unquestionably seek only to enjoy the fruits of American society as it now exists, their quest cannot objectively be satisfied within the framework of existing political and economic relations. The young Negro who would demonstrate his way into the labor market may be motivated by a thoroughly bourgeois ambition and thoroughly "capitalist" considerations, but he will end up having to favor a great expansion of the public sector of the economy. At any rate, that is the position the movement will be forced to take as it looks at the number of jobs being generated by the private economy, and if it is to remain true to the masses of Negroes.

The revolutionary character of the Negro's struggle is manifest in the fact that this struggle may have done more to democratize life for whites than for Negroes. Clearly, it was the sit-in movement of young Southern Negroes which, as it galvanized white students, banished the ugliest features of McCarthyism from the American campus and resurrected political debate. It was not until Negroes assaulted *de facto* school segregation in the urban centers that the issue of quality education for *all* children stirred into motion. Finally, it seems reasonably clear that the civil rights movement, directly and through the resurgence of social conscience it kindled, did more to initiate the war on poverty than any other single force.

It will be—it has been—argued that these by-products of the Negro struggle are not revolutionary. But the term revolutionary, as I am using it, does not connote violence; it refers to the qualitative transformation of fundamental institutions, more or less rapidly, to the point where the social and economic structure which they comprised can no longer be said to be the same. The Negro struggle has hardly run its course; and it will not stop moving until it has been utterly defeated or won substantial equality. But I fail to see how the movement can be victorious in the absence of radical programs for full employment, abolition of slums, the reconstruction of our educational system, new definitions of work and leisure. Adding up the cost of such programs. we can only conclude that we are talking about a refashioning of our political economy. It has been estimated, for example, that the price of replacing New York City's slums with public housing would be $17 billion. Again, a multi-billion dollar federal public-works program, dwarfing the currently proposed $2 billion program, is required to reabsorb unskilled and semi-skilled workers into the labor market—and this must be done if Negro workers in these categories are to be employed. "Preferential treatment" cannot help them.

I am not trying here to delineate a total program, only to suggest the scope of economic reforms which are most immediately related to the plight of the Negro community. One could speculate on their political implications—whether, for example, they do not indicate the obsolescence of state government and the superiority of regional structures as viable units of planning. Such speculations aside, it is clear that Negro needs cannot be satisfied unless we go beyond what has so far been placed on the agenda. How are these radical objectives to be achieved? The answer is simple, deceptively so: *through political power*.

There is a strong moralistic strain in the civil rights movement which would remind us that power corrupts, forgetting that the absence of power also corrupts. But this is not the view I want to debate here, for it is waning. Our problem is posed by those who accept the need for political power but do not understand the nature of the object and therefore lack sound strategies for achieving it; they tend to confuse political institutions with lunch counters.

A handful of Negroes, acting alone, could integrate a lunch counter by strategically locating their bodies so as *directly* to interrupt the operation of the proprietor's will; their numbers were relatively unimportant. In politics, however, such a confrontation is difficult because the interests involved are merely *represented*. In the execution of a political decision a direct confrontation may ensue (as when federal marshals escorted James Meredith into the University of Mississippi—to turn from an example of non-violent coercion to one of force backed up with the threat of violence). But in arriving at a political decision, numbers and organizations are crucial, especially for the economically disenfranchised. (Needless to say, I am assuming that the forms of political democracy exist in America, however imperfectly, that they are valued, and that elitist or putschist conceptions of exercising power are beyond the pale of discussion of the civil rights movement.)

Neither that movement nor the country's twenty million black people can win political power alone. We need allies. The future of the Negro struggle depends on whether the contradictions of this society can be resolved by a coalition of progressive forces which becomes the *effective* political majority in the United States. I speak of the coalition which staged the March on Washington, passed the Civil Rights Act, and laid the basis for the Johnson landslide—Negroes, trade unionists, liberals, and religious groups.

There are those who argue that a coalition strategy would force the Negro to surrender his political independence to white liberals, that he would be neutralized, deprived of his cutting edge, absorbed into the Establishment. Some who take this position urged last year that votes be withheld from the Johnson–Humphrey ticket as a demonstration of the Negro's political power. Curiously enough, these people who sought to demonstrate power through the non-exercise of it, also point to the Negro "swing vote" in crucial urban areas as the source of the Negro's independent political power. But here they are closer to being right: the urban Negro vote will grow in importance in the coming years. If there is anything positive in the spread of the ghetto, it is the potential political power base thus created and to realize this potential is one of the most challenging and urgent tasks before the civil rights movement. If the movement can wrest leadership of the ghetto vote from the machines, it will have acquired an organized constituency such as other major groups in our society now have.

But we must also remember that the effectiveness of a swing vote depends solely on "other" votes. It derives its power from them. In that sense, it can never be "independent," but must opt for one candidate or the other, even if by default. Thus coalitions are inescapable, however tentative they may be. And this is the case in all but those few situations in which Negroes running on an independent ticket might conceivably win. "Independence," in other words, is not a value in itself. The issue is which coalition to join and how to make it responsive to your program. Necessarily there will be compromise. But the difference between expediency and morality in politics is the difference between selling out a principle and making smaller concessions to win larger ones. The leader who shrinks from this task reveals not his purity but his lack of political sense.

The task of molding a political movement out of the March on Washington coalition is not simple, but no alternatives have been advanced. We need to choose our allies on the basis of common political objectives. It has become fashionable in some no-win Negro circles to decry the white liberal as the main enemy (his hypocrisy is what sustains racism);

by virtue of this reverse recitation of the reactionary's litany (liberalism leads to socialism, which leads to Communism) the Negro is left in majestic isolation, except for a tiny band of fervent white initiates. But the objective fact is that *Eastland and Goldwater* are the main enemies—they and the opponents of civil rights, of the war on poverty, of medicare, of social security, of federal aid to education, of unions, and so forth. The labor movement, despite its obvious faults, has been the largest single organized force in this country pushing for progressive social legislation. And where the Negro-labor-liberal axis is weak, as in the farm belt, it was the religious groups that were most influential in rallying support for the Civil Rights Bill.

The durability of the coalition was interestingly tested during the election. I do not believe that the Johnson landslide proved the "white backlash" to be a myth. It proved, rather, that economic interests are more fundamental than prejudice: the backlashers decided that loss of social security was, after all, too high a price to pay for a slap at the Negro. This lesson was a valuable first step in re-educating such people, and it must be kept alive, for the civil rights movement will be advanced only to the degree that social and economic welfare gets to be inextricably entangled with civil rights.

The 1964 elections marked a turning point in American politics. The Democratic landslide was not merely the result of a negative reaction to Goldwaterism; it was also the expression of a majority liberal consensus. The near unanimity with which Negro voters joined in that expression was, I am convinced, a vindication of the July twenty-fifth statement by Negro leaders calling for a strategic turn toward political action and a temporary curtailment of mass demonstrations. Despite the controversy surrounding the statement, the instinctive response it met with in the community is suggested by the fact that demonstrations were down 75 per cent as compared with the same period in 1963. But should so high a percentage of Negro voters have gone to Johnson, or should they have held back to narrow his margin of victory and thus give greater visibility to our swing vote? How has our loyalty changed things? Certainly the Negro vote had higher visibility in 1960, when a switch of only 7 per cent from the Republican column of 1956 elected President Kennedy. But the slimness of Kennedy's victory—of his "mandate"—dictated a go-slow approach on civil rights, at least until the Birmingham upheaval.

Although Johnson's popular majority was so large that he

could have won without such overwhelming Negro support, that support was important from several angles. Beyond adding to Johnson's total national margin, it was specifically responsible for his victories in Virginia, Florida, Tennessee, and Arkansas. Goldwater took only those states where fewer than 45 per cent of elgible Negroes were registered. That Johnson would have won those states had Negro voting rights been enforced is a lesson not likely to be lost on a man who would have been happy with a unanimous electoral college. In any case, the 1.6 million Southern Negroes who voted have had a shattering impact on the Southern political party structure, as illustrated in the changed composition of the Southern congressional delegation. The "backlash" gave the Republicans five House seats in Alabama, one in Georgia, and one in Mississippi. But on the Democratic side, seven segregationists were defeated while all nine Southerners who voted for the Civil Rights Act were re-elected. It may be premature to predict a Southern Democratic Party of Negroes and white moderates and a Republican Party of refugee racists and economic conservatives, but there certainly is a strong tendency toward such a realignment; and an additional 3.6 million Negroes of voting age in the eleven Southern states are still to be heard from. Even the tendency toward disintegration of the Democratic party's racist wing defines a new context for Presidential and liberal strategy in the congressional battles ahead. Thus the Negro vote (North as well as South), while not decisive in the Presidential race, was enormously effective. It was a dramatic element of a historic mandate which contains vast possibilities and dangers that will fundamentally affect the future course of the civil rights movement.

The liberal congressional sweep raises hope for an assault on the seniority system, Rule Twenty-two, and other citadels of Dixiecrat-Republican power. The overwhelming of this conservative coalition should also mean progress on much bottlenecked legislation of profound interest to the movement (e.g., bills by Senators Clark and Nelson on planning, manpower, and employment). Moreover, the irrelevance of the South to Johnson's victory gives the President more freedom to act than his predecessor had and more leverage to the movement to pressure for executive action in Mississippi and other racist strongholds.

None of this *guarantees* vigorous executive or legislative action, for the other side of the Johnson landslide is that it has a Gaullist quality. Goldwater's capture of the Republican

party forced into the Democratic camp many disparate elements which do not belong there, Big Business being the
major example. Johnson, who wants to be President "of all
people," may try to keep his new coalition together by stick-
ing close to the political center. But if he decides to do this,
it is unlikely that even his political genius will be able to
hold together a coalition so inherently unstable and rife with
contradictions. It must come apart. Should it do so while
Johnson is pursuing a centrist course, then the mandate will
have been wastefully dissipated. However, if the mandate is
seized upon to set fundamental changes in motion, then the
basis can be laid for a new mandate, a new coalition including
hitherto inert and dispossessed strata of the population.

Here is where the cutting edge of the civil rights movement
can be applied. We must see to it that the reorganization of
the "consensus party" proceeds along lines which will make
it an effective vehicle for social reconstruction, a role it cannot play so long as it furnishes Southern racism with its
national political power. (One of Barry Goldwater's few attractive ideas was that the Dixiecrats belong with him in the
same party.) And nowhere has the civil rights movement's
political cutting edge been more magnificently demonstrated
than at Atlantic City, where the Mississippi Freedom Democratic Party not only secured recognition as a bona fide component of the national party, but in the process routed the
representatives of the most rabid racists—the white Mississippi and Alabama delegations. While I still believe that the
FDP made a tactical error in spurning the compromise, there
is no question that they launched a political revolution whose
logic is the displacement of Dixiecrat power. They launched
that revolution within a major political institution and as part
of a coalitional effort.

The role of the civil rights movement in the reorganization
of American political life is programmatic as well as strategic.
We are challenged now to broaden our social vision, to develop functional programs with concrete objectives. We need
to propose alternatives to technological unemployment, urban
decay, and the rest. We need to be calling for public works
and training, for national economic planning, for federal aid
to education, for attractive public housing—all this on a
sufficiently massive scale to make a difference. We need to
protest the notion that our integration into American life,
so long delayed, must now proceed in an atmosphere of competitive scarcity instead of in the security of abundance which
technology makes possible. We cannot claim to have answers

to all the complex problems of modern society. That is too much to ask for a movement still battling barbarism in Mississippi. But we can agitate the right questions by probing at the contradictions which still stand in the way of the "Great Society." The questions having been asked, motion must begin in the larger society, for there is a limit to what Negroes can do alone.

Black Power: A Creative Necessity*

By NATHAN WRIGHT, JR.

The theme of "black power," in spite of much recent publicity, is not new to the American scene. Nor is it likely in the foreseeable future to come to a definite end, regardless of the outcome of the current debate concerning the propriety of the term.

"Black power" has been a continuing refrain in the history of the American Negro. The slave uprisings, which were more frequent than historians often relate, continually reiterated the black power theme. It was the clarion call of the rebel John Brown and the abolitionist Frederick Douglass. Again, the sophisticated and angered W. E. B. Du Bois and the militant visionary Marcus Garvey addressed themselves to the issue of the black man's co-operative strength and dignity. A. Philip Randolph's Brotherhood of Sleeping Car Porters came together, was held together and became a major leverage in American political and economic life through a commitment to what militants today speak of as black power.

To what precisely does the theme black power speak? In the Negro churches, it has most often addressed itself to a kind of black solidarity in a holy war where in an imminent latter day the saints of light, who have withstood the evil onslaughts of the powers of darkness, will receive their due reward. Howard Thurman in his recent and perhaps his greatest book, *The Luminous Darkness*, speaks of the perception of his early youth that white humanity was beyond the pale of his morality. Such widespread feelings of the mystical uniqueness of the Negro in his corporate life have been the backdrop for the political thrusts which we identify most often as black power. In its first several decades of militancy, the

* Reprinted from *The Catholic World*, CCIV (October, 1966), pp. 46–51. By permission of *The Catholic World* and the author.

National Association for the Advancement of Colored People could be fairly identified with the alleged dissidents of today who speak of the critical force of the Negro's united strength.

Reference to such an idea today is subjected to the frequent criticism that it is open to misunderstanding, is subject to individual interpretation; and therefore may be misleading. Because black power speaks—as it has done over several centuries—to the Negro's recognition and aggressive assertion of his own fundamental sense of dignity, integrity and worth, it must have at least flexible implications; for no two individuals can perceive of and assert their own validity and place in precisely identical ways. The belligerent Negro by nature will tend to express his own sense of being and relationship in bellicose ways; the more temperate Negro will tend to use more temperate means. Nonetheless, there may be an apparently realistic danger in a mass rallying to the theme of black power. The Negro people over the years have been encouraged by many means to suppress and sublimate their natural feelings of conflict and frustration. In this light, under a long-postponed and new-found freedom, the potential catharsis inherent in the current call to the banners of black power may be fraught with not unexpected and painful excess. Black power may be seen to be a logical and perhaps much needed expression of the Negro's awakening to self-awareness by an overly delayed and awkward stretching of his arms and flexing of his muscles, as he looks half-bewildered at his newly felt but as yet untested and unmeasured political and moral strength.

Interestingly, those who oppose the use of the term "black power" have often raised the objection that Negroes court annihilation once black power comes face to face with white power. Such a vision of the armed conflict of two opposing and ludicrously unequal camps represents both a misreading of the intent of those who espouse black power and a failure to understand the necessary dynamics of social and moral progress.

Ethnocentrism, or the consciousness of in-group solidarity, with a consequent sense of pride and power, is one of the strongest of human sentiments. What an in-group or an ethnic community may be is defined by the culture of which such a group is a part. The American culture has defined a number of ethnic groups, including notably the Jews, the Irish and the Scotch-Irish, who represent religious, national or a combination of religious and national groupings. All of these groups have intensive pride in their own membership; and this is given expression in a variety of ways. There are several singular and significant differences in the circumstances of the Negro's place or role as an ethnic group in American life. The Negro's ability to express his sense of pride has been circumscribed.

Perhaps nowhere has this been more flagrant than in the well-nigh completely successful attempts of the white community, with the encouragement and complicity of the nation's social scientists, to have the Negro forget that he is by and large a European-American Indian-black African hybrid. The Negro has been encouraged to forget—as in my own family— that the Hickmans and the Wrights (our family names) were of British stock, and that the varying shades of color and different textures of hair are a reflection of variegated ethnic ancestry. By culture, almost completely, and by race to a fairly considerable degree, the overwhelming majority of American Negroes are of a white European background.

Yet the Negro's sense of limited racial and cultural pride has been restricted to his supposed African origins in a veiled and uncertain past. Rare is the writer of an American textbook in sociology or history who attributes to the Negro anything other than pure African descent, except in the semi-derogatory sense of illegitimacy. Even here, illegitimacy is an occurrence common to family strains, and is simply heightened in varying degrees and by diverse means among the rootless and the oppressed. "Black power" may be seen as a form of ethnocentrism, albeit falling into a trap set by the historically racist-bound American culture.

The Negro's sense of pride is further blunted by the seemingly un-American assumption that the Negro's position of social and economic inferiority is immutable. The "last hired-first fired" concept here may be seen to be not the multiplication of individual behavior but the logical expression of a way of life which rejects the Negro's sense of worth. The Negro himself has purchased stock in this endeavor. Partly by recoil in self-defense and partly by imposed design, the American Negro has eschewed social equality. No major civil rights leader, even today, espouses as a major plank in his platform social equality, at the very heart of which is the matter of inter-marriage. Yet, economic survival and advancement, as well as a sense of pride, depend in no small degree upon relationships of a blood and legal variety.

Because of the lack of social contacts, Negroes today are isolated from jobs, not only at the bottom of the ladder but from those so desperately needed at the top. Whom one knows is for white Americans as important as what one knows. For Negro Americans, the failure to know people in those intimate and familial relationships which spell care, concern and mutual economic responsibility means growing isolation from the economic and social fruits of American life which are theoretically their due inheritance.

The renewed impetus toward the concept of black power here reflects the apparent readiness of many Negro Americans to give a perhaps still illusory implementation to their now hoarse, hackneyed and desperate cry of "All! Here! Now!"

A story is told of an advertisement for what was billed to be the most unusual show on earth. The day finally came for the great performance; and an audience in curious expectancy was treated to a one-minute show of symbolic behavior. Twelve Negroes were simply tugging hard at a rope. When those who had come for the show demanded an explanation, the producer simply asked, "Where on earth have you ever seen twelve Negroes pulling together?"

What is apparently true of the American Negro is true of all ethnic groups. People are all unique; only at critical and measured points do corporate interests emerge. For the Negro this has been both bane and blessing. Hence with the current controversy over the use of the term "black power" a consensus is sought where no agreement need legitimately exist. The fact is that—in spite of the massive economic and social signs and indications of the monumental failure of the American people to close the gap between Negro and white advancement—many Negroes are content with the current drift and trend of things.

Negroes, as all Americans, are generally better off today than they were at the end of World War II. The awareness of this fact leads not only many Negroes representative of the "man in the street" but also a substantial portion of recognized Negro leadership to speak with apparent integrity of the "progress" and "gains" which Negroes are making. Yet the American economy generally has been growing by greater degrees than has the Negro's alleged "progress." This leads other Negroes of a different type of perceptiveness and of equal integrity to reject the term "progress" with as great a degree of disdain as that which some have rejected the term black power.

The willingness to speak to the affirmative implications of black power may be in precise relationship to one's conception of Negro progress. On this issue, Negroes are not, and doubtless will not be, agreed. The figures for the relative income of non-whites in relation to whites over a recent fifteen-year period are as follows:

1949	51.05%	1957	53.50%
1950	54.25%	1958	51.15%
1951	52.66%	1959	51.69%
1952	56.83%	1960	55.41%
1953	56.03%	1961	53.35%
1954	55.34%	1962	53.39%
1955	55.35%	1963	52.92%
1956	52.61%		

The fact that there is no clear statistical trend suggests that—even if the figures may be radically improved for 1964 to 1966—the idea of a relative and secure indication of "progress" is for the Negro an illusory reality.

Further, the current programs under the auspices of the Office of Economic Opportunity and the extensive efforts of private and civic agencies on behalf of Negro employment and upgrading are largely in the direction of lower echelon and "make-work" jobs. These jobs serve a basic and necessary purpose of enabling Negroes to survive and of postponing the day of massive revolt. In our present circumstance, this is no mean purpose and must be given the fullest encouragement. Nonetheless, the catapulting of significant numbers of available, qualified Negroes into positions of high economic value and extensive influence at policy-making levels in our business, educational and civic structure remains neglected in a way which may reach perilous proportions. A sad fact which must be contemplated by all is that, in spite of all our efforts in the Negro's behalf in the recent past, his relative stake in the benefits of the American good life has not improved; at the same time his perceptions of his own worth and due inheritance have tremendously increased. This suggests the possibility of a heightened polarization within the Negro community. Middle-class Negroes who have bettered their status understandably will be under the illusion and spell of progress because of the tangible and unmistakable reality of their own personal progress. On the other hand, there may be in the days ahead growing masses of the disinherited, feeling isolated and neglected, believing themselves to be forgotten by their traditional leadership, and ever more willing to spell out in word and deed the implications of black power in terms of the frustration and depth of deprivation which they perceive to be their lot.

Some economists believe that the economic system which is traditional to our culture calls for a fluid reservoir of untapped resources at its base. If such a reservoir is needed—

as may be perceived from its continued existence—the rudimentary economic problem becomes a potentially explosive social problem when the group at the bottom is not heterogeneous—but is composed of one group which includes well-trained personnel who should not be there but are, because of social injustice. Such has been and is the Negro's plight. Even with increased education, only a relatively small proportion of the economic gap is closed. In most communities in America, it is still true that only after most white unemployed find employment are the Negro unemployed given basic consideration. In our large cities, there has been a recent rise from a 25% to a 34% unemployment rate among Negroes between the ages of 16 and 21 while the rates for white youth in the same age category have been going steadily down.

The differing situations of Negro Americans have thus brought about differing attitudes toward the problems of the present and the future. Human nature historically has not been fundamentally altruistic in sharing power. Thus, to hope that the aspiring and upwardly mobile Negro and those in the secure white community will voluntarily side with those who perceive themselves as the disinherited may represent the height of folly. The cry, "black power!" says "my share!" to some. For others, it gives the totally unfounded illusion of threatening an accustomed, or hopefully to be increased, abundance.

The question of the feasibility of the use of black power is mainly a rhetorical one. It is not a question of *whether* Negroes can express black power, but a *necessity*—in the sense that the Negro—as all who grow into responsible selfhood must do—assert his own inherent sense of worth and being. Several centuries of admittedly crippling segregation and discrimination have not left the American Negro unaffected. He has been limited by this evil process, and it is he alone who must stake his claim to the worth which for centuries he has been denied. In giving expression to his own new-found self-realization, the American Negro must stand alone. No one may do this for him or with him. It is so with our children; it is true also with rising social groups. Here one may appropriate the famed "hand" analogy of Booker T. Washington in claiming that today all Americans—white and black—must be as one "hand" in all that pertains to the extension of the corporate, national good life. But we must be as separate as the fingers of the hand in doing that which each group must do for itself, staking its claim in its own unpredictable and variegated way to its own due dignity and worth.

What, then, is the white man's role? It is a changeless law of human life that each man must claim for himself the dignity of his own adulthood. Those who would deny to the Negro this privilege would consciously or unconsciously will for the Negro that he be less than what he should be. What he would do for himself today has been the privilege of all other Americans since the "shot heard around the world." If the black man has any power in American life, it is black power; and so the term is simply descriptive of a contemporary and hopefully growing reality in American life. As the Negro's response to the term black power is mixed, so is that of the white community. Many would applaud what they perceive to be the Negro's coming at last into his own. Others who have been close to the American Negro, who find themselves in positions of influence in national and local civil rights groups, may understandably regret the current impetus toward black power. Thus, to carry the analogy of growth into adulthood further, the lament of the white liberal (and consequently of organizations in which he has significant control) may be not unlike the lament of a foster parent who contemplates losing as a child the one to whom he has become accustomed to giving succor. In the movement toward black power, the white liberal's perceived reluctance must be understood and appreciated by the Negro as the action of one who historically has extended the hand of friendship and upon whose help, once the dust of self-assertion has settled, the Negro must continue to rely.

To what strategic ends—aside from eventual growth and an ultimate furtherance of self-respect—can the movement toward black power lead? There are several.

(1) *National self-interest.* The Negro's current restless and aggressive protest (as yet relatively mild and self-destructive) points to what may become a massive, irrational, ultimate and widespread response to the continued arbitrary isolation of the masses of the nation's Negro poor from the economic mainstream of American life. Either we develop all of the nation's human resources to their full productive potential and then open opportunities for their effective utilization for our mutual benefit, or we create liabilities which become a growing burden upon both this and succeeding generations.

In this light, the contemporary impetus toward black power may be seen as a restorative and conserving force in American life, calling America to save itself from the folly of a myopic vision of what America in human terms is destined and called to be.

(2) *Urban improvement.* The life of our cities needs to be redeemed. The Negro's often angry protests show that social palliatives no longer apply. New and creative answers must be found for the sores which fester in the heart of city life. Our urban schools, with their contemporary racial unrest, remind us that the basic planning and administration at every level must be sensitive to, and representative of, the concerns of those who are served. Schools with proprietors removed from their constituents, as our urban systems tend now to be, are as potentially insidious as absentee landlords. Answers to the Negro's anxious pleas for improved quality education may provide much-needed and hard-to-find handles for meeting the needs of all.

(3) *Marginal insights.* The Negro's present protest speaks to neglected dimensions of democracy. To a considerable degree outside the center of American life, the Negro may be seen in the unique and enviable position of bringing new and saving perspectives to basic issues in our national life. One such issue is the extension of the meaning of equality. Our religious and national heritage, as well as the persistent experience of family life, speaks to the equitable principle of taking from each as he is able and providing for each as is his need. Those who are benighted deserve our richest and best resources to enable them to progress toward standing alone. Can a truly democratic society reach for less than this humane goal? By virtue of his rich experience at the margin of American life, the American Negro can provide fresh insights into the common inheritance to which we owe allegiance. Here a uniquely black power may provide rich resources for us all.

(4) *Changed status.* Inevitably, a changed perception of the Negro's own position creates a changed racial situation. When the nature of the problem is altered, new challenges await us which can provide some new foundations in exchange for the old from which little that can be called true progress was achieved.

New conditions and uncharted paths are always fraught with peril. We cannot specifically foretell what the future holds for any implication or consequence of black power. But the assertion of human dignity and worth—as we may learn from experience with our own sons and daughters—while creating times of testing, are productive of much good, growth and gain.

Hopefully, the days ahead, as well as the more distant

future, may be entrusted with their own problems as we build today the human aspect of our corporate life. It is in this context that we may come to see and accept as a creative necessity the current focus on black power.

Black Americans and the Press: Comment*

By CHARLES EVERS

We Mississippians are between the river and the deep blue sea, and I'm going to talk about what the press has done for us there. But in doing this, there is the risk that we may all wind up walking out saying "the hell with the press."

The press has been and is one of the worst enemies, along with the police, that the Negro has in Mississippi. I can only speak for Mississippi, not Los Angeles or Chicago, because Mississippi is the only place I really know about.

Every newspaper in Mississippi—with one exception—has damned the Negro. That one exception is the Greenville *Delta Democrat-Times*. Hodding Carter and his parents down through the years have tried to do what was fair. But the rest of the papers have picked out all the things that the Negro may have done wrong and blown them into the biggest balloon you can imagine. The editors down there always come out with racist statements and have caused more unrest and humiliation for Mississippi Negroes than any other single institution I can think of.

The paper there in Jackson is the worst in the nation. The editor himself writes inflammatory statements like these: "The way to keep the nigger down is to visit him the night before the election." If a Negro who is down and out and hungry makes the mistake of stealing a chicken, they write it to sound like he stole the First National Bank. The things that you would read in the newspapers, hear over our radio and TV stations are almost unbelievable.

* Reprinted from *The Black American and the Press*, 1968. By permission of the Ward Ritchie Press and the author.

When Sidney Poitier won an Oscar, the newscaster on a Jackson station said "Although he won it, well, you know, we don't approve of it." Can you imagine that, a newscaster saying "he won it, but we know he doesn't deserve it and we don't approve of it."

The newscasters call us "niggers" openly. This wasn't yesterday, it was today, and the FCC hasn't done anything about it. We have filed a complaint with the FCC against WLBT in Jackson because of their unfair reporting. But many of the television station reporters go around, trying to find the wrong and evil and the worst part of the Negro, and that's how they show us on the six o'clock news.

As Hodding can tell you, my brother Medgar and I were struggling for a long time, but it wasn't until the national and international press began to come into Mississippi that we were able to get people to start seeing what was happening in Mississippi.

I remember very clearly a speech I gave in Nashville in 1964. I said "If the whites don't stop beating and mistreating and burning our churches and killing our brothers and our sisters, we're going to shoot back." What did the headlines say the next day? "Evers Says Negroes Will Shoot Whites." This type of thing goes on all the time.

Now I don't agree with a lot of the things that Stokely Carmichael says, but the press doesn't print what Stokely really says. They don't print it all; they print just enough to mislead. And they don't ask why he says these things. Like all the rest of us, he's a victim of the press.

All we ask the press to do is to be fair, to point out the evils that the whites bring on us and point out the good we are trying to do. When Stokely or I say things, just print what we say and why we say it; don't cut it up and make it sound different.

Let me make it clear: I am not a Black Nationalist. I am not an extremist one way or the other. I just believe that every American should be treated equally. I could never go around preaching against the whites what they have preached against us. But America is falling apart today because of the hatred and bigotry and racism. What is destroying us is the way you treat us. Medgar and I always believed in democracy and I don't care what anybody says, I still believe in it, and I'll always believe in it. But I don't believe we can make it work with us Negroes on the outside.

The only way we're going to destroy the evils that exist in America is for all of us to get in there and knock the hell out of them. Hate is so destructive, it destroys everything—and it has no color lines. It destroys black and white, Indian, Japanese, and Chinese.

My brother Medgar was shot down for no reason other than that he wanted to be an American. That's the kind of thing hate produces. I can't teach hate; I want no part of hate because I personally have suffered too much from hate and I know what hate will do.

The press can eliminate a lot of hate by printing the truth, by telling white America what it is really like to be a Negro and that this type of thing cannot exist. White Americans are sick and their minds are twisted. We've got to straighten them out and heal them; we've got to save America because it is our home as well as the white's. It's not a white man's country; it belongs to all of us. For example, the press doesn't show the contribution we Negroes are making in Vietnam.

Instead, the press destroys everything that we try to do. For instance you never show the times we go in and try to reason and negotiate with the whites in Mississippi. You only show us marching and cussing and picketing; it's only news when we are calling whites a bunch of racists and bigots, hunkies or what not. You don't explain that we're doing that because we are frustrated as a result of the whites not listening to us.

You jump on Stokely and ride him right down, but you follow George Wallace around like he was something good to eat. Dr. King spoke once or twice against the Vietnam war and you play it up continually, but then there's old Senator Eastland who has disavowed and disobeyed every law in the book and you never mention it.

Since my brother was killed, 45 Negroes have been murdered in Mississippi. But you don't report that; it's not important.

No, gentlemen of the press, you've done a great injustice to the Negro cause. Now, since you have done that injustice, I beg you to change and give us an equal chance.

JAMES FORMAN,

Activist, Social Reformer

James Forman grew up in Chicago but spent much time in the delta of Mississippi with his grandparents. After graduating from Englewood High School in Chicago, he spent four years in the air force and, later, earned a B.S. degree in political science and public administration from Roosevelt University.

Forman attended the Institute of African Affairs at Boston University before heading for the Deep South to help the sharecroppers in the area where he visited his grandparents as a child. He raised money and collected clothing for the people. Soon afterward, he was asked to become head of a student organization—SNCC. He served as its executive secretary until 1966 when Carmichael came into the picture. After resigning his post, he became actively involved in international politics. He delivered a paper in Zambia on racism, colonialism, and apartheid. Forman has also appeared before the UN Fourth Committee to make comparisons between colonialism in the United States and in South Africa.

Forman has written a book, Sammy Younge, Jr., and has served as minister of foreign affairs for the Black Panther Party. His ideas had their greatest impact when he delivered "The Black Manifesto" which calls for $500 million in reparations from white churches and synagogues.

"IT WILL ULTIMATELY BE BY FORCE AND POWER THAT WE WILL WIN."

The Black Manifesto*

We the black people assembled in Detroit, Michigan, for the National Black Economic Development Conference are fully aware that we have been forced to come together because racist white America has exploited our resources, our minds, our bodies, our labor. For centuries we have been forced to live as colonized people inside the United States, victimized by the most vicious, racist system in the world. We have helped to build the most industrialized country in the world.

We are therefore demanding of the white Christian churches and Jewish synagogues, which are part and parcel of the system of capitalism, that they begin to pay reparations to black people in this country. We are demanding $500,000,000 from the Christian white churches and the Jewish synagogues. This total comes to fifteen dollars per nigger. This is a low estimate, for we maintain there are probably more than 30,000,000 black people in this country. Fifteen dollars a nigger is not a large sum of money, and we know that the churches and synagogues have a tremendous wealth and its membership, white America, has profited and still exploits black people. We are also not unaware that the exploitation of colored people around the world is aided and abetted by the white Christian churches and synagogues. This demand for $500,000,000 is not an idle resolution or empty words. Fifteen dollars for every black brother and sister in the United States is only a beginning of the reparations due us as people who have been exploited and degraded, brutalized, killed and persecuted. Underneath all this exploitation, the racism of this country has produced a psychological effect upon us that we are

* The Black Manifesto was delivered and adopted by the National Black Economic Development Conference in Detroit, Michigan, on April 26, 1969.

394

beginning to shake off. We are no longer afraid to demand our full rights as a people in this decadent society.

We are demanding $500,000,000 to be spent in the following way:

(1) We call for the establishment of a southern land bank to help our brothers and sisters who have to leave their land because of racist pressure, and for people who want to establish cooperative farms but who have no funds. We have seen too many farmers evicted from their homes because they have dared to defy the white racism of this country. We need money for land. We must fight for massive sums of money for this southern land bank. We call for $200,000,000 to implement this program.

(2) We call for the establishment of four major publishing and printing industries in the United States to be funded with ten million dollars each. These publishing houses are to located in Detroit, Atlanta, Los Angeles, and New York. They will help to generate capital for further cooperative investments in the black community, provide jobs and an alternative to the white-dominated and controlled printing field.

(3) We call for the establishment of four of the most advanced scientific and futuristic audio-visual networks to be located in Detroit, Chicago, Cleveland and Washington, D.C. These TV networks will provide an alternative to the racist propaganda that fills the current television networks. Each of these TV networks will be funded by ten million dollars each.

(4) We call for a research skills center which will provide research on the problems of black people. This center must be funded with no less than thirty million dollars.

(5) We call for the establishment of a training center for the teaching of skills in community organization, photography, movie making, television making and repair, radio building and repair and all other skills needed in communication. This training center shall be funded with no less than ten million dollars.

(6) We recognize the role of the National Welfare Rights Organization, and we intend to work with them. We call for ten million dollars to assist in the organization of welfare recipients. We want to organize welfare workers in this country so that they may demand more money from the government and better administration of the welfare system of this country.

(7) We call for $20,000,000 to establish a National Black Labor Strike and Defense Fund. This is necessary for the

protection of black workers and their families who are fighting racist working conditions in this country.

(8) We call for the establishment of the International Black Appeal (IBA). This International Black Appeal will be funded with no less than $20,000,000. The IBA is charged with producing more capital for the establishment of cooperative businesses in the United States and in Africa, our Motherland. The International Black Appeal is one of the most important demands that we are making, for we know that it can generate and raise funds throughout the United States and help our African brothers. The IBA is charged with three functions and shall be headed by James Forman:

(a) Raising money for the program of the National Black Economic Development Conference.
(b) The development of cooperatives in African countries and support of African liberation movements.
(c) Establishment of a Black Anti-Defamation League which will protect our African image.

(9) We call for the establishment of a black university to be founded with $130,000,000, to be located in the South. Negotiations are presently under way with a southern university.

(10) We demand that IFCO allocate all unused funds in the planning budget to implement the demands of this conference.

In order to win our demands, we are aware that we will have to have massive support, therefore:

(1) We call upon all black people throughout the United States to consider themselves as members of the National Black Economic Development Conference and to act in unity to help force the racist white Christian churches and Jewish synagogues to implement these demands.

(2) We call upon all the concerned black people across the country to contact black workers, black women, black students and the black unemployed, community groups, welfare organizations, teachers' organizations, church leaders and organizations, explaining how these demands are vital to the black community of the United States. Pressure by whatever means necessary should be applied to the white power structure. All black people should act boldly in confronting our white oppressors and demanding this modest reparation of fifteen dollars per black man.

(3) Delegates and members of the National Black Economic Development Conference are urged to call press conferences in the cities and to attempt to get as many black organizations as possible to support the demands of the conference. The quick use of the press in the local areas will heighten the tension, and these demands must be attempted to be won in a short period of time, although we are prepared for protracted and long-range struggle.

(4) We call for the total disruption of selected church-sponsored agencies operating anywhere in the United States and the world. Black workers, black women, black students and the black unemployed are encouraged to seize the offices, telephones, and printing apparatus of all church-sponsored agencies and to hold these in trusteeship until our demands are met.

(5) We call upon all delegates and members of the National Black Economic Development Conference to stage sit-in demonstrations at selected black and white churches. This is not to be interpreted as a continuation of the sit-in movement of the early sixties, but we know that active confrontation inside white churches is possible and will strengthen the possibility of meeting our demands. Such confrontation can take the form of reading the Black Manifesto instead of a sermon, or passing it out to church members. The principle of self-defense should be applied if attacked.

(6) On May 4, 1969, or a date thereafter, depending upon local conditions, we call upon black people to commence the disruption of the racist churches and synagogues throughout the United States.

(7) We call upon IFCO to serve as a central staff to coordinate the mandate of the conference and to reproduce and distribute en masse literature, leaflets, news items, press releases and other material.

(8) We call upon all delegates to find within the white community those forces which will work under the leadership of blacks to implement these demands by whatever means necessary. By taking such actions, white Americans will demonstrate concretely that they are willing to fight the white skin privilege and the white supremacy and racism which has forced us as black people to make these demands.

(9) We call upon all white Christians and Jews to practice patience, tolerance, understanding and nonviolence as they have encouraged, advised and demanded that we as black people should do throughout our entire enforced slavery in the United States. The true test of their faith

and belief in the Cross and the words of the prophets will certainly be put to a test as we seek legitimate and extremely modest reparations for our role in developing the industrial base of the western world through our slave labor. But we are no longer slaves, we are men and women, proud of our African heritage, determined to have our dignity.

(10) We are so proud of our African heritage and realize concretely that our struggle is not only to make revolution in the United States but to protect our brothers and sisters in Africa and to help them rid themselves of racism, capitalism and imperialism by whatever means necessary, including armed struggle. We are and must be willing to fight the defamation of our African image wherever it rears its ugly head. We are therefore charging the steering committee to create a black Anti-Defamation League to be founded by money raised from the International Black Appeal.

(11) We fully recognize that revolution in the United States and Africa, our Motherland, is more than a one-dimensional operation. It will require the total integration of the political, economic and military components, and therefore we call upon all our brothers and sisters who have acquired training and expertise in the fields of engineering, electronics, research, community organization, physics, biology, chemistry, mathematics, medicine, military science and warfare to assist the National Black Economic Development Conference in the implementation of its program.

(12) To implement these demands we must have a fearless leadership. We must have a leadership which is willing to battle the church establishment to implement these demands. To win our demands we will have to declare war on the white Christian churches and synagogues, and this means we may have to fight the total government structure of this country. Let no one here think that these demands will be met by our mere stating them. For the sake of the churches and synagogues, we hope that they have the wisdom to understand that these demands are modest and reasonable. But if the white Christians and Jews are not willing to meet our demands through peace and goodwill, then we declare war, and we are prepared to fight by whatever means necessary. We are, therefore, proposing the election of the following steering committee:*

*This list was later revised, more church representatives were added.

Lucius Walker	Mark Comfort
Renny Freeman	Earl Allen
Luke Tripp	Robert Browne
Howard Fuller	Vincent Harding
James Forman	Mike Hamlin
John Watson	Len Holt
Dan Aldridge	Peter Bernard
John Williams	Michael Wright
Ken Cockrel	Muhammed Kenyatta
Chuck Wooten	Mel Jackson
Fannie Lou Hamer	Howard Moore
Julian Bond	Harold Homes

Brothers and sisters, we are no longer shuffling our feet and scratching our heads. We are tall, black and proud.

And we say to the white Christian churches and Jewish synagogues, to the government of this country and to all the white racist imperialists who compose it, there is only one thing left that you can do to further degrade black people and that is to kill us. But we have been dying too long for this country. We have died in every war. We are dying in Vietnam today fighting the wrong enemy.

The new black man wants to live, and to live means that we must not become static or merely believe in self-defense. We must boldly go out and attack the white Western world at its power centers. The white Christian churches are another form of government in this country, and they are used by the government in this country to exploit the people of Latin America, Asia and Africa, but the day is soon coming to an end. Therefore, brothers and sisters, the demands we make upon the white Christian churches and the Jewish synagogues are small demands. They represent fifteen dollars per black person in these United States. We can legitimately demand this from the church power structure. We must demand more from the United States Government.

But to win our demands from the church, which is linked up with the United States Government, we must not forget that it will ultimately be by force and power that we will win.

We are not threatening the churches. We are saying that we know the churches came with the military might of the colonizers and have been sustained by the military might of the colonizers. Hence, if the churches in colonial territories were established by military might, we know deep within our hearts that we must be prepared to use force to get our demands. We are not saying that this is the road we want to take. It is not, but let us be very clear that we are not opposed to force and we are not opposed to violence. We were captured in Africa by violence. We were kept in bondage and political servitude and forced to work as slaves by the military machinery and the Christian church working hand in hand.

We recognize that in issuing this Manifesto we must prepare for a long-range educational campaign in all communities of this country, but we know that the Christian churches have contributed to our oppression in white America. We do not intend to abuse our black brothers and sisters in black churches who have uncritically accepted Christianity. We want them to understand how the racist white Christian church with its hypocritical declarations and doctrines of brotherhood has abused our trust and faith. An attack on the religious beliefs of black people is not our major objective, even though we know that we were not Christians when we were brought to this country, but that Christianity was used to help enslave us. Our objective in issuing this Manifesto is to force the racist white Christian church to begin the payment of reparations which are due to all black people, not only by the church but also by private business and the United States Government. We see this focus on the Christian church as an effort around which all black people can unite.

Our demands are negotiable, but they cannot be minimized, they can only be increased, and the church is asked to come up with larger sums of money than we are asking. Our slogans are:

All Roads Must Lead to Revolution
Unite with Whomever You Can Unite
Neutralize Wherever Possible
Fight Our Enemies Relentlessly
Victory to the People
Life and Good Health to Mankind
Resistance to Domination by the White Christian Churches
    and the Jewish Synagogues
Revolutionary Black Power
We Shall Win Without a Doubt

Divine Libel*

By DICK GREGORY

The National Black Economic Development Conference
timed the attack upon the white churches and synagogues per-
fectly. The Black Manifesto was issued right after the Vatican
pronouncement reevaluating the status of certain saints. Although immediate response to the $500 million reparation
demand was not all that it could or should be, I understand a
group of Roman Catholics decided to make modest reparation
on their own and offered to send one million used St. Christopher medals to Harlem.

Basically, the Black Manifesto is an historical reminder to
the white religious establishment. It points out the history of
performance of white churches and synagogues and highlights
the contradictions between words and deeds. Religious rhetoric has spoken of man's freedom and lifting the yoke of
bondage, while the performance of the religious establishment
has been to form an unholy alliance with a worldwide system
of oppression.

The contradiction between words and deeds runs deep in
the history of white Christianity. I got my first taste of that
contradiction when I was very young. A white Christian minister came up to me one day and said, "Boy"—that's how I
know he was a white Christian—"what do you want to do
when you grow up?" I said, "Oh, Mr. White Christian, I want
to go to Africa and visit my ancestors." With a look of pious
horror, Mr. White Christian said, "Why would you want to
have anything to do with those uncivilized people? Your ancestors are cannibals."

Reflecting my childhood innocence, I said, "Canni—who?"
"Cannibals, boy. Your ancestors eat folks."

* Reprinted from *Black Manifesto: Religion, Racism, and Reparations,* 1969. By permission of Sheed and Ward, Inc., and the author.

"Oooee. You mean they eat real live people?"

I was so shocked and ashamed that I followed Mr. White Christian into his church to pray. I fell on my knees and asked God to forgive my ancestors. "Please, God," I prayed, "forgive my ancestors for being so uncivilized that they eat people."

Mr. White Christian heard my prayer and came over to me. "We don't usually let colored boys in this church," he said. "But I like the way you pray. I want you to stay and have communion with us." "Thank you, Mr. White Christian," I said, "but what's communion?" "Just get down on your knees and I'll show you," Mr. White Christian replied.

So I got down on my knees at the altar rail with the other folks, and Mr. White Christian handed me a piece of bread and a cup of grape juice and said, "This is his body and this is his blood." So I decided then and there I would have to amend my prayer to include many more people!

Observing the history of the performance of white Christian missionaries first aroused my curiosity about the strange power of the Bible. It seemed to me that the pattern was clear. When the white Christian missionaries went to Africa, the white folks had the Bibles and the natives had the land. When the missionaries pulled out, they had the land and the natives had the Bibles. Now that's a pretty good trick if you can pull it off. I've often wondered if I could try the same pattern with the Board of Directors of General Motors. I'd walk into the board meeting with my Bible under my arm. Naturally, the directors would own the corporation. If I could find the magic formula that worked so well for the missionaries, when I left the meeting, I'd own the corporation and each director would have a Bible.

The Black Manifesto seems to have no quarrel with the words of the Bible. It merely traces the history of colonization, oppression and economic exploitation which results wherever those words are read by the religious establishment. Since the Bible has been used to exploit and the religious establishment has become wealthy, it is entirely just to demand that some of the wealth be divested back into the hands of the exploited. That's reparation in a nutshell.

Considering the history of economic exploitation and the vast stores of wealth held by the white churches and synagogues of this nation, the $500 million reparation demand of the National Black Economic Development Conference is a modest sum indeed. One cannot help wondering what God himself—the Boss of all Bosses—would demand if he ever took the religious establishment into court on charges of defa-

mation of character. A divine libel action would surely demand
a much larger sum from the churches for what they have been
doing in God's name for the past twenty centuries.

Speaking through the prophet Amos, the Boss is on record
concerning his feelings about religious folks who "trample
upon the poor" and give certain sacred activities priority over
the demands of justice. "I hate, I despise your feasts," said
the prophet Amos, "and I take no delight in your solemn
assemblies. . . . Take away from me the noise of your songs;
to the melody of your harps I will not listen. But let justice
roll down like waters, and righteousness like an overflowing
stream."

Exhibit "A" in a divine libel action would no doubt be a
selection of the most popular pictures of Jesus adorning the
walls of church sanctuaries and Sunday School classrooms
throughout the nation. What price would God demand from
the churches for having the audacity to lighten the color of
his son's skin, straighten out his nappy hair, and portray him
as a clean white hippie in a suburban setting? Surely the Boss
would "take no delight" in such adornments.

And surely the Boss would reject the songs and melodies of
today's solemn assemblies. Church folks will gather in solemn
assembly and sing the words, "Were you there when they
crucified my Lord?" And when they sing those words, they
have an expression on their faces that suggests that they *would*
have been there—on the Hill of the Skull standing at the foot
of the Cross—if they had the chance. But it is so cheap and
easy to sing about what you would have done two thousand
years too late. The question is what you *will* do and *are* doing
right now.

When decent, thinking people lay their bodies on the line
for their beliefs and truth and justice are crucified in the
streets of this nation, are white church folks there in the same
numbers as attend the solemn assemblies? If the Russians or
Chinese took over this country tomorrow and rolled tanks
into the streets and issued a decree that anyone caught going
to church the following Sunday morning would be mowed
down with machine guns, would most church folks attend?
You know what would happen. Older church folk who never
missed a day of church in their lives would wake up sick that
Sunday morning. And, ironically, morally determined youth
who never *attended* church in their lives would decide to worship that Sunday!

In their solemn assemblies, church folks will sing *The Battle
Hymn of the Republic* and *Onward Christian Soldiers*. Remember the words? "As he *died* to make men holy, let us *die*

to make men free." Church folks will sing those words and do just the reverse. They will *kill* and sanction killing to make men free. Church folks seem to believe that a "Christian soldier" is a Marine who prays. But that's a distortion for which the Boss would surely demand reparation. The words of both songs are really talking about a man who will follow the cause of right to his death.

But church folks will twist their religious language to justify almost anything. I came from a family where I was expected to go to church on Sunday. I used to sit next to so many people who *loved* God—until the chips were down. They were so busy *loving* God superficially that it never occurred to them to *respect* him and his word. My momma was like that. If she had respected God and the Bible, things would have been different at my house. The Ten Commandments clearly and unequivocally say, "Thou shalt not steal." Yet momma used to bring home food which she stole from the pantry of the white folks she was working for. She would cook it, serve it, and then *demand* that we kids pray over it. One day I took momma down into the basement where I hid the things I had stolen. I said, "Here, momma, You pray over what I have stolen and then I'll go back to the table and pray over what you have stolen." Momma didn't know that I was a better thief than she was. I just couldn't justify mine.

Then one day, when I was in my teens, I got caught snatching a pocketbook. I came back to my religious home and told momma what had happened. She went to the white folks and got a lawyer. The next day in court, my momma sat and watched me put my hand on that Bible which she said she loved. She heard me solemnly swear to tell "the truth, the whole truth, and nothing but the truth, so help me God." For the next two hours she listened to me lie to beat the case. And when that judge said, "not guilty," my momma jumped up and shouted, "Thank God." If that isn't using the Creator to justify stealing, I don't know what is. Testimony in a divine libel suit would no doubt be riddled with phrases like, "by their fruits you shall know them," highlighting the contradiction between word and deed in the religious establishment.

If the Boss took legal action against the religious establishment, he certainly would cite property holdings as a supreme example of "trampling upon the poor." The religious establishment is not only a wealthy property owner, but also enjoys a tax exempt status which places a larger tax burden upon the poor, those least able to afford any tax payment whatsoever. Nor has the religious community raised a united cry of moral indignation against the inequity of the tax structure in this country which allows the super-rich to escape tax payment through loopholes designed to protect wealth and power.

Many white church folks are morally indignant over the large numbers of black people, and other poor people, on relief. But they accept so easily the immorality of tax injustices in this country. I know about tax loopholes since I am in a high income bracket. It is possible for me to take an entire nightclub audience out for dinner, and it won't cost me a quarter because I can write it off my income tax as publicity expense. Yet some poor white or black woman who needs to write off her baby's milk expense does not enjoy the same privilege.

The wealthiest families in this nation pay no income tax at all. The hardest hit are middle-income taxpayers, those in the $10,000-to-$20,000 bracket. The higher up the income bracket a man climbs, the less tax he pays. Many millionaires in this country pay absolutely no income tax. Oil depletion allowances make it possible for big oil companies to earn a half-billion dollars without paying a penny of taxes.

During his day in court, the Boss would surely read off a list of church contributors (much like James Forman has done), condemning the church's grateful acceptance of immoral funds. The Mafia has always been known to pay its church dues (although organized crime is as responsible as any other single source for the continued misery of the poor).

New York State Senator John H. Hughes recently estimated that $223 million is siphoned out of the New York City ghettos of Central Harlem, the South Bronx and Bedford-Stuyvesant annually by racketeers. He compared that statistic with an estimated $272 million in welfare funds funneled into the same areas by government agencies. Insisting that gambling and narcotics peddling gives organized crime a stranglehold on the ghettos, Senator Hughes said: "This hold is so tight that until it is broken little by way of economic improvement can be expected, no matter how much money and effort the state devotes to the improvement of these areas."

A divine libel suit would surely "hate and despise" a religious establishment which can continue to build and decorate buildings while human beings starve to death daily. Nor could the Boss possibly approve of silence in the religious community while billions of dollars are sent to the moon and the plates of America's hungry remain empty. It should be easier to place food in a man's stomach than to place a man on the moon. At least in the feeding process you have gravity working on your side.

Yet church folks rejoice in space exploration and enjoy

hearing the astronauts read the Bible to them from outer space. The closest the religious establishment will get to really being concerned about hunger is to advocate programs of planned parenthood and, in protestantism at least, to push the Pill in the world's ghettos.

But the Boss's Son said, "Feed my sheep." He didn't say control the flock's reproduction. The Pill is merely an unnatural cop out to cover up the fact that about one-fourth of the world's land *could* be cultivated if money and training were made available by the haves to the have-nots. This land just simply is not used today. If it were, the world's food production would multiply four times. Even if the 10 percent of the world's land that *is* used for agriculture were *fully* utilized, ten times the present world population might be fed.

It is nature's law that man plants the seed to start the process of natural growth. It is true both of crop cultivation and human reproduction. With proper "seed" money, financial and technological commitment, the world could be fed and the Pill could be discarded as an unnatural resource.

Which leads to what would probably be the Boss's strongest indictment against the contemporary religious establishment. A divine libel suit would cite the religious community for failing to teach a proper respect for nature, which is the same, really, as teaching a respect for the divine. If man respected nature with a religious passion, he could not abuse her resources, pollute the natural environment and continue to undo creation through arrogant disrespect for human habitation.

If men were ever to become infused with a profound respect for nature, they would respect themselves and each other as nature's creatures. The Boss's Son hinted at that concept when he urged men to love their neighbors as *themselves*. That kind of self-love and self-respect would lead to an end of slaughter on the highways of America as well as on the battlefields of the world. And it would surely hasten the day when *all* forms of oppression and exploitation would be seen basically as expressions of self-denial opposed to the natural created order of life and leading ultimately only in the direction of self-destruction.

Yet the religious community consistently refused to embrace a concept of total respect for nature and nature's creatures. Some courageous members of the religious community will speak out against the war in Vietnam, or work to ban the bomb. But such actions are partial solutions when compared with the natural human problem. Church folks have the answer if they will only listen to it. "Thou shalt not kill." If church folks would believe that commandment, not only would they all become vegetarians, but they would see respect for nature in its proper perspective.

Personally, I am not opposed to war, nor am I opposed to the existence of national armies. But I believe the commandment. I am opposed to *killing*. Nations who feel that they must settle their differences through competitive combat may do so if that "war" does not involve killing. National leaders settling their differences at the chess or checkerboard would be a humane, even if risky, military strategy. Of course, competitive combat is never a lasting or even desirable solution. The power of right should stand on its own and should not need the representation of either military might or wit.

The presence of an army has value in a civilized nation, though a civilized military should not be involved in killing. An army is necessary, for example, to clean up after national disasters—hurricanes, tornadoes, floods, earthquakes, and the like. After every such natural disaster, the National Guard is called in to restore peace and order, to hold in check the looting and theft which always accompanies natural disorder. But that military function does not need to involve killing. The current irony in America is that the National Guard is called in after the "spontaneous combustion" of ghetto revolts but is ordered to kill rather than restore order, thus exacerbating a disaster rather than healing it.

The only road to world peace and to a climate of respect for nature is to render the concept of killing irrelevant. A peaceful world order cannot exist where any form of killing is allowed or justified. A world ban on capital punishment is more important than a ban on the bomb. Stop killing. That is the answer.

To talk of banning the bomb is pointless, because we already *have* the bomb. We might just as well urge men to "Forget the wheel." But if the idea of killing is eliminated from man's mind, the bomb will never be used. And if church folk were really concerned about escaping indictment in a divine libel action, they would be working to expand man's mind to envision a human order where killing has no place.

More important than petitions to ban the bomb are programs to feed a starving humanity, medical programs to heal a disease-ridden mankind, humanitarian approaches to world need which leave no time for military preoccupation.

Such a humanitarian world emphasis would lift the vision and enlist the energies of the new generation. The instinctive moral thirst of the youth of the world would be quenched. In years to come, youth would have been raised in an atmosphere enabling them to choose for themselves never again to

drink of destruction, and the bomb will have been banned to
its rightful status of irrelevance.

The Black Manifesto has caused the religious establishment
in this country to feel the sting of indictment for past sins.
But the white churches and synagogues should thank God that
the indictment has been so restrained. If members of the religious community have any doubts about the justice of the
reparation demand, they should try looking at themselves
through the eyes of their Creator and doubt *would* fade into
horror.

Discussion and Study Questions

1. In what ways is black an "attitude," according to Mrs. Chisholm?

2. Analyze Mrs. Chisholm's definition of social revolution. How does it differ in strategy and purpose from the political liberationism of Rustin, the institutional reforms of Innis, and the intellectual liberation advocated by Hare?

3. What is the distinction between individual racism and institutionalized racism? Why is it important to those who advocate social reform?

4. What are the arguments which "The Black Manifesto" uses to justify its demands for reparations from white churches and synagogues? Are they symbolically or literally true?

5. In what ways does the church contribute to the continued misery of the poor, according to Gregory?

6. Relate the difference in profession to the differences in style, rhetoric and perspective of Gregory, Jones, and Jackson, each of whom surveys the same phenomenon of racism.

7. How does Rustin propose that the black protest movement be transformed into a political movement?

8. Rustin analyzes the 1964 Presidential election in view of the Negro "swing" vote. Can you do the same for the last election? What effects seem visible from such a vote, if there was one?

9. What is the focal point around which Bond sees a possibility of uniting the various peoples within this country?

10. In what way does Evers indicate that the press acts as a formulator of opinions? Can you think of any current examples which defend or refute Evers' position?

Revolutionary
Action

Revolutionary Action

The ideas and thoughts presented in this part call for a sudden and drastic change of existing social, political, and economic institutions. Many black spokesmen have become disillusioned with the familiar tactics of mass demonstration and political maneuvering. As a result they have become less concerned with the means by which the needed change can be accomplished. In fact, many of the essays take the position that this country was bred on violence and has been perpetuated by the same. They indicate that if the required change must be brought about through violent tactics, then so be it. Other essays point out the need to use violence as a defense against the extensive and pervasive evils of this system.

Jones advocates a nationalistic revolution leading to the destruction of America as it now is and to the creation of absolute political and economic power for Blacks. Newton's essay, written in prison, alludes to the evils of capitalism which profits from poverty. He views all oppressed people as prisoners who must come to realize that this society is corrupt, illegitimate, and thus in need of being overthrown. In an interview Seale calls for a revolutionary struggle which uses ethnic, political and class alliances against those who perpetuate tyranny, oppression, and poverty. Bond's responses in the same interview point more specifically toward changes within the existing system. The essay by Cleaver calls for the creation of new political machinery in order to carry out the revolution against capitalistic exploitation and racism. Carmichael's essay urges Blacks to gain collective power as a goal. He implies that such power might be necessary to destroy certain aspects of the system. Brown states that meaningful change can only come about through the destruction of the system. For him, revolution is the only cure for oppression and colonization.

The Legacy of Malcolm X, and the Coming of the Black Nation*

By LEROI JONES

Malcolm X's greatest contribution, other than to propose a path to internationalism and hence, the entrance of the American Black Man into a world-wide allegiance against the white man (in most recent times he proposed to do it using a certain kind of white liberal as a lever), was to preach Black Consciousness to the Black Man. As a minister for the Nation of Islam, Malcolm talked about a black consciousness that took its form from religion. In his last days he talked of another black consciousness that proposed politics as its moving energy.

But one very important aspect of Malcolm's earlier counsels was his explicit call for a National Consciousness among Black People. And this aspect of Malcolm's philosophy certainly did abide throughout his days. The feeling that somehow the Black Man was different, as being, as a being, and finally, in our own time, as judge. And Malcolm propounded these differences as life anecdote and religious (political) truth and made the consideration of Nationalist ideas significant and powerful in our day.

Another very important aspect of Malcolm's earlier (or the Honorable Elijah Muhammad's) philosophy was the whole concept of land and land-control as central to any talk of "freedom" or "independence." The Muslim tack of asking for land within the continental United States in which Black People could set up their own nation, was given a special appeal by Malcolm, even though the request was seen by most

*Reprinted from *Home: Social Essays,* 1966. By permission of William Morrow and Company, Inc., and the author.

people outside the movement as "just talk" or the amusing howls of a gadfly.

But the whole importance of this insistence on land is just now beginning to be understood. Malcolm said many times that when you speak about revolution you're talking about land—changing the ownership or usership of some specific land which you think is yours. But any talk of Nationalism also must take this concept of land and its primary importance into consideration because, finally, any Nationalism which is not intent on restoring or securing autonomous space for a people, i.e., a nation, is at the very least shortsighted.

Elijah Muhammad has said, "We want our people in America, whose parents or grandparents were descendants from slaves, to be allowed to establish a separate state or territory of their own—either on this continent or elsewhere. We believe that our former slavemasters are obligated to provide such land and that the area must be fertile and minerally rich." And the Black Muslims seem separate from most Black People because the Muslims have a national consciousness based on their aspirations for land. Most of the Nationalist movements in this country advocate that that land is in Africa, and Black People should return there, or they propose nothing about land at all. It is impossible to be a Nationalist without talking about land. Otherwise, your Nationalism is a misnamed kind of "difficult" opposition to what the white man has done, rather than the advocation of another people becoming the rulers of themselves, and sooner or later the rest of the world.

The Muslims moved from the Back-to-Africa concept of Marcus Garvey (the first large movement by Black People back to a National Consciousness, which was, finally, only viable when the Black Man focused on Africa as literally "back home") to the concept of a Black National Consciousness existing in this land the Black captives had begun to identify as home. (Even in Garvey's time, there was not a very large percentage of Black People who really wanted to leave.) Certainly, the newly emerging Black bourgeoisie would have nothing to do with "returning" to Africa. They were already created in the image of white people, as they still are, and wanted nothing to do with Black.

What the Muslims wanted was a profound change. The National Consciousness focused on actual (nonabstract) land, identifying a people, in a land where they lived. Garvey wanted to go back to Jordan. A real one. The Nation of Islam wanted Jordan closer. Before these two thrusts, the Black Man in America, as he was Christianized, believed Jordan was the sky, like pie, and absolutely supernatural.

Malcolm, then, wanted to give the National Consciousness its political embodiment, and send it out to influence the newly forming third world, in which this consciousness was to be included. The concept of Blackness, the concept of the National Consciousness, the proposal of a political (and diplomatic) form for this aggregate of Black spirit, these are the things given to us by Garvey, through Elijah Muhammad and finally given motion into still another area of Black response by Malcolm X.

Malcolm's legacy to Black People is what he moved toward, as the accretion of his own spiritual learning and the movement of Black People in general, through the natural hope, a rise to social understanding within the new context of the white nation and its decline under hypocrisy and natural "oppositeness" which has pushed all of us toward "new" ideas. We are all the products of national spirit and worldview. We are drawn by the vibrations of the entire nation. If there were no bourgeois Negroes, none of us would be drawn to that image. They, bourgeois Negroes, were shaped through the purposive actions of a national attitude, and finally, by the demands of a particular culture.

At which point we must consider what cultural attitudes are, what culture is, and what National Consciousness has to do with these, i.e., if we want to understand what Malcolm X was pointing toward, and why the Black Man now must move in that direction since the world will not let him move in any other way. The Black Man is possessed by the energies of historic necessity and the bursting into flower of a National Black Cultural Consciousness, and with that, in a living future, the shouldering to power of Black culture and, finally, Black Men . . . and then, Black ideals, which are different descriptions of a God. A righteous sanctity, out of which worlds are built.

What the Black Man must do now is look down at the ground upon which he stands, and claim it as his own. It is not abstract. Look down! Pick up the earth, or jab your fingernails into the concrete. It is real and it is yours, if you want it.

But to want it, as our own, is the present direction. To want what we are and where we are, but rearranged by our own consciousness. That is why it was necessary first to recrystallize national aspirations behind a Garvey. The Africans who first came here were replaced by Americans, or people responding to Western stimuli and then Americans. In order

for the Americans to find out that they had come from another place, were, hence, alien, the Garvey times had to come.
Elijah said we must have a place, to be, ourselves. Malcolm
made it contemporarily secular.

So that now we must find the flesh of our spiritual creation.
We must be *conscious*. And to be conscious is to be *cultured*,
processed in specific virtues and genius. We must respond to
this National Consciousness with our souls, and use the correspondence to come into our own.

The Black Man will always be frustrated until he has land
(A Land!) of his own. All the thought processes and emotional
orientation of "national liberation movements"—from slave
uprisings onward—have always given motion to a Black National (and Cultural) Consciousness. These movements proposed that judgments were being made by Black sensibility,
and that these judgments were *necessarily* different from those
of the white sensibility—different, and after all is said and
done, inimical.

Men are what their culture predicts (enforces). Culture is,
simply, the way men live. How they have come to live. What
they are formed by. Their total experience, and its implications and theories. Its paths.

The Black Man's paths are alien to the white man. Black
Culture is alien to the white man. Art and religion are the
results and idealized supernumeraries of culture. Culture in
this sense, as Sapir said, is "The National Genius," whether
it be a way of fixing rice or killing a man.

I said in *Blues People:* "Culture is simply how one lives and
is connected to history by habit." Here is a graphic structure
of the relationships and total context of culture:

GOD

RELIGION

CULTURE

ART

POLITICS

NATION

MAN

God is man idealized (humanist definition). Religion is the aspiration of man toward an idealized existence. An existence in which the functions of God and man are harmonious, even identical. Art is the movement forward, the understanding progress of man. It is feeling and making. A nation (social order) is made the way people *feel* it should be made. A face is too. Politics is man's aspiration toward an order. Religion is too. Art is an ordering as well. And all these categories are spiritual, but are also the result of the body, at one point, serving as a container of feeling. The soul is no less sensitive.

Nations are races. (In America, white people have become a nation, an identity, a race.) Political integration in America will not work because the Black Man is played on by special forces. His life, from his organs, i.e., the life of the body, what it needs, what it wants, to become, is different—and for this reason racial is biological, finally. We are a different *species.* A species that is evolving to world power and philosophical domination of the world. The world will move the way Black People move!

If we take the teachings of Garvey, Elijah Muhammad and Malcolm X (as well as Frazier, Du Bois and Fanon), we know for certain that the solution of the Black Man's problems will come only through Black National Consciousness. We also know that the focus of change will be racial. (If we *feel* differently, we have different *ideas.* Race is feeling. Where the body, and the organs come in. Culture is the preservation of these feelings in superrational to rational form. Art is one method of expressing these feelings and identifying the form, as an emotional phenomenon.) In order for the Black Man in the West to absolutely know himself, it is necessary for him to see himself first as culturally separate from the white man. That is, to be conscious of this separation and use the strength it proposes.

Western Culture (the way white people live and think) is passing. If the Black Man cannot identify himself as separate, and understand what this means, he will perish along with Western Culture and the white man.

What a culture produces, is, and refers to, is an image—a picture of a process, since it is a form of a process: movement seen. The changing of images, of references, is the Black Man's way back to the racial integrity of the captured African, which is where we must take ourselves, in feeling, to be truly the warriors we propose to be. To form an absolutely rational attitude toward West man, and West thought. Which is what is needed. To see the white man as separate and as enemy. To make a fight according to the absolute realities of the world as it is.

Good-Bad, Beautiful-Ugly, are all formed as the result of image. The mores, customs, of a place are the result of experience, and a common reference for defining it—common images. The three white men in the film *Gunga Din* who kill off hundreds of Indians, Greek hero-style, are part of an image of white men. The various black porters, gigglers, ghost-chumps and punkish Indians, etc., that inhabit the public image the white man has fashioned to characterize Black Men are references by Black Men to the identity of Black Men in the West, since that's what is run on them each day by white magic, i.e., television, movies, radio, etc.—the Mass Media (the *Daily News* does it with flicks and adjectives).

The song title "A White Man's Heaven Is a Black Man's Hell" describes how complete an image reversal is necessary in the West. Because for many Black People, the white man has succeeded in making this hell seem like heaven. But Black youth are much better off in this regard than their parents. They are the ones who need the least image reversal.

The Black artist, in this context, is desperately needed to change the images his people identify with, by asserting Black feeling, Black mind, Black judgment. The Black intellectual, in this same context, is needed to change the interpretation of facts toward the Black Man's best interests, instead of merely tagging along reciting white judgments of the world.

Art, Religion, and Politics are impressive vectors of a culture. Art describes a culture. Black artists must have an image of what the Black sensibility is in this land. Religion elevates a culture. The Black Man must aspire to Blackness. God is man idealized. The Black Man must idealize himself as Black and idealize and aspire to that. Politics gives a social order to the culture, i.e., makes relationships within the culture definable for the functioning organism. The Black Man must seek a Black politics, an ordering of the world that is beneficial to his culture, to his interiorization and judgment of the world. This is strength. And we are hordes.

Black People are a race, a culture, a Nation. The legacy of Malcolm X is that we know we can move from where we are. Our land is where we live. (Even the Muslims have made this statement about Harlem.) If we are a separate Nation, we must make that separateness where we are. There are Black cities all over this white nation. Nations within nations. In order for the Black Man to survive he must not only identify himself as a unique being, but take steps to insure that this being has, what the Germans call *Lebensraum* ("living room") literally space in which to exist and develop.

The concepts of National Consciousness and the Black Nation, after the death of Malik, have moved to the point where now some Black People are demanding national sovereignty as well as National (and Cultural) Consciousness. In Harlem, for instance, as director of the Black Arts Repertory Theatre School, I have issued a call for a Black Nation. In Harlem, where 600,000 Black People reside.

The first act must be the nationalization of all properties and resources belonging to white people, within the boundaries of the Black Nation. (All the large concentrations of Black People in the West are already nations. All that is missing is the consciousness of this state of affairs. All that is missing is that the Black Man take control. As Margaret Walker said in her poem "For My People": *A race of men must rise, and take control*.)

Nationalization means that all properties and resources must be harnessed to the needs of the Nation. In the case of the coming Black Nation, all these materials must be harnessed to the needs of Black People. In Harlem, it is almost common knowledge that the Jews, etc., will go the next time there's a large "disturbance," like they say. But there must be machinery set up to transfer the power potential of these retail businesses, small industries, etc., so that they may benefit Black People.

Along with nationalization of foreign-owned businesses (which includes Italian underworld businesses, some of which, like the policy racket, can be transformed into a national lottery, with the monies staying with Black People, or as in the case of heroin-selling, completely abolished) must come the nationalization of all political voices setting up to function within the community/Nation.

No white politicians can be allowed to function within the Nation. Black politicians doing funny servant business for whites, must be eliminated. Black People must have absolute political and economic control. In other words they must have absolute control over their lives and destinies.

These moves are toward the working form of any autonomous nation. And it is this that the Black Man must have. An autonomous Nation. His own forms: treaties, agreements, laws.

These are moves that the conscious Black Man (artist, intellectual, Nationalist, religious thinker, dude with "common sense") must prepare the people for. And the people must be prepared for moves they themselves are already making. And moves they have already made must be explained and analyzed. They, the people, are the bodies. . . . Where are the heads?

And it is *the heads* that are needed for the next move Black People will make. The move to Nationhood. The exact method of transformation is simple logistics.

What we are speaking about again is sovereignty. Sovereignty and independence. And when we speak of these things, we can understand just how far Malik went. The point now is to take ourselves the rest of the way.

Only a united Black Consciousness can save Black People from annihilation at the white man's hands. And no other nation on earth is safe, unless the Black Man in America is safe. Not even the Chinese can be absolutely certain of their continued sovereignty as long as the white man is alive. And there is only one people on the planet who can slay the white man. The people who know him best. His ex-slaves.

State/Meant*

By LEROI JONES

The Black Artist's role in America is to aid in the destruction of America as he knows it. His role is to report and reflect so precisely the nature of the society, and of himself in that society, that other men will be moved by the exactness of his rendering and, if they are black men, grow strong through this moving, having seen their own strength, and weakness; and if they are white men, tremble, curse, and go mad, because they will be drenched with the filth of their evil.

The Black Artist must draw out of his soul the correct image of the world. He must use this image to band his brothers and sisters together in common understanding of the nature of the world (and the nature of America) and the nature of the human soul.

The Black Artist must demonstrate sweet life, how it differs from the deathly grip of the White Eyes. The Black Artist must teach the White Eyes their deaths, and teach the black man how to bring these deaths about.

We are unfair, and unfair.
We are black magicians, black art
s we make in black labs of the heart.

The fair are
fair, and death
ly white.

The day will not save them
and we own
the night.

* Reprinted from *Home: Social Essays*, 1966, by permission of William Morrow and Company, Inc., and the author.

HUEY P. NEWTON,

Black Panther Founder-Leader

Huey P. Newton was born in a small Louisiana town on February 17, 1942. He was the youngest of seven children in his working class family. When Huey was three the family moved to Oakland, California, where he attended the public schools. While in high school he was jailed for the first time for defending himself with a hammer. Upon completing high school Huey attended Merrit College in California. From his experiences and his associations there he became instrumental in founding the Black Panther Party in 1965. He serves as the minister of defense for this organization, which is growing in popularity. Newton has served a prison term for the alleged killing of a white policeman, a decision which has since been reversed. His influence among the black youth of this country has continued to increase, however, and even at his young age, he is a spokesman for many black Americans.

With the Black Panther Party, he is committed to a struggle for black self-determination, to a political and economic structure that truly relates to and meets the needs of the people, and to action to regain the dignity and freedom of blacks and of oppressed people everywhere. Like Cleaver his perspective is not only ethnic, it is international.

"AS LONG AS THE PEOPLE RECOGNIZE THE BEAUTY OF THEIR HUMAN SPIRITS AND MOVE AGAINST SUPPRESSION AND EXPLOITATION THEY WILL BE CARRYING OUT ONE OF THE MOST BEAUTIFUL IDEAS OF ALL TIMES."

In Defense of Self Defense*

Introduction:

Huey P. Newton's column in The Black Panther *Newspaper was entitled "In Defense of Self Defense." The following articles by the minister of defense were taken from those columns.*

"In Defense of Self Defense."   June 20, 1967.

Laws and rules have always been made to serve people. Rules of society are set up by people so that they will be able to function in a harmonious way. In other words, in order to promote the general welfare of society, rules and laws are established by men. Rules should serve men, and not men serve rules. Much of the time, the laws and rules which officials attempt to inflict upon poor people are non-functional in relation to the status of the poor in society.

These officials are blind to the fact that people should not respect rules that are not serving them. It is the duty of the poor to write and construct rules and laws that are in their better interests. This is one of the basic human rights of all men.

Before 1776, white people were colonized by the English. The English government had certain laws and rules that the colonized Americans viewed as not in their best interests but as a colonized people. At that time the English government felt that the colonized Americans had no right to establish laws to promote the general welfare of the people living here in America. The colonized American felt he had no choice but to raise the gun in defense of the welfare of the colonized people. At this time, he made certain laws insuring his protection from external and internal aggressions from governments and agencies. One such form of protection was

*Reprinted from *The Black Panther* Newspaper, June 20, 1967. By permission of the Black Panther Party and the author.

the Declaration of Independence, which states: ". . . whenever any government becomes destructive to these ends, it is
the right of the people to alter or to abolish it, and to institute
a new government, laying its foundations on such principles
and organizing its powers in such forms as to them shall seem
most likely to effect their safety and happiness."

Now these same colonized white people, these ex-slaves,
robbers, and thieves, have denied the colonized black man
the right to even speak of abolishing this oppressive system
which the white colonized American created. They have carried their madness to the four corners of the earth, and now
there is universal rebellion against their continued rule and
power. The Black people in America are the only people who
can free the world, loosen the yoke of colonialism and destroy
the war machine. As long as the wheels of the imperialistic
war machine are turning there is no country that can defeat
this monster of the West. But Black people can make a
malfunction of this machine from within. Black people can
destroy the machinery that's enslaving the world. America
cannot stand to fight every Black country in the world and
fight a civil war at the same time. It is militarily impossible
to do both of these things at once.

The slavery of Blacks in this country provides the oil for
the machinery of war that America uses to enslave the peoples of the world. Without this oil the machinery cannot
function. We are the driving shaft; we are in such a strategic
position in this machinery that, once we become dislocated,
the functioning of the remainder of the machinery breaks
down.

Penned up in the ghettos of America, surrounded by his
[white colonizer's] factories and all the physical components of
his economic system, we have been made into "the wretched
of the earth," who are relegated to the position of spectators
while the white racists run their international con game on
the suffering peoples. We have been brainwashed to believe
that we are powerless and that there is nothing we can do
for ourselves to bring about a speedy liberation for our
people. We have been taught that we must please our oppressors, that we are only ten per cent of the population, and
therefore, we must confine our tactics to categories calculated
not to disturb the sleep of our tormentors.

The power structure inflicts pain and brutality upon the
peoples and then provides controlled outlets for the pain in
ways least likely to upset them or interfere with the process
of exploitation. The people must repudiate the channels established as tricks and deceitful snares by the exploiting op-

pressors. The people must oppose everything the oppressor supports and support everything that he opposes. If Black people go about their struggle for liberation in the way that the oppressor dictates and sponsors, then we will have degenerated to the level of grovelling flunkies for the oppressor himself. When the oppressor makes a vicious attack against freedom fighters because of the way that such freedom fighters choose to go about their liberation, then we know we are moving in the direction of our liberation. The racist dog oppressors have no rights which oppressed Black people are bound to respect. As long as the racist dogs pollute the earth with the evil of their actions, they do not deserve any respect at all, and the rules of their game, written in the people's blood, are beneath contempt.

The oppressor must be harassed until his doom. He must have no peace by day or by night. The slaves have always outnumbered the slavemasters. The power of the oppressor rests upon the submission of the people. When Black people really unite and rise up in all their splendid millions, they will have the strength to smash injustice. We do not understand the power in our numbers. We are millions and millions of Black people scattered across the continent and throughout the Western hemisphere. There are more Black people in America than the total population of many countries that now enjoy full membership in the United Nations. They have power and their power is based primarily on the fact that they are organized and united with each other. They are recognized by the powers of the world.

We, with all our numbers, are recognized by no one. In fact, we do not even recognize our own selves. We are unaware of the potential power latent in our numbers. In 1967, in the midst of a hostile racist nation whose hidden racism is rising to the surface at a phenomenal speed, we are still so blind to our critical fight for our very survival that we are continuing to function in petty, futile ways. Divided, confused, fighting among ourselves, we are still in the elementary stage of throwing rocks, sticks, empty wine bottles and beer cans at racist cops who lie in wait for a chance to murder unarmed Black people. The racist cops have worked out a system for suppressing these spontaneous rebellions that flare up from the anger, frustration, and desperation of the masses of Black people. We can no longer afford the dubious luxury of the terrible casualties wantonly inflicted upon us by the cops during these spontaneous rebellions.

Black people must now move, from the grassroots up through the perfumed circles of the Black bourgeoisie, to seize by any means necessary a proportionate share of the power vested and collected in the structure of America. We must organize and unite to combat by long resistance the brutal force used against us daily. The power structure depends upon the use of force within retaliation. This is why they have made it a felony to teach guerilla warfare. This is why they want the people unarmed.

The racist dog oppressor fears the armed people; they fear most of all Black people armed with weapons and the ideology of the Black Panther Party for Self Defense. An unarmed people are slaves or are subject to slavery at any given moment. If a government is not afraid of the people it will arm the people from foreign aggression. Black people are held captive in the midst of their oppressors. There is a world of difference between thirty million unarmed, submissive Black people and thirty million Black people armed with freedom and defense guns and the strategic methods of liberation.

When a mechanic wants to fix a broken-down car engine, he must have the necessary tools to do the job. When the people move for liberation, they must have the basic tool of liberation: the gun. Only with the power of the gun can the Black masses halt the terror and brutality perpetuated against them by the armed racist power structure; and in one sense only by the power of the gun can the whole world be transformed into the earthly paradise dreamed of by the people from time immemorial. One successful practitioner of the art and science of national liberation and self defense, Brother Mao Tse-Tung, put it this way: "We are advocates of the abolition of war, we do not want war; but war can only be abolished through war, and in order to get rid of the gun it is necessary to take up the gun."

The blood, sweat, tears and suffering of Black people are the foundations of the wealth and power of the United States of America. We were forced to build America, and if forced to, we will tear it down. The immediate result of this destruction will be suffering and bloodshed. But the end result will be the perpetual peace for all mankind.

Prison, Where Is Thy Victory?*

When a person studies mathematics, he learns that there are many mathematical laws which determine the approach he must take to solving the problems presented to him. In the study of geometry, one of the first laws a person learns is that "the whole is not greater than the sum of its parts." This means simply that one cannot have a geometrical figure such as a circle or a square which in its totality, contains more than it does when broken down into smaller parts. Therefore, if all the smaller parts add up to a certain amount, the entire figure cannot add up to a larger amount. The prison cannot have a victory over the prisoner, because those in charge take the same kind of approach to the prisoner and assume if they have the whole body in a cell that they have there all that makes up the person. But a prisoner is not a geometrical figure, and an approach which is successful in mathematics, is wholly unsuccessful when dealing with human beings.

In the case of the human, we are not dealing only with the single individual, we are also dealing with the ideas and beliefs which have motivated him and which sustain him, even when his body is confined. In the case of humanity the whole is much greater than its parts, because the whole includes the body which is measurable and confinable, and also the ideas which cannot be measured and which cannot be confined. The ideas are not only within the mind of the prisoner where they cannot be seen nor controlled, the ideas are also within the people. The ideas which can and will sustain our movement for total freedom and dignity of the people, cannot be imprisoned, for they are to be found in the people, all the people, wherever they are. As long as the people live by the ideas of freedom and dignity there will

*Reprinted from *The Black Panther* Newspaper, July 12, 1969. By permission of *The Black Panther* Newspaper and the author.

be no prison which can hold our movement down. Ideas move from one person to another in the association of brothers and sisters who recognize that a most evil system of capitalism has set us against each other, when our real enemy is the exploiter who profits from our poverty. When we realize such an idea then we come to love and appreciate our brothers and sisters who we may have seen as enemies, and those exploiters who we may have seen as friends are revealed for what they truly are to all oppressed people. The people are the idea, the respect and dignity of the people, as they move toward their freedom is the sustaining force which reaches into and out of the prison. The walls, the bars, the guns and the guards can never encircle or hold down the idea of the people. And the people must always carry forward the idea which is their dignity and their beauty.

The prison operates with the idea that when it has a person's body it has his entire being—since the whole cannot be greater than the sum of its parts. They put the body in a cell, and seem to get some sense of relief and security from that fact. The idea of prison victory then, is that when the person in jail begins to act, think, and believe the way they want him to, then they have won the battle and the person is then "rehabilitated." But this cannot be the case, because those who operate the prisons have failed to examine their own beliefs thoroughly, and they fail to understand the types of people they attempt to control. Therefore, even when the prison thinks it has won the victory, there is no victory.

There are two types of prisoners. The largest number are those who accept the legitimacy of the assumptions upon which the society is based. They wish to acquire the same goals as everybody else, money, power, greed, and conspicuous consumption. In order to do so, however, they adopt techniques and methods which the society has defined as illegitimate. When this is discovered such people are put in jail. They may be called "illegitimate capitalists" since their aim is to acquire everything this capitalistic society defines as legitimate. The second type of prisoner, is the one who rejects the legitimacy of the assumptions upon which the society is based. He argues that the people at the bottom of the society are exploited for the profit and advantage of those at the top. Thus, the oppressed exist, and will always be used to maintain the privileged status of the exploiters. There is no sacredness, there is no dignity in either exploiting or being exploited. Although this system may make the society function at a high level of technological efficiency, it is an illegitimate system, since it rests upon the suffering of humans who are as worthy and as dignified as those who do not suffer. Thus, the second type of prisoner says that the society is corrupt and illegitimate and must be overthrown. This second type of prisoner is the political prisoner. They do not accept the legitimacy of the society and cannot participate in its corrupting exploitation, whether they are in the prison or on the block.

The prison cannot gain a victory over either type of prisoner no matter how hard it tries. The "illegitimate capitalist" recognizes that if he plays the game the prison wants him to play, he will have his time reduced and be released to continue his activities. Therefore, he is willing to go through the prison programs and do the things he is told. He is willing to say the things the prison authorities want to hear. The prison assumes he is "rehabilitated" and ready for the society. The prisoner has really played the prison's game so that he can be released to resume pursuit of his capitalistic goals. There is no victory, for the prisoner from the gitgo accepted the idea of the society. He pretends to accept the idea of the prison as a part of the game he has always played.

The prison cannot gain a victory over the political prisoner because he has nothing to be rehabilitated from or to. He refuses to accept the legitimacy of the system and refuses to participate. To participate is to admit that the society is legitimate because of its exploitation of the oppressed. This is the idea which the political prisoner does not accept, this is the idea for which he has been imprisoned, and this is the reason why he cannot cooperate with the system. The political prisoner will, in fact, serve his time just as will the "illegitimate capitalist." Yet the idea which motivated and sustained the political prisoner rests in the people, all the prison has, is a body.

The dignity and beauty of man rests in the human spirit which makes him more than simply a physical being. This spirit must never be suppressed for exploitation by others. As long as the people recognize the beauty of their human spirits and move against suppression and exploitation, they will be carrying out one of the most beautiful ideas of all time. Because the human whole is much greater than the sum of its parts, the ideas will always be among the people. The prison cannot be victorious because walls, bars and guards cannot conquer or hold down an idea.

POWER TO THE PEOPLE:
BLACK POWER TO BLACK PEOPLE, AND PANTHER POWER
TO THE VANGUARD.

BOBBY SEALE, *Black Panther*

Bobby Seale is one of the cofounders with Newton of the Black Panther Party in Oakland, California. Like Newton, he has spent a great deal of time in jail. He was one of the defendants in the Chicago conspiracy trial of 1970. As a result of his repeated attacks on the judicial system during this trial, he was sentenced to four years for contempt. He is also involved in a trial in Connecticut for allegedly kidnapping and murdering another Black Panther.

Seale sees a revolution as being the primary means to accomplish a socialist form of government in the United States. With him and other Panthers, the party has evolved into a political revolutionary group. Aside from their political agitation, however, they have promoted many programs for ghetto youth, including lunches for children, drug clinics, and patrols of potentially explosive riot areas.

"YOU DON'T FIGHT RACISM WITH RACISM. THE BEST WAY TO FIGHT RACISM IS WITH SOLIDARITY."

Other Voices, Other Strategies*

Interviews with Julian Bond and Bobby Seale

Where does the black American go from here in his drive for a racially equal society? What should he do?

BOND: We should develop greater unity in the black community. There ought to be at least a community-wide concensus of what ought to be done, politically, socially, economically and educationally. In Atlanta we're going to have two black candidates running in the same congressional district. Two black candidates can only hurt the prospect of one's being elected.

SEALE: Black people, brothers and sisters in this country, have to move to a level of revolutionary struggle in terms of what we understand to be the true enemy, the enemy who perpetuates tyranny and oppression, poverty and the wretched conditions that we're subjected to in the black community. This enemy, as Eldridge [Cleaver] always puts it, is at three levels of oppression: the big-time, tycooning, avaricious businessmen, the lying, demagogic, trick politicians, and the fascist pig cops, militia, and pig agents who work for the avaricious, demagogic ruling class. Black people's direction should be to wage a relentless revolutionary struggle against the three levels of oppression. But it can't be handled alone by blacks. We need alliances with those whose own self-interest is to seek communities free of disorders.

*Reprinted from *Time*, XCV (April 6, 1970), pp. 23–27. By permission of Time, Inc., and the authors.

What do you think will happen in the next decade to the black drive for a racially equal society?

BOND: I tend to be pessimistic. While income for blacks has been increasing, it has not been increasing apace with income for whites. The gap is getting wider. I think that's going to continue. The physical aspects of poverty may be eliminated in the next several decades. Slum housing may disappear. Then people will find it easier to ignore poverty because it won't be an eyesore.

Politically, you're going to see many more black elected city officials. Baltimore could have a black mayor. So could Detroit, Newark, Los Angeles and Kansas City. We're coming into politics that same way the Irish did. The Irish used politics to lift themselves up as a group, controlling New York at one time, Boston at another. Now, the city itself is just not a healthy animal any more. So we are taking it over at a time when no one wants it. We are seizing on a dead horse. At best it is a mixed blessing.

Southern black people are going to become more and more political on a local level. You're going to see more and more black people running for public office. In Northern communities the black population is going to be farther away from any accommodation with the white community. I don't think you will see riots on the scale of Watts, Detroit and Newark. The police forces have too many armaments, like helicopters and tanks that shoot through whole rows of buildings. The techniques learned in Viet Nam are being brought back to this country, ready for use against the local insurgents. You will see incidents of terror from the black community, aimed at property—the physical manifestations of oppression in the black community—like a savings and loan institution that has been particularly vicious in its practices. But the black community has discovered that the percentage in a riot, although it is a very fine political expression of discontent, is a losing one. The only loss is a loss to us.

SEALE: First, you have no pat blueprint for revolution. Second, I see the power structure moving into a fascist state, George Orwell's *1984*, where they say, "Big Brother is watching you." They will move to take away constitutional rights, not only from black people, but, as we can see with the Chicago Seven, from white people too. And at the same time, I see a lot of black, white, red and brown people becoming politically educated and moving to oppose the fascist regime that's being built.

What are your recommendations for achieving black goals in the next ten years?

BOND: We should end the war first. We should not only redirect the money (which President Nixon says won't happen) but redirect the minds that are used to plot the war. Second, Congress has to make good on its promises of almost 30 years ago that every American will live in a decent home. Third, you must guarantee full employment. You have to provide income maintenance for those who cannot earn an income. You need make-work programs. We should break the control of the unions over the skilled trades. It's ridiculous that in a city like New York you have so much difficulty getting a plumber. Why couldn't the plumbers' union let some blacks in? Fourth, we must improve the quality of primary and secondary schools, particularly among minority people. In some schools, a kid goes to school twelve years and comes out on the fifth-grade level.

SEALE: When we speak of what is to be accomplished, we have to deal with an understanding that the political, economic and social injustices that exist have to be solved with some practical program. The Panther party's free-breakfast program for children and its attack on hunger are related to where we're going. There are 15 million people in this country who are hungry, and 50% of them are black, and when you move in this fashion, you start taking care of the children, because they will have to sustain the struggle.

What it's going to entail, though, is black people institutionalizing such programs in the community, where they have control over them. Even the poor white people have to oppose the system with these kinds of programs. It's a need for cooperative housing, cooperative marketing, more unity with the workers. The workers are going to have to start demanding a 30-hour work week with the same 40-hour pay. The poor oppressed are predominantly white unemployed. The courts have to be controlled more by the people, and the constitutional rights of the people are going to have to be secured.

Is a second civil war, or a race war between blacks and whites in America, a possibility or an inevitability?

BOND: I don't think it's inevitable. It is a possibility. This great mass of white middle America is getting more and more uptight. It is prone to answer violence with violence. But I don't see a civil war in the sense of two defined groups opposing each other violently. The black group is so small that it would render itself almost impotent. I just don't think we could carry it off.

SEALE: I don't think there's going to be a race war. Here in the streets, we can see that young middle-class people are opposing the Establishment in the manner that black people have.

What is your prescription for ending white racism in America?

BOND: It is part of the human condition, but it can be controlled. Government is the force to control it. If Government doesn't sanction it, its manifestations will be less severe. Some predicted that when lunch counters were integrated, blood would flow in the streets. But the Government said the counters would integrate. As resentful as white people were, and as much as white people dislike black people, blood didn't flow. There was no official Government sanction for it. Unfortunately, the Federal Government is sanctioning more racism today than five or ten years ago. You see the Moynihan memo, you see Nixon trying to kill the Voting Rights Act of '65 and trying to reverse the very slow process of desegregation. You see Congress trying to curb the work foundations have done among poor people. This is giving rise to overt acts of racism, like attacking school buses.

SEALE: What you have to do to end white racism is civilize white America. You have to educate the masses of white America to the trick bag that the power structure's putting them into.

What value is there in the notion of black nationalism or black separation?

BOND: There are separatists who say it is possible for us to control a black community. We should control the school system, the police system, hopefully the economy, so that money both flows in and stays in the community. That kind of separatism is going to increase. The last decade has done more for racial consciousness among black people than anything else. It makes it easier for us to be a mental nation, a nation within a nation. We're a nation separate and apart in our problems and have to be dealt with separate and apart. And we have to think of ourselves as different from the whole.

SEALE: You don't fight racism with racism. The best way to fight racism is with solidarity. When you talk of black separation it is not a point of whether we dig black separation. The fact of the matter is that now we are already separated. So we're not concerned with abstract, false notions of integration. Nor are we concerned with abstract, false notions of separation. We are concerned with the political, economic and social evils.

Revolution in the White Mother Country & National Liberation in the Black Colony*

By ELDRIDGE CLEAVER

The Black Panther Party believes that the era in which we now struggle can be characterized as the Age of the Showdown—between Oppressed People Everywhere and the Racist Imperial Power Structure. This era can be further defined as that in which significant sectors of the exploiting population have turned away from the system, have declared war upon the system that has warped their lives and tainted their existence at the same time that it was doing the same thing and worse to those whom it oppresses. We recognize these alienated people as allies or potential allies in a struggle against a common enemy.

We start with the basic definition: that black people in America are a colonized people in every sense of the term and that white America is an organized Imperialist force holding black people in colonial bondage. From this definition our task becomes clearer: what we need is a revolution in the white mother country and national liberation for the black colony. To achieve these ends we believe that political and military machinery that does not exist now and has never existed must be created. We need functional machinery that is able to deal with these two inter-related sets of political dynamics which, strictly speaking, make up the total political situation on the North American continent. Ideally, we need a revolutionary organization that is able, guided by a revolutionary ideology and comprehending the necessity involved, to move in two directions at the same

* Reprinted from *The North American Review*, V (July-August, 1968), pp. 13–15. By permission of *The North American Review* and the author.

time. We are here tonight because we believe that the Peace and Freedom Party is the beginning of the answer to one half of this equation and that the Black Panther Party is the beginning of the answer to the other half. We do not delude ourselves with the notion that we have found or that we represent or that anybody else has found or represents any final solutions to age-old problems, but we do feel that the Peace and Freedom Party and the Black Panther Party have made a significant breakthrough and have indisputably upped the ante.

The Coalition

The Black Panther Party and the Peace and Freedom Party in the Bay Area have been experimenting over the past few months with a very narrow coalition around a very broad subject. The focal point of the coalition is now, and has always been, the case of Huey P. Newton, Minister of Defense, Creator, and Leader of the Black Panther Party. Although the coalition has been narrow and limited, tentative and viewed with mutual suspicion, it has in fact unleashed political forces with explosive impact and national implications. It is a fact that in a very short time these infant political facts have become forces with which the old, established forces must contend. We must recall that the Peace and Freedom Party has been on the ballot only a couple of months, it is less than a year old, and is still wearing the diaper of its liberal democratic parentage. The Black Panther Party is less than two years old and the coalition of which we speak is less than five months old. For newborn children we are already doing a man-size job. This is a source of great optimism and enthusiasm for us, because if in our infancy we are able to do a man-size job, we can dream that when we grow to maturity we can do the giant-size work that history has cut out for us.

The coalition between our two fraternal parties is based upon Carmichael's dictum of specific coalitions for specific purposes. We think that this dictum is functional and proper and that it provides a basis for unlimited action with no strings attached. On the basis of this dictum, we think that ultimately we can develop a specific coalition for the specific purpose of destroying capitalistic exploitation and racism. We have freedom to move as far and with such speed as our understanding and imagination and commitment will allow us. We believe that cooperation between revolutionary forces in the mother country and their counterpart in the black colony is absolutely and unequivocally desirable and necessary. We believe that it is suicidal and nonsensical for such potential allies to remain aloof and isolated from each other any longer. All that is needed is for those who fulfill the vanguard function to supply the form of this cooperation. We believe that henceforth the form of cooperation between revolutionary forces in the mother country and those in the colony must be on a coalition basis. We believe that all black colonial subjects should be members of the Black Panther Party, and that all American citizens should be members of the Peace and Freedom Party. We invite other oppressed and colonized people in America to organize themselves and to join our coalition as equal partners. We feel that it is a political mistake of the first order to try and develop a multi-national, all-inclusive political party at this time; to do so would only compound existing confusion and erect new obstacles to the real work that can and must be done.

The Dual Status of Black People in Babylon

Black people in North America have always been plagued by a dual status. We were both slave and Christian, we were both free and segregated, we are both integrated and colonized. In the past this duality has worked to our disadvantage. It kept us running around in circles. Today we propose to turn it to our advantage, in the manner that we have turned our blackness from a disadvantage into a rallying point of advantage. Yesterday we were black and oppressed; today our blackness is a tool for our liberation. Our dual status gives us a mythical right of citizenship and the concrete reality of our situation has given us the national consciousness of an oppressed and colonized people. We intend to use them both wisely. The citizenship that we have on paper we will use through the mechanism of our coalition with the Peace and Freedom Party. We will use our papier-mâché right to vote to help strengthen the Peace and Freedom Party and to help it attain its objectives within the framework of political realities in the mother country. Our major emphasis, or direction, and our perspective, however, are inward—into the black heart of the colony. Our goal is to organize black people for national liberation. In this, our primary task, political reality in the white mother country can only have pe-

ripheral and supportive importance. The duality of our status
dictates the duality of our strategy.

The Black Plebiscite

As our major political objective, the Black Panther Party
is calling for a Black Plebiscite, a United Nations-supervised
plebiscite to be held throughout the black colony, in which
only black colonial subjects will be allowed to participate.
The plebiscite is for the purpose of determining the will of
black people as to their national destiny. In the past many
people and organizations have stated what they believed the
will of black people to be. The Black Panther Party believes
that it is the right of black people to state for themselves
the destiny they desire. We feel that the burning question
to which only such a plebiscite can supply the answer is:
Whether the black people want to be integrated into Babylon,
or whether they want to be separated into a sovereign nation
of their own, with full status and rights with the other nations
of the world, including UN membership and diplomatic
recognition by the other nations of the world. Through
our Minister of Foreign Affairs, James Forman, we have
conducted a preliminary poll of certain key members of
the UN and have learned to our utter satisfaction but
not to our surprise, that they are receptive to the idea
of the Black Plebiscite. In our perspective on our struggle for
liberation, the Black Plebiscite would play a key function. In
the colonial analogy, it would correspond to the role of the
first or the key political campaign that happened in all countries emerging from colonial bondage. In Guinea the political
focus was provided by the campaign against De Gaulle's
Constitution. In Ghana it was the national election that placed
Kwame Nkrumah at the head of the government. The campaign leading to the Plebiscite would be the means of solidly
organizing Afro-America along national lines. Committees
organized by people on both sides of the national question
will spring up throughout the black colony. The issue will
be hotly debated, and people will be organized around the
issues involved. The entire political fabric of the mother
country would be thrown into a crisis. The argument of those
who oppose black national independence would be that blacks
do not need it because they are citizens of white America.
Our argument would be simply to point out the facts, the
reality of the black man's status in white America. Here our
coalition with the Peace and Freedom Party will become

functional because the members of the Peace and Freedom Party whom we will have strategically helped to elect could argue for our position within the Senate and House of Representatives, the State Legislatures, and the city councils.

For those who view the land question, that is, the absence of geographical boundaries of our dispersed colony, as an insuperable obstacle to nationhood, we say that we will hold the land in question in abeyance. We follow the dictum of Osagyefo Kwame Nkrumah, "Seek ye first the political kingdom, and all other things shall be added unto you." What the black man in Babylon needs is organized black power, and with that political power he can carve out his place in the sun—and it won't be on a reservation or in the gas chambers, as certain madmen propose and certain other panic-stricken people fear.

Electoral Politics

We have offered our leader, Minister of Defense Huey P. Newton, as a candidate for the Seventh Congressional District of Alameda County and we have offered our Chairman, Bobby Seale, as a candidate for the Seventeenth Assembly District. In San Francisco, we have offered our Communications Secretary, Kathleen Cleaver, for a candidate in the Eighteenth Assembly District. The advantages in doing this are manifold. First and foremost, we are interested in setting Huey P. Newton free. By running Huey P. Newton for Congress we are uniting the revolutionary political arena with the conventional political arena, and thereby obliterating the distinction between the two. We are able to focus attention in all our campaigns on a revolutionary leader with a revolutionary program within the conventional political context. In over-sophisticated and decadent "revolutionary" circles, this is called "heightening the consciousness of the masses." In practical terms, this kind of campaign becomes another tool for political organization for black power. Our main purpose in entering the political arena is to send the jackass back to the farm and the elephant back to the zoo. We want to put the Establishment up tight. We want to put the black lackeys and bootlickers of the Demo/Republican Party out of business; some of them will be sent back to the farm, and others can also go to the zoo with the elephants. We want to pull people out of the Democratic Party, out of the Republican Party, and swell the ranks of the Black Panther Party and the Peace and Freedom Party on the basis already outlined.

Toward Black Liberation*

By STOKELY CARMICHAEL

One of the most pointed illustrations of the need for Black Power, as a positive and redemptive force in a society degenerating into a form of totalitarianism, is to be made by examining the history of distortion that the concept has received in national media of publicity. In this "debate," as in everything else that affects our lives, Negroes are dependent on, and at the discretion of, forces and institutions within the white society which have little interest in representing us honestly. Our experience with the national press has been that where they have managed to escape a meretricious special interest in "Git Whitey" sensationalism and race-war mongering, individual reporters and commentators have been conditioned by the enveloping racism of the society to the point where they are incapable even of objective observation and reporting of racial *incidents*, much less the analysis of *ideas*. But this limitation of vision and perceptions is an inevitable consequence of the dictatorship of definition, interpretation and consciousness, along with the censorship of history that the society has inflicted upon the Negro—and itself.

Our concern for black power addresses itself directly to this problem, the necessity to reclaim our history and our identity from the cultural terrorism and depredation of self-justifying white guilt.

To do this we shall have to struggle for the right to create our own terms through which to define ourselves and our relationship to the society, and to have these terms recognized. This is the first necessity of a free people, and the first right that any oppressor must suspend. The white fathers of American racism know this—instinctively it seems—as is

* Reprinted from *The Massachusetts Review*, VII (1966), pp. 639–51. By permission of The Massachusetts Review, Inc., and the author.

indicated by the continuous record of the distortion and omission in their dealings with the red and black men. In the same way that southern apologists for the "Jim Crow" society have so obscured, muddied and misrepresented the record of the reconstruction period, until it is almost impossible to tell what really happened, their contemporary counterparts are busy doing the same thing with the recent history of the civil rights movement.

In 1964, for example, the National Democratic Party, led by L. B. Johnson and Hubert H. Humphrey, cynically undermined the efforts of Mississippi's Black population to achieve some degree of political representation. Yet, whenever the events of that convention are recalled by the press, one sees only that version fabricated by the press agents of the Democratic Party. A year later the House of Representatives in an even more vulgar display of political racism made a mockery of the political rights of Mississippi's Negroes when it failed to unseat the Mississippi Delegation to the House which had been elected through a process which methodically and systematically excluded over 450,000 voting-age Negroes, almost one half of the total electorate of the state. Whenever this event is mentioned in print it is in terms which leaves one with the rather curious impression that somehow the oppressed Negro people of Mississippi are at fault for confronting the Congress with a situation in which they had no alternative but to endorse Mississippi's racist political practices.

I mention these two examples because, having been directly involved in them, I can see very clearly the discrepancies between what happened, and the versions that are finding their way into general acceptance as a kind of popular mythology. Thus the victimization of the Negro takes place in two phases—first it occurs in fact and deed, then, and this is equally sinister, in the official recording of those facts.

The "Black Power" program and concept which is being articulated by SNCC, CORE, and a host of community organizations in the ghettoes of the North and South has not escaped that process. The white press has been busy articulating their own analyses, their own interpretations, and criticisms of their own creations. For example, while the press had given wide and sensational dissemination to attacks made by figures in the Civil Rights movement—foremost among which are Roy Wilkins of the NAACP and Whitney Young of the Urban League—and to the hysterical ranting about black racism made by the political chameleon that now serves as Vice-President, it has generally failed to give accounts of the reasonable and productive dialogue which is taking place in the Negro community, and in certain important areas in the white religious and intellectual community. A national committee of influential Negro Churchmen affiliated with the National Council of Churches, despite their obvious respectability and responsibility, had to resort to a paid advertisement to articulate their position, while anyone shouting the hysterical yappings of "Black Racism" got ample space. Thus the American people have gotten at best a superficial and misleading account of the very terms and tenor of this debate. I wish to quote briefly from the statement by the national committee of Churchmen which I suspect that the majority of Americans will not have seen. This statement appeared in the *New York Times* of July 31, 1966.

We an informal group of Negro Churchmen in America are deeply disturbed about the crisis brought upon our country by historic distortions of important human realities in the controversy about "black power." What we see shining through the variety of rhetoric is not anything new but the same old problem of power and race which has faced our beloved country since 1619.

. . . The conscience of black men is corrupted because, having no power to implement the demands of conscience, the concern for justice in the absence of justice becomes a chaotic self-surrender. Powerlessness breeds a race of beggars. We are faced now with a situation where powerless conscience meets conscience-less power, threatening the very foundations of our Nation.

. . . We deplore the overt violence of riots, but we feel it is more important to focus on the real sources of these eruptions. These sources may be abetted inside the Ghetto, but their basic cause lies in the silent and covert violence which white middleclass America inflicts upon the victims of the inner city.

. . . In short; the failure of American leaders to use American power to create equal opportunity *in life* as well as *law,* this is the real problem and not the anguished cry for black power.

. . . Without the capacity to *participate with power,* i.e., to have some organized political and economic strength to really influence people with whom one interacts—integration is not meaningful.

. . . America has asked its Negro citizens to fight for opportunity as *individuals,* whereas at certain points in our history what we have needed most has been opportunity for the *whole group,* not just for selected and approved Negroes.

. . . We must not apologize for the existence of this form of group power, for we have been oppressed as a group and not as individuals. We will not find our way out of that oppression until both we and America accept the need for Negro Americans, as well as for Jews, Italians, Poles, and white Anglosaxon Protestants, among others to have and to wield group power.

Traditionally, for each new ethnic group, the route to social and political integration into America's pluralistic society, has been through the organization of their own institutions with which to represent their communal needs within the larger society. This is simply stating what the advocates of black power are saying. The strident outcry, *particularly* from the liberal community, that has been evoked by this proposal can only be understood by examining the historic relationship between Negro and White power in this country.

Negroes are defined by two forces, their blackness and their powerlessness. There have been traditionally two communities in America. The White community, which controlled and defined the forms that all institutions within the society would take, and the Negro community which has been excluded from participation in the power decisions that shaped the society, and has traditionally been dependent upon, and subservient to the White community.

This has not been accidental. The history of every institution of this society indicates that a major concern in the ordering and structuring of the society has been the maintaining of the Negro community in its condition of dependence and oppression. This has not been on the level of individual acts of discrimination between individual whites against individual Negroes, but as total acts by the White community against the Negro community. This fact cannot be too strongly emphasized—that racist assumptions of white superiority have been so deeply ingrained in the structure of the society that it infuses its entire functioning, and is so much a part of the national subconscious that it is taken for granted and is frequently not even recognized.

Let me give an example of the difference between individual racism and institutionalized racism, and the society's response to both. When unidentified white terrorists bomb a Negro Church and kill five children, that is an act of individual racism, widely deplored by most segments of the society. But when in that same city, Birmingham, Alabama, not five but 500 Negro babies die each year because of a lack of proper food, shelter and medical facilities, and thousands more are destroyed and maimed physically, emotionally and intellectually because of conditions of poverty and deprivation in the ghetto, that is a function of institutionalized racism. But the society either pretends it doesn't know of this situation, or is incapable of doing anything meaningful about it. And this resistance to doing anything meaningful about conditions in that ghetto comes from the fact that the ghetto is itself a product of a combination of forces and special interests in the white community, and the groups that have access to the resources and power to change that situation benefit, politically and economically, from the existence of that ghetto.

It is more than a figure of speech to say that the Negro community in America is the victim of white imperialism and colonial exploitation. This is in practical economic and political terms true. There are over 20 million black people comprising ten percent of this nation. They for the most part live in well-defined areas of the country—in the shanty-towns and rural black belt areas of the South, and increasingly in the slums of northern and western industrial cities. If one goes into any Negro community, whether it be in Jackson, Miss., Cambridge, Md., or Harlem, N.Y., one will find that the same combination of political, economic, and social forces are at work. The people in the Negro community do not control the resources of the community, its political decision, its law enforcement, its housing standards; and even the physical ownership of the land, houses, and stores *lies outside that community*.

It is white power that makes the laws, and it is violent white power in the form of armed white cops that enforces those laws with guns and nightsticks. The vast majority of Negroes in this country live in these captive communities and must endure these conditions of oppression because, and only because, *they are black and powerless*. I do not suppose that at any point the men who control the power and resources of this country ever sat down and designed these black enclaves, and formally articulated the terms of their colonial and dependent status, as was done, for example, by the Apartheid government of South Africa. Yet, one can not distinguish between one ghetto and another. As one moves from city to city it is as though some malignant racist planning-unit had done precisely this—designed each one from the same master blueprint. And indeed, if the ghetto had been formally and deliberately planned, instead of growing spontaneously and inevitably from the racist functioning of the various institutions that combine to make the society, it would be somehow less frightening. The situation would be less frightening because, if these ghettoes were the result of design and conspiracy, one could understand their similarity as being artificial and consciously imposed, rather than the result of identical patterns of white racism which repeat themselves in cities as distant as Boston and Birmingham. Without bothering to list the historic factors which contribute to this pattern—economic exploitation, political impotence, discrimination in employment and education—one can see that to correct this pattern will require far-reaching changes in the basic power-relationships and the ingrained social patterns within the society. The question is, of course, what kinds of changes are necessary, and how is it possible to bring them about?

In recent years the answer to these questions which has been given by most articulate groups of Negroes and their white allies, the "liberals" of all stripes, has been in terms of something called "integration." According to the advocates of integration, social justice will be accomplished by "integrating the Negro into the mainstream institutions of the society from which he has been traditionally excluded." It is very significant that each time I have heard this formulation it has been in terms of "the Negro," the individual Negro, rather than in terms of the community.

This concept of integration had to be based on the assumption that there was nothing of value in the Negro community and that little of value could be created among Negroes, so the thing to do was to siphon off the "acceptable" Negroes into the surrounding middle-class white community. Thus the goal of the movement for integration was simply to loosen up the restrictions barring the entry of Negroes into the white community. Goals around which the struggle took place, such as public accommodation, open housing, job opportunity on the executive level (which is easier to deal with than the problem of semi-skilled and blue collar jobs which involve more far-reaching economic adjustments), are quite simply middle-class goals, articulated by a tiny group of Negroes who had middleclass aspirations. It is true that the student demonstrations in the South during the early sixties, out of which SNCC came, had a similar orientation. But while it is hardly a concern of a black sharecropper, dishwasher, or welfare recipient whether a certain fifteen-dollar-a-day motel offers accommodations to Negroes, the overt symbols of white superiority and the imposed limitations on the Negro community had to be destroyed. Now, black people must look beyond these goals, to the issue of collective power.

H. RAP BROWN,

Organizer, Revolutionary

H. Rap Brown first became involved in the Black Movement in 1960 in Baton Rouge, Louisiana, his home town. He attended Southern University there for a while before becoming interested in the Student Nonviolent Coordinating Committee's Mississippi Summer Project, and the Mississippi Freedom Democratic Party. Brown worked for the library in the U.S. Department of Agriculture for a short while in 1964, but later took a position at Howard University, trying to promote cooperative relations between black college students and the blacks on the street. In 1966–67 he worked in Alabama as a SNCC representative, again organizing black people to gain power through group action. He succeeded Stokely Carmichael as chairman of SNCC in 1967 and in July of that year Brown, already a controversial black spokesman, was invited to speak at Cambridge, Massachusetts. It was also around this time that he ran afoul of the law and was charged with conspiring to incite a riot and illegal transporting of guns.

Like so many other blacks who advocate revolutionary action, Brown has withdrawn from the public scene with felonious charges pending against him. Thus, although he, as the others, is presently incommunicado, his influence among black activists seems to be intact.

"VIOLENCE IS AS AMERICAN AS CHERRY PIE."

Excerpts From

Die Nigger Die*

Our job is not to convert whites. If whites are dedicated to revolution then they can be used in the struggle. However, if they impede the struggle and are proven to be a problem then it is up to us to deal with them as with all problems. Our job now is to project what should be our common goal—the destruction of a system that makes slavery profitable.

Now there're a lot of people who say that the way you change laws is to destroy the power structure. I say you got to go beyond that. If you destroy the power structure, it can always be replaced by another power structure, whether it's white or Black. The power structure serves the system and the system is the thing which demands exploitation of people. You have to destroy the system. You can destroy the power structure and leave the system intact. But if you get the system, you got the power structure. That's the job which confronts us.

However we may twist our words and regardless of our personal, subjective feelings—the truth of the matter is that we cannot end racism, capitalism, colonialism and imperialism until the reins of state power are in the hands of those people who understand that the wealth, the total wealth of any country and the world, belongs equally to all people. Societies and countries based on the profit motive will never insure a new humanism or eliminate poverty and racism. However we may twist our words and regardless of our personal feelings—the stark reality remains that the power necessary to end racism, colonialism, capitalism and imperialism will only come through long, protracted, bloody, brutal and violent wars with our oppressors.

* Reprinted from *Die Nigger Die*, 1969. By permission of The Dial Press and the author.

Liberation movements must be based upon political principles that give meaning and substance to the struggle of the masses of people, and it is this struggle that advances the creation of a people's ideology. Liberation movements from the very beginning must be dedicated to principles that speak to the needs of the poor and oppressed, or must evolve into this type of movement with these principles while the fighting is going on, for it is not evident that those who fight will assume power and implement decisions that appropriate the wealth of countries for all people. Rather to the contrary: the absence of these revolutionary political principles relates to the fact that some new rulers have settled for a new flag, a new style of dress, a seat in the UN, and/or accommodation with former colonial powers. A negotiated independence.

We must draw from all ideologies those principles which benefit the majority of mankind. We cannot limit ourselves to just one concept or ideology that was relevant in some other revolution. Certain changes have made even some of the most advanced ideologies obsolete.

This country has always used negroes as a political tool against Blacks. Without a common Black political doctrine, america will use (and is using) Blacks against Blacks. Blackness must be political in our behalf. Individuals can no longer be immune to public political criticism because they are "Black and proud." There must be revolutionary political criticism of counter-revolutionary positions and acts. Some individuals who gain popularity in Black america are later used as tools by white america. In most cases, white political interest comes as a result of the existing popularity of Black individuals. Understand, popularity does not reflect correctness. Blackness alone is not revolutionary.

If we examine Cleveland, Ohio, Gary, Indiana, Washington, D.C., and many other areas populated predominately by Blacks we can see a tactic being used that has often been tried in Africa, Vietnam and other oppressed countries. It is called neo-colonialism. In other words, when white structures and institutions are threatened whites protect their economic and political interests and maintain control by using members of the oppressed people as their spokesmen. They set up puppet governments headed by individuals with white interests in mind. These people oppress their own kind for their personal gain. These puppet leaders are as dangerous as those whom they represent. The only constructive thing a Black mayor can do is to organize Blacks to destroy the system that oppresses Black people. We must never permit anyone, white or Black, to destroy with impunity the product of a single drop of the blood and sweat of our people.

White folks realize now that they can concede Blackness and still exercise control. This country says, "Yes, you may be Black; but, you must be american," which means we are as responsible for oppression as whites. This country says, "Yeah, you may have Black heroes; but, we must approve of them." So, they publicize negroes who have been beneficial to this country. The tactic of co-opting is being used to its fullest. White folks will co-opt dog shit if it's to their advantage. Today, niggers are tomming and don't even know they're tomming. We must say as Fidel Castro says, "No liberalism whatsoever! No softening whatsoever! A revolutionary people, a political people—a strong people—this is what is needed throughout these years. . . . What do the dangers or the sacrifices of a man or of a nation matter when the destiny of humanity is at stake?"

*   *   *

Our dream is one of liberation, a right of self-determination, a dream of denied freedom; no more, no less. Our fire says we are no longer dreaming of freedom, we are exercising our rights to be free (at the expense of anybody who gets in our way). You see, freedom is absolute. You're either free or you're a slave. There is nothing in between freedom and slavery. There's no such thing as second-class citizens. That's like telling me you can be a little bit pregnant. Freedom is as absolute as truth. You're either lying or telling the truth. We were born free. We must exercise our right to be free.

Today I will talk about two things—colonialism and revolution. In other words, sickness and cure. The united states redefined colonialism. It not only went to Africa and exploited the land and its people; it brought Black people here and continues its exploitation; and it drove the native American Indians by murder and wholesale genocide into reservations (and now this is romanticized on t.v. as cowboys and Indians). America is the ultimate denial of the theory of man's continuous evolution. This country represents everything that humans have suffered from, their every affliction. The very fact that a place like this can exist appalls most of mankind. This country is the world's slop jar. America's very existence offends me. For Black people it is not a question of leaving or separating—given our historical experiences, we know better than anyone that the animal that is america must be destroyed. Through capitalism, this country establishes colonies; but, not colonies in the old sense, but like franchises. The Philippines, Venezuela, Vietnam, Puerto Rico and other countries are to the united states what dope is to Harlem; bloods use it, but the Mafia owns it. It just goes to show you, you give the cracker an inch, he wants a yard, give him a yard, and he'll BURN A CROSS ON IT, every time. There is no difference between Harlem and Puerto Rico, or Harlem and Vietnam, except that in Vietnam people are fighting for their liberation. (That is, armed struggle.)

Let's examine that war in Vietnam. My position, on that war, is that Black folks ain't got no business shooting other Black folks for white folks. If we must fight, then our war is here at home. We can't let white folks decide for us who our enemy is. We must decide who our enemy is and how to deal with him. Black cats must say that if Lynch'em Burn Johnson can stay here and keep the Vietcong off Ladybird, then we can stay here and keep the crackers off our women. We must refuse to participate in the war of genocide against people of color: a war that also commits genocide against us. Black men are being used on the front lines at a disproportionate rate. Forty-five percent of the casualties are Black. That's genocide! We cannot let our Black brothers fight in Vietnam because we need them here to fight with us. If we can die defending our motherland, we can die defending our mothers. It is the Black man's will to be free that has made him fight for this country. The army is to kill people. We have to decide if we will be killers; when we decide, we have to decide who we are going to kill, and when.

We are the greatest victims of colonial rule. We are exposed to this country's strongest institutions every day. We find that what is called "education" is not education at all. What it is, is white nationalist propaganda. Black people are made to hate themselves. I saw a brother on the corner once, trying to figure out what was wrong with his skin—it didn't match his flesh-colored bandaid.

Media is used against us in total. The W.P.P. (white power people, or the white power press, or white people's power—take your choice) all victimize Blacks. The rebellion's aftermath brought demands in the white press not for the resolution of historic grievances of oppressed Blacks but for the guillotining of Carmichael or myself. The negro press is no better. They wait for white folks to tell them what to say. The tactic of media is to make you an enemy of the people. Enemies of the people are always vulnerable. The reason Malcolm could be killed and Black folks didn't revolt is that the press had made Malcolm an enemy of the people. More negroes were scared of Malcolm than whites. The reason they could give Muhammad Ali the maximum sentence and fine was because the press had made him an enemy of the people. The reason Adam Powell could be politically lynched and Black folks didn't revolt, was because Adam had been made an enemy of the people. Negroes believe anything the press says.

Anything you don't control can be used as a weapon against you. Education is used as a weapon against us. News media is used as a weapon against us. Athletics. We dominate in athletics, but we don't control them. Therefore the negro athlete is used as a weapon against us. This country realizes that the athlete has an image in our community. So they get some ol' boot-licking, shuffling, money-mad negro, who can run or jump, and they tell him, "Go control your people. If we can't control athletes, we can sure cripple 'em." Brothers ought to break him up so bad, until he'll have to die to get well. The same thing goes for entertainers. Teach them that if they can't say the right thing, then don't say nothing.

Another thing that is used effectively against Blacks is the court system. There is no justice in this country for Black people. Justice is a joke, and it stinks of hypocrisy. Lyndon Johnson is Hitler's illegitimate child and J. Edgar Hoover is his half-sister. Justice means "just-us-white-folks." There is no redress of grievance for Blacks in this country. When the government becomes the lawbreaker, people must become law enforcers. What happened at the Algiers Motel must not be allowed to be repeated. The tribunal to be held must be made legal by the people. If the murderers are found guilty, and they should be, the brothers should carry out the execution.

When we begin to put all of these things together, we begin to understand what america is doing. Genocide can be seen in the mass removal of Blacks from the streets, by placing them in jails. Yes, the courts conspire to commit genocide. Black people are in the majority in most jails in this country. Concentration camps have been established and maintained throughout this country. They were established as a result of the McCarran Act of 1950. There is a book called *Concentration Camps, U.S.A.** that's written by Charles R. Allen—who is white. (I say this because it usually bridges the credibility gap; you don't believe what Black folks say but you believe white folks.) It is in your interest that you read it, because your not knowing what's going to happen doesn't make it any the less true. Me and Carmichael can't fill all them camps. They must be planning on taking somebody else.

* Charles R. Allen, *Concentration Camps, U.S.A.* New York: Marzani and Munsell, 1966.

This country is waging a genocidal war against people of color; domestic and foreign. This is a country that pays white farmers for not growing food and dumps surplus food in the ocean. Birth control, as it's practiced by governmental programs dealing with the masses of poor, can't be called anything else but an attempt at genocide. Birth control should be an individual decision. It should not be forced by a government.

We have not made any progress since we have been in this country. We are still slaves! Concessions are not to be confused with progress. Whites have made concessions only out of political necessity. This country only loosens its hold on Black people to get a better grip. Whites and negroes talk of progress, and point to Thurgood Marshall. He is a concession; white folks put him there, and can remove him when they get ready. James O. Eastland, a red-neck camel-breath moldy old cracker from Mississippi, subjected Thurgood to a level of questioning that was unheard of before. What he was really saying was, "You might be the top nigger in the country, but you are still a nigger to me." They gave negroes an astronaut; but, I bet they lose that nigger in space. [Note: He was killed in a jet crash while landing.] We have not made any progress. Negroes go for anything white folks tell them or sell them.

There must be a re-evaluation of politics. What is considered politics in this country is meaningless to black people. Politics, as defined by the geographical and influential boundaries of this country, is irrelevant to masses of people. The vote is used as a tool of oppression. Camus raises a very good point. He says, "What better way to enslave a man, than give him the vote and call him free." In other words, what does it profit a man to be able to vote, and not be able to choose his candidates. Politics in this country is not bipartisan; politics is very partial—partial toward whites with money. The only politics that should be relevant to us is the politics of revolution.

Everything must relate to the struggle as a political form. Culture must be political. Nationalism alone is not a political doctrine. Nationalism has to be a part of a political doctrine. Without vanguard political direction cultural movements bring economic and/or political liberalism, not revolution. We must move to define the difference between political nationalism and cultural nationalism. We must move from Black awareness to revolutionary motion. "To be Black is necessary but not sufficient." Every negro is a potential traitor; and every Black man is only a potential revolutionary—with emphasis on potential. To be Black is not to be revolutionary. When you begin to stress culture without politics, people can become so hooked up in the beauty of themselves that they have no desire to fight. It becomes ego-gratifying just to be Black. Vanguard groups can't afford to go around stressing culture without politics, the real test now is preparation for, and initiation of, struggle.

Today we see the Black world divided on the question of ideology. Throughout Africa the lack of common political motion divides people against people and insures opportunism by certain leaders. Inside the united states this is a paramount problem where groups of Blacks are struggling in various ways for liberation. This struggle is being checked through the lack of a common political objective. The concept of Black Power, for instance, has been diluted and prostituted to the point where even the most conservative negroes are now for Black Power. "Whitey" Young, dictator of the urban league, preaches for Black pride and acclaims that Black Power is attainable through Black capitalism. A lot of cats said the blood is coming home, but look again, he's still following his master. Floyd McKissick, former director of CORE, who once argued for Black Power maintains that Black people need Black capitalism. The united states government is in the process of giving tax incentives to those who start Black businesses and invest in Black areas; and the unlimited Ford Foundation, which has been trying to buy up the Movement for years, and which funds everything from Black television programs to experiments in school decentralization, has recently declared that it will place some of its investment portfolio in developing Black capitalism. All Black folks considering revolutionary work must be aware of these pitfalls. We must study how revolutions are aborted, how independence movements are stifled, how people are cheated of the fruits of their efforts, how the foot soldier or the Mau Mau gets betrayed by the bourgeois nationalist— these are things that all revolutionaries must understand. (January, 1969)

At this stage of struggle the greatest danger comes from within. It has become profitable, fashionable and even necessary to be Black. In that order. Militancy is second to Blackness. However, to be militant is not to be revolutionary. Upon close examination, I find the thrust of most militancy is toward reform, not revolution. A militant in this case is one who never stops talking.

Militancy, too, must be political. We must begin to see ours as the struggle of oppressed people. We are not the only oppressed people in this country. We are a vanguard force in the revolution because we have been the most dispossessed. The Mexican-American, the Puerto Rican, the American Indian, Japanese-American, poor whites; all these groups have reason to fight. Repression will force them to fight. However, it is doubtful that poor whites can overcome racism. We hold the key to liberation around the world. The freedom of people around the world depends upon what we do. This is true, because this country is the chief oppressor around the world. If we view this country as an octopus, then we see that her tentacles stretch around the globe. Like in Vietnam, Africa, Latin America. . . . If these countries cut off a tentacle, it can be replaced. But we got his eye; we live in the belly of the monster. So it's up to us to destroy its brain. When we do this not only will Africa be free but all people oppressed by "the man." It is because of america's racism and greed that Black people and people of color around the world are oppressed.

The question of violence has been cleared up. This country was born of violence. Violence is as american as cherry pie. Black people have always been violent, but our violence has always been directed toward each other. If nonviolence is to be practiced, then it should be practiced in our community and end there. Violence is a necessary part of revolutionary struggle. Nonviolence as it is advocated by negroes is merely a preparation for genocide. Some negroes are so sold on nonviolence that if they received a letter from the White House saying to report to concentration camps, they would not hesitate. They'd be there on time! If we examine what happened to the Jews, we find that it was not the Germans who first began to remove Jews. It was other Jews! We must be prepared to fight anyone who threatens our survival. Black and white. The rebellions taught Blacks the value of retaliatory violence. The most successful rebellion was held in Plainfield. It was successful in the sense that white violence was minimized. The only death that occurred in Plainfield was that of a white racist cop. We know how sensitive america is about the killing of policemen—especially white policemen. But both National Guardsmen and local police were afraid to shoot up the Black community because the brothers had just stolen two crates of guns. Each one of these guns would shoot seven times before you load it, which makes it hard to hold it; eight times before you cock it, and it takes a man to stop it. The very fact that white folks fear guns shows the value of being armed. Power, indeed, must come from the barrel of a gun.

We can no longer allow threats of death to immobilize us. Death is no stranger to Black folks. We've been dying ever since we got here. To all the brothers and sisters who are here, ours may be to do and die, but for the little brothers and sisters, theirs should be but the reason why. This country has delivered an ultimatum to Black people; america says to Blacks: you either fight to live or you will live to die. I say to america, Fuck It! Freedom or Death.

Power to the People.

Discussion and Study Questions

1. Why does Carmichael find the goals of integration so objectionable? In this sense, how does he justify the early goals of SNCC in their protests against public accommodations laws in the South?

2. Is Brown expressing attitudes toward the press similar to Evers? If so, how do you account for the difference in rhetoric and psychological perspective?

3. How does Brown's idea of "neo-colonialism" fit into the scheme of colonized peoples as clarified by Cleaver, Forman, Jones, and others?

4. What is the Black Plebiscite which Cleaver envisions? Why is it necessary?

5. What is the nature and basis of the coalition between the Peace and Freedom Party and the Black Panther Party that is advocated by Cleaver?

6. The word assimilation is used frequently in the essays in this text. What does it connote to many black spokesmen? Why is it viewed with hostility by the more militant spokesmen and the separatists?

7. Can you explain why Newton seems to feel that black people are the only people who can free the world?

8. Explain the two types of prisoners as Newton sees them. Why can't the prisons rehabilitate either type?

9. To what extent do Newton and King agree in their definitions of unjust laws? Explain the differences in their techniques of resistance.

10. In what ways do the essays in this section suggest that black communities in America are victims of colonial exploitation?

SIGNET Titles of Special Interest

☐ **TO BE YOUNG GIFTED AND BLACK by Lorraine Hansberry. Adapted by Robert Nemiroff.** By the author of **A Raisin in the Sun,** here is Miss Hansberry's unique view of the human spirit, and her unwavering belief in the possibilities innate in human nature. "She knows more about the bloody world than any living playwright . . ."**—Rex Reed** (#Y5318—$1.25)

☐ **BLACK LIKE ME by John Howard Griffin.** The startling, penetrating, first-hand account of a white man who learned what it is like to live as a Negro in the South. Winner of the **Saturday Review** Anisfield-Wolf Award. (#Q4871—95¢)

☐ **SHADOW AND ACT edited by Ralph Ellison.** Essays on writers and writing, on music and on humanity and individual responsibility. "As an artist he has an expressive range that rises in a swinging arc from brown study to hard talk to soaring lyricism."**—Saturday Review** (#Q3022—95¢)

☐ **THE MAN WHO CRIED I AM by John Williams.** The most powerful novel about Blacks in America since Ralph Ellison's **Invisible Man.** Mr. Williams tells the brute truth about the Black man's realistic role in American society. (#Q3616—95¢)

MENTOR and SIGNET Biographies
of Special Interest

☐ **ELY: TOO BLACK, TOO WHITE (abridged) by Ely Green.** The unforgettable biography of a man whom nature blessed with every gift—and America damned for the color of his skin. "Unlike any other story of race . . . poignant and powerful."—**Saturday Review**
(#MJ1075—$1.95)

☐ **NARRATIVE OF THE LIFE OF FREDERICK DOUGLASS, AN AMERICAN SLAVE. Written by Himself with a Preface by William Lloyd Garrison.** In the tradition of the best-selling **The Confessions of Nat Turner,** an escaped slave who organized an insurrection and lived to tell the world his harrowing story boldly discloses the nightmare world of the pre-Civil War slave in the South. (#P4633—60¢)

☐ **DOWN THESE MEAN STREETS by Piri Thomas.** A powerful autobiography, unanimously praised by the critics, this is the story of one man's journey from childhood to maturity in the violent world of Spanish Harlem.
(#Y4532—$1.25)

☐ **MANCHILD IN THE PROMISED LAND by Claude Brown.** The extraordinary autobiography of a child of Harlem who pulled himself up from the gang wars, the pot smoking, the stealing, the dope pushing to become a law student at one of America's leading universities.
(#Y4737—$1.25)

MENTOR and SIGNET Titles of Special Interest

☐ **ANCIENT AFRICAN KINGDOMS by Margaret Shinnie.** A comprehensive book, combining the efforts of the anthropologist, the archaeologist and the historian to give the reader a clear picture of the culture of ancient Africa. Includes numerous photographs, maps and drawings. (#MY1037—$1.25)

☐ **THE CHRONOLOGICAL HISTORY OF THE NEGRO IN AMERICA edited by Mort Bergman.** An enlightening account of the history of the Black people in America. The four sections covered are **Slavery, Reconstruction, Separate but Equal** and finally **Deliberate Speed** which goes to modern times. (#MW937—$1.50)

☐ **EARLY AMERICAN VIEWS ON NEGRO SLAVERY. From the Letters and Papers of the Founders of the Republic edited by Matthew C. Mellon. Introduction by Richard B. Morris.** The opinions and beliefs of Franklin, Washington, Jefferson, Hamilton, Adams and Madison on slavery, the slave trade and race relations. (#MY920—$1.25)

☐ **THE NEGRO REVOLUTION. From Its African Genesis to the Death of Martin Luther King by Robert Goldstone.** Robert Goldstone has written a provocative and well-documented analysis of Black history in this definitive work. He traces the plight of the Black people from Africa through the Civil War, post-Civil War on to the civil rights movement of today. (#Q3915—95¢)

MENTOR and SIGNET Plays
You Will Want to Read

☐ **BLACK QUARTET: Four New Black Plays by Ed Bullins, Ben Caldwell, Ronald Milner and LeRoi Jones.** Four powerful plays by the most brilliant Black playwrights of our time. Includes an introduction by Clayton Riley and a photographic insert. (#MY1160—$1.25)

☐ **THE SANDBOX AND THE DEATH OF BESSIE SMITH by Edward Albee.** Two explosive off-Broadway hits, one about a scathing domestic tragedy, the other baring the ugly circumstances surrounding the death of a great Black blues singer. (#P2339—60¢)

☐ **A RAISIN IN THE SUN and THE SIGN IN SIDNEY BRUSTEIN'S WINDOW by Lorraine Hansberry.** Two outstanding plays: one, winner of the New York Drama Critics Award, about a young Black father's struggle to break free from the barriers of prejudice, the other, portraying a modern-day intellectual's challenge of the negation and detachment of his fellow intellectuals. With a Foreword by John Braine and an Introduction by Robert Nemiroff. (#Q4111—95¢)

☐ **IN WHITE AMERICA by Martin Duberman.** Text and supporting documents of the moving off-Broadway play about the American Black's centuries-old legacy of pain and discrimination. (#T4534—75¢)

MENTOR and SIGNET Titles of Special Interest

☐ **BEYOND THE ANGRY BLACK edited by John A. Williams.** In this gripping collection of stories, articles and poems, some of America's best known authors—black and white—answer the unasked questions raised by the lack of racial communication in all phases of life. Included are **Langston Hughes, Chester Himes and Carrie Allen Young.** (#MY1058—$1.25)

☐ **CHRONICLES OF BLACK PROTEST edited by Bradford Chambers.** A superlative documentary on Black Power from the pens of **Booker T. Washington, Stokely Carmichael, Malcolm X, Martin Luther King, Nat Turner,** etc. (#MQ907—95¢)

☐ **PREJUDICE: TWENTY TALES OF OPPRESSION AND LIBERATION edited by Charles R. Larson.** The twenty stories in this powerful anthology have one common theme as their concern—racial prejudice. The writers represent ten different countries. Included are **Albert Camus, Flannery O'Connor** and **Anatole France.** A biographical sketch of each author is included. (#MW1070—$1.50)

☐ **36 CHILDREN by Herbert Kohl.** "An extraordinary and heartening account . . . Mr. Kohl tells, with great simplicity and honesty, what it is like to be a teacher in a public school in Harlem."—The New York Times (#Q3684—95¢)

THE NEW AMERICAN LIBRARY, INC.,
P.O. Box 999, Bergenfield, New Jersey 07621

Please send me the MENTOR and SIGNET BOOKS I have checked above. I am enclosing $_____(check or money order—no currency or C.O.D.'s). Please include the list price plus 15¢ a copy to cover handling and mailing costs. (Prices and numbers are subject to change without notice.)

Name_____

Address_____

City_____State_____Zip Code_____

Allow at least 3 weeks for delivery